PENGUIN BOOKS

UNDERSTANDING THE MUSLIM MIND

Rajmohan Gandhi was born in 1935. He was chief editor of *Himmat*, a Bombay weekly, from 1964 to 1981. He is also the author of a highly regarded biography of C. Rajagopalachari, independent India's first Indian head of State.

He lives, at present, with his wife and two children in Madras, where he is the resident editor of the *Indian Express*.

RAJMOHAN GANDHI

UNDERSTANDING
THE MUSLIM MIND

PENGUIN BOOKS

Penguin Books India (P) Ltd., 210 Chiranjiv Towers, 43 Nehru Place, New Delhi-110 019
Penguin Books Ltd, 27 Wrights Lane, London W8 5TZ, England
Penguin Books USA Inc., 375 Hudson Street, New York, New York 10014, USA
Penguin Books Australia Ltd, Ringwood, Victoria, Australia
Penguin Books Canada Ltd, 10 Alcorn Avenue, Toronto, Ontario, Canada M4V 3B2
Penguin Books (NZ) Ltd, 182–190 Wairau Road, Auckland 10, New Zealand

First Published in the USA by the State University of New York Press, Albany 1986
First published in India as *Eight Lives : A Study of the Hindu-Muslim Encounter* by Roli
Books International 1986
Published in Penguin Books 1987
10 9 8 7 6 5
Copyright © Rajmohan Gandhi 1986
All rights reserved
Not for sale in the United States of America
Made and printed in India by
Ananda Offset Private Limited, Calcutta

CONTENTS

CONTENTS

For Sonu, Bhaiya, Leela, Divya, Amrita,
Supriya, Debu and all those whose
forebears, famous or unknown, shed tears,
sweat and blood on the earth of India,
Pakistan and Bangladesh.

PREFACE

Any nuclear clash between India and Pakistan (may God forbid it) would, in part, be due to history. Though living side by side for centuries, the subcontinent's Hindus and Muslims have never adequately understood or trusted one another, and killings, partition and wars have resulted. All the same, even if man's folly sets off a series of nuclear explosions on the subcontinent, it is unlikely that they will wipe out either the entire Hindu population, or the entire Muslim population, or each side's habit of blaming the other. Hindus and Muslims will remain, and so will the Hindu-Muslim question. A fresh look at the Hindu-Muslim relationship is therefore not hard to justify.

Not that India-Pakistan or India-Bangladesh relations can be equated with the Hindu-Muslim encounter. Both communities live in all three countries, even if Hindu numbers in Pakistan are negligible, and Muslim participation in India's conflicts with Pakistan has always been more than nominal. But the two subjects, how the neighbouring nations get along and how the neighbouring communities do, are not unconnected.

Though the Muslim question has pursued me from my childhood, I allowed a lot of time to pass before attempting a serious understanding of the subcontinent's Muslims. Like many of my compatriots I mouthed the fact that India was the world's second largest Muslim country but I had not cared to study the history of the subcontinent's Muslims or the impulses that moved them.

I was ignorant but not, I recognized with some concern, more so than most of my non-Muslim compatriots, including highly educated ones. Thus, to give only two revealing examples, they did not know, as I had not known, that the Qur'an contained a verse that unambiguously frowned upon compulsion in religion, or that it spoke more than once of God sending prophets to all nations and peoples. Muslims have been similarly uninformed about Hindu beliefs and points of view. Hence these pages, an attempt to reduce the understanding gap or scale the separating wall.

A stimulus for this attempt was the research I had to do for a biography of Chakravarty Rajagopalachari, or Rajaji, as he is better known, who strove for freedom and became, following the Raj's withdrawal, India's first Indian head of state. Rajaji's stance on the Hindu-Muslim question was criticized as appeasing by his colleagues in the Indian National Congress, but it did not satisfy Muslim League, the body that demanded and won Pakistan. My study for the biography underlined for me the fact that the Hindu-Muslim question is central in our sub-continent's affairs. It has broken hopes, hearts and India's unity. It had to be understood.

Passions, however, overtake our understanding. We take sides before we have grasped what happened and is happening. We are merely more polarized, not better informed, after we have read and talked of disputes of the Shah Bano or Babari Masjid/Ram Janmabhoomi kind. Our communal riots have many dimensions, including the commercial, the political, and the criminal, but it is undeniable that they fuel polarization and also feed on it. "Ahmedabad," a Congress (I) MP assesses, (*India Today*, November 30, 1986) "is divided into two parts—Hindu Ahmedabad and Muslim Ahmedabad." A nation cannot be judged by a city, nor a city by a season, but the wall, the *lathi* and the knife are not, alas, figments of the imagination.

History will not dissolve resentments and suspicions. Selective history will, in fact, harden them. Yet a frank and non-partisan look at the past can at least tell us of the blocks to Hindu-Muslim partnership, and tell us, too, of what went wrong, and why, in the efforts to remove them. If it informs us of times when the other side, too, was large-hearted, and of other times when our side also was small-minded, that awareness may make us, whoever we are, less prickly. History will then have served the cause of national, and subcontinental, understanding.

This book consists of the biographies of eight Muslims who

were prominent on the subcontinent's stage in the hundred years following the 1857 Rising. It will be seen from the list at the end of the book, of works and documents consulted, that I was able to study a number of Muslim authors, including many Pakistanis and Bangladeshis. Yet it was not my purpose to produce a Hindu's summary of the Muslim view of the history of the last 150 years. Neither was it to provide a Hindu refutation of the Muslim view. The intention was to look, as honestly and fairly as I could, at the lives of the eight, and through them at the Muslim mind, and to share what I saw with others. I admit that I hoped that study would show that bridge-building was not a rootless cause. Whether or not this hope was fulfilled will be apparent from the pages that follow.

I am grateful to all those, dead or alive, whose works I have consulted, but except where they are attributed to others the opinions expressed are, of course, mine. Stanley Wolpert's *Jinnah of Pakistan* was published soon after I commenced my study but I intentionally postponed looking at it until my Jinnah sketch, easily the longest in this book, was completed. I did not want my interpretation to be influenced by, or become a reaction to, another current assessment. I have, however, incorporated one of Wolpert's opinions in my final Jinnah text.

For the grant, facilities and atmosphere of the Woodrow Wilson Center for Scholars, Washington D.C., where I spent eight months in 1984-85 working on this book, I offer my sincere thanks.

Usha Gandhi, my wife, has fully shared this endeavour, typed a fair portion of the text, pointed out errors and demanded that my meaning should be clear. My thanks to her were not always whole-hearted, but they are now.

Rajmohan Gandhi
Madras
November 24, 1986

UNDERSTANDING
THE MUSLIM MIND

CHAPTER 1

HINDUS AND MUSLIMS

The Muslim question nagged me from my depths, and from an early age. *"Hamid Saheb, main sharminda hoon."* (Mr. Hamid, I am ashamed.") So I, a twelve-year-old, heard my father say in 1947. He, Devadas Gandhi, editor of the *Hindustan Times*, was speaking in our second-floor Connaught Circus flat, directly above the paper's offices, to his Muslim friend, an official of Jamia Millia, the Muslim college with a nationalist bent.

We think of 1947, accurately, as the year of our independence from British rule but that is not quite how the future will look upon it. Unless I am greatly mistaken, our descendants will regard the transfer of power as less significant than the inhumanity to which many Hindus, Muslims and Sikhs allowed themselves to sink that year. It is a year of our shame, not a year of our achievement.

Places in the north and east of what was still undivided India vied with one another in the capacity to kill, maim, rape, abduct, burn, loot, expel. Even if you were a boy of twelve you knew that Delhi had not scored too badly and that in Delhi the Muslims were the victims. Apart from the stories you heard and the headlines you read, you also saw columns of smoke rising from different points on the skyline; you listened to gunfire from time to time; and you fraternized with rifle-holding soldiers positioned along the terraces of the building in which you lived.

Now, after 38 years, I can still see Hamid Saheb clearly in his stiff white khadi cap, grave face, small black beard, brown achkan and white churidars, saying very little, conveying his pain through his silences and somewhat surprised and moved (or so I imagined) by what my father had said.

Let me go back a little further, to 1944-46, when I heard elders speak of a Great Obstacle going by the name of Jinnah who was threatening to block everyone's path if he wasn't given Pakistan and who obviously meant what he said. I didn't much like my picture of him but he intrigued me. I saw him twice, once in 1945 outside the Viceroy's house in Simla, where he arrived in a rickshaw drawn by four men, and the second time at a football match in Delhi in what must have been early 1947.

I had heard or read that Jinnah would give away the cups and had wandered off alone to the ground to see the game and also to see the Great Obstacle again. I sensed that I would be a lone Hindu boy in a Muslim crowd and was a bit apprehensive, but curiosity was the stronger emotion and I wove my way toward him.

At the end of the match he gave a speech, looking thin and old and wearing a cap, long coat and loose trousers. I have no memory of what he said, only of rousing slogans being chanted, doubtless in his honour.

August 15, 1947. I had stayed awake to hear the sound of midnight on the radio, which would also be the sound of freedom. That day or the next, walking down Barakhamba Road and looking around me, I actually imagined that heads were suddenly higher and backs straighter; and I consciously straightened my own back. I think I also looked for whites to see if they were walking with bent heads but didn't find any.

My school was on Barakhamba Road, a few hundred yards from Connaught Circus. I belonged to Akbar House but soon after August 15 my House vanished — the school didn't want to keep a Muslim name any longer. Along with most of the school's Muslim pupils, emperor Akbar had gone to Pakistan.

I was hurt, more no doubt because the House I was loyal to and fervent about had disappeared and less because of the school's fall from broadmindedness. All the same I was unhappy and I listened approvingly to a master who murmured his dissatisfaction with the change. He was the only one to do so.

Chaudhri Muhammad Ali, father of one of my classmates who left for Pakistan, Javid Akhtar, later became Prime Minister. Arif, a boy not from my school but a companion in rounds of cricket played on any vacant neighborhood patch, also vanished from one day to the next. "Be careful of Arif," an aunt had warned me. "He may be carrying a knife." I assumed Arif had gone to Pakistan.

By this time some Hindu and Sikh refugees from Pakistan, victims of Muslim violence, were urging my grandfather, Mahatma Gandhi, to go to Pakistan himself or to retire to a Himalaya cave. "You didn't stop Pakistan," they told him. "And you didn't save the lives or honour of our relatives. We curse you."

The Mahatma wanted to go to Pakistan and said so in a message to Jinnah, who was the new nation's Governor General and unquestioned leader. But the sighs and fears of Delhi's Muslims held Bapu. And in January 1948 he decided to stop eating and not resume until Delhi's Muslims felt secure again.

He was 78 and sad. Delhi's Sikhs and Hindus were angry and bitter. Why should they save the life of the old man who had given in to their oppressors?

"Do not fast," my father had pleaded, in a letter to his father. "You life is more valuable than your death can be." "Thank you for your love," the Mahatma had replied, "but it is selfish love. It is attachment."

We tried to brace ourselves for the inevitable. The fast reached its sixth day. Fighting my anxiety, I was playing table tennis on the terrace of the neighbours on our floor, the Pandyas. Suddenly the worry left me and I was at peace. I felt sure the fast would be broken! It was, that same day. The Hindus and Sikhs who had been so angry a few days earlier had met the Mahatma's conditions.

Twelve days later it was sports day in our school. My new House, Subhash, had done well and I had contributed my share to the result. When my brother Ramu and I reached home in the evening our father's secretary Kali Prasad met us at the entrance. "Bapuji has been shot dead." A Hindu who saw the Mahatma as a betrayer of Hindu honour had killed him.

Three years later a *Hindustan Times* sub-editor ran up to our flat to show my father a sheet hot off the teleprinter. I had opened the door and he showed it to me first. "Flash," it said. "Liaqat Ali Khan, Prime Minister of Pakistan, has been shot at. More to follow." I looked at the sub-editor for a couple of seconds and said, "I hope what follows is news of his death."

Liaqat Ali Khan had done me or mine no harm. Our paths had never crossed. But he was Pakistan's Prime Minister and Pakistan was India's enemy. Moreover, making a heartless remark put a 16-year-old in the category of real men, didn't it? And in the category of smart men. But the sub-editor did not smile. Not smiling, he made me feel small. The vanity and ill-will that masqueraded in my heart as manliness stood exposed. *Main sharminda hoon*. And always will be.

* * *

Hindu-Muslim strife, and coldness, is an ancient tale that began in 712 A.D. when Muhammad bin Qasim, son-in-law of the Governor of Iraq, conquered Sind and declared it a Muslim state. In Qasim's Sind Hindus were inferior in status to Muslims and had to pay the *jizia*, a poll-tax not levied on Muslims. Between the years 1000 and 1026 Sultan Mahmud of Ghazni in what is now Afghanistan raided India seventeen times, broke idols in Hindu temples, took away a store of riches and annexed an area around Lahore. A scholar in Mahmud's court who accompanied him to India, al-Beruni, noted that because of the ruination at Mahmud's hands the Hindus "cherished the most inveterate aversion towards all Muslims."[1]

Al-Beruni also saw that while apparently resigned to their humiliation, the Hindus looked upon the invaders as outcastes and "recoiled from the touch of the impure barbarian Muslims."[2] Muhammad Ghori (1174-1206) extended Muslim rule eastward; from his days until 1857 there was always a Muslim king on the throne of Delhi. But a hundred years after Ghori the Muslim traveller Ibn Battutah observed that Hindus in Malabar ensured that "no Muslim should enter their house or use their utensils for eating purposes" and that "if a Muslim is fed out of their vessels the Hindus either break the vessels or give them away to the Mussulmans."[3]

The Pakistani historian, Ishtiaq Husain Qureshi, has given his terse view of the distance between Hindus and Muslims down the ages:

> They have lived with minimum contacts. There has been little inter-marriage, because Islam forbids it with the Hindus and the Hindus are bound by their rules of caste. Except in a small sector of the highly Westernized class, inter-dining has been unthinkable. The festivals provide no social occasion for coming together, instead they have often given a pretext for rioting. The communities have remained different not only in religion but in everything, culture, outlook on life, dress, cookery, furniture and domestic utensils. There has been no sense of a common history. The heroes of the Muslim conquest and the rebels against Muslim domination inspire contradictory feelings among Muslims and Hindus. Common bondage to the British did not always inspire the same feelings at all times.[4]

Some students of history, Hindu and Muslim, have argued that though India had succeeded in integrating foreign elements that had entered India before the Muslims (Greeks, Scythians, Kushans and others), she could not "Indianise" the Muslims. Asserting this, Hafeez Malik of Pakistan adds that Muslims "were a distinct and separate cultural and political entity."[5] A group of Hindu historians examining the Muslim Sultanate of Delhi (1206-1526) state that

> ... unlike the previous invaders the Muslims did not merge themselves with the Hindus and thus for the first time the population of India was divided into two separate units with marked distinctions. This was the historic beginning of the Hindu-Muslim problem that led after more than six hundred years to the creation of Pakistan.[6]

Malik is frank. "*Jizia*," he says, "symbolized the inferior status of the Hindus."[7] And he quotes Shivaji's letter to Aurangzeb in which the Maratha chief reminded the last of the major Mughals that his great-grandfather Akbar had abolished the *jizia* and told Aurangzeb that in re-imposing the tax "the emperor of India was envying the bowl of beggars and taking money from Brahmins, monks, paupers and the famished." Shivaji went on to say: "Many of your forts and provinces have gone out of your possession, and the rest will soon do so, because there will be no slackness on my part in ruining and devastating them."[8]

Malik concludes that "the pattern of relations between Hindus and Muslims since the early days of Muslim rule was essentially that of conflict."[9] Holding a similar view, Dr. Ambedkar described a recent twenty-year period (1920-1940) as one of "civil war between Hindus and Muslims interrupted by brief intervals of armed peace."[10]

The belief in Hindus-Muslim incompatibility, not, as we have seen, held by Muslims alone, was a factor in Pakistan's creation. "Was," asks Malik, "a *modus vivendi* between Hindus and Muslims in one state at all possible in the light of the preceding twelve hundred years of history?" "The Muslim answer," he says, "has been emphatically in the negative." As Ambedkar saw it:

> In segregating themselves the Muslims were influenced by some mysterious feeling, the source of which they could not define, and guided by a hidden hand which they could not see. This mysterious feeling and this hidden hand was no other than their pre-appointed destiny, symbolized by Pakistan . . . [12]

In other words, Pakistan was inevitable, essential, destined. Perhaps it was. Even if it was not, it has been there for about 40 years, and we must wish it well. I certainly do. Yet two questions remain. Is a *modus vivendi* between Hindus and Muslims spread over three independent states (India, Pakistan and Bangladesh) impossible? Secondly, and this is relevant not just for India with its 90 million Muslims (11.4 percent of the population) but also for Bangladesh with its 11 million Hindus (12.1 percent of the population), can we afford not to search for a *modus vivendi*, no matter how elusive, between Muslims and Hindus in one state? Actually the question is not wholly without relevance even in Pakistan, where though only 1.4 percent of the population, roughly 1.25 million Hindus still live.

To the first question there can only be one answer. As Malik says in the final lines of his book, *Moslem Nationalism in India and Pakistan*:

> The leaders of India and Pakistan have the obligation to protect the
> liberties and cultural heritages of their respective nations. They can
> protect them only if they learn to cooperate and compromise with
> each other.[13]

He would no doubt add Bangladesh (his book was published in 1963,
before the separation) and agree also that the obligation falls on peoples
as well as leaders.

India and Pakistan have clashed thrice since their emergence as free
nations. Officials of the two countries talk with one another from time to
time. So do the rulers, though less often. But no one has ever spoken of
India and Pakistan as friendly neighbours. Trade between the two is
minimal, and though one can with effort move from one country to the
other, there is no direct flight between New Delhi and Pakistan's capital,
Islamabad.

The Indo-Pak boundary is always tense and, in Kashmir, disputed.
The two countries, both poor, commit precious parts of their budgets to
defence. Stories of a Pakistani hand behind Indian troubles are readily
believed in India. In Pakistan the easiest way to discredit a political rival
is to call him pro-Indian.

In both lands rulers have found that a democratic process can be suspended, or a long-promised reform withheld, by the simple expedient of
claiming that a conflict with the neighbour was likely. Both countries
assert they are non-aligned and would no doubt like to be, but Pakistan
has strategic and defence links with the U.S.A. and India a treaty with
the Soviet Union.

A super-power conflict is not likely to leave the subcontinent alone, nor
is it wholly inconceivable that an Indo-Pak clash would initiate a super-
power conflict. And though India and Pakistan may not be insane enough
to throw nuclear bombs at each other, they probably have the necessary
ability. India did explode a nuclear device in 1974, and Pakistan is widely
thought to be near to doing so. It follows that people everywhere, and
not just those living on the subcontinent, have a stake in "cooperation and
compromise" there.

What about Hindu-Muslim cooperation within a state? An examination
of the question may remind Pakistanis and Bangladeshis of discussions
that preceded Pakistan's emergence. But I do not go into it here only to
see all over again if Pakistan was avoidable. My intention is to test the
foundations, such as they are, for lasting amity in today's India; as noted
earlier, this may have relevance for Bangladesh and Pakistan too. If nothing
else, the communal violence that has continued to scar independent India

calls for a fresh look at the Hindu-Muslim relationship. It is noteworthy, also, that in a 1980 book Malik states that "despite the creation of Pakistan in 1947 the problem for the Indic Muslims has remained unsolved."[14] (By Indic he means the subcontinent's.) Of course, some elements of the story of Pakistan's creation will figure in these pages: apart from being of historical interest, they have a bearing on current Hindu-Muslim questions. Moreover, attitudes toward Pakistan, real or perceived, are an ingredient in today's Hindu-Muslim relationship.

We have seen that the Muslim proponents of Pakistan did not think that a Hindu-Muslim partnership could take place satisfactorily or at a deep level, and that some Hindus agreed with them. Two other Hindus who did so were V.D. Savarkar and Lajpat Rai. Presiding over a Hindu Mahasabha session in 1939, Savarkar said: "Let us bravely face the unpleasant facts. There are two nations in India, the Hindus and the Muslims."[15] Lajpat Rai, who chaired a 1920 session of Congress, thought that Muslim history and Muslim law constituted "an effective bar" to.Hindu-Muslim unity.[16]

Altaf Husain Hali, the poet, thought differently. This author of the famed *Musaddas*, the long poem, published in 1879, portraying the rise, fall and future hope of Islam, "pleaded," says S.M. Ikram in his *Modern Muslim India and the Birth of Pakistan*, "for Hindu-Muslim unity in all stages of his life."[17] In *Patriotism* Hali says:

> If you desire the good of your country,
> Then do not consider any compatriot a stranger,
> Be he a Muslim or a Hindu,
> Be he a Buddhist or a Brahmoo.[18]

The perspective of *Musaddas* is broad:

> This was the first teaching of the Book of Guidance [the Quran].
> That all humanity is the family of God;
> He alone is the friend of the Lord
> Who is friendly to the Lord's creations.
> What is devotion, religion, faith?
> That man should help his brother man.[19]

Hali's *Musaddas* "took Muslim India by storm and struck a responsive chord in the heart of every thoughtful Muslim." His verses throb with love for the Prophet — "the shelter for the poor and the protection of the weak; for the orphans a guardian, champion of the slaves" — and anguish at "the ruined garden of Islam." Hali is not a minor figure in the story of Indian Islam. A hundred years ago he was, in Ikram's words, "the national poet of Indian Moslems."[20]

Of Hakim Ajmal Khan (1863-1928), physician, poet, calligraphist, educator and political leader, the historian Muhammad Mujeeb has written:

> His belief in Hindu-Muslim unity was not a matter of policy, it was a part of his heritage; it was in his blood, and the substance of his everyday life. He was completely broken when he found the two communities moving further apart in spite of his best efforts to bring them together.[21]

Mujeeb concedes that Ajmal Khan, who presided over the Muslim League in 1919 and the Indian National Congress in 1922, was "no more representative of the generality of Indian Muslims than the Red Fort is of domestic architecture." Among other things, Ajmal Khan did not mind being called a "nationalist" Muslim and the bond between him and Gandhi survived the deep strains to which Mujeeb refers.

Not that all Muslims who broke with Gandhi and Congress lost their belief in the possibility of Hindu-Muslim unity. One who did not was Choudhry Khaliquzzaman, who headed the Muslim League in the U.P. and later in Pakistan. While not regretting his espousal of Pakistan, he held that the Muslim presence in India had led to "the evolution of a common culture and a common social life."[22] That "the Muslims were forced by circumstances to seek the partition of the country" was, in his view, more "a great irony" than an outcome of incompatibility.

It was an irony because, says Khaliquzzaman, "the Muslims had endeavoured for centuries to unite India."[23] Though this endeavour was linked to Muslim rule, which meant minority rule, there is truth in the remark. Many Muslims found Pakistan a thrill but partition sad; they had been heirs, some of them at any rate, to a tradition of a composite Indian or Hindustani culture. This culture had influenced Delhi and areas near it ever since the reign of Akbar (1556-1605), a Hindu wife of whom gave birth to his son and successor Jahangir. Jahangir's Hindu wife was in turn the mother of emperor Shahjehan; and even Aurangzeb the devout (fanatical to others) married a Hindu noblewoman. The mother of the last Mughal, Bahadur Shah II (1837-1857), was a Hindu too, called Lalbai. These Hindu wives were all converted to Islam;* nonetheless, they were vehicles for an infusion of Hindu culture into the Red Fort. Culture also

---

*In Akbar's case, the Hindu wives "were allowed to practise their own religions rites inside the palace."[24]

flowed the other way. Many Hindu men took to the Muslim *achkan* (long coat) and *pajama* (loose trousers) and Hindus of both sexes sought favours from the tombs of Muslim saints.

It was common for the Muslim ruler to celebrate Holi, Rakhi, Dussehra and Diwali and to fete Hindus and Muslim together. But the most significant fusion was over language. The court, Hindu and Muslim subjects and Muslim and Hindu poets increasingly used a new language that was evolving, Urdu, which had strong Persian and Arabic flavours but was, in Hali's words, "based on Hindi." "All its verbs, prepositions, conjunctions and the greater part of its nouns," added Hali, "are derived from Hindi."[25] In Khaliquzzaman's estimate, "Urdu contained about seventy-five percent words of Hindi and Sanskrit origin."[26]

If men like Khaliquzzaman perceived a composite culture, they also seemed to value such personal experiences as they had had of Hindu-Muslim friendship. Recalls Khaliquzzaman:

> I had now been the chairman of the Lucknow Municipal Board for seven years. The Hindu members of the Board continued to support me loyally. Now that I am at the fag end of my life I have to thank them. Pandit Rahasbihari Tiwari, who was the President of the Lucknow Hindu Mahasabha and had always opposed my election as chairman, asked me to see him in hospital.

> I found him very weak, suffering from consumption. He took my hands in his, with tears in his eyes, and asked his son, Bhirgudat Tiwari, to touch my feet and treat me as his father after he had gone. On the way back to my house I felt very miserable. I was meeting nothing but affection from my Hindu friends personally but in matters of public policies I had failed to convince them.[27]

But even if he desired Hindu-Muslim unity, the Indian Muslim was afraid of the future. Demands for elected legislatures, increasingly voiced by the Indian National Congress, founded in 1885, troubled him. He was not less keen for India's political progress, for independence from white rule, than the Hindu. Perhaps he was keener, for his elders were always reminding him that the English had toppled a Mughal from the Delhi throne that Muslims had occupied for 650 years. But he was nervous about the self-rule talk. Congress wasn't asking for restoration of the Delhi throne to the heirs of pre-British rulers; it was (more and more) asking for one-man-one-vote, for democracy, for rule by majority parties in elected legislatures.

Since Hindus were easily the majority community, democracy — the Muslim thought — would mean Hindu rule. Right from the start the Indian National Congress sought to persuade the Muslim that this equation was incorrect, that self-rule would be Indian, not Hindu, rule and that Muslims would have their due share in it. But the concept of a share in ruling was outside the Indian Muslim's experience. He knew from 650 years of history what being a ruler meant; and he knew from current experience what being a subject meant. But sharing power was a new thought and, given the Hindu majority, a frightening one. The Muslim feared the phrase might merely be a cloak for Hindu rule.

Was there any guarantee, he asked himself, that Hindu rule would suit him more than British rule? The latter had been unpleasant enough, especially in the four or five decades following the 1857 Rising, for which the British had blamed the Muslims more than the Hindus. But since then there had been an improvement.

As for Hindu rule, the Muslim saw risks in it. Only a section of Hindus had subscribed to the composite culture. Wouldn't the rest, a majority, yield to urgings to recall the past? Might they not see Muslims as aliens, indeed as aliens tarred with the anti-Hindu excesses of men like Mahmud of Ghazni and desire revenge? In estimating their prospects under majority rule, India's Muslims were influenced by their reading of history, which, among other things, reminded them of Spain. There the dynamism of Islam had established a Muslim state in the 11th century; when power eventually returned to the Christian majority, the Muslim minority suffered greatly.

To a lesser extent, Muslim psychology was also coloured by the traditional Muslim belief in a nexus between state and religion. Wasn't Islam both a personal religion and a polity? Some Indian Muslims thought that a self-governing India had to be either a Muslim or a Hindu country; it could not be religiously neutral. True, the Briton ruling India had not imposed an official religion but he was an outsider; if he left, India would need a state faith. Though some Muslims (and Hindus) entertained such a view, it was not really a lesson provided by the history of Muslim rule in India.

It is a fact that many Muslim rulers levied the *jizia* (though several did not) and at least one (Firoz Shah Tughlak, 1351-1358) fostered conversions by offering to withdraw it, but the tax exempted a non-Muslim from military service and entitled him, at least in principle, to the ruler's protection. Most Muslim rulers had to call Islam the official religion; without such an affirmation they would have alienated the *ulama*, the body of Islamic scholars and interpreters, which was seldom without influence, and also strengthened the hands of their Muslim rivals and challengers, of whom there never seemed to be a shortage. (One reason for this was that Islamic tradition offered no clear guidelines on succession rights.) In practice, however, every Muslim ruler needed Hindu administrators and soldiers, and some Hindu support was often crucial to the foiling of a Muslim rival's designs.

The need for Hindu goodwill softened the Muslim state. For one thing, this state did not clash with Hindu wealth. In fact, while affluent Hindus could accumulate riches and bequeath them at will, the Muslim nobleman could forfeit his wealth if he lost the ruler's pleasure. At least one *jizia*-levying sultan, Jalaluddin Khilji (1290-1296), lamented that

> . . . during our rule the enemies of God and the enemies of the Prophet live under our eyes and in our capital in the most sophisticated and grand manner, in dignity and plenty, enjoying pleasures and abundance, and are held in esteem and honour among the Muslims.[28]

Hindu temples were defaced by Muslim rulers — and also preserved by them. If some rulers permitted the sacrifice of cows, others, out of an understanding of Hindu sentiment, discouraged cow-killing. The Hindu assumption that Muslims were outcastes was not always concealed but the Muslim rulers chose not to react angrily to it; they just ignored it. And though some conversions, frequently short-lived, were obtained at swordpoint, and others through the lure of honours, decorations and money, many more were the outcome of the Hindu caste system and the selfless, appealing lives of Muslim *sufis*. Especially in Bengal, though not only there, despised and neglected untouchables welcomed Muslim *sufis* and embraced Islam; the claim that men were equal under Islam's roof attracted them. In many cases whole sub-castes or clans imitated their chief and accepted Islam. The gain the chief sought might have been spiritual or mundane; the rest simply displayed clan loyalty. That Islam was the creed of the ruling race no doubt played a part with many converts but forcible conversion was never the policy of India's Muslim rulers.

Akbar's bid for Hindu-Muslim unity was bold, too bold in fact. Not only did he abolish the *jizia* and create, by appointing Hindus to vital posts in the empire, a mixed governing class, he also allowed his enemies to charge that the emperor sought to dilute Islam out of recognition. His great-grandson Dara Shikoh, the eldest son of emperor Shahjehan and the apple of his father's eye, believed in what he called "the mingling of the two oceans," translated portions of the *Upanishads* and declared that the latter were of divine origin. But in the battle for succession the broadminded but weak and moody Dara lost out to his self-controlled and puritanical younger brother, Aurangzeb.

Not only did Aurangzeb re-impose, for whatever reason, the hated *jizia*;

his regime saw the destruction of many a Hindu temple, the execution of Hindus and Sikhs, including the ninth Sikh Teacher, Guru Tegh Bahadur, and two sons of the tenth Guru, and the humiliation of many of his non-Muslim subjects. His clashes, offensive or defensive, with the Rajputs, Sikhs and Marathas and with Muslim chieftains in the south ate the life out of the Mughal empire; and his policies induced hate in Hindus and Sikhs. That he realized what had happened, and also sensed his personal responsibility, is indicated in the letter he wrote in his last days to his favourite son Kam Baksh:

> Son of my soul.... Now I am going alone. I grieve for your helplessness. But what is the use? I have greatly sinned, and I know not what torment awaits me.... Let not Muslims be slain and reproach fall on my useless head. I commit you and your sons to God's care. I am sore troubled.[29]

If we except Aurangzeb and his unfortunate excess of zeal, we can agree with Mujeeb that the Mughal state "was Islamic only in the sense that the ruler was a Muslim and the ruling party mainly Muslim."[30] No doubt the government promoted the interest of the ruling class, and that class happened to be mainly Muslim, but the state was not a theocracy. Because it was not, Shivaji could, in that letter to Aurangzeb in which he defied the emperor, speak warmly of Akbar, Jahangir and Shahjehan, and add:

> Well, your majesty! If you believe in the true Heavenly Book and word of God (i.e., the Quran), you will find there *Rabb-ul-alamin* (God of all men) and not *Rabb-ul-Musalmin* (God of Muslims).... To show bigotry... is like altering a word in the Holy Book.[31]

* * *

If Islam rode across India with the sword and spoke from the throne, it also walked with the sufi and spoke in gentler cadences from the hut. The sufis, Muslim mystics, talked of the love of God and the brotherhood of man, of the shortness of life and the length of eternity. As has been noted, some of them won converts. But others seemed more interested in whether a man would turn to God and to things of the spirit and less in whether he would become a Muslim. Their thoughts took root; their language did not seem alien. Numerous Hindu admirers and disciples were drawn to them and, after their death, to their tombs. Likewise, many Muslims, in Qureshi's words, "felt attracted to the Bhakti saints" who spoke of the emptiness of mere ritual, a view "familiar to the Muslims through their own sufis."[32]

Together the sufis and the Bhakti poets brought Hindus and Muslims closer at the grassroots. Affirming, often in memorable verse, that there was no difference between Hindus and Muslims, or between Ram and Rahim, or between Hinduism and Islam, some of these mystics refused to accept either the Hindu or the Muslim label for themselves. The best known among them is, of course, the fifteenth-century saint-poet, Kabir, but there were others as well. The orthodox in both communities warned the faithful against persons who denied the existence of differences and questioned the value of externals. That inward belief was not possible without outward observance was the position of Shaikh Ahmed of Sirhind, the brilliant purist (1562-1624) who reacted against Akbar's heterodoxy. But the sufis did not fall in line. Despite orthodox warnings the message of the Muslim sufis and the Hindu Bhakti school reached and uplifted large sections of the common folk, Muslim and Hindu, and tended to unite them. Of course, there were other sections, equally large perhaps, that they could not reach.

A historian like Qureshi holds that Islam in India was put at risk by those who placed "the ritual and the communal sense . . . at a discount" and taught "that the external aspects of religion had no significance."* However, he agrees that the sufis and the Bhakti school "rendered great service." They "strengthened the forces of conciliation" and created a "harmony . . . by reaching the hearts of the people" that "the monarchs could not, even with the most strenuous efforts, have achieved."[34]

Whether the Muslim in India is a Muslim or an Indian first is a question he has always faced. That it should arise is natural. For one thing, the first Muslims were Arabs, Turks, Central Asians, Afghans or Persians. They were outsiders. (But so were the first Hindus.) Secondly, Mecca stirs the heart of any Muslim who takes Islam seriously as no place in India can; if he is a Shi-ite, Karbala and Najaf in Iraq will move him almost as much. Thirdly, the Muslim is taught that he is part of a world-wide community of the faithful and that nationalism is a sin; in actual practice this sin might disfigure the relations between one Muslim country and another but he should not lose faith in Islam's larger brotherhood.

A Muslim occupant of the Delhi throne was apt on occasion to profess allegiance to the caliph of Islam ("God's viceregent on earth") of his time. This caliph might be real or nominal or even a puppet; he might live in Baghdad or Cairo; but a link with him was expected to enhance, in Muslim

---

*As an example Qureshi quotes a verse of Amir Khusrau (1253-1325): "Love has converted me into an infidel, I no longer need Islam; Every vein in my body is a thread, I do not require the sacred thread of the Brahmin." Adds Qureshi: "Khusrau's orthodoxy was beyond doubt and his meaning was clear to the disciplined sufis, but not to the populace."[33]

eyes, the status of the ruler of Delhi. So there were times when coins minted in Delhi bore a distant Arab's name.

The Hindu, on the other hand, loved, even venerated, the land, rivers and mountains of India. His supposed Central Asian origins never figured in the lore on which he was raised. India was his soil, his sacred earth. The Muslim, especially when wanting an argument or provoked into one, charged that the Hindu's devotion to India amounted to a worship of earth and clay and was merely another instance of his idolatry.

Only God, the One God, knows the heart of man. Only He knows when a person's love, devotion or reverence for another, or for a place, slips fatally into the worship of humans or things.

Apart from Hindus, several Muslim communities in India kneel before special objects.[35] Mirza Mazhar of Delhi (1702-1781), a sufi and an accomplished swordsman and cutter ("he knew almost fifty different ways of cutting a *shalwar*"), held that "the prostration of Hindus before their idols was an expression of reverence and not an association of any gods with the True God."[36] Doubtless he was in a tiny minority among Muslim scholars, but was he wholly wrong? Is the answer unrelated to what is in the heart of the prostrating man? The True God knows the truth . . .

The devout Muslim never worshipped India but he often lost his heart to her. The poet Masud Salman was born in 1048 in Lahore and lived there. His father had served the invading Mahmud of Ghazni. When he was forty, Salman found himself in a prison in Ghazni and pined for the city of his birth:

> Thou knowest that I lie in grievous bonds, O Lord!
> thou knowest that I am weak and feeble, O Lord!
> My spirit goes out in longing for Lahore, O Lord!
> O Lord, how I crave for it.[37]

Two hundred years later Amir Khusrau wrote *The Third Sky* in which, in Mujeeb's words, he "likens India to Paradise, and shows that because of its fruits, flowers and climate it is better than any other country." Says Khusrau:

> The Indians excel in science and wisdom; they are the inventors of numerals, the creators of the *Panchatantra*, the great book of worldly wisdom that has been translated into Persian, Turkish, Arabic and Dari; their music surpasses the music of any other country.

Then, referring to the sin of *sati*, he speaks of the "noble" courage of "a woman dying willingly for her dead husband."[38]

His pessimism about the prospects of India's Muslims under democracy did not sour the poet Hali's sentiment about his land. "Farewell to thee, O ever-green garden of India," he wrote at the end of the last century. "We foreigners have stayed long in this country as your guests."[39]

India's Muslims were and are attached to India for the simplest of reasons: they and their forefathers were born in the land. Descendants of non-Indians are but a tiny percentage of India's Muslim population. They were a small element, likewise, in the Muslim population of undivided India. The great majority are descendants of converts of Indian origin. This means that the ethnic roots of most of the subcontinent's Muslims are no different from the ethnic origins of the Hindus, a factor that people from both communities tend to forget. India is wholly different from the period when Muslims were, in the main, alien conquerors. Today, for the most part, Muslims and Hindus are the same ethnically: where they are not, they share a long common tie to the same stretch of land. If partnership is our goal, these factors will help.

"I belong to two circles of equal size, but which are not concentric. One is India and the other is the Muslim world."[40] This was said in 1930 by the colourful Maulana Muhammad Ali, who for a period had been one of Mahatma Gandhi's closest colleagues. His words probably represent the sentiments of many Indian Muslims today. They imply a problem only if we assume that India and Islam have a stake in a conflict with each other. The Muslims of post-1947 India have not been slow to work, speak or fight for their country. They would hesitate if India were to clash with Islam but in the context of our times it is not easy to see why such a clash should occur. If we rule out such a confrontation, we can see the Indian Muslim's "extra-territorial" involvement as a national opportunity. It gives us ready links with the Muslim world, which is not without influence and wealth. Moreover, this "extra-territorial" involvement of our Muslims causes the rest of us also to think beyond India's borders, a useful thing that does not come naturally to us.

Can, then, Hindus and Muslims live as partners? For a credible answer we need a fuller inquiry, which can assume one of a number of shapes. Thus one may compare Hinduism and Islam as religions. Or the history of Hindu-Muslim relations in a part of India may be surveyed. The sad sequence of violent clashes involving the two communities may be studied. Or one may focus on, say, the number, acceptance and impact of Hindu-Muslim marriages in a particular place and period, or on the proportion of Muslims in various job categories. One may look for Hindu strands in the literature and art of Indian Muslims or for Islamic influence in modern Hindu writings and art. And so forth. The number of possible approaches is large.

I have chosen the path of studying eight Muslims who have influenced the subcontinent in this century. Their lives as a whole and their interaction with Hindus may help us in measuring the possibility of Hindu-Muslim partnership. Three of the eight I have selected, Sayyid Ahmed Khan, Iqbal and Jinnah, are national heroes in Pakistan, which also respects the memory of Liaqat Ali Khan, its first Prime Minister. Muhammad Ali was a rocket in the subcontinent's skies in the early twenties. Abul Kalam Azad and Zakir Hussin stood by India's nationalist movement and were honoured by free India. Fazlul Huq, "the Bengal tiger," moved the 1940 Pakistan resolution of the Muslim League but something of the impulse behind the Bangladesh of a later period can be seen in his relationship with Jinnah. Together the eight represent a fairly broad geographical and ideological spectrum. Some among them aroused less controversy than others but none was "neutral." All had foes, and the subcontinent's Hindus responded differently to each of them.

Inevitably, we will look longer at some periods than at others. Phases or years when Hindu-Muslim unity seemed striking, or an accord appeared to be close at hand, or hopes were destroyed, or paths separated, will demand special attention. One of our aims, though it may not be fully realizable, will be an impartial scrutiny of some of the milestones of the Hindu-Muslim story between 1857 and 1957. Despite the passage of years, these milestones continue to arouse controversy and even heat.

We will attempt to see, among other things, whether recent Muslim figures seen by Hindus in general as foes, obstacles or disappointments may not, on closer study, emerge with positive qualities. We will seek facts, and endeavour to avoid that "adroit marshalling of selected facts so as to create the maximum goodwill" which, as Muhammad Mujeeb, that brilliant but careful historian, warns, can "easily become an evasion of truth and deprive the Indians as a people of the courage to face reality."[1] If the reality as it emerges injures hope and demolishes dreams, so be it. It would be wiser to live without bridges, if their construction is found impossible, than to venture out on a bridge laid out without probing the shores.

The first of the eight, Sayyid Ahmed Khan, died before the end of the last century, the only one of the eight to do so. In his youth he was at the heart of the (dying) Mughal empire; in his age he clashed with the Indian National Congress, the body that was to inherit power from the British Raj. The past and the present come together in his person.

CHAPTER 2

SAYYID AHMED KHAN

(1817–1898)

He is hailed, and assailed, as the founder of Muslim separatism on the subcontinent. He is blamed, and praised, as a modernizer of Islam. Later in this chapter we shall try to see whether or not these descriptions are valid. His name lives regardless, and so does the title the Raj gave him. Almost ninety years after his death and forty years after Indian independence he is still Sir Sayyid (or Syed). But, thanks no doubt to Islam's discouragement of sculpture, we do not fully know what he looked like. Fortunately a man called George Graham, a police officer of the Raj and a friend and contemporary of Sayyid Ahmed, painted a picture. In an unusual book, perhaps the first "by a Victorian Englishman in praise of a 'native',"[1] Graham described the· Sayyid Ahmed of ripe years:

> He is of middle height and of massive build, weighing upwards of nineteen stone. His face is leonine — a rugged witness to his determination and energy.... He has a hearty laugh, and enjoys a joke as much as any man.
>
> He has been a widower for many years, and has had only one wife. He informed me the other day, with a twinkle in his eye, that "he might marry again!" "But," he said, "she must be English, in order that I may mix more freely in English society, and she must be eighty years old, and have lost all her teeth!"
>
> He is a born orator. His lips quiver with suppressed emotion; the voice and figure follow suit. Up at 4 a.m. he ... works far into the night.[2]

Akbar Shah II was the Mughal "emperor" when, in 1817, Sayyid Ahmed Khan was born in Delhi, where 160,000 people lived at the time. But the empire was dead and Akbar Shah, pitied but respected by the populace, lived in the Red Fort under British sufferance. His court-hall echoed to the sounds of grandiose titles but he had neither power nor riches. Screened by a high wall, hundreds of his relatives lived in a ghetto inside the Fort. At times they would shout from their rooftops, "*Bhukay martay hain, bhukay martay hain.*" ("We die of hunger.") One of Akbar Shah's sons built himself a European-style house and wore European uniforms but others of the Muslim nobility and professional elites—the *sharif*—tried to counter their humiliation by sneering at the West's presence, by applauding verses or composing them, or by lifting their elbows and recalling Muslim glory.

One who did not do this was the capable Khwaja Farid, Sayyid Ahmed's maternal grandfather. Realizing that the British were in India to stay, he served them in Calcutta and also at their missions in Iran and Burma. Recognizing Farid's standing with the British, Akbar Shah made him First Minister. Farid was in this position for eight years or so, his main task being to balance the budget of the royal household. It was in Farid's large *haveli* (residence) and under his eye that Sayyid Ahmed was raised, for Sayyid Ahmed's father, Mir Muttaqi, a descendant of the Prophet, had become a recluse. An ancestor of his had officered for Aurangzeb but Muttaqi rejected the positions and titles offered to him by Akbar Shah.

Though Farid and his daughter Aziz-al-Nisa were undoubtedly greater influences on Sayyid Ahmed than his father, Muttaqi also played a part, taking his boy occasionally to meet the emperor, with whom he was on frank but friendly terms, or a mystic. He gave his son the link with the sufi tradition which the scholar Troll discerns in Sayyid Ahmed's eventual religious thought.[3]

Sayyid Ahmed and his brothers and sisters were taught to avoid the company of the children of the working class ("They will corrupt your Urdu"), and to turn up "immaculately clean" for their post-dinner lesson in Persian, Urdu or mathematics with Khwaja Farid in "the brightly lit *diwan khana* (drawing room)." A child who even accidentally stained the freshly laundered white sheet covering the Persian carpet was "chased out of the room like a dog." If Farid instructed his grandchildren to remember their class, he also gave them an example or two of Hindu-Muslim trust. Thus his long-serving Hindu manager, Maluk Chand, from whom Farid took advice "on sensitive issues," received a brother's share in Farid's will.

The remarkable Aziz-al-Nisa, on her part, asked the big-built Sayyid Ahmed to forgive a man who had injured him (Sayyid Ahmed had been "bent upon revenge"); and she ordered Sayyid Ahmed out of the house until he had obtained the pardon of an aged servant he had slapped. When at age 38 she lost her eldest son she simply said, "*Khuda ki marzi* ('It is God's will')," unrolled her prayer mat and with tears running down her cheeks knelt down to beg for God's solace.[4]

Though Sayyid Ahmed learned some mathematics and Arabic from an uncle, and aspects of oriental medicine from a family friend, he did not learn English or join the secular Delhi College, which the Raj had started at the end of the 18th century. The *ulama* called English schools "abodes of ignorance" and the prejudice must have affected even the "liberal" Farid and his young grandson. No Muslim of their time could be wholly open to the language or institutions of those who had extinguished the empire. Not that the white man was the Muslim empire's sole destroyer. Muslim jealousies and Maratha, Sikh and Rajput arms had played their crucial roles in debilitating it. All the same, the white man's overlordship was a wounding reality, and self-respecting Muslims were not eager to embrace his creations.

Sayyid Ahmed kept clear of Delhi College but not of the pleasures that Delhi offered to the youths of the nobility; marriage at age eighteen did not steady him. If, as is likely, he hoped that carnal gratification might soothe hurt pride, he was not the first, nor the last, to nurse the vain wish. "In the days of irresponsibility, with the exception of a few individuals, hardly anyone knew of his deeds," says the poet Hali, who became Sayyid Ahmed's friend. "Members of the *sharif* culture did whatever they did surreptitiously."[5]

The death of his older brother, to whom he had been devoted, shocked and sobered him; Sayyid Ahmed grew a beard and stopped wearing bright clothes. Soon his father died and Farid's successors at the imperial court withdrew the grants that the family was receiving in Muttaqi's name and Sayyid Ahmed had to find a job. He became a functionary in the Raj's courts and served in a string of North Indian towns, first as a reader and later as Munsif or junior judge. He worked hard and ably at his posts, and he wrote.

His energy was vast. Tract followed tract. His early education may have been limited but Sayyid Ahmed set himself hard tasks and accomplished them. He hoped that writing would add to his income. This did not happen; all the same, people spoke of the quality of the young man's Urdu, and of his commonsense and scholarship. When Sayyid Ahmed was twenty-five the new "emperor," Bahadur Shah, gave him the honorifics his father had turned down. The titles and prefixes with which a lord of the mighty Mughal empire used to be flattered were now conferred on a Munsif whose "monthly salary of barely 100 rupees was paid by the East India Company."[6]

Five years later Sayyid Ahmed's *Athar al-Sanadid*, a survey of Delhi's monuments, was published, followed, in 1855, by his version of *Ain-i-Akbari*, the 16th-century work of emperor Akbar's minister, Abul Fazl. "These two works," says Mujeeb, who is not liberal with praise, "entitle Sayyid Ahmed to a high position among the scholars of the world."[7] Sayyid Ahmed's writings in this period of Mughal downfall breathe of pride in bygone eras; like other *sharif* Muslims he too turned to the past to compensate for decline; unlike most of them he did so with skill. There are other points that we may note. Sayyid Ahmed's heart embraces Delhi and does not travel to the Persian or Arab territories his ancestors left behind. Compiling a chronology of Delhi's kings, he begins with the ancient Hindu ones. Looking for a figure to study and admire, he selects Akbar rather than Aurangzeb.

At least one of Sayyid Ahmed's contemporaries, the celebrated poet Ghalib, was unimpressed by the new edition of *Ain-i-Akbari*. Not that Ghalib would have preferred a reminder of Aurangzeb; the poet merely felt that the people to study were the British. In a *taqriz* (review poem) that he sent to Sayyid Ahmed, Ghalib said:

> You waste your time.
> Put aside the *Ain*, and parley with me;
> Open thine eyes, and examine the Englishmen,
> Their style, their manner, their trade and their art.[8]

Sayyid Ahmed indignantly returned the *taqriz* to Ghalib. But 1857 would produce a Sayyid Ahmed who agreed with it. That year, when Delhi was briefly held by rebels, and some other places too yielded to the Rising, Sayyid Ahmed was in Bijnor, an area that the ruler of Oudh had handed over to the Raj in 1801. A man called Shakespeare was the collector, the district's chief. On May 20 Nawab Mahmud Khan, who had won over some sentries of the Raj, seized control. A plucky Sayyid Ahmed confronted Mahmud and obtained safe passage out of the district for the European men, women and children trapped there, including Shakespeare and his family. Thanks to Sayyid Ahmed's persuasiveness, Mahmud conceded for a while that he was ruling the district "on behalf of the British" but soon an independent state of Bijnor was announced. The population, with a 2-to-1 Hindu-Muslim ratio, seemed willing to support Mahmud, who apparently asked Sayyid Ahmed to leave the British and join his service. Sayyid Ahmed replied. "By God, Nawab Sahib, I say that British sovereignty cannot be eliminated from India."[9]

Sayyid Ahmed proved right. The rebellion was suppressed in Bijnor, Delhi and elsewhere. In Bijnor, though not only there, British officers "pitted Hindus against Muslims" to facilitate the Raj's return.[10] What followed was not attractive. Reprisals for the cruel killings of white men, women and children, were, in their turn, harsh and indiscriminate. Because he had allowed himself to be used by the rebels, Bahadur Shah was deposed and exiled to Burma, and two of his sons were executed in his presence. Properties of suspects were confiscated all over India. Large populations were driven out of recaptured Delhi. Because it housed the Muslim nobility, the ground between the Red Fort and Jama Masjid was razed and ploughed up. Some maddened officers of the Raj saw no need for trials and killed suspects on their own; a "special commission" tried 3306 persons of whom 2025 were convicted. Of these 392 were hung. "The dust of Delhi thirsts for Muslim blood," wailed Ghalib, who had criticized the rebellion.[11] As was admitted by Colonel George Graham of the Raj's police, "At the dreadful time many innocent men, I grieve to say, suffered for the sins of the guilty."[12]

Among the guiltless victims were an uncle and cousin of Sayyid Ahmed's, slain by pro-British Sikh soldiers. Their house adjoined the home where Aziz-al-Nisa lived. Reaching there in September 1857, Sayyid Ahmed heard that his mother had taken refuge in a *syce*'s (horse-attendant's) house. He went there and called out, "Mother!" She cried: "Why have you come here? All are being killed. You will be killed also!" He then found out that she had been living on horses' grain and had not had any water for three days. Fetching a jug of water, he encountered an old female servant of his mother's, also intensely thirsty. When he poured out some water for her, the faithful old woman told him his mother's need was greater. Sayyid Ahmed made the servant drink, but she died in a few moments. Aziz-al-Nisa died a month later in Meerut, where Sayyid Ahmed had taken her.[13]

The Raj rewarded Sayyid Ahmed and would for decades speak of him as its "foremost loyal Mohammedan." He had gambled right. And he had been courageous. But he was miserable. His misery was part guilt, part sorrow. He had, after all, taken the British side against his people. Implementing the Raj's policy, he had even encouraged Bijnor's Hindu landlords in their bid to undermine Nawab Mahmud Khan. Now the heirs of the Mughals, including his kin, lay dead or battered. Feeling "that India was no place for a self-respecting Muslim,"[14] Sayyid Ahmed bitterly turned down an offer from Shakespeare of a large estate forfeited by a rebel talukdar of Bijnor. It was an episode that Sayyid Ahmed would recall:

> I said to myself that there was no one more wretched than myself. Our nation suffered like this, and I, at their expense, should become a talukdar! I declined this offer and said to Shakespeare that I no longer desired to live in India. Believe me, this grief aged me prematurely and my hair turned grey.[15]

He contemplated migrating to Egypt but an 1858 experience in Moradabad, where he was posted at the time, changed him. He found himself amidst thousands of Muslims who had come together for mourning, saw their plight and found a purpose.

> Then and there it occurred to me that my personal flight to a place of safety was contrary to all feelings of compassion and manhood. No, I must share the troubles of my nation; and whatever the afflictions there might be, I must help to alleviate them. . . . Then I decided not to leave the country.[16]

It was a classic transformation. Until Moradabad Sayyid Ahmed was the centre of his life. He focussed on Sayyid Ahmed's pleasures and successes, Sayyid Ahmed's guilts and sorrows. With Moradabad the centre changed; he started to focus on the community's condition. Concern grew into passion, and Abd al-Haqq, "the father of Urdu," would write effusively but not without a core of truth:

> Farhad did not love Shirin and Nal did not love Damayanti as much as Sayyid Ahmed loved his *qaum*. Sleeping or waking, standing or sitting, this and this alone was his devotional exercise. He reached the mystical stage of annihilation in the *qaum*.[17]

There is another way of seeing the change. Hitherto Sayyid Ahmed was studying the past and seeking inspiration from it; now he would look at the present and seek tasks for it. Sayyid Ahmed the realist had felt all along, like his grandfather Farid, that the British were in India for good. If this was so, the *qaum*'s future lay in reconciliation with the British. Sayyid Ahmed the lover of the *qaum* pursued this goal. "It is my heartfelt desire and prayer to God," he said in 1859, "that our Government and the people of India be so connected together as to be of one accord."[18]

Peace between India and the Raj would assist the *qaum*; it would also resolve the tension in Sayyid Ahmed's spirit following the 1857 events.

Sayyid Ahmed worked at both ends of the Raj-*qaum* relationship. In 1858 he wrote a memorandum, *Asbab-i-Baghawat-i-Hind* ("The Causes for India's Revolt"), which was frank about the Raj's errors. In it he recalled the ruler-subject cordiality of the Akbar era, contrasting it with the "injury done to the subjects and their alienation" during Aurangzeb's time, and added: "The English Government has existed for more than a century and to the present hour has not secured the peoples' affection."[19] Also, he wrote, "the manner of punishing" Indian soldiers who had won medals for loyalty to the East India Company but who out of religious scruple had refused to bite cartridges was "most wrong." These soldiers saw "their hands and feet manacled, looked at their medals and wept."[20] Above all, "the absence of any Indian representing the Indian point of view in the upper councils governing the country" had proved costly.[21] In 1858, only a year after what the Raj had termed the Mutiny, these were provocative words. Acting with discretion, Sayyid Ahmed sent the memo to the Raj's custodians in India and England but did not circulate it among Indians.

The memo was not without repercussions. Officials in London perused it; and there is some evidence that it encouraged Allan O. Hume, the civil servant, in his launching of the Indian National Congress, which took place in 1885.[22] Then, two years after *Asbab*, Sayyid Ahmed brought out *Loyal Mahomedans of India*, which pointed out to the Raj that not all Muslims had backed the Rising.

As for the *qaum*, Sayyid Ahmed asked it to broaden its mind and to "examine the style and art of Englishmen." "The student will discover," he said in a 1863 lecture to a Muslim audience in Calcutta, "that truth is many-sided, and that the world is a good deal wider than his own sect, or society or class."[23] Ignorance was the enemy: "If the natives of India had known anything of the mighty power which England possess, . . . the unhappy events of 1857 would never have occurred."[24] Sayyid Ahmed did more than exhort; he supplied tools. A school was started in Moradabad in 1858 and another in Ghazipur, following Sayyid Ahmed's posting there, both financed by Hindus as well as Muslims and serving all communities. An Urdu commentary on the Bible appeared, written by him; it sought to show the closeness between Islam and Christianity. Sayyid Ahmed had purchased a press in Ghazipur to print it.

In 1864 came the Translation Society, soon to be renamed the Scientific Society, through which Sayyid Ahmed hoped to "bring the knowledge and literature of the nations of the Western world within reach of the immense masses of the people of the Eastern."[25] In time the Society, which had as its patron the Duke of Argyll, Secretary of State for India, would translate forty books dealing with, among other subjects, electricity, meteorology and agriculture. When, along with Sayyid Ahmed, the Society moved to Aligarh, it acquired land there for agricultural experiments; it also acquired, in the person of Raja Jaikishan Das, a Hindu, an able backer. And Sayyid Ahmed himself had acquired a motto. According to Graham, whose friendship with Sayyid Ahmed began in this period, the motto was: "Educate, educate, educate."[26]

* * *

Yet just whom was he striving to educate or reconcile with the Raj? The Muslims of India? Or all Indians? The answer is, now the one, now the other. He never chose to learn English, and in his Urdu (as in the Urdu of many others) the word *qaum* at times meant the Muslims of India, at other times Hindus and Muslims together.

It only rarely meant the global brotherhood of Islam. Though he enunciated the Islamic theory that "it was irrelevant whether a believer was white or black, Turkish or Tadjhik, an Arab or a Chinese, a Punjabi or a Hindustani,"[27] Sayyid Ahmed frontally opposed the idea of a continuing *Khilafat*: "The Turkish *khalifa*'s sovereignty does not extend over us. We are residents of India and subjects of the British Government."[28] India was the land he was involved with, and on one occasion he said that the word Hindu could designate all those living in India, Muslims as well as Hindus.[29] When he had Muslims alone in mind, his *qaum* was the Indian Muslim community, not "the *ummah* of common belief."[30]

Again, when the Viceroy, Lord Lawrence, gave Sayyid Ahmed a gold medal in 1886, services to "his countrymen" were cited,[31] not services to the Muslim community. The Moradabad and Ghazipur schools were "Indian" rather than "Muslim," and the Scientific Society was more than a body for Muslims. When, after 1861, three Indians, all non-Muslims, were included in the Viceroy's Legislative Council, Sayyid Ahmed said that he "rejoiced" and expressed "thanks to the Almighty" that the three had "discharged their duties manfully and right well."[32] That the three — the rulers of Patiala and Benares and Sir Dinkar Rao — belonged to a class for which Sayyid Ahmed felt instinctive warmth does not cancel the picture of a man interested in India, and not just in Muslims.

Other elements strengthen the picture. In 1866 Sayyid Ahmed, no doubt inspired by the British Indian Association started in 1851 in Calcutta, launches the British India Association in Aligarh, where he is now transferred. Once more it is a joint Muslim-Hindu affair. Indians, he says at the inauguration, should "honestly, openly and respectfully speak out their grievances" to their British rulers; and he refers to "the great God above" who is "equally the God of the Jew, the Hindu, the Christian and the Mohammedan."[33] The association's petitions are educational, economic — and non-communal. It seeks a vernacular (not Muslim) university in the North-West Provinces (roughly today's U.P.) where "the arts, sciences and other . . . European literature may be taught . . . in Urdu."[34] In 1867, though still a functionary of the Raj, he leads a walk-out at an Agra ceremony because Indian guests have been assigned inferior places; Hindus and Muslims leave with him.

Now, however, the picture receives a shaking, or at least Sayyid Ahmed does. He finds some Hindus in Benares, his latest posting, campaigning for the substitution of Hindi for Urdu in the courts. To Sayyid Ahmed Urdu "is a memento of the Muslim rule in this country,"[35] and the heart of any common Hindu-Muslim culture. He is hurt, even bitter, and his old friend Shakespeare, also posted in Benares, finds that "for the first time" Sayyid Ahmed is speaking about "the welfare of Muslims alone."

"Before this," says Shakespeare, "you were always keen about the welfare of your countrymen in general." Replies Sayyid Ahmed:

> Now I am convinced that both these communities will not join whole-heartedly in anything. . . . On account of the so-called "educated" people, hostility between the two communities will increase immensely in the future. He who lives will see."[36]

There was a fresh jolt when a few Hindu members of the Scientific Society wanted Hindi to replace Urdu in the Society's publications. Sayyid Ahmed saw it as "a proposal which will make Hindu-Muslim unity impossible."[37] Fruit as well as cement of friendship, Urdu was now being seen as a Muslim rather than an Indian possession. Ignoring its largely indigenous vocabulary, some Hindus stressed Urdu's alien associations; they were assisted by Muslims who loaded their Urdu with ornate Arabic and Persian expressions.

The poet Hali urged both communities to adopt "the simple, spoken language of Delhi, which was current among the city's Hindus and Muslims";[38] and Mahatma Gandhi was to say later that if there could be a common language for all, it would be the language of Hali's *Plaint of a Widow*.[39] Urdu and Hindi would have fused into one language in two scripts if such words had been heeded.

Sayyid Ahmed was grieved and upset by these signs of a rejection of Urdu, but he was always capable of recapturing his belief in cooperation.

In 1869, on his first voyage to Britain, he would write of "the men and women of Hindustan, who are really one . . ."[40]

* * *

Graham the police officer had suggested the journey, and when Mahmud, Sayyid Ahmed's son, was granted the North-West Provinces' first scholarship to Cambridge, Sayyid Ahmed took furlough and crossed the seas with him. Hamed, the other son, also went along, as did a young friend, Khudadad Beg, and a servant called Chajju.* Sayyid Ahmed was fifty-two, white-bearded and keen to discover the Occident. He described his journey and discoveries in letters to Raja Jaikishan Das and others, which were published in the *Aligarh Institute Gazette*, the journal of the Scientific Society. The party travelled by train to Jubbulpore; by bullock-cart from there to Nagpur, a matter of "three days and three nights"; by train to Bombay, Sayyid Ahmed noting the tunnels it had to go through, "rather the work of Titans than of men"; by the P. & O. ship *Baroda* to Suez; thence by train to Alexandria; by the *Poona* to Marseilles; by train again, via Paris, to Calais, where they crossed the English Channel.

Sayyid Ahmed wrote that on the *Baroda* "we ate freely of mutton, beef, chickens and pigeons," as the manner of killing was "also lawful for Mohammedans." He added:

> At our first meal sherry and claret glasses were alongside our plates, and we turned them upside down. The steward thinking that we drank wine, brought us a bottle; and thinking that I must be the great man of the party, having a long white beard, began pouring some out for me. I said, "No, no," and he stopped, but gave me the names of a number of other wines. I kept on saying "No, no! only cold water," and he then removed the wine glasses and brought us ice water, the liquor made by the Almighty for mankind.[41]

On a Sunday Sayyid Ahmed saw that "all the English assembled on deck and seated themselves on chairs and the clergyman read prayers." Later he described the occasion:

> I stood silently and respectfully near them, walking every now and then. I saw the way God was prayed to, and admired His catholicity. Some men bow down to idols; others address him seated in chairs, with head uncovered; some address Him with head covered and beads on, with hands clasped in profound respect; many abuse Him but He cares not for this.[42]

---

*It is not clear whether Chajju was a Hindu or a Muslim.

When a passenger died and Sayyid Ahmed saw his body was lowered into the waters, he reflected: "When man dies, do what you like — burn him, commit him to the deep, bury him in the earth— what has been has been, and what is to be is to be."[43] A Hindu or Christian or Jew might have told himself the same thing, but other reactions of his were uniquely Muslim. "Early on Friday," he observed, "the Arabian coast came in sight, greatly to my delight. As I gazed upon it, I thought of God having caused our blessed Prophet to be born in it." The ship passed "quite close to Messina, the capital of Sicily." Wrote Sayyid Ahmed: "At one time Sicily was for long in the hands of the Mohammedans, but I could not see any buildings built by our race. That there must be some traces of our oc-cupation is, I think, certain."[44]

Entering the continent, Sayyid Ahmed noted with awe "the beauty of the buildings, the brilliancy of the lamps and the number of well-dressed, good-looking men and women" that he saw in Marseilles and Paris. He was "struck dumb with amazement" by "the life-like fidelity" of the paint-ings at the Palace of Versailles; compared with this palace's canals, "the famous canal in the Delhi Fort in whose waters I used in former days to play was undoubtedly far inferior."[45]

Sayyid Ahmed spent seventeen months in England. His friend Graham, also on furlough, took him to the Derby. Lord Lawrence, no longer Viceroy, called on him. Sayyid Ahmed saw Queen Victoria opening a viaduct, met Carlyle, attended the last reading given by Charles Dickens, and received the Star of India from the Duke of Argyll.

He was impressed that servants in England were educated, and wrote about the maids in the house where he had rented rooms:

> The first, Anne Smith, is very clever, reads the papers and does her work like a watch or machine. . . . She calls us all "sir." Khudadad Beg she calls Mr. Beg, and on her hearing that that was not his full name, said, "Sir, please pardon me, but your full name is very dif-ficult." There was great fun over this, and we have all taken to calling Khudadad Beg "Mr. Beg". . . The other, Elizabeth Matthews, very young and modest, maid-of-all-work, in spite of her poverty invariably buys a half-penny paper called the "Echo.[46]

He sought "the cause of England's civilisation" and found it in the fact that "all the arts and sciences are in the language of the country." Ac-cordingly, Indians desirous of "bettering India" should have "the whole of the arts and sciences translated into their own language." "This," he told his friends in India, "is truth, this is the truth, this is the truth"; and he wished it "written in gigantic letters on the Himalayas."[47]

England's attainments, the literacy of her coachmen and cabmen, conversations at the clubs and homes where he dined and the riches of her "famous mansions, museums, engineering works and gun-foundries" bowled him over. He delivered himself of remarks that could not have appealed to the readers of the *Aligarh Institute Gazette*:

> Without flattering the English, I can truly say that the natives of India, high and low, merchants and petty shopkeepers, educated and illiterate, when contrasted with the English in education, manners and uprightness, are as like them as a dirty animal is to an able and handsome man.[48]

He himself, however, had been wounded by what Sir William Muir, Governor of the North-West Provinces, had written in his *Life of Mohammed*. To prepare a rebuttal Sayyid Ahmed spent months in London's libraries, and to find money for publishing it he instructed, from London, the sale of his library in India. He also visited Cambridge and Oxford, and several private schools including Eton and Harrow, and set his mind on a modern college for India's Muslims. There he would raise an advanced elite; and through a journal to be called *Tahdhib-al-Akhlaq* or *Mohammedan Social Reformer*, for which he prepared blocks in England, he would reform a *qaum*'s manners. He gathered that Addison and Steele had done that through the *Tatler* and the *Spectator*. If that Moradabad experience had shifted his focus from the past to the present, England moved it from the present to the future.

His relationship with the Raj was a many-tiered affair. At one level he was a loyal employee — in his own words, "one of her Majesty's subordinate judges of the Uncovenanted Service," nursing "fidelity and attachment to the British Government and to my most gracious Sovereign."[49] At another level, as a student of history, he deemed British rule over India both desirable and permanent, and British achievements worthy of emulation. At a third level he was a proud representative of Hindustan and Mughal scion who found it natural that a duke or a lord should be entertaining him. At a fourth level he was a Muslim convinced of the excellence of his religion, telling an English friend while in England: "My religion is Islam and I believe in it firmly. . . . Islam does not approve of limited monarchy or hereditary kingship."[50]

His relationship with his *qaum* or *qaums* was also complex, and his seemingly insulting words reflected his impatience with a people he cared for. They had not come up to the West's standards; he hoped to rebuke or shame them into change. "Hindustanis" had the potential, he wrote from England, "to become, if not the superior, at least the equal of England."[51] Sensing his inner sentiments, many Indians would back him despite his uncomplimentary remarks.

* * *

Returning to Benares in October 1870, Sayyid Ahmed "settled down in a large house on the banks of the Barna river" and lived, somewhat to Graham's disappointment, "in European style." "Asiatics who have lived in England seem to prefer our habits," observed Graham, who had come back to his post. Apprehensive that "petty slights" from Britons in India might undo the effects of England, where Sayyid Ahmed "had everywhere been well received," Graham invited him to dinner in his home in the company of the Judge of Benares, Sayyid Ahmed's English superior, and other "English ladies and gentlemen." Graham thought that "this was the first occasion on which a Mohammedan gentleman had dined at a private (British) dinner party in India."[52]

The proud Hindustani had in fact imagined a slight — he had heard in England that Sir William Muir, the North-West's Governor, had accused him of falsehood. An offended Sayyid Ahmed refused to report his return to Muir, the man who had recommended Mahmud's name for Cambridge and Sayyid Ahmed's for the Star of India. When Muir learned of Sayyid Ahmed's feelings he wrote, "I should never have dreamt of imputing to you anything approaching a misstatement of facts." What Sayyid Ahmed had heard, said Muir, was a mistranslation of his remark. The oriental was assuaged. "I see now how wrong I was," he replied.[53]

The first issue of *Tahdhib-i-Akhlaq* appeared on December 24, 1870, within three months of Sayyid Ahmed's return to India. Two days later a committee that would launch the Aligarh college swung into action. The journal raised a storm, for Sayyid Ahmed was saying in it that the slavery that Muslims had practised in their past was forbidden by the Qur'an; that polygamy was permissible only if the husband was sure he could be equally just to each wife; that interest on Government Promissory Notes and loans was not prohibited; that dressing like non-Muslims and eating like them was not forbidden; and that contemporary Muslims were entitled to practise *ijtihad*, or independent judgment, on modern questions not covered by the Qur'an or some authentic *hadith*. Questioning the traditional story that the Prophet had one night been physically carried from Mecca to Jerusalem, he argued that the lines cited in support for it referred to a dream.[54]

He had, in Ikram's words, "assailed the pride of people who had lost everything except that"; some called him "Kafir" (infidel) or "atheist" or

"Kristan" (Christian). Yet if he made enemies he also, to quote Ikram again, "caused a deep stir in the still waters of the Muslim community."[55] And even those who never forgave Sayyid Ahmed his religious views seemed to hail the journal's bare and simple Urdu.

* * *

"After 1857," writes Jawaharlal Nehru in his autobiography, "the heavy hand of the British fell more on the Muslims than on the Hindus. They considered the Muslims more aggressive and militant, possessing memories of recent rule in India and therefore more dangerous."[56] The Muslims in turn were sullen toward the Raj. In this situation a reconciler like Sayyid Ahmed was of value to the British. They assisted him with his college. Muir, the Governor, released 75 acres in Aligarh, formerly used by the British military. Lord Northbrook the Vicerory gave Rs 10,000 from his personal funds. Lord Lytton, his successor, laid the foundation stone in January 1877. And a Briton observing the ceremony bestowed the unofficial title, "Leader of advanced Islam in India," on Sayyid Ahmed, who had retired the previous year from the judicial service of the Raj and settled in Aligarh.[57] Help also came from the Indian rich, including the Muslim rule of Rampur, the Sikh ruler of Patiala and the Hindu ruler of Vizianagaram. The small Indian too was approached; Sayyid Ahmed would go door-to-door with a bag round his neck or recite poetry for a fee or even sell lottery tickets.

The Raj was not uniformly helpful. Some Aligarh-based officials tried unsuccessfully to block the transfer of the 75 acres (the proud Hindustani refused thereafter to have social dealings with them), while others successfully vetoed Sayyid Ahmed's wish for a university rather than a college. The Mohammedan Anglo-Oriental College, as it was called, or MAO, offered arts, science and law courses—in English. Sayyid Ahmed said that his earlier faith in vernacular teaching had been a "fallacy";[58] for one thing, he said, translations were scarce and hard to produce. Indeed he now urged the government to "abolish in *toto* the system of imparting instruction in the Indian vernacular."[59] The difficulty of obtaining the Raj's support for a college that taught in Urdu played a part in the about-turn, as did the realization that young Muslims needed an English education to rise in government service.

Yet MAO was not as reformist or modern as his journal the *Reformer*. He saw the college not as a vehicle for his ideas but simply as a place where "Mussalmans may acquire an English education without prejudice to their religion."[60] There was no question, for instance, of women being considered for admission. Though Muir had spoken in Aligarh, even before the college got going, of "the necessity of educating your girls,"[61] Sayyid Ahmed argued that "no satisfactory education can be provided for Mahammedan females until a large number of Mohammedan males received a sound education."[62]

Also, Sayyid Ahmed announced that the religious education of the boys would be handled not by him but by a committee of orthodox Muslims. The assurance was kept, and Sayyid Ahmed ensured that no controversial religious opinion of his fell into any student's hands. He would not let his reformist views confuse the youth.[63]

Most histories of the college (which became a university in 1920) begin with an assertion of Muslim aloofness from modern English education in the nineteenth century and its corollary of a disproportionate Hindu weightage in the Raj's schools, colleges and offices. Sayyid Ahmed himself regularly made the assertion. According to him, many Muslims of the time believed that the schools and colleges of the Raj were meant for the spread of Christianity and that even "the study of English by a Mussalman" came close to "the embracing of Christianity."[64] Hafeez Malik, who sees Sayyid Ahmed as a father of Muslim separatism on the subcontinent and admires him in that role, concludes nonetheless, on the basis of a detailed study, that "the Muslims' repudiation of modern education was a myth that Sir Sayyid himself created and then assiduously disseminated."[65] Pointing out that "from 1882 to 1898 Muslim graduates of (Sayyid Ahmed's) MAO College totalled 122, while those of (the Government-run) Allahabad University were 250," Malik adds, "It is intriguing to hypothesize that even in the absence of Sir Sayyid modern education among Muslims would have spread."[66]

Acknowledging that in Bengal, Orissa and parts of Sayyid Ahmed's North-West province, Muslim participation "in college and university education" was "discouraging," Malik ascribes the result to "widespread poverty among the Muslims" rather than to "religious prejudice." And he claims that in places like Bombay, the Awadh and Punjab, Muslims responded "positively" to British education. Malik's inference is that Sayyid Ahmed "wanted to see not merely a 'just' and proportionate representation of Muslims in modern schools but their largest possible number."[67]

Sayyid Ahmed's own tables seem to tell a somewhat different tale,[68] and there is no reason to doubt the realism of the woeful picture that William Hunter paints, in his *The Indian Mussalmans*, of Muslim poverty, joblessness and "neglect of modern education" in the Bengal of the 1860s and early 1870s. Writing in 1872, Hunter said: "There is now scarcely a Government office in Calcutta in which a Muhammadan can hope for any post above the rank of porter, messenger, filler of ink-pots and mender of pens." "Some years ago," added Hunter, "out of three hundred boys in the English College (Calcutta), not one per cent were Muslim."[69]

Two sets of figures can easily conflict.* What is indisputable is that Sayyid Ahmed urged Muslims to support and join *his* "modern" college; he did not exhort them to join the Raj's modern institutions. This suggests that Muslim control of Muslim education was as much his aim as modernity. It is a reading confirmed by what Sayyid Ahmed said in 1882:

> After a full consideration of the question in all its bearings, I have come to the conclusion that the native public cannot obtain suitable education unless the people take the entire management of their education into their own hands.... The Government should ... withdraw its interference.[70]

Because he wants a Muslim college, and wants Muslims to join and support it, he hands over religious teaching to an orthodox committee. And because the Muslim community senses Sayyid Ahmed's Muslimness, it forgives him his heterodox views and supports the college. The role of the orthodox committee helps, of course, as does Sayyid Ahmed's insistence that all Muslim students shall pray five times a day and wear a red fez. Hali's appreciative reference to Sayyid Ahmed in his *Musaddas*, which comes out in 1879, "steadies Muslim opinion."[71] The abuses of enemies ("Infidel!" "Satan!" etc.) are in vain. The college progresses, and Sayyid Ahmed himself is not shaken or slowed down by "anonymous letters in which the writers said they had sworn on the Koran to take his life."[72]

MAO would belong to the *qaum* (the Muslim *qaum*) and not to any sect within it. Observers would be "struck by the sight of the Shia and Sunni praying-places side by side."[73] MAO was Muslim but not only for Muslims. Hindus were welcome to join it as day scholars and were assured exemption from the rules and religious courses mandatory for Muslims. To win Hindu confidence Sayyid Ahmed forbade the slaughter of cows on the campus. In 1887 three of the managing committee of eleven were Hindus; in 1894 two of the seven Indian teachers were Hindus; and in some of the early years of the college Hindu students even outnumbered Muslim ones. Sayyid Ahmed said "that Hindus and Mussalmans are equally entitled to get scholarships" in MAO and at least on one occasion he announced a gold medal from his own pocket to go to "the Hindu

---

*The more so if they do not belong to an identical period. Sayyid Ahmed speaks of a period earlier than the one Malik analyzes. Compare Malik's *Sir Sayyid*, pages 116–72, with Sayyid Ahmed's table in Shan Muhammad's *Sir Syed*, page 56.

student who may pass the approaching B.A. Examination in the First Class." Thrilled by such gestures, Hali said in verse that one who had not seen Hindu-Muslim love could find it at MAO — a sweeping remark but with a grain of truth.[74]

Yet in time the campus's tradition of Hindu-Muslim friendship would be violated. Even if the campus itself might remain fairly free of communal violence, the shadow of recurring Hindu-Muslim disturbances in Aligarh town would fall over it. MAO (or Aligarh Muslim University) would produce rows of Muslim government servants, including many who performed important tasks in the Pakistan that would emerge fifty years after Sayyid Ahmed's death. It would educate popular leaders like the Ali brothers, Shaukat and Muhammad, and leaders of government like Liaqat Ali and Khwaja Nazimuddin. But it would eventually symbolize neither the modernity that had become Sayyid Ahmed's goal while in England nor the religious reforms that he espoused after his return, but Muslim solidarity and conservatism. Some called it Muslim nationalism and thanked God for it; others regretted it and called it Muslim communalism. Sayyid Ahmed's vision was, at best, only partially fulfilled.

* * *

With the launching of MAO Sayyid Ahmed was seen as a national figure and a leader of the Indian Muslims. Lytton named him to the Imperial Legislative Council, as, in his turn, did Ripon, Lytton's successor as Viceroy. In the Council Sayyid Ahmed initiated a bill favouring powers for compulsory vaccination against smallpox and give vigorous backing to a measure to end racial discrimination in Indian courts. The proud Hindustani opposed his friend Graham when the latter criticized a proposal by Allan Octavian Hume, another of the Raj's custodians, for a native volunteer corps in India. "In not allowing the natives to become volunteers," said Sayyid Ahmed in a letter to Graham, "the Government means to say that they do not trust the natives of India." He then proceeded to remind Graham of the saying, "If you want us to trust you, you should also trust us."[75]

Now and again an incident would offend or embitter the Mughal scion; at times he would wonder whether "our European friends, conquerors of this country," would ever "condescend to sit down on the same bench with a conquered Indian."[76] But though he never concealed his hurt at haughtiness, he refused to be provoked into opposition to the British: 1857 and its aftermath were always fresh in his mind. Rebellion was folly and loyalty rewarding. These maxims he never flouted, and the Raj on its part nurtured the loyal.

Viceroys and Governors visited Aligarh and praised MAO. Sayyid

Ahmed was put on the Education and Public Service Commissions. His son Sayyid Mahmud became a judge. Good jobs awaited MAO graduates. A *qaum* that had been in the depths of despair was beginning to acquire influence. Sayyid Ahmed thought and claimed that his strategy was working, and some of his *qaum* felt that Sayyid Ahmed had steered it successfully across perilous and unknown waters. He was their sensible captain. Because of him the Muslim community did not feel "the void created by the disappearance of Muslim rule."[77]

Himself possessing the Raj's ear, he was not keen on the masses obtaining it. "Adult franchise," "open competition for jobs" and "one-man-one-vote," phrases that were beginning to be heard, made him uneasy. They made sense in an educated and homogeneous nation but India was neither. Indians possessed neither the maturity nor the unity that democracy demanded. In India it would lead to rule by the lower classes and to Hindu rule.

In part it was a class reaction. "Men of good family," he said, "would never like to trust their lives and prosperity to people of low rank, with whose humble origins they are well acquainted." But it was also a *qaum* reaction:

> Now suppose that all the English were to leave India. Then who would be rulers of India? Is it possible that two *qaums*—the Muslim and Hindu—could sit on the same throne? Most certainly no. It is necessary that one of them will conquer the other and thrust it down.[78]

When Lord Ripon's Local Self-Government Bill was before the Council Sayyid Ahmed made a successful plea for separate nomination of Muslims to local boards and district councils. His speech on the occasion deserves to be quoted at some length:

> The system of representation by election, in countries where the population is composed of one race and one creed, is no doubt the best system that can be adopted.
>
> But, my lord, in a country like India, where caste distinctions still flourish, where there is no fusion of the various races, where religious distinctions are still violent, where education in its modern sense has still not made an equal or proportionate progress among all sections of the population, I am convinced that the introduction of the principle of election, pure and simple, [to] the local boards and district councils would be attended with evils of great significance. . . .
>
> The larger community would totally override the interests of the smaller community . . . and the measures might make the differences of race and creed more violent than ever.[79]

This speech was made in January 1883, almost three years before the founding of the Indian National Congress, largely the inspiration of Allan Octavian Hume, the man whose advocacy of an Indian volunteer corps had appealed to Sayyid Ahmed. Congress's founders — Hume and his Indian and British friends — were loyal to the Raj but believed in constructive criticism. Lord Dufferin, the Viceroy at the time, encouraged Hume; there were signs of popular discontent and he thought Congress might serve as a safety-valve. Among Congress's aims was "the eradication of all possible racial, religious or provincial prejudices," but its demands, voiced at its first session, for "the admission of a considerable proportion of elected members" to the Legislative Councils and for facilitating a wider entry of Indians into the I.C.S. went against Sayyid Ahmed's grain.[80]

He was silent for two years but when a Muslim, Badruddin Tyabji, was named Congress President, Sayyid Ahmed spoke out. Congress was clearly bidding for Muslim support, and Sayyid Ahmed felt he ought to give the *qaum* a steer. He attacked Congress's demands. Elections would be inappropriate because "the Viceroy cannot address members of the lower classes as 'my honourable colleagues', nor can he invite them to grand dinners."[81] Also, "because their population is four times as numerous, Hindus will have four votes to every one Muslim vote. How will the Mohammedan guard his interests?"[82] Open exams for the I.C.S. would be unfair because "one *qaum* (the Bengali) is far ahead of the others in western education." "Can the Mohammedans compete with the Bengalis in higher English education?" he asked.[83]

Aware of Sayyid Ahmed's influence Tyabji and Hume tried to allay his fears. Tyabji said in a letter to Sayyid Ahmed:

> If any proposal is made which would subject the Mussalmans to the Hindus or would vest the exclusive power in Hindus to the detriment of the Mussalmans, I would oppose it with all my strength, but the Congress proposes to do no such thing. It aims are and must be for the benefit of all communities equally.

Tyabji added that it "passed [his] comprehension" that Sayyid Ahmed should think that Congress "was composed of Bengali Babus alone"; not only the Hindus but the Muslims of Bombay and Madras presidencies were taking an active part in it, he argued.[84] But Sayyid Ahmed was not going to be budged. He countered:

> I do not understand what the words 'National Congress' mean. . . . You regard the doings of the misnamed National Congress as bene-

ficial to India, but I am sorry to say that I regard them as injurious not only to my community but also to India at large.[85]

Sayyid Ahmed's determined opposition and the support he was receiving made a mark on Tyabji, who wrote to Hume of his regret that "the Mahomedans have been split into two factions." Added Tyabji: "I have come to the distinct conclusion after the most careful consideration of which I am capable that it is time to cease holding the Congress every year."[86] The drastic recommendation was not heeded, but it is noteworthy that Tyabji made it.

In Jawaharlal Nehru's view, Sayyid Ahmed, who was knighted in 1888, "was not opposed to the National Congress because he considered it predominantly a Hindu organisation; he opposed it because he thought it was politically too aggressive."[87] The scholar W.C. Smith agrees and says that Sayyid Ahmed "opposed the Congress and advised Muslims to stay out of it because it was too disrespectful, not because it was too Hindu."[88] Malik, on the other hand, speaks of the "Hindu middle class which was the main prop of the All-India National Congress,"[89] and implies that Sayyid Ahmed's aloofness from Congress was linked to its "Hindu" character. However, there is no reference in Sayyid Ahmed's numerous criticisms of Congress to its supposed Hinduness. He was against Congress because he did not want to disturb the Raj-*qaum* equilibrium for which he had carefully and successfully laboured.

The truth of Nehru's view is confirmed by the fact that Sayyid Ahmed sought and obtained Hindu backing for his opposition of Congress. Many a Hindu raja and talukdar of the North expressed himself against Congress's "disloyal demonstrations";[90] rather like Sayyid Ahmed, the Maharaja of Benares argued that "representative institutions was an occidental idea."[91] Sayyid Ahmed gave such Hindus, and Muslims who thought similarly, a platform for airing their views, the United Indian Patriotic Association, formed by him in 1888. Within a month fifty local groups joined the apex body; accounts of their meetings, at which Congress was invariably denounced, were "published with great pride" by the *Aligarh Institute Gazette*.[92] Malik is wrong. Sayyid Ahmed had mounted a Hindustani, not a Muslim, campaign against Congress.

* * *

The platform seemed to change toward the end of Sayyid Ahmed's life. In December 1893 the Patriotic Association gave place to the Mohammedan Defence Association (MDA), with Theodore Beck, principal of MAO, as its secretary. As Ikram notes, Sayyid Ahmed gave "little time" to the new body.[93] In Hali's bulky biography of Sir Sayyid there is no reference to it. Yet there is no doubt that Sayyid Ahmed had blessed it. In Ikram's view, he did so because Hindu-Muslim riots took place in Bombay in 1893 and were followed by a Hindu revivalist movement that encouraged the playing of festival music on the streets. If, as happened at times, this music was played before mosques, Muslims were offended. The movement also asked for a ban on cow slaughter. "Muslims who refused to abide by the Hindu sentiment in favour of the cow were subjected to a severe economic boycott," says Ikram.[94] If this could happen under the Raj, what would be the fate of Muslims under Hindu rule? As Ikram sees it, this reasoning led Sayyid Ahmed to the MDA.

Questioning the analysis, the historian Tara Chand says that "the doubtful credit for twisting Sir Syed's original policy and directing it into communalist channels must be given to Principal Beck and his English colleagues."[95] Shibli, the influential poet who taught at MAO, believed that "Sir Syed was not a flatterer but whatever he did in politics was due to the British influence."[96] "Beck assiduously tried to wean Sir Syed away from nationalism, and to evoke in him enthusiasm for a rapprochement between the Muslims and the Government," say Asoka Mehta and Achyut Patwardhan, the socialists, in their book, *The Communal Triangle*.[97]

We must turn to the facts. Theodore Beck, a Quaker's son, was a bright Cambridge student and president of the Cambridge Union when Sayyid Ahmed's son Mahmud recruited him. On his arrival in Aligarh at the end of 1883 he was seen by another Briton as "a pretty little young man with pink cheeks and blue eyes."[98] He persuaded two other presidents of the Cambridge Union to join him at MAO, his brother-in-law Walter Raleigh, later "a famous professor of English at Oxford,"[99] and Harold Cox. Other Cambridge men who before long also taught at Aligarh included T.W. Arnold, later to rise to eminence in scholarship, and Theodore Morison, principal from 1899, when Beck died, to 1905.

An American scholar, David Lelyveld, has delved into the lives and backgrounds of these Cambridge graduates who were to mould the early MAO generations. He finds that Beck was a "Tory radical" and Cox a socialist in the Union debates. Beck was against the House of Lords and for Irish Home Rule, women's rights and a classless society. He also denounced British rule in India and supported a motion moved by Morison that "John Bull is a revolting national ideal."[100]

Lelyveld's conclusion is that Beck "was a man more influenced than influencing," and that "under intense indoctrination from Sayyid Mahmud on the voyage out (to India), and anxious to give himself heart and soul to the Aligarh cause, Beck had abandoned his undergraduate sympathy for Indian nationalism."[101] A desire "to devote his life to restoring a people who once thronged the palaces of the great Moghul" captured Beck.[102] Shortly after his arrival in Aligarh, he wrote to Raleigh a letter that summed up his conversion to what Lelyveld calls the Aligarh party line:

> The Muhammadans were, you know, for two centuries the rulers of Upper India. . . . (After Britain came) the most downtrodden of the Hindoos, the Bengalis, eagerly embraced the opportunities of English education, while the proud Muhammadans held sulkily aloof. . . . Accordingly, our founder, Syed Ahmed Khan, set to work to mould the opinion of his countrymen.[103]

Sayyid Ahmed's Legislative Council remarks against "the principle of election, pure and simple" were made before Congress was founded and, as Ikram points out, "full eleven months before Theodore Beck set foot on Indian soil."[104] Lelyveld's finding that Beck was "more influenced than influencing" has to be accepted as a fair description of at least the initial phase of the Sayyid Ahmed-Beck relationship. Later on Beck became confident and assertive and in some ways more zealous than Sayyid Ahmed: as Lelyveld puts it, "The British professors enforced attendance at prayers with a determination unmatched by their pious Muslim predecessors."[105]

Talented, dedicated and mixing freely with the boys in the hostel and on the sports field, they were effective promoters of a Raj-*qaum* understanding. Moreover, Beck meddled in politics in a way that principals rarely do. He opposed Congress publicly and strongly; he said that "the English and the Mahomedans should become united in a firm alliance," and he assailed what he called "the anti-cowkilling movement."[106] Beck, not Sayyid Ahmed, founded the MDA; Beck, in Ikram's phrase, was the new body's "life and soul."[107] In Sayyid Ahmed's last years, Beck ran the college, giving rise to the saying: "*Qaum Khuda Ki, College Sir Syed Ka, Hukm Beck Bahadur Ka.*" ("The *qaum* is God's, the college Sir Sayyid's, the rule Beck's.")[108]

None of this makes Sayyid Ahmed an instrument in Beck's hands. He was ever the proud Hindustani. If anything, as Ikram says, Sayyid Ahmed's "obstinate and self-willed nature . . . increased with the years." On the other hand, it should be noted that, Ikram's words notwithstanding, the stir against cow-killing troubled Beck more than it seems to have troubled Sayyid Ahmed. Shan Muhammad for one quotes Sayyid Ahmed as saying in 1897: "If by abandoning cow-slaughter more Hindu and Muslim co-operation is achieved, it is a thousand times better than sticking to the practice."[109] Shan Muhammad also contrasts a Beck statement of 1895 on Hindu-Muslim unity with a remark that Sayyid Ahmed made in 1897, a year before his death. Said Beck: "Anglo-Muhammadan friendship was possible but friendship between Muslims and the followers of Hindu and Sikh religions was impossible."[110] And Sayyid Ahmed: "Without any doubt, I want friendship, unity and love between the two communities."[111] Taken together, the evidence shows that Beck had little to do with Sayyid Ahmed's stand against Congress; but it suggests that without him the MDA might not have been formed.

* * *

Numerous guests, Muslims, Hindus, Sikhs and Britons, visited him in his large house. It was filled with books and furnished in the European style by the Cambridge-educated Mahmud. Practising what he preached, Sayyid Ahmed had adopted British clothes and table manners. However, his serious writing was done on the floor. While calling himself "an illiterate," "ignorant" and "not qualified,"[112] he continued to write on Islam. Between 1880 and 1888 four volumes of a commentary on the Qur'an appeared. Says Ikram:

> When writing his Commentary, for some time he had given up going to bed. He would sit and work on the floor, surrounded by books and try to keep himself awake by drinking cups of tea. When sleep overpowered him, he would take a book for a pillow and sleep on the floor for an hour or so and again resume his work.[113]

The Commentary was as provocative as his previous religious writing, but it was written to shield Islam, not to undermine it. His loyalty was confirmed by remarks in the last phase of his life. In 1884 he said, "I am an utter nothing, yet I am a descendant of the Messenger who is the mercy of the two worlds. I shall walk on the path of my ancestor."[114] But it was more than a matter of descent. He reaffirmed Islam, he claimed, "not because I was born in a Muslim home," but because "considerable reflection and thought with an open mind" had given him "full certainty" about his faith.[115] When a schoolboy praised the old man's achievements, Sayyid Ahmed replied: "My dear boy, should you progress sky-high, yet not remain a Muslim in the process, then of what use will all this prosperity be to you?"[116]

The scholar Muhammad Umar al-din insists that "Sir Sayyid was first and last a religious man."[117] Christian Troll's admirable research leaves him with "no doubt that a genuinely religious concern played a central role in [Sayyid Ahmed's] life."[118] Mujeeb does not quite agree. In his view Sayyid Ahmed's was basically the non-religious mind of one who "sought to achieve essentially secular values." "He desired," says Mujeeb, "a position of honour for the Muslims in India and felt, quite correctly, that the traditional view of Islam was a real hindrance to progress."[119]

Sayyid Ahmed himself once said that from his "earliest childhood [his] mind could have developed in no other direction but the religious one."[120] He also said that there was a practical motive for his commentary. Having "striven to spread" education "in the English sciences" among Muslim youths, it was his duty now "to do whatever was in my power" to rid "the original luminous face of Islam" of "the black stains" of irrationalities read into it or added to it. If this was not done, the ones educated by him would be "disaffected towards Islam."[121]

Whatever the impulse, the results were significant. Thus Mujeeb thinks that Sayyid Ahmed's "insight and sincerity enabled him to pick out a few issues which religious thinkers had been evading."[122] Sayyid Ahmed questioned the authenticity of several Traditions (*hadith*) and declared that he was as capable as the learned jurists of the past at interpreting Islam. *Taqlid*, acceptance of the old interpretations, was not binding. "We should resolve upon investigating all matters," he wrote, "whether they concern religion or worldly life. We must remember that circumstances keep on changing and we are daily faced with new problems and needs."[123] He believed wholly in the Qur'an, he said, and in the One God and in Muhammad as the last Prophet, but this was because he had found that the Qur'an was in conformity with nature. This did not, he added, surprise him, for the "word of God" and the "work of God' had to harmonize.[124]

Still, the Qur'an had to be studied in the light of reason if Islam was to retain the educated in its fold. "It does not satisfy the mind of the doubter," said Sayyid Ahmed, "to simply say that in Islam this has been taught in this way and has to be accepted."[125] And he saw the educated and believing Muslim of the future as having "philosophy in his right hand and natural science in the left and, crowning his head, the *kalimah*, 'There is no deity but God'."[126] The ethics Sayyid Ahmed advocates in his commentary gives "due importance," in Troll's words, "to the intentions of the heart" and goes beyond "mere formalism and legalism." Troll thinks that this emphasis may reflect the sufi tradition which was a part of Sayyid Ahmed's early life.[127]

We saw earlier that he was vilified for the religious views he had expressed in the *Reformer*. The commentary invited less hostility because his opinions were no longer new. Still, it is of interest to note what the head of the influential Muslim theological school of Deoband said in 1889. Maulana Rashid Ahmed was asked if Muslims could join the Congress, which included Hindus, and also if they could join the MDA. The Maulana replied: "Sayyid Ahmed administers sweet poison that is fatal. Therefore do not join him. You may join with the Hindus."[128]

To Malik Sayyid Ahmed's "greatest achievement" is that he liberalized and modernized Islam. Malik claims that while traditionally Islam applied equally to secular and religious affairs, Sayyid Ahmed, giving a modern orientation, laid down that "religion deals only with spiritual matters."[129] Mujeeb not only does not go so far; he criticizes Sayyid Ahmed for putting his college ahead of religious and social reform. In Mujeeb's strong words:

> It appeared as if he had made a bargain, and asked his community to accept his college, where the "new" education was offered, on condition that new ideas on Islam were not offered as a part of this education. . . . The higher value was discarded for the lower, a few hundred acres of dusty land and buildings without character were exchanged for the infinite spaces of religious and moral speculation; the reconstruction of the social and economic life of a whole community was sacrificed to secure recruitment in the lower grades of government service for the sons of a few hundred Muslim families.[130]

From the other extreme some people told Sayyid Ahmed that he was putting his college at risk by continuing to express his theological ideas. To one of them Sayyid Ahmed sent a memorable reply not long before his death:

> Satan, our enemy, deceives us. We are asked to believe that we are performing noble deeds and now, if we utter an unpopular truth, people will be scared, and our noble work will suffer. . . . To suppress or fight shy of the truth, and still to expect that virtue will flourish, is like sowing barley and expecting wheat to grow.[131]

Rash to some, to Mujeeb a person who settled for something smaller than what he had glimpsed, true, as others saw him, to himself, Sayyid Ahmed was, in poet Iqbal's simple words, "the first Indian Muslim to react to the modern age."[132]

* * *

At least two scholars, J.N. Farquhar and Christian Troll, have detected a parallel between Sayyid Ahmed's and Raja Ram Mohan Roy's positions vis-a-vis the Raj. Both saw God's hand in much of the Bible, while disagreeing with the divinity of Christ, and both favoured an India-Raj understanding. Troll says that the parallel could be "mere coincidence" or "the effect of a common historical situation" or "perhaps a result" of an "influence" that Ram Mohan Roy might have had on Sayyid Ahmed.[133] Sayyid Ahmed has related that he saw the Bengali reformer when the latter called on the Mughal emperor in Delhi in 1830. The Raja re-enters the story in 1869, when a fellow passenger on Sayyid Ahmed's voyage to Britain, a Miss Carpenter of Bristol, told him that Ram Mohan Roy had died in her father's home. Sayyid Ahmed mentioned the fact in one of his letters home, with a warm reference to the Raja.[134] But no evidence exists of a borrowing of ideas that may, or may not, have taken place.

His acquaintance with Hindu religious texts was not close, but two statements by him disclose a catholicity of mind. In an 1880 article in the *Reformer* he wrote: "Look at the sayings of the writers of the Hindu Vedas, where the Unity and attributes of that God which is spotless and who appears in the form of light, *Jyoti-swarupa Nirwikara*, are stated."[135]

On another occasion he said: "It is absurd to believe that the prophets appeared only in Arabia and Palestine to reform a handful of Arabs or Jews, and that God condemned the peoples of Africa, America and Asia to ignorance." A prophet of God had to be followed; "it was immaterial whether the prophet was from China, America, Mongolia, Africa, India or Iran."[136]

The Muslim *qaum* in India was no doubt his first concern but Jinnah's biographer Bolitho surely went too far when he called Sayyid Ahmed "the first Muslim in India who dared to speak of 'partition'."[137] Neither the idea nor the word had suggested itself to Sayyid Ahmed. Some have held that the concept of Pakistan, even if never mentioned by him, was implicit in Sayyid Ahmed's attitude.[138] But it is hard to discern even a "hidden" or latent Pakistan in the following statements, all made in the last twenty years of his life, when he was objecting to "election, pure and simple" and campaigning against Congress:

> O Hindus and Musalmans, do you inhabit any country other than India? Do you not both live here and are you not buried in this land or cremated on the ghats of this land? Remember that Hindu and Musalman are words of religious significance, otherwise Hindus, Musalmans and Christians who live in this country all constitute one nation.[139]

> Centuries have passed since God desired that Hindus and Musalmans may share the climate and the produce of this land and live and die on it together. So it appears to be the will of God that these two communities may live together in this country as friends, or even like two brothers. They form the two eyes of the pretty face of India.[140]

> It is our desire that between the Hindus and Muslims of India friendship, fraternal feeling and love may grow daily and such progress may be achieved in their mutual social relations that, except only in mosques, and temples, the Muslims and Hindus be not distinguished.[141]

What is termed *qaum* among Muslims is termed thus not with reference to country or race but rather purely with reference to religion.[142]

I have frequently said that India is a beautiful bride and Hindus and Muslims are her two eyes. . . . If one of them is lost, this beautiful bride will become ugly . . .[143]

His efforts for Hindu-Muslim friendship were noticed. Colvin, the Governor of his province, visited MAO and was glad that "the Hindu scholar is as readily received as the Mahomedan."[144] Hindu citizens of Aligarh thought that Sayyid Ahmed, "our distinguished countryman," had "infused toleration in the Mohamedan community."[145] The Indian Association of Lahore, comprising Muslims, Hindus and Sikhs, felt in 1884 that Sayyid Ahmed's "conduct throughout has been stainless of bias or bigotry."[146] If Raja Jaikishan Das was his close friend, it was because he had found Sayyid Ahmed as considerate to Hindus as he was to Muslims when, in 1880, he was asked by the British to organize famine relief in Moradabad district. Dr. Bhagwan Das claims that "the aim of Syed was not merely to reconcile the Muslims to the Government but also to reconcile them to this country and to the Hindu community."[147]

The Muslin *qaum* may have come first with him. All the same, he never ceased to speak of bonds with the other *qaum*. This was more than an exercise in sentimentality. In the phrase of the Pakistani historian, Ishtiaq H. Qureshi, Sayyid Ahmed's "greatest asset was a realism which removed the cobwebs of sentimental loose thinking."[148]

Sayyid Ahmed's realism taught him that recovering India from Queen Victoria was out of the question. His vision told him that if Muslims qualified themselves they would eventually sit beside Britons at the level of decision-makers. In 1883 Graham found it "a right pleasant sight" to see the Viceroy, Lord Ripon, seated on Sayyid Ahmed's right at an Aligarh luncheon, and Sayyid Mahmud on the Viceroy's right.[149] The scene was symbolic of a change in India. The *qaum* had recovered influence. Sayyid Ahmed had enabled it to do so.

There were blows in the last three years. First a bitter division arose on who should run MAO after Sayyid Ahmed. An enraged Sayyid Ahmed challenged the man who tried to block his wishes to "a duel in Paris."[150] Then Mahmud, experiencing a nervous breakdown, quarrelled with his father. The college accountant, a Hindu, forged cheques and stole a lakh of rupees. Admissions fell drastically.

On March 27, 1898, Sayyid Ahmed died in sadness. Fortunately, his successors were able to save and strengthen the college. They were helped by the fresh memory of a man who had restored the morale of a crushed *qaum*.

Chapter 3

Muhammad Iqbal

(1876 – 1938)

You created the night (*Man is talking to God*)
— I lit the lamp;
You created clay — I moulded the cup;
You made the wilderness; I cultivated flower-beds.
I made a mirror from a rock,
and from poison I extracted a sweet beverage.*

An infidel before his idol with wakeful heart
is better than the religious man asleep in the mosque.**

You do not understand it, stupid ascetic,
That a single frenzied error of the heart is the envy
Of a hundred prostrations.***

Is it a wonder that the creator of the Urdu and Persian originals of such verse is seen as a remarkable thinker-poet? "The appeal of his poetry," says Mujeeb (and let us remember that Mujeeb weighs his words), "was stupendous."[1] Muhammad Iqbal is also, at least to a man like Fazlur Rahman, the Pakistani scholar, "the most daring intellectual modernist the Muslim world has produced.[2]

To Wilfred Cantwell Smith, writing in 1946, Iqbal's laudation of man and his picture of God as a co-worker with man represented a theological

---

Payam-i-Mashriq ("Message from the East"), published in 1923.
***Jawid Namah* ("Book of Eternity"), published in 1932.
****Dil* ("Heart"), published in 1924.

revolution, indeed "the most important and most necessary revolution" of modern Islam. Why? Because it recognizes "the traditional remoteness of God [as] an error." "It puts God back in the world, now, with us, facing our problems from within, creating a new and better world with us and through us."[3]

"Muhammad Iqbal summoned the sleeping Muslims to awake." The words are Smith's but the thought has been expressed by many a writer.[4] Yet those who heeded his call or claimed that they were heeding it did opposing things; they "diverge[d] utterly, from Muslim socialists to reactionaries of the deepest dye."[5]

Writing eleven years later, Smith described Iqbal's 1912 poem *Shikwah* ("Complaint") as "superlatively significant," but added: "The historical consequence of his (Iqbal's) impact seems on the whole to have served to weaken liberalism among Indian Muslims."[6] In the appraisal of Mujeeb, Iqbal the thinker celebrates personality but Iqbal the practical guide asks the Muslim "not to look for other than the explicit meaning of doctrine and law, for God Himself is the jeweller who has cut the jewel of the *shariah*." Instead of redefining good works, this Iqbal merely walks "the beaten track of Muslim history and thought."[7]

* * *

Iqbal was born in Sialkot, a Punjab town between Lahore and the state of Jammu and Kashmir. His family, Kashmiri Brahmin in origin, was "not so long ago converted" from Hinduism to Islam.[8] Shaikh Rafiq, Iqbal's grandfather, was a pedlar of shawls. Rafiq's son Nur Muhammad did not or could not go to school and became a tailor and embroiderer. His skin was red, his beard white, his eyes penetrating, his nature mystically inclined. He belonged to a sufi order. His friends called him the *anparh* (uneducated) philosopher. Noticing his skill as a tailor, a local official purchased a Singer sewing machine, a recent wonder, and lent it to Nur Muhammad. But Iman Bibi, the tailor's wife, had strict notions of right and wrong. Having heard that the official had bought the Singer with illicit money, she refused to accept what her husband earned from it. Nur Muhammad gave up the Singer and became a cap-embroiderer; successful in this role, he soon employed other workmen.

Muhammad Iqbal was born to Nur Muhammad and Iman Bibi. He had three sisters and a brother, older by sixteen years, Atta Muhammad. Thanks to his father-in-law, a retired soldier, Atta Muhammad joined the army as an overseer of mechanical works; his income enabled Iqbal to go to school and college.

An impression of the atmosphere in which Iqbal was raised may be had from lines he wrote later, possibly based on a true incident of the boy

Iqbal hitting a beggar and demanding alms. "The harvest of his beggary spilled from his hands . . . and tears rolled down my father's cheeks. He said: 'On the day of Resurrection the beggar will cry and the Prophet will ask me why the young Muslim entrusted to my care, that heap of clay, did not become a man.' " Iqbal has his father say:

> Reflect a little, son, and bring to mind
> The last great gathering of the Prophet's fold:
> Look once again on my white beard, and see
> How now I tremble between fear and hope;
> Do not thy father this foul injury,
> O put him not to shame before his lord!
> Thou art a bud burst from Muhammad's branch . . . [9]

At sixteen, Iqbal entered Sialkot's Scottish Mission College (now called Murray College) and was married to Karim Bibi, daughter of a physician. She gave birth to two daughters and a son. One of the girls died soon after birth, the other at age nineteen after a series of illnesses. The boy, Aftab, would become an international corporate lawyer. When he was nineteen, Iqbal moved to Government College, Lahore, where he studied Arabic, English literature and philosophy under the guidance of Thomas Arnold, who had left Aligarh's MAO to join the Lahore College. At Aligarh Arnold had completed *The Preaching of Islam*, perhaps the first book by a Westerner to note that there was such a thing as Islam's peaceful spread, even if it had not been the only reality.

In turn Aligarh had noted (in the words of Arnold's colleague at MAO, Shibli), that "it is not the sword of Europe alone which conquered the nations of the world" and found in Arnold "the best living example of Europe's praiseworthy character."[10] Arnold's warmth and his understanding of Islamic culture captured Iqbal; he also induced in Iqbal the desire to pursue higher studies in Europe. When in 1904 Arnold left Lahore for London, Iqbal composed *Nala-i-Firaq* ("Lament of Separation").

Recognition of Iqbal's poetic talent had come six years earlier. At the age of twenty-two, he went to a *mushaira* (poetical symposium) in Lahore's Hakiman Bazar and recited the verse: "His Grace gathered them as pearls, so shining and bright — the beads of perspiration of my remorse." Mirza Gorgani, a noted poet who was present, simply exclaimed: "Iqbal! Such beautiful verse at your age!"[11]

At twenty-three Iqbal started teaching Arabic, history, and economics in Lahore — for Rs 73 a month. Law and the civil services gave better rewards and tempted him but he failed a law exam and was declared medically unfit for a bureaucratic post he sought. These disappointments were bitter blows, for Iqbal's was a proud spirit, but they saved him for greater things.

Another hurtful stroke was a criminal charge against Atta Muhammad, now an officer in the department of military works. Convinced that his brother was being framed, Iqbal, twenty-seven at the time, put together the facts as he knew them and sent them directly to Lord Curzon, the Viceroy; Curzon intervened and the charge was withdrawn. Also, Iqbal composed a touching ode to the sufi saint, Nizamuddin Auliya, beseeching him to intercede with Allah and rescue Atta Muhammad from the snares of enemies. The ode, *Berg-i-gul*, became a feature at annual festivals associated with the saint and a verse from it hung beside the saint's tomb in Delhi. Two years later, while on his way to Europe, Iqbal recited another ode at the saint's grave, *Iltaja-i-Musafir* ("The Traveller's Request"). These gestures are of some interest in the light of Iqbal's subsequent attacks on sufism and on the Ahmadi group that Atta Muhammad joined.

Many Indians had heard the name of Iqbal by 1905, when he left for Europe. This was because of poems like *Nala-i-yatim* ("The Orphan's Cry"); *Abr-i-Gauhar Bar* ("Blessed Showers), dedicated to the Prophet; *Taswir-i-Dard* ("Portrait of Anguish"); *Parinde ki Faryad* ("The Bird's I ament"); *Tarana-i-Hindi* ("Anthem of India"); and *Naya Shivala* ("The New Temple").

Parinde, a caged bird's longing for open skies, was about India's servitude. And in *Taswir*, *Tarana* and *Naya Shivala* Iqbal cried for Muslim-Hindu unity. *Tarana* is the widely popular song *Saare Jahaan Se Achha*; it would not be wrong to call it India's unofficial national anthem. One reason for its unending life is the sincerity it breathes. In *Naya Shivala* Iqbal said:

> I shall tell the truth, O Brahman, but take it not
>   as an offence;
> The idols in they temple have decayed.
> Thou has learnt from these images to bear ill-will
>   to thine own people,
> And God has taught the *mullah* (Muslim preacher)
>   the ways of strife.
>
> O Brahman, to thee images of stone embody the divine,
> For me, every particle of my country's dust is a
>   divinity.
> Come, let us remove all signs of division
>   and build a new temple in our land.

> Let us raise its pinnacle till it touches the lapel
> of the sky . . .
> The salvation of all earth-dwellers is in love.[12]

The new temple is in India but it is not India. Iqbal conceived it not as the shrine of a new faith merging Hinduism and Islam but simply as an altar of love — of India and between Indians. Before long Iqbal would become the poet of Islam rather than of India. He would even revoke *Tarana-i-Hindi* and write *Tarana-i-Milli* ("The Muslim Anthem") to take its place. But it is difficult not to agree with Mujeeb that Iqbal's "longing for unity among the Indian people," which expressed itself in his 1900-1905 poems, had "a deep spiritual basis and did not derive from any transitory political sentiment."[13]

* * *

In three years in Europe, Iqbal studied philosophy at Cambridge and law at London's Lincoln Inn. He also wrote a dissertation on Persian metaphysics for which Munich University awarded him a doctorate. "I have made up my mind to give up poetry," he told his friend Abdul Qadir, who was with him in Europe. Fortunately, his old teacher Arnold talked Iqbal out of concentrating wholly on "something more useful."[14] But Iqbal switched, while in England, from Urdu to Persian as the language of his poetry. Later he wrote:

> The Language of Hind is sweet as sugar,
> Yet sweeter is the fashion of Persian speech.
> My mind was enchanted by its loveliness.
> My pen became as a twig of the Burning Bush.
> Because of the loftiness of my thoughts,
> Persian alone is suitable to them.[15]

Iqbal knew, as did his Indian audience, that his Urdu had comfortably borne the weight of his lofty thoughts. Perhaps, as Malik suggests, Iqbal, who wanted a wider audience, saw Persian "as the lingua franca of the Muslim World."[16]

In Europe Iqbal fell in love with Atiya Fyzee, a young woman from an aristocratic Muslim family of Bombay. They spent time together in Cambridge, London and Germany. Miss Fyzee has spoken of the Iqbal of this period as self-assertive and gregarious but also, on occasion, as a lost or solemn mystic. Once he told her, "I am pragmatic and utilitarian outside but a mystic inside." Atiya Fyzee was attractive, intelligent and ahead of her time. When she went back to India Iqbal sent her a poem, *Wisal* ("Union"):

Hark ye Nightingale!
> the flower I was restlessly in search of
> I fortunately got.
When I heard your melody I invariably blushed.
Like mercury my heart was in constant flux.
Perhaps the sin of love made it so impatient...
I gained freedom in my captivity.[17]

But only in the world of dreams. In a letter to Miss Fyzee Iqbal claimed that "as a human being I have a right to happiness," that "the dead barren leaves of books" around him were not giving it to him, and that he had "sufficient fire" in his "soul to burn them up and all social conventions as well." But he did not marry her. She accused him of "indifference" and "hypocrisy." He protested, "I wish I could turn inside outward in order to give you a better view of my soul." But he never proposed.

Miss Fyzee later blamed Indian traditions and said that "Iqbal was not in India what he had been in Europe." "His genius was corroded and constricted" in India, she held, adding that India never saw the "intellectual brilliance" that Iqbal "exercised so well" in Europe. In Malik's view the marriage did not occur because the avant-garde Miss Fyzee "would have been completely out of place" in Punjab's conservative milieu, and also because Iqbal would not marry above his social class.[18]

* * *

Europe's vitality hit Iqbal. He found active people who had "the confident restlessness whereby if they did not like a thing, they changed it."[19] Henceforth, Iqbal would sing of action and satirize passivity. He would ask his people to "glow with the sunbeams of desire," and to learn from the wave, which says of itself,

> When I am rolling, I exist,
> When I rest, I am no more.[20]

"By virtue of their will to action," Iqbal would soon write, "the western nations are preeminent among the nations of the world. For this reason, and in order to appreciate the secret of life, their literature and ideas are the best guides for the nations of the east."[21] Not only the West's life but also its thought was worth looking at. Iqbal probed Bergson's notions of dynamism and Nietzsche's philosophy of self-assertion; he would adopt some ideas and reject others.

The West's vigour was admirable to Iqbal but not its merciless competition between man and man, and nation and nation. True, some in the

West spoke the language of socialism, which, rejecting competition, appealed to a part of Iqbal's spirit; it could not satisfy all of it because atheism seemed integral to European socialism. "Love is dead in the West," Iqbal wrote, "because thought has become irreligious."[22] While in Europe Iqbal composed the lines:

> The European tavern-keeper's wine brings jubilee,
> It has not sorrow's ecstasy: give home-brewed wine to me.[2]

Iqbal's mind demanded a final solution, a model for a new world. Where, he asked himself, was action to be found without destruction, and cohesion instead of nationalistic competition? The answer he gave himself was, "Not, despite all its energy, in Europe, but in Islam." Nationalism, after all, had crumbled before Islam in the religion's early history. Also, Iqbal saw Islam as "a successful opponent of the race idea, which is probably the hardest barrier in the way of the humanitarian ideal."[24]

Iqbal did not, or could not, see the heterogeneous Indian society with its oft-conflicting communities growing into a great example. On the other hand, early Islam, especially that which existed under the first four caliphs, had been inspiring; if they understood Islam aright, and in its supranational character, tomorrow's Muslims might build the ideal world. His European sojourn redefined his *qaum* for life. The focus shifted from Indians to the global community of Muslims.

Islam's proud past had spoken to Iqbal as he faced a vibrant Europe. Perhaps too, he recalled his childhood, when his father had told him that he was "a bud burst from Muhammad's branch." Iqbal accepted the sweeping view that "modern Western thought is a direct descendant of the glorious medieval intellectual culture of Islam, disseminated through Spain and Sicily."[25] Two poems that he wrote before he was back in India disclose the fervour of his strengthened faith. In the first he said:

> The silence of Mecca has proclaimed to the expectant
>   world at last,
> That the compact made with the desert-dwellers shall
>   be enforced again.
> That lion which emerged out of the wilderness and
>   upset the Empire of Rome,
> I hear from the angels, shall awaken once more.[26]

The second was written after he sighted Sicily from the ship that was taking him back. We observed Sayyid Ahmed's reaction to Sicily in the last chapter but Iqbal's is perhaps the more noteworthy. His ancestors were Hindu Brahmins, whereas Sayyid Ahmed could speak of his "Arab blood."

> Weep to thy heart's content, O blood-weeping eye!
> Yonder is visible the grave of Muslim culture.
> Once this place was the tent of those dwellers of the desert
> For whose ship the ocean was a playground,
> Who raised earthquakes in the courts of mighty emperors,
> Whose electric touch . . .
> Broke the chains of superstition.
> Tell me of thy anguish.
> I am the dust raised by that caravan which once broke
>   its journey here.
> Rouse me by telling the tale of bygone days.
> I shall carry they gift to India,
> And make others weep as I weep now.[27]

Shortly after his return to India Iqbal "politely declined" an opportunity to associate himself with an Amritsar based Hindu-Muslim-Sikh body. He explained:

> I have myself been of the view that religious differences should disappear from this country and even now act on this principle in my private life. But now I think that the preservation of their separate national entities is desirable for both the Hindus and Muslims. The vision of a common nationhood for India is a beautiful ideal and has a poetic appeal . . . but appears incapable of fulfilment.[28]

Iqbal's marriage with Karim Bibi was not a success. "My life is extremely miserable," he wrote Miss Fyzee in 1909, not long after he was back home. "They forced my wife upon me," he added.[29] The long separation and Iqbal's relationship with Miss Fyzee had not helped. Karim Bibi moved out in 1916 but Iqbal supported her until his death in 1938. Karim Bibi lived until 1946. It would appear that in 1909 Iqbal married two other women, Sardar Begum and Mukhtar Begum, "the niece of a very wealthy businessman," but Iqbal did not bring Sardar Begum home. Some hold that she had not been married to him — that only an engagement ceremony had taken place, not a marriage. But Sardar Begum obviously felt differently, for she chided Iqbal in a letter: "I was married to you, a second marriage is now inconceivable to me. I will remain in my present state until I die, and on the day of Judgment will hold you [responsible for ruining my life]." Her determination worked; Iqbal married, or remarried, her in 1913. Mukhtar Begum died in 1924, Sardar Begum in 1935, at age 37, having given Iqbal love, devotion, a son (Javid) and a daughter (Munira).[30]

* * *

It was "pure Islam" that Iqbal had seen as the final answer, not the "corrupted" Islam that so many Muslims and even Iqbal himself had been practising. In pure Islam there was no room (Iqbal now held) for venerating tombs of sufi saints; indeed, there was little room in it for sufism. His research for his Munich dissertation on Persian metaphysics seemed to tell Iqbal that *tasawwuf* or sufism "has no solid, historical foundation in original Islam."[31] He asked a close friend, Khwajah Hasan Nizami, custodian of the shrine to which he had addressed the odes, to convince him that *tasawwuf* was intrinsic to Islam. The material Nizami provided did not satisfy Iqbal, who is supposed to have concluded that "so far as Islam was concerned, *tasawwuf* was an alien and even an unhealthy growth."[32] However, Iqbal would speak off and on about "true" sufism or Islamic mysticism. He would use the sufi phrase *ishq* (absorbing love) and the sufi notion of Perfect Man in the philosophy he was developing. And his denunciation of the sufi poet Hafiz of Iran,

Beware of Hafiz the drinker,
His cup is full of the poison of death.
He is a Muslim but his belief wears the thread of the unbeliever.
The beloved's eyelashes make holes in his faith.

would be climaxed by the pejorative verdict that "Hafiz was not a sufi."[33]

Scholars disagree on the origin of the Persian word *tasawwuf*, from which the phrases sufi and sufism are derived. Some believe that the root was *suf* (wool), the cloth the early sufis wore; others think that it grew out of *safa* (purity), which they sought to realize. *Tariqah*, often used as a synonym for *tasawwuf*, means a (or the) way. Sufi teachers have used the symbol of a circle to depict the relation between the *shariah*, the divine law, and the *tariqah*, the way. As Nasr, a sympathetic student of sufism, puts it:

The circumference is the *Shariah* whose totality comprises the whole of the Muslim community. Every Muslim by virtue of accepting the divine law is as a point on the circumference. The radii symbolize the *tariqahs*. Each radius is a path from the circumference to the centre. As sufis say, there are as many paths to God as there are children of Adam....

At the centre is the *Haqiqah*, or Truth, which is the source of both the *Tariqah* and the *Shariah*. The law and way have both been brought into being independently by God who is the Truth. To participate in the Shariah is to live in the reflection of the Centre or Unity. It is the necessary and sufficient cause for living a whole life and being "saved." But there are always those who cannot only live in the reflection of the Centre but must seek to reach it. Their Islam is to walk upon the path to the Centre . . . to attain that final End or Goal.[34]

Sufism's attractions are not hard to understand. It responded to a personal hunger for God. It seemed to stress the eternal and not just the historical, God's love and not just His power, the state of a man's heart and not just his behaviour, the spirit rather than the letter. It flowed out in poetry, and was in turn strengthened by it. As Fazlur Rahman, who is sufficiently wary of sufism to say that "sufi spirituality as a whole is no better than a form of spiritual deliquency," admits: "The systems of the *ulama* had become rigid and their legal casuistry and empty theological pedantry drove the serious-minded men of religion and originality into the sufi fold."[35] Rahman is speaking of the 10th and 11th centuries but it is obvious that what he describes can happen any time and has happened often.

The risks of sufism are also easy to see. Won't men be inclined to forget the *shariah* in their anxiety over the *tariqah*? And if there are as many paths to God as there are children of Adam (or radii in a circle), what happens to the distinctiveness and solidarity of Islam? And if, as some sufis maintained, "the true mystic has but one guide — the inner light," isn't there scope for excess and even anarchy? Rahman, for instance, speaks of the "self-righteous intuitive certainty" of sufis, of their "incorrigible way of knowing independently of intellectual knowledge," and of their freedom from "the check and control" of the *ulama*.[37] And Smith refers to sufism's oscillations between "the serene insight of the saint" and the "anxious abracadabra of the charlatan."[38] From the start, however, sufis claimed Qur'anic sanction for their beliefs and practices.

An important milestone was the feat of the scholar al-Ghazali, who died in the year 1111: he obtained the *ulama*'s recognition for sufism. A sufi himself, al-Ghazali ("this greatest figure in medieval Islam," as Rahman calls him), "was a great reformer of sufism . . . putting it at the service of orthodox religion."[39] He castigated the many sufis who sought ecstatic delirium, and said that the verities of Islam could be the only object of sufism. Simultaneously, however, he said that it was only through "the life of the heart" that faith could really be acquired.[40] Neither the *ulama* nor the sufis were prepared to submit wholly or for all time to the careful balance al-Ghazali prescribed. For Islam the problem appears to survive: it cannot ban *tasawwuf* but neither can it give *tasawwuf* free rein.

Another conspicous medieval figure, the Hispano-Arab philosopher Ibn al-Arabi (1165-1240), symbolizes sufism's uneasy place in Islam. Al-Arabi successfully taught that the key Qur'anic notion of *tawhid* (the unity or oneness or single-ness of God) had two other important meanings, one spiritual and the other philosophical. The spiritual meaning was that a Muslim should seek union with God. Philosophically it meant the unity of being or existence — *wahdat-ul-wujud*. The universe was the outer aspect of God, who was the inner aspect. In the deepest sense, said al-Arabi, man too was close to divinity; in support of his view he quoted the Qur'anic verse, "We (God) are nearer to him (Prophet Muhammad) than the great artery," and the Tradition of the Prophet that said that God created Adam in the image of Himself.[41] Eventually, purists would allege that al-Arabi was teaching Greek pantheism, but some Muslim scholars would disagree.[42] In any case, al-Arabi's ideas "became so common among Muslims," says the scholar Nuruddin, "that almost all learned people with an inclination toward Sufism came under its spell. Arabic, Persian and Urdu poets injected these ideas into their verses."[43] In Nuruddin's view, "Muslim mysticism was Hellenized" by al-Arabi. His ideas became part of sufistic Islam because of what Rahman calls his "imaginative genius";[44] but al-Arabi was helped also by the fact that the Arabic expression *tawhid* could connote both oneness and union.

Al-Arabi was followed by the mystic poet Jalaluddin Rumi who died in 1273. The author of what is at times called "the sufi Qur'an," a poetic work of "surpassing beauty" — the expression of Rahman, no admirer of sufism[45] — Rumi knew just how to offend purists. He has the Almighty say to Moses: "I have bestowed on everyone a particular mode of worship; I have given everyone a peculiar form of expression. The idiom of Hindustan is excellent for Hindus . . ."[46] Some 500 years later a mystic from Sind, Shah Abdul Latif, would commit an identical "error." "When the truth is one and the beloved the same, why should men fight over the means?" he wrote. Asked what religion he followed, he replied, "All or none."[47] Rumi and Latif were by no means the only ones to say what they did.

Future purists, and some contemporary ones, would see such men as diluting, confusing, even betraying Islam. Akbar the Great Mughal and the great eclectic was, in this view, the king of offenders. Pitting his learning and intellect against the trend, Shaikh Ahmad of Sirhind (1564-1624), himself a sufi, presented an Islam free of Greek philosophy, Persian mysticism and Indian compromise and became the purists' hero. He remains that today. (Unfortunately for Islamic unity, he also attacked what he called the heresy of the Shi-ites).

As a sufi's son Iqbal had regularly recited some of al-Arabi's verses. He had even taken, at his father's hands, the oath of discipleship in the Qadiriya order of sufis. Though his distance from sufism was widening, he had paid a glowing tribute to al-Arabi in the introduction to his Munich thesis. The new Iqbal was dramatically different. He repudiated sufism, refused to recruit disciples, denounced al-Arabi, deplored Akbar's mix of religions and in an Urdu poem thanked God for the Shaikh of Sirhind:

> I stood by the Reformer's tomb: that dust
> at whose least speck stars hang their heads.
> Dust shrouding that knower of things unknown
> Whom Allah sent in season to keep watch
> In India on the treasure-house of Islam.[48]

In a private notebook he wrote: "The history of the preceding Muslim dynasties had taught Aurangzeb that the strength of Islam in India did not depend, as his ancestor Akbar had thought, so much on the goodwill of the people of this land as on the strength of the ruling race."[49] Tennyson had noted the sentiment behind Akbar's withdrawal of the *jizia* — "I will reap no revenue from the field of unbelief"[50] — but it was Aurangzeb whom Iqbal would hail as

> The last arrow in our quiver left
> In the affray of faith with unbelief, . . .
> An Abraham in India's idol-house.[51]

In Iqbal's new purism there was a very human, and attractive, inconsistency, if indeed it was that. He went in 1923 to the tomb of the Shaikh of Sirhind and prayed there for a son. A boy was born in the following year; when he was ten Iqbal took him to the mausoleum. The son, Javid, has recalled: "Father took me inside and sat close to the grave of the saint, and recited the Qur'an. His sad voice vibrated through the dark dome and tears streamed down his cheeks . . ."[52]

Iqbal opposed sufism because too many sufis had forgotten the circumference—the *shariah*—where they had, or should have, stood; they were too busy advancing on their radius toward God, the Centre. They encouraged the belief that all religions were the same. Their notions, said Iqbal, were pantheistic and, he added, akin to the cry of the Vedantist,

"*Aham Brahma Asmi.*"[53] Converts to Islam that sufis won in India retained different forms of idolatry. Like Buddhists and some Hindus, the sufis fostered the goal of the self's annihilation in the Supreme Being, using the simile of a drop losing itself in the ocean. But Iqbal wanted man to be a pearl, not a drop of water, a servant of God, not merged with God. He sought conquest for man, not effacement. Prayer could enable the individual personality to "discover its situation" in relation to God, but union (*wisal*) with God, was neither possible nor desirable. Said Iqbal:

> *Tasawwuf* is always the sign of decline of a nation. Greek mysticism, Persian mysticism, Indian mysticism — all are signs of decline of these nations; the same is true of Islamic mysticism. . . . Any philosophy or religious teaching that prevents the blossoming of the human personality is worthless.[54]

Hafiz's had been the opposite refrain:

> To have self-decoration and self-conceit is to be
> an infidel.
> One thing I tell thee, don't see toward thee,
> thou wilt be free.[55]

Iqbal wants man to acquire some of God's attributes and to accept God as a co-worker but he celebrates *firaq*, separation:

> In the state of burning and passion, separation is
> better than union;
> In union the death of desire; in separation the
> enjoyment of seeking.[56]

Yet is Iqbal's man really content to stay on the circumference, letting his personality grow, discovering his position vis-a-vis God but avoiding the Almighty's touch or embrace? Iqbal's proud, blossoming, conquering man is not inhuman; he is not without hunger for contact with the Divine. The apostle of *firaq* achieves contact, though not *wisal*, through an ingenious device and without accepting a humble status for man. Iqbal's man will not and must not rest his head on God's shoulder; but he will let God find some peace on his (man's) person:

> More blissful than a thousand pious acts
> — Is for Thee and me to come a step nearer by way
>   of friendship.
> Come, rest a while in my bosom
> From the toil and weariness of Godhood.[57]

There are places where Iqbal speaks like a sufi, as in remarks such as "Faith is God-intoxication" and "Faith gives the strength to sit in fire like Abraham."[58] The passage quoted earlier where he assails *tasawwuf* ends nonetheless with a positive reference to what Iqbal calls "pure Islamic *tasawwuf*," in which "the divine injunctions become imperatives ensuing from one's own wishes."[59] A close friend of Iqbal, Mirza Jalaluddin, sees the poet as a sufi, though not a saintly one. He adds:

> In the last years of his life he had to a great extent withdrawn himself
> from the world and adopted the ways of a dervish. Oblivious to the
> material world, Iqbal lost himself in his own spiritual reverie.[60]

We are not ready yet to define Iqbal's message or describe his place in the history of Islamic thought. Before attempting to do so we will have to look at his philosophy of *khudi* — of ego, self or personality, as it has been differently translated — and at more of Iqbal's statements on Islam. We can note, however, that Fazlur Rahman, one of the subcontinent's leading Islamic modernists, a critic of the fundamentalist *Jamaat-i-Islami* but also a purist in his own way, speaks of Iqbal as "the most serious Muslim philosophical thinker of modern times" and yet holds that Iqbal's teaching threw "its overwhelming weight on the revivalist side."[61]

Also, we can note that Wilfred Cantwell Smith, at first sympathetic to Marxism and later to Christianity and throughout a close student of Islam on the subcontinent, says that "any modern Muslim who would talk about religion must begin where Iqbal left off"[62] — and that Barbara Metcalf, an American scholar, calls Iqbal a "scripturalist," by which she means one focussing on "principles, on texts, on rules that could be generalized, on religious laws . . . " and opposing "local cults and festivals."[63]

We are ready, however, to speak with certainty of some things that Iqbal was not. He was not one of those sufis or "Muslim seekers of religious truth," referred to by the historian Tara Chand, who "travelled with Hindu seekers" and "came to see the oneness of the quest, and the identity of their pursuits, and discovered that in the depths of religious conscious-ness there is little room for distinction."[64] He was not like the poet Kabir, who held that

The Muslim's *namaz* is as different from a
Hindu's *puja*
As a bracelet's gold is from gold in an ear-ring.[65]

Nor was Iqbal like Akbar's minister Abul Fazl, who wrote of the Hindus:

They one and all believe in the unity of the Godhead, and although
they hold images in high veneration, yet they are by no means idol-
ators. I have myself frequently discoursed upon the subject with many
learned and upright men of this religion, and comprehend their doctrine, which is that the images are only representations to whom they
turn, whilst at prayer, to prevent their thoughts from wandering.[66]

* * *

"The idea of *khudi* gives us a standard of value," said Iqbal in his *Asrar-
i-khudi* ("Secrets of the Self"). "It settles the problem of good and evil.
That which fortifies *khudi* is good, that which weakens it is bad."[67] He
despised the static ascetic and praised the restless conqueror, looked upon
tension as dynamic and relaxation as soporific, and saw strong personalities
constituting the ideal society of the future. "Cut the head of *khudi* with
the sword," Rumi had advised;[68] and many a Persian and Urdu (and Hindi)
poet had hungered for release from the "prison of self"; but Iqbal almost
idolized self. He clarified, however, that his *khudi* was not vanity or arrogance but "self-realisation and self-assertion." It was a deep impulse
within man, "a silent force anxious to come into action."[69] Reviewing the
English version of *Asrar-i-khudi*, E.M. Forster wrote:

Iqbal has been influenced by Nietzsche. He tries to find, in that rather
shaky ideal of the superman, a guide through the intricacies of conduct. His couplets urge us to live dangerously. We are to be stone,
not glass; diamonds, not dewdrops; tigers, not sheep.... As a guide
to conduct Nietzsche is at a discount in Europe. The drawback of
being a superman is that your neighbours observe your efforts and
try to be superman too.[70]

Iqbal admired Nietzsche and wrote that the German had the ability of
"divine seeing."[71] But he claimed that it was the sufi concept of the perfect
man rather than Nietzsche's superman that had influenced him. In any
case, the personality that Iqbal celebrates is different from the superman.
He is not an aristocrat above "a herd which he must proudly rise and
reign" over.[72] Iqbal's hero can emerge from any class; Iqbal moreover,
wants "the entire people to be made up of strong, wilful personalities."[73]
Finally, whereas God is absent in Nietzsche's world, Iqbal's strong individual is striving to acquire the attributes of the Ultimate Ego, God.

All the same, forceful individuals made their mark on Iqbal. After calling on Mussolini in 1932, Iqbal wrote a poem in which he admired the dictator's "vitality" and "the magnetic quality of his bright eyes."[74] (After meeting Mussolini at about the same time, Gandhi had commented that the Duce's eyes were shifty.) Admiring Mustafa Kemal's rise in the Turkey of the early 1920s, Iqbal said: "Among the Musim nations of today, Turkey alone has shaken off its dogmatic slumber, and attained to self-consciousness."[75] However, Iqbal attacked Mussolini when he invaded Abyssinia; and he expressed dissatisfaction with Kemal's absolute rule. He wrote:

> The morning breeze is still in search of a garden.
> Ill lodged in Ataturk, the soul of the east is still
>   in search of a body.[76]

We should note, too, that what gave Iqbal lasting pride in Islam's past were not "the magnificent empires of Damascus, Baghdad and Spain" but "the simple democratic community under the first four caliphs." Of conquest by force he wrote: "That Muslim peoples have fought and conquered like other people and that some of their leaders have screened their personal ambition behind the veil of religion, I do not deny; but I am absolutely sure that territorial conquest was no part of the original programme of Islam."[77] Iqbal was aware of the brevity of the sword's success:

> Alexander stormed like lightning,
> And we all know that he suddenly died.
> Nadir Shah robbed Delhi of its treasures;
>   and a single stroke
> Of the sword put an end to his short history.[78]

Iqbal's personality development was for men only. Even at "his most poetic, his most progressive, his most inclusively utopian" moments, says Smith, Iqbal left the women of the world out of his dynamic new world. Smith adds: "For women he wanted no activism, no freedom. Iqbal kept his own wives in seclusion (*pardah*) and untiringly he preached to the world his conception of the ideal woman." Of the Prophet's daughter Iqbal wrote:

> The chaste Fatimah is the harvest of the field
>   of submission,
> is a perfect model for mothers.
> So touched was her heart for the poor,

That she sold her own wrap . . .
She who might command the spirits of heaven and hell
Merged her own will in the will of her husband.
Her upbringing was in courtesy and forbearance;
And, murmuring the Qur'an, she ground corn.[79]

In one of his last major works, *Javid-Namah* ("Book of Eternity"), Iqbal satirizes a westernized woman of the subcontinent. She is addressing simple women:

Ladies! Mothers! Sisters!
How long shall you live as beloveds?
Belovedness is sheer privation:
It is suffering of oppression and tyranny.[80]

And yet Iqbal was aware of the problem. Only he did not know how to answer it. In "Woman" he says:

I too at the oppression of women am most sorrowful;
But the problem is intricate, no solution do I find
     possible.[81]

* * *

It is possible to find holes in Iqbal's *khudi* theory. Islam means submission or surrender. Iqbal seems to laud it in woman and to ignore the need for it in man. For him he covets ascendance, defiance, assertion. We may not be fully convinced even if Iqbal were to apply his theory to all. Strong personalities are impressive but also hurtful to weaker personalities around them. We marvel when man defies nature; but we also want him at times to defy his own nature. It is good to hear man say yes to life — and also good to hear him say no to a cruel desire. Moreover, shouldn't weaker personalities be protected from the excesses of the strong? Iqbal appears to meet this, or some of it, with his emphasis on obedience to the *shariah*, and with his reference to self-control. But this solution lacks the enthusiasm Iqbal exudes while speaking of *khudi*. He is excited like a discoverer when he extolls *khudi*; when reminding us of the law, he is the dutiful reciter of given truth. What is missing is an aspect of *ishq*, or love, a stress on helping the neighbour's personality, and not just your own, to grow.

Yet who can deny that passivity was and is the east's flaw? Iqbal attacked it with fire and brilliance. He also attacked it in sweeping language, but the assault was certainly called for. We should note, too, that Iqbal's man-the-hero, self-confident and adventurous, is also, in some of the poet's verses, filled with a sense of loneliness and inadequacy. To become, in the Qur'anic phrase, a viceregent of God may be man's destiny, but there are times when Iqbal's man is "a particle of dust" or "a piteous creature." At one place Iqbal asks God:

> Is Man, the Man I know, lord of the lands and seas?
> What shall I say about this piteous creature?
> Is he the masterpiece Thy hands have wrought?[82]

Iqbal speaks unqualifiedly but doubt or an amendment often hides nearby. The American scholar Sheila McDonough writes of Iqbal's "awareness of the finitude of his or anyone's ideas and beliefs in the face of the awesome strangeness of the cosmos that confronts us." She quotes a significant sentence from him:

> As a plant growing on the bank of a stream hearest not the sweet, silver music which sustains it from beneath, so man growing on the brink of infinity listeneth not to the Divine undertone that maketh the life and harmony of his soul.[83]

Always growing, always travelling, Iqbal may not have reached the station of Total Truth. Yet from his position on the brink of infinity he caught valuable snatches of its undertone and repeated them. There is at least a part of us where they strike a responsive chord.

* * * *

In Iqbal's concept of personality there is, as Mujeeb says, "an element of the universal." Eventually, however, in Iqbal's thought, "the self and mankind become the Muslim and the Muslim community."[84] Moreover, the Muslim finds his true individuality when he dissolves his "I" in the *qaum*. Man must remain a diamond in God's ocean, but a Muslim should be happy to become a drop in the waters of his community. Dissolution is proper in this special context; here it will lead to fulfillment. Accordingly, Muslims in India should work for "the development, preservation and consolidation of the communal ego."[85]

A European critic called Dickinson complained. He wrote: "While Mr. Iqbal's philosophy is universal, his application of it is particular and exclusive. Only Muslims are worthy of the Kingdom. The rest of the world is either to be absorbed or excluded." Iqbal answered thus:

The humanitarian ideal is always universal in poetry and philosophy but if you work it out in actual life you must start with a society exclusive in the sense of having a creed and well-defined outline, but ever enlarging its limits by example and persuasion. Such a society in my belief is Islam. . . .

All men and not Muslims alone are meant for the Kingdom of God on earth, provided they say goodbye to their idols of race and nationality and treat one another as personalities . . . [86]

What then commanded Iqbal's loyalty and yearnings? A future society of individuals embodying Iqbal's ideals? Or, to use Smith's words, "the empirical Muslim community as the Government of India census recognize it?" Smith thought that Iqbal "confused the two."[87] The poet himself felt that he had to start somewhere, with something actual, to reach the goal, and that he would do so with the Muslims of India. Despite his abhorrence of nationalism, the practical focus of Iqbal's concern was the Muslim community of India, not the larger brotherhood of Islam. This *qaum* would be the first stone of the new house Iqbal envisioned.

He would work with and for the Muslims of India because he saw them as "like-minded"; he did not think, to use his phrases, that "social tradition" or "unity of language" or "ethnic or geographic unity" would give "inner cohesion" to India or to a joint Hindu-Muslim community.[88] This Iqbal presented as his frank and considered opinion, but perhaps we should also remember his statement that "all men and not Muslims alone are meant for the Kingdom of God." It imparts some flexibility to Iqbal's new world.

The spirit of this statement can be found in at least two of Iqbal's poems written in his poet-of-Islam phase:

> The dervish intoxicated with the love of God is
> neither of the east nor of the west,
> My home is neither Delhi, nor Isfahan nor Samarkand.
> I utter only those words which I consider to be true,
> I am neither a blind follower in the mosque, nor a
> creature of today's civilisation.[89]
>
> Religion consists in burning from head to foot in
> search of Truth,
> Its end is love,
> The 'infidel' and the 'faithful' are all creatures
> of God;
> A devotee of Love takes into the breadth of his soul
> both 'infidelity' and 'faith'.[90]

A few more vignettes and verses will complete our picture of Iqbal's Muslimness. His conception of the Prophet and of Arab Islam is what

Iqbal gloried in; his Indian ethnicity did not come in the way. His son Javid Iqbal recalled: "Someone sitting in the room said that I should recite Hali's verses about the Prophet, which ran thus, 'The One called Mercy among the Prophets.' Before the second verse could be uttered, father was moved to tears." Adds Javid: "He narrated stories from Islamic history. . . . He told me that the ancestors of Napoleon originally hailed from Arabia and that the Arabs had shown Vasco da Gama the route to India."[91]

Visiting Spain in 1932, Iqbal called it "the treasure-house of Muslims' blood and the sacred land of Islam." At the mosque of Corboba, which had been converted into a Church in 1236, he raised his hands in entreaty to Allah, tears trickled down his cheeks, and a poem came to him:

> All Art's wonders arise only to vanish once more;
> All things built on this earth sink as if built on sand!
> Yet some gleams of immortal life
> Show where a servant of God wrought into some high shape
> A work whose perfection is bright with the splendour of love.
> Shrine of Cordoba! from love all your existence is sprung,
> Love that can know no end, stranger to Then-and-now.[92]

At Spain's Al-Hamra Palace he returned to his theme of man-the-hero. "Whichever way I looked," Iqbal afterwards, "I saw the inscription, 'He is the Dominant.' I said to myself 'Here Allah is dominant all over. It would make sense to see man, too, dominate somewhere'."[93]

But in *Shikwah*, which Iqbal recited in 1911, the verse that Smith selects as superlatively significant, the poet is neither stirred nor self-assertive. He is baffled and angry. More than any other people, the Muslims have promoted worship of the One God, and what has God done in return?

> There are nations beside us; there are sinners amongst
>   them too,
> Humble folk and those intoxicated with pride, slothful,
>   careless and clever,
> Hundreds who detest Thy Name,
> But Thy Grace descends on their dwellings;
> And nothing but the lightning strikes us![94]

Though, believing in its cohesion, he had selected the Muslim community of India as the starting block for his new world, the community often failed to live up to his expectations. It would disappoint and at times embitter him. Once he even wrote: "Ever since their political fall, the

Mussalmans of India have undergone a rapid ethical deterioration. Of all the Muslims communities of the world they are probably the meanest in point of character."[95]

* * *

This votary of restlessness and adorer of man's dynamism shied away from the role of a religious reformer. "At one time, he was a vigorous champion of all reforms that were necessary to improve the position of Muslims," says Ikram, but this historian is disappointed at what became, in his words, "Iqbal's energetic advocacy of unreformed orthodoxy."[96] Ikram thinks that a part was played by India's emotional climate in the years following Iqbal's return from Europe. In this phase Muslims in India were under the influence of the poets Shibli Nomani and Akbar Allahabadi and the scholar-editor Abul Kalam Azad, all of whom spoke of the ignominy of remaining under an alien, non-Muslim thumb. Iqbal accepted their line, which was opposed to Sayyid Ahmed's. Europe had stimulated Iqbal's mind but of Aligarh-style modern education he now wrote:

> This new wine will weaken the mind still further;
> This new light will only intensify the darkness.[97]

To Akbar, who aimed his eloquent sarcasm at Sayyid Ahmed's followers, Iqbal said: "I see you with the eyes of a disciple towards his spiritual guide." In Ikram's view, Iqbal "wrote poems frankly in imitation of Akbar."[98]

When Britain and Turkey found themselves on opposite sides of a world war, Azad and Akbar and a large number of Indian Muslims sympathized with Turkey: not only was it a Muslim land, its Sultan was the caliph of all Sunni Muslims, including those in India, and was the custodian of Islam's sacred places in Arabia. Britain's post-war attitudes to a defeated Turkey offended Indian Muslims; a new security measure, the Rowlatt act, offended Hindus and Muslims alike. Gandhi, who had returned to India from South Africa in 1915, seized this opportunity to unite Hindus and Muslims in a nationalist struggle. There were unprecedented manifestations of Hindu-Muslim partnership in the caliphate or Khilafat movement, as it was called. "For a very brief period Iqbal was attracted by the movement," records Ikram.[99] In some short poems he praised the Mahatma. But the movement could not retain him.

In 1922 he was knighted by the Raj. This was a recognition of his poetry but Iqbal's acceptance of an English title at the height of the Khilafat movement symbolized his break with Indian nationalism and evoked caustic comment:

> Pity! Iqbal stooped to knighthood from an Allama (scholar).
> Formerly he was the crown of the community;
> Hark another news! Iqbal has become a knight of the
>   (British) crown.[100]

Iqbal broke with the political line of the Khilafat movement but not with the religious conservativism of most Khilafatists. At times he seemed torn between conviction and expediency. In 1925, in a letter to a friend, he said:

> I had written an English essay on *Ijtihad* (exercise of judgment), which was read in a meeting here and God willing will be published, but some people called me a Kafir. We shall talk at length about this affair, when you come to Lahore. In these days, particularly in India, one must move with very great circumspection.[101]

This essay was never published, but it is possible that some of its ideas were included in Iqbal's *Reconstruction of Religious Thought in Islam*, which came out in 1930. In this work he defends the right of "the present generation of Muslim liberals to reinterpret the foundational legal principles in the light of their own experience and the altered conditions of modern life." Iqbal adds: "Each generation, guided but unhampered by the work of its precedessors, should be permitted to solve its own problems."[102]

These words offer strong encouragement to reformers, who have frequently quoted them, but Iqbal managed to say contrary things as well and warned against liberalism. Long after the death of the Khilafat movement, he continued to show "very great circumspection." Mujeeb summarizes Iqbal's eventual position in these words: "Some change might be made somewhere but caution is more necessary than courage."[103] In Smith's view, Iqbal is "most venturesome when he is enunciating principles. But on the specific question of women, Islamic customs of eating and drinking and so on, he hesitates to innovate. . . . He can be found upholding the canon law and condemning the moderns who would not practise it in full."[104]

Yet perhaps we are unfair to Iqbal if we explain his attitude in terms only of carefulness. When he sings of the *shariah* it is his heart, not his head, that guides him:

> Who would master the sun and stars,
> Let him make himself a prisoner of Law!

The star moves towards its goal
With head bowed in surrender to a law.
O thou that art emancipated...
Adorn thy feet once more with the same fine silver chain.[105]

We have earlier noted Iqbal's anxiety to rid Islam of what he saw as impurities connected with sufism. He also opposed the Ahmadi movement, chiefly because of the charge that its founder claimed (or at any rate did not clearly deny) that he was a prophet. To Iqbal this ruled out a place for Ahmadis in the world of Islam, which could only admit those who believed that prophethood came to an end with Muhammad. So when his brother Atta Muhammad became an Ahmadi he was no longer a Muslim in Iqbal's eyes.

Those who spoke of themselves as loyal Muslims and votaries of the law appealed to Iqbal, whether or not they shared all his deepest convictions. One such was an able young writer named Abul Ala Maudoodi. The poet encouraged Maudoodi to move to the town of Pathankot, where the future initiator of the *Jamaat-i-Islami* "found an endowed estate, complete with a printing press, at his service."[106] Following partition Maudoodi opted for Pakistan where he led a movement for turning the new nation into an Islamic state, where "the entire programme of Islam and not merely a fragment of it" might be translated into practice, with the help, if required, of the coercive power of the state.[107]

According to the American scholar Freeland Abbott, Maudoodi believed that "one must observe Islamic forms implicitly, for while form without spirit is meaningless, ... the existence of form is the only evidence that the proper spirit might also be present."[108] This was scarcely the beat of Iqbal's throbbing heart, of the poet whose celebration of man's personality was linked to its liberation, and who believed that "to delight in creation is the law of life."[109] Still, the fact remains that Iqbal encourged Maudoodi. On the other hand, Iqbal also hoped, it would seem, to write a book called 'Reconstruction of Islamic Jurisprudence' where he would interpret items in the *shariah* "in the altered conditions of modern life." Unluckily, death intervened.[110]

If liberals, conservatives and reactionaries alike can quote Iqbal in aid, so can socialists. Once he said, "Bolshevism plus God is almost identical with Islam."[111] In *Lenin in God's Presence*, Iqbal's Lenin expresses all the wrath and grief of the poor; in a subsequent poem Allah orders the angels to ruin the rich and succour the serfs. Communism's denial of God bothered Iqbal but he saw it as a reaction against the corruption of the Russian Orthodox church:

Russian atheism was inspired from on high
To disrupt the old heathen idols of the bigots.[112]

Lovers of democracy, too, can cite Iqbal's statements. "Islam," he wrote, "has a horror of personal authority"; and he regarded "the absolute equality of all the members of the community" as a basic principle of a Muslim constitution. And yet Iqbal also made the remark that in a democracy "men are counted but not weighed" and pointed out that "even the brains of two hundred donkeys do not produce the thought of a man."[113]

We are in a position now to describe Iqbal's philosophical and religious legacy. He dared — and hesitated. He sang with impudence and acted with prudence. His wings take us to new worlds; but he is also with us, plodding, if we want to walk on the beaten track. He envisioned a brotherhood of mankind but absorbed himself, at times with frightening intensity, in the Muslim *qaum* in India. His imprints are powerful — and point to different directions.

* * *

Iqbal's deeds frequently belied his words. The lion and the eagle were saluted in his verses (and vegetarians ridiculed) but the poet himself "could not stand the sight of blood," as his son has testified. His poems exhorted action, but he himself performed no physical activity besides "walking up and down the courtyard of his house." As Javid recalls:

> He hated going out, but loved to sit on his sofa or recline on his bed reading or taking notes. . . . Many friends and admirers used to call on father, usually in the evening. Chairs were placed around his bed; he loved to chat with his friends while smoking his hookah.[114]

He sang of *ishq* but hardly ever kissed his children. Islam was his passionate faith and his *qaum* had become his world, yet two of his closest personal friends were Sikhs, Sir Jogendra Singh and Umrao Singh; and on one occasion he pulled a young Hindu "from the abyss of despair" and from the edge of suicide by offering him

> a flash of a loving glance, a cheering eye-twinkle
> and an amusing dialectic based on the doctrine of *karma*.[115]

He was not greedy. And often he was short of money. Though he practised law to supplement his income from poetry, he turned down cases if there was any risk of losing time for friends or his art. He bought prints by European masters to encourage Javid's interest in painting but when the boy asked his father, who was in Europe at the time, to buy him a gramophone, Iqbal composed a verse asking the boy to learn his speech not from a soundbox but from "the rose and tulip's long silence." Added Iqbal:

> No gifts of the Franks' clever glass-blowers ask!
> From India's own clay mould your cup and your flask...
> The way of the hermit, not fortune, is mine;
> Sell not your soul! in a beggar's rags shine.[116]

The opponent of sufism remained a mystic at heart, at times moved to tears while hearing, or reciting, Rumi's verses about true sufis. An admirer quoted Iqbal's verse:

> The memory of the homeland became a sadness without cause.
> Sometimes it transformed itself into a desire to look at beauty and
>   sometimes into passionate pursuits.

and asked the poet to confirm that the lines showed Iqbal's nostalgia for Lahore and Sialkot while in Europe. That was not what they meant, replied Iqbal; he was referring, he added, to "that pre-earthly home from which all come to live in this terrestrial world."[117]

All students of Iqbal's life speak of his recurring sadness. "His soul remained deeply embedded in sadness," writes Rahbar, adding: "This hidden transcendental sadness in the midst of Iqbal's vivacious conversations provided that magnetic touch of drama in his personal presence that attracted people to him."[118] Earlier we had noted Iqbal's lament that the West's wine had no sorrow to offer; but he himself seldom lacked its flavour. Readings of the Qur'an or a reference to the Prophet might occasion it, or some lines of verse, his own or another's, recited by him or to him.

Once, while relating to a group of friends the Tradition about the Prophet's companions' envy of antelopes who had kissed the Prophet's feet, Iqbal became speechless and his voice faltered when he came to Muhammad's reaction: "Prostrate before Allah alone and as for your elders, only respect them." After he had composed himself Iqbal said, "There is a not a better sentence in the literature of the whole world." As Rahbar puts it, "Iqbal's gifts of charming physique, sense of humour and brilliant conversation were the steel, stone and mortar of the dam that checked the torrent of tears. However, this dam would burst every now and then . . . "[119]

"The place for love is not the pulpit but the gibbet," Iqbal wrote not long before his death.[120] This was a reference to the 9th century mystic, Hallaj, who had been put to death because of his controversial views. Imagining him to be a pantheist, Iqbal had once condemned Hallaj's views, but later he interpreted these views as an affirmation of *khudi* and tended to identify himself with Hallaj. In *Javid-Namah* ("Book of Eternity"), Hallaj says to Iqbal:

> The voice of resurrection shot its call
> Forth in my breast; I saw a people who were
> Hastening to their graves; the reality of
> Self they did reject . . .
> My friend, fear for thyself,
> Thou too repeatest what I did . . . [121]

When Reynold Nicholson, who had been with Iqbal in Cambridge, wrote asking the poet's permission to translate *Asrar-i-khudi*, Iqbal "could not control his tears."[122] Someone present wanted to know why Iqbal was moved. The poet replied: "My people, whose self-hood I wanted to resurrect, neither care to appreciate it nor recognise its value. Europeans, for whom this book was not intended, want to understand my message." Iqbal's melancholy would show itself in "weeping without apparent cause," as Javid would observe, and in remarks like, "No one ever comes and sits with me."[123]

In fact, he was seldom left alone. People made a path to his door to taste his talk and not because he was famous. "From morning to evening this man sat on a plain bedstead or an armchair, wearing simple clothes, and the influx of visitors continued." He "never displayed any symptom of boredom with anyone's presence" and no one could find Iqbal dull. Leg-pulling, innocent naughtiness and hearty laughter were the marks, and religion almost always the subject, of Iqbal's conversation, which was mostly in Punjabi or in an Urdu with a natural Punjabi accent.

The humour of Iqbal's Urdu or Punjabi talk cannot be reproduced in English, but the setting has been described by Rahbar:

> His style of answering the *salaam* of visitors was seemingly cold. He
> would only lift his right hand, letting it drop casually. But the glow
> of warmth would appear soon on his face. When stimulated he would
> indicate his desire for conversation by muttering "hmm." This mas-
> terly announcement would alert his admirers to the infinite possibil-
> ities of a conversational advance. . . . During intervals of silence he

would comb his hair with his fingers and occasionally say "Ya Allah".
... Usually half-open, his eyes would open fully with the rise of his
enthusiasm.[124]

Adds Rahbar: "In his heart Iqbal was more thankful for this chain of
admiring visitors than for anything else. His audience came to him; what
more can a performing artist of conversation want!"[125]

At times Iqbal's talk would take place in the home of his friend, Mirza
Jalaluddin, where the company was likely to include Jogendra Singh and
Umrao Singh. "For their entertainment they arranged private sitar concerts and exchanged witticisms with each other."[126] Occasionally the melody and rhythm of the players would stimulate Iqbal into composition.
In Rahbar's words, "At the first signs of the approach of his inspiration,
the musicians would discontinue their piece and improvise some gentle
instrumental accompaniment to suit the recitation by the poet."[127]

Inspiration also, of course, arrived at home, where everyone, including
the children, had to be silent; sometimes it arrived in the middle of the
night. Recalls Javid:

> When inspiration came to him, the colour of his face changed and he
> gave the impression of suffering from physical discomfort. During
> the late hours of the night he frequently called Ali Baksh, his servant,
> by clapping his hands, and told him to bring his pen and notebook.
> As he wrote verses in his notebood, his face relaxed, as if he had been
> relieved of great pain.[128]

* * *

Winging, Iqbal sang of a transnational Islamic brotherhood but his feet
were on Punjab's good earth, where he was pushed into politics. "Your
prestige must be used for what you believe in," his friends told him. And
he saw himself as a practical leader and not just a visionary. In 1926,
though he hardly campaigned and stayed indoors, he was elected to the
Punjab Legislative Council from a Muslim seat. Three years later he made
a significant and indeed historic speech as president of the All India Muslim
League, to which we shall presently turn. In 1931 and 1932 he took part
in Round Table conferences held in London to discuss political reforms
for India. In 1935, two days after Iqbal and his family had moved to the
first house they ever owned, Sardar Begum died. Javid has described the
pathetic scene:

> The two of us (Javid, 11 and Munira, 5), wept bitterly. Holding each
> other's hand, we went to our father's room. He was lying in bed, for
> he was not in good health. He had also lost his voice and could not

speak clearly. Munira and I stood at the door, not knowing what to do. He noticed us and asked us to come closer. When we came near him, he asked us to sit on his right and left sides. Then, placing his hands affectionately on our shoulders, he said rather angrily to me: "You must not cry like this. Remember that you are a man — and men do not cry." He then kissed both of us on the forehead — probably for the first time in his life.[129]

* * *

At the end of 1930 Iqbal expressed a hope that seemed discordant to almost everyone who heard of it, but it was destined to be fulfilled. Presiding over a session in Lucknow of the Muslim League, he said:

> I would like to see the Punjab, Northwest Frontier Province, Sind and Baluchistan amalgamated into a single state. . . . The formation of a consolidated North Western Indian Muslim state appears to me to be the final destiny of the Muslims, at least of North West India.[130]

What lay behind the wish? One factor was his view of the Indian scene. In 1927 he had said:

> The talk of a united nationalism is futile. The word has existed on the lips of the people of this country for the last fifty years, and like a hen it has cackled a great deal without laying a single egg. . . . In this country one community is always aiming at the destruction of the other community.[131]

But the stronger influence was Iqbal's vision of a homogeneous Muslim state that would commence a global brotherhood. The First World War had seen the liquidation of the Turkish empire; now, thought Iqbal, it was up to the Muslims of India to raise Islam's flag. "Indian Muslims," the poet said some time before his 1930 address, "who happen to be a more numerous people than the Muslims of all other Asiatic countries put together, ought to consider themselves the greatest asset of Islam."[132] As the Pakistani scholar, Riffat Hassan, puts it, Iqbal saw the new Muslim state as "only a means to achieving a universal brotherhood of man baptized with love."[133]

Iqbal's accent was on initiation, not separation; on getting going with a new society, not on getting out of India. He saw practical advantages in a consolidated Muslim state in India but his primary impulse was idealistic. Whether the people of the state Iqbal had proposed were capable of fulfilling his vision was another question. It is possible to accuse Iqbal of excessive idealism but he was not actuated by dislike of the Hindus. We should note that the state Iqbal had in mind was, in his words at

Lucknow, a "Muslim India within India" and not one that would sever all links.[134] He was willing to be seen as a believer in a "communalism of a higher kind" but he clarified that "the principle that each group is entitled to free development on its own lines is not inspired by any feeling of narrow communalism." Iqbal added: "I entertain the highest respect for the customs, laws and religious and social institutions of other communities. Nay, it is my duty, according to the teachings of the Qur'an, even to defend their places of worship if need be."[135]

The new state would be a Muslim state but "Hindus should not fear" that there would be "a kind of religious rule" in it.[136] Two other points connected with Iqbal's scheme are of interest. One, he said that he was willing to exclude from it Punjab's Hindu-majority eastern districts, something that Jinnah, as we shall see later, was not prepared to do. Two, the Muslim-majority areas of the subcontinent's eastern wing were left out of Iqbal's scheme. Clearly, Iqbal saw better prospects for his ideological concept in a compact area with an undiluted Muslim majority. We shall discover that with Jinnah the emphasis was less on ideology and more on parity with non-Muslims. It was Jinnah's historic role to achieve Pakistan but his belief in a Muslim homeland was not as unqualified as Iqbal's.

Jinnah had played a prominent part in a 1916 Congress-League understanding in favour of, among other things, separate electorates for Muslims all over India and "weightage" in Punjab for the province's Hindu and Sikh minorities. Iqbal welcomed the separate electorates but opposed the reduction of Muslim influence in Punjab. Then, in the late twenties, Jinnah proposed a League-Congress settlement that, among other things, would do away with separate electorates in return for "weightage" for Muslims in all-India politics. Why Congress did not accept Jinnah's proposals will form part of the Jinnah chapter; here we should note that Iqbal also opposed the Jinnah terms. Believing in the two-nation theory, the poet rejected joint Hindu-Muslim electorates.

In 1936-37, Iqbal and Jinnah wrote several letters to each other. The ones from the poet were published by Jinnah in 1946. No copies of the letters to Iqbal from Jinnah appear to exist. The correspondence related to an announcement by Jawaharlal Nehru, Congress president at this juncture, of a Congress drive for "mass contact" with Muslims, and to Nehru's declaration of his socialist hopes. Affirming that "the atheistic socialism of Jawaharlal is not likely to receive much response from the Muslims," Iqbal nonetheless proposes a counter. In his view "the best reply" that Jinnah can give Nehru is to declare "a separate federation of Muslim provinces" as the Muslim goal and the goal of the League.

Why should not "the Muslims of North-West India and Bengal," asked

Iqbal, "be considered as nations entitled to self-determination?" By now he is thinking of Bengal, too, as a Muslim nation, though separate from the one in the North-West. In these letters Iqbal seems also to advocate a form of Islamic socialism: "the Shariat of Islam" makes "the right to subsistence" obligatory, but Islamic laws could only be enforced by "free Muslim states," which should develop the code of Islam "in the light of modern ideas." Finally, Iqbal asks Jinnah to hold the next annual session of the League in Lahore, and not in any of the Muslim-minority provinces, which could be "ignored" for the time being.

Not yet ready to ask for partition, Jinnah did not accept any of Iqbal's recommendations. He chose Lucknow, capital of the U.P., a Muslim-minority province, as the venue for the next League rally. In the middle of 1937 Congress ministries were elected to power in all Hindu-majority provinces. This had led to Muslim fears of "Hindu Raj." Legitimate or unjustified, these fears gave the League an opportunity in provinces like the U.P. that Jinnah was determined to grab.

Another consideration influencing Jinnah was the power of Sir Sikander Hyat Khan, who had become Premier of Punjab as the leader of the Unionist party, which was supported by affluent Muslims, Hindus and Sikhs. Jinnah wanted to woo Sikander, whereas Iqbal's was proposing a strategy of enlisting the poor and ousting the Unionists from power.[137] Eventually, in 1940, the League held a session in Lahore and adopted a separate Muslim state or states as its goal. But Iqbal was dead by then, and in his presidential address Jinnah did not refer to Iqbal or his scheme.

Nehru, in his *Discovery of India*, says that a few months before his death Iqbal commented to him, "What is there in common between Jinnah and you? He is a politician, you are a patriot."[138] And Edward Thompson, the British writer, claims that toward the end of his life Iqbal had spoken to him of his "very serious reservations" about the separate Muslim state then being talked of.[139] What are we to infer from these observations? They confirm that the Iqbal-Jinnah relationship was not always smooth, and also that the two had different conceptions of the Pakistan-to-come. They do not, however, disprove Iqbal's zeal for a Muslim homeland, or the significance he and Jinnah attached to each other. It is undeniable that Iqbal had written to Jinnah in 1937 that the latter "alone" could guide India's Muslims, and that later Jinnah described Iqbal as one who "stood like a rock."[140]

There was astringency between Iqbal and Sikander. Aware that an Iqbal Day was to be observed in the poet's honour, and aware too of Iqbal's poor health and finances, Premier Sikander said in December 1937:

Today, after years of deep slumber, Muslims are awake; this is largely due to the message of Iqbal.... I would propose that in the cities where Iqbal Day is celebrated the citizens should collect money and present it to the great poet.

Hitting back at a foe's display of kindness, the proud Iqbal said: "The needs of the people as a whole are far more pressing than the needs of a private individual even though his work may have been a source of inspiration to most people." If people wanted to honour him, continued Iqbal, they should "establish a chair for Islamic research on modern lines in the local Islamia college." Expressing the hope that his proposal "will meet with the Premier's approval," Iqbal offered "a humble contribution of one hundred rupees" towards implementing it.[141]

* * *

Though he took his Punjab politics seriously and also played a part in two major rounds of talks in London on India's future, Iqbal was more a visionary than a politician. And his vision was a poet's vision. His intense concern with God, man and the world was a poet's concern. In Hadi Hussain's arresting words, Iqbal's "God is the archetypal poet, the supreme creative artist, incessantly creating out of a grand passion of self-expression." Iqbal's ideal man, adds Hussain,

> ... is God's apprentice and helpmate in this creative activity, always adding to the Master's work and daring even to improve upon it.... His universe is that perfect poem yet to be written, which God and man are writing in collaboration.[142]

Muhammad Iqbal is one of this century's great poets. The darling of his poetry is not nature or beautiful woman but man in motion:

> To reach no end, to travel on
> Without a stop is everlasting life.
> Our range is from the ceiling of the skies
> To the sea's floor, and Time and Space are both
> Dust lying in our path.[143]

To some other poets and servants of God it is man who is dust, but, powdered with gold-dust, Iqbal's man in motion is proud — even as Iqbal himself was. Meeting him in Lahore, the King of Afghanistan said, "So you are Iqbal. I am amazed. I had pictured you with a beard." Retorted Iqbal, "My surprise is greater than yours. You are a military general. I had pictured you with a giant's physique, but you are so lean and puny."[144]

When he had company he liked, the proud poet relaxed and laughed at life. One Ramadan evening, when two friends visited him just before the hour of breaking the fast, Iqbal clapped his hands and asked the responding servant, Rehma, to bring "oranges, dates, sweetmeats and savouries." "Please," protested Maulana Salik, one of the visitors, "no formality is necessary. Just some dates will suffice." "But let me at least impress you with a big list," said Iqbal. A man who was present adds: "Rehma considered a word-by-word fulfilment of Iqbal's instructions unnecessary and contented himself with meeting the wishes of Maulana Salik."[145]

On New Year's day in 1938, Iqbal the universalist spoke from the Lahore station of All India Radio:

> Only one unity is dependable, and that unity is the brotherhood of man, which is above race, nationality, colour or language.... So long as men do not demonstrate by their actions that they believe that the whole world is the family of God. . . . the beautiful ideals of liberty, equality and fraternity will never materialize.[146]

Iqbal was ill now, attacked by asthma. On April 20, 1938, he responded to a young admirer's request by reciting a quatrain he had composed a few months earlier:

> The departed melody may or may not come.
> The breeze from Hejaz* may or may not come.
> The days of this *faqir* have come to an end,
> Another wise one may or may not come.[147]

Some hours after Iqbal had recited it Javid went up to his father but by this time Iqbal was too ill to recognize his 14-year-old son. "Who are you?" asked the poet. "I am Javid," said the boy. Iqbal smiled and, turning to a friend, said, "Chaudhari Sahib, please see to it that he learns the passage 'Addressed to Javid' which appears near the end of my *Javid-Namah* ('Book of Eternity')."[148] Shortly afterwards Iqbal died.

Among the lines that this passionate Muslim had addressed to his son are:

> The man of love, who sees men with God's eye,
> Loves heathen and believer equally.

---

*Arabia

Give both of them a warm place in your heart.
Woe to the heart if heart from heart should part.

Among the Muslims you will seek in vain
The faith, the ecstasy of days bygone...
Show me a single man who is drunk with God.
Distinguish men of faith from men of hate.
Seek out a man of God for your soul mate.[149]

Chapter 4

Muhammad Ali

(1878–1931)

Between 1919 and 1921 Hindus and Muslims united as never before. "The scenes that took place," says Ikram, the Pakistani historian, "cannot be easily imagined by those who did not see them. The Hindus and Musims literally drank water from one cup."[1] Writing of this at the time, a Muslim professor spoke of "a wonderful phenomenon, undreamed of, unimagined, unhoped by the wildest hopes of man."[2] Presiding at a Muslim League session in December 1919, Hakim Ajmal Khan, one of the founders of the Muslim body, said: "If thankfulness can be expressed in words, let me in the name of the Indian Muslim community thank the Hindus from the bottom of my heart."[3]

How this Muslim-Hindu alliance came about and then came apart are stories linked to Muhammad Ali, whose brilliant, stormy and sad life commenced in 1878 in the principality of Rampur, which lay 150 miles to the east of Delhi. The boy was the fifth son of Abdul Ali, "a favourite courtier of Nawab Yusuf Ali Khan, the ruler of Rampur."[4] Abdul Ali's father Ilahi Bakhsh too had been a Rampur courtier. During the 1857 Rising, Bakhsh and his ruler sided with the British, who rewarded Bakhsh with a piece of land. Abdul Ali lived beyond his means, offering hospitality to friends and flatterers in his property's *mardana*, or male quarters, and amusing them with quail-fights. The extended family's women and children lived in the secluded *zenana*, the women "whiling away their time cutting betel nuts, chewing betel leaves, supervising servants and gossiping about trivial events in the neighbourhood."[5]

Abdul Ali died of cholera when he was 30, his wife 27, Muhammad Ali 2 — and his debt Rs 30,000. Luckily, there was a tough and bold side to Muhammad Ali's illiterate mother Abadi Bano Begum, later Bi Amman to many in India. The young widow clothed her children in humble material and raised them on simple food and the Prophet's sayings, but also sent her boys to the English school in the nearby town of Bareilly. The uncle managing the family's affairs said he wouldn't pay for turning the boys into infidels; Bi Amman countered by pawning her personal jewellery with the assistance of the maid of a Hindu neighbour.

From Bareilly Muhammad Ali, a dark-eyed, good-looking lad with a dreamy look and an idle walk, and an older brother, Shaukat Ali, went to Aligarh, seat of MAO and of a school linked to it. Shaukat, tall, broad and bearded, became captain of the cricket eleven but Muhammad Ali, though clearly bright, seemed less of an ornament. Muhammad Ali has recalled.

> Being senior to me by the somewhat large margin of six years and having been the captain of the famous cricket eleven of the Aligarh College, besides being the secretary of the College union and many other things which made him a very big "boss" indeed, [Shaukat] had not condescended to take much notice of an inconsequential schoolboy like me. This was in spite of the fact that I regularly earned a small scholarship and thereby helped him to dress as a smart cricket captain should, for which even our joint pocket money, which of course he pocketed for both of us, did not apparently suffice. And on the few occasions on which he did take notice of his little brother, the little brother ardently prayed for perfectly uninterrupted obscurity, for these were the occasions when some of my schoolmates complained to him of my militancy and I became in turn the object of even more militant attentions from by big brother. . . . Although he did not in those days breaks the scales as he did in the gaol on our imprisonment, he turned them at a heavy enough weight as my tingling ears, when he had soundly boxed them, could honestly testify . . .

An impish precocious wordy victim of hurtful blows — this was Muhammad Ali all his life. There is only one important element of his personality that the quotation does not suggest: his life-long romance with Islam. It started early. Being a schoolboy Muhammad Ali was not entitled to attend the lectures on the Qur'an that Shibli Nomani was giving in MAO's Principal's Hall, but he heard them from behind a door. Learning of the boy's interest, and of a talent the boy had for versifying, Shibli sent for him. The boy's answers to Shibli's questions were satisfactory; thereafter, Muhammad Ali attended the lectures as an invitee, a lone schoolboy amidst scores of college students and lectures.

He cut classes and, after entering college, made flippant speeches in the Union. In the theology hour he wrote droll verse or drew caricatures of the teacher. But when the results were out, the B.A. results of Allahabad University, to which MAO was affiliated at the time, Muhammad Ali's name was at the top of the list. Where did one go from there? To England, if possible, and then to the I.C.S. Shaukat, who had entered the provincial civil service of the U.P., said he would bear the burden of an Oxford education for Muhammad Ali.

Muhammad Ali made it to Oxford and was enrolled at Lincoln College. According to his contemporaries, Indian and British, he "lived in style" in England, liked modish clothes and being photographed, was "very quick in making friends" and seen by some as likely to get into trouble.[7] But his affair with Islam was continuing, after a fashion. In his words:

> I had been greatly attracted by a new translation of the Qur'an into good easily intelligible Urdu; and had had a copy sent on to me at Oxford. Fired by my own religious zeal and financed by a generous brother, I had the Qur'an bound most sumptuously by the book-binder of the Bodleian, and it looked superb on the otherwise meagerly furnished book-shelf in my college room. But alas for the inconsistency of human nature, the Qur'an which I had so eagerly sent for from home, remained far too often a mere ornament of my book-shelf . . .[8]

He spoke in some Union debates. An excess of modesty not being his fault, he called the circle of students to which he belonged the *Nauratan*, or the set of nine jewels, after the style of Akbar the emperor. The nine included Hindus, of whom a son of the ruler of Baroda was one, Muslims and a Parsi. However, to his and Shaukat's distress, Muhammad Ali failed to gain admission into the I.C.S. Why did he fail? "Thanks to an English spring, and a young man's more or less foolish fancy," says Muhammad Ali.[9] But he stops there and cheats posterity of information on what the spring did or what the fancy was. In any case, the fulfilment of an earlier wish was round the corner. The girl he had wanted to wed, a cousin, was waiting for him in India. Bi Amman, who had endorsed her son's choice, was sure that marriage would banish Muhammad Ali's grief over the I.C.S. tests. Muhammad Ali returned to India to marry, went to Oxford again and came back a few months later with an honors degree in modern history. Now he was Muhammad Ali, B.A. (Oxford), easily the first man from Rampur with that title, and very proud of it.

He wanted to teach at MAO but the British principal saw signs of an agitator in Muhammad Ali and would not accept him. Rampur's ruler made him chief educational officer but the intrigues of the feudal set-up "disgusted" Muhammad Ali into resigning in less than a year. Thanks, however, to Prince Fateh Singh, his *Nauratan* colleague at Oxford, Muhammad Ali was taken into the civil service of Baroda. Its ruler Sayaji Rao Gaekwar (1875-1936) was forward-looking: he gave Muhammad Ali discretion in his tasks and liberty to write, speak and travel.

The young bureaucrat helped the state's revenues to grow and acquired a reputation for humour, fluency in English and a passion for matching neckties with handkerchiefs. But a civil servant's anonymity did not suit him; without the freedom to speak and write Muhammad Ali would have given less than the seven years he gave to the state.

Part of his message at this juncture was that the British were not devils. Some of them were acting under "generous impulses." Indeed, wrote Muhammad Ali in 1907, " . . . hardly any Indian patriot has rendered India such valuable services as Burke and Bright, Macaulay and Bentinck." He added: "But all cannot take the wings of angels. Because the average Englishman lacks the fluffy growth on his shoulder blades, is it any reason to credit him with the cloven foot?" The fault of the white man in India was not Machiavellianism but insularity: "He was avoiding the touch of a sixth of the whole human race."[10]

He did not see a conflict between sentiments for Islam and for India. Hindu-Muslim tension was a reality but, observed Muhammad Ali, "The greater portion of bigotry agitates not the bosoms of the ignorant and the illiterate but excites to fury and to madness the little-learned of the land."[11] Another diagnosis of his was that "it is not the love of our religion that makes us quarrel with our fellow countrymen of other faiths, but self-love and petty personal ambition."[12] He told India's Muslim community that,

> . . . while the pressing needs of the present may inevitably bring it now and then into conflict with other elements in the body politic . . . ultimately all communal interests had to be adjusted in order to harmonize the paramount interests of India.[13]

A vision for India accompanied his romance with Islam:

> Here in this country of hundreds of millions of human beings, intensely attached to religion and yet infinitely split up into communities, sects and denominations, Providence [has] created for us the mission of solving a unique problem and working out a new synthesis, a Federation of Faiths.[14]

Sprinkled among his long sentences were quotable epigrams or metaphors. Conservative Muslims reluctant to ask the Raj for free and compulsory education were told by him: "The best form of freedom is free education, and the most pleasing compulsion is compulsory education."[15] And Hindus who disliked the small percentage of Persian and Arabic words in Urdu were addressed thus:

> Did Muslims bring Urdu from Arabia or Persia or Afghanistan? No, it was in the Indian camp and market-place that they picked it up, and eighty per cent of the words used in their daily intercourse are such as will have no meaning for an Arab or a Persian or a Turk or an Afghan. . . . No Hindu banker will throw away pure gold and silver simply because it might have been minted in Arabia or Persia. . . . Hindus of the U.P. and Punjab should not object to words of Persian and Arabic origin, branding them as *bideshi* and foreign.[16]

In 1906 the Aga Khan led a Muslim deputation to the Viceroy, Lord Minto, in Simla. The group asked for a clear commitment that Muslims would be allowed to choose, by their separate vote, Muslim representatives in the elected bodies that the Raj was contemplating. In addition, the group asked for "adequate Muslim representation" which would take into account "not merely the numerical strength" of India's Muslims but also "their political importance" and "the value of the contribution which they make to the defence of the empire."[17] Minto agreed, and the Act of 1909 providing for the elected bodies incorporated his pledges: only Muslim votes would select Musim legislators, and there would be more Muslim seats than was warranted by numbers alone. India would be compartmentalized; a decisive step had been taken.

The Muslim seats assured in Simla called for a Muslim political party. Within months of the meeting with Minto the All India Muslim League was born in Dacca. At the opening meeting, chaired by the Nawab of Dacca, the Aga Khan was made the League's permanent president. Muhammad Ali, who was given leave by the Gaekwar to attend the occasion, played a part, providing "necessary clarifications" to those who had misgivings and later writing the official report of the first session.[18]

The League's slogan was: "defence, not defiance, loyalty, not sedition; education, not agitation."[19] This was by no means the emphasis of Congress, which had been founded in 1885 and was seen by the Raj as increasingly radical. In the circumstances it was natural for the allegation to emerge that clever British practitioners of divide-and-rule had fathered the League. A passage in a book subsequently written by Lady Minto seemed to confirm the charge: she quoted a British official who described the Viceroy's response to the Muslim deputation as "nothing less than the pulling back of 62 million people from joining the ranks of the seditious opposition."[20] But delight at an event does not prove paternity. The Raj was glad at the League's launching and indeed assisted it,* but the impulse for separate representation and the desire for weightage were indigenous to many Muslims.

Though he took an active part in the League's founding, Muhammad Ali "advised his co-religionists to work for unity" with Hindus. In lectures delivered immediately after the Dacca meeting he explained that he would "never advocate the cause of any association likely to disintegrate the people." The League, he argued, was "an effort at integration."[21]

Fateh Singh, son of Sayaji Rao and a "jewel" along with Muhammad Ali at Oxford, died when Muhammad Ali had spent five years in Baroda state. The Hindu prince was only 24. Muhammad Ali cried like a baby and wrote a lament in Urdu verse. Two years later he left Baroda for Calcutta, still India's capital, to start *The Comrade*, a weekly in English that announced that it would be no one's partisan and everyone's friend. Fateh Singh's absence had made Baroda less of a magnet; more important, Muhammad Ali had to express himself, and not just occasionally. The move was courageous, for he had no funds, and he nearly abandoned it when a lucrative offer of a ministership in another princely state reached him shortly before he was to leave for Calcutta. One of the Raj's custodians, Sir Michael O'Dwyer, who would soon become Punjab's Governor, pressed Muhammad Ali to accept the offer. If *The Comrade* had to appear, added O'Dwyer, it could be produced in the new state. Though Muhammad Ali said no to the Raja and to Sir Michael, he had been greatly tempted; and when on arrival in Calcutta he found another telegram from the Raja, he took care not to open it until the first issue of *The Comrade* was on sale in the streets. *The Comrade*'s motto was:

> Stand upright, speak thy thought, declare
> The truth thou hast that all may share.
> Be bold, proclaim it everywhere;
> They only live who dare.[22]

And its policy, as outlined in the opening number of January 14, 1911, included "the frank recognition of yawning differences that divide" Hindus and Muslims. "But," added Muhammad Ali,

---

*Here some Pakistanis would point out that several British officials, including the Viceroy at the time, assisted the founding of Congress. Later this help was regretted; it had been given in the belief that free venting of views would make violence less likely.

... if the Muslims or the Hindus attempt to achieve succees in opposition to or even without the cooperation of one another, they will not only fail but fail ignominiously. When the statesmen and philanthropists of Europe, with all its wars of interests and national jealousies, do not despair of abolishing war, shall we despair of Indian nationality? We may not create today the partriotic fervour of Japan with its forty millions of homogeneous people. But a concordat like that of Canada is not without the bounds of practicability.... This ... no easy task ... is one worthy of the sons and daughters of India.[23]

Written and edited by one man and produced on expensive paper, *The Comrade* quickly gained circulation and influence. A Bengali journalist commented, referring to the paper's look, that Muhammad Ali had "taught the Bengali journalists that clothes make all the difference in the world."[24] But it was more than appearance. In Mujeeb's words, Muhammad Ali's English, "written with ease and confidence and displaying familiarity with British life and literature, impressed [his readers]." He reviewed books, wrote humorous pieces, commented on events. Says Mujeeb:

> The initial bias in his favour was not affected by the involved sentences, the constant digressions, the egoistic references to himself, because scattered all over, without any literary design and almost without intention, were witty remarks, epigrams, amusing anecdotes.[25]

European officials, too, became subscribers and Lady Hardinge, the wife of the Viceroy, would phone if an issue was delayed. After twenty months, *The Comrade* moved to Delhi, the Raj's new capital. Before long it acquired a sister, an Urdu-language daily named *Hamdard*. For *Hamdard* Muhammad Ali imported machinery and type faces from Beirut and Cairo, but the public found the script unfamiliar and *Hamdard* had to switch to calligraphy and litho, the traditional form of Urdu printing. His Urdu writing was not as effective as his English but it enabled him to speak to his *qaum*.

As Mujeeb puts it, Muhammad Ali felt himself "the equal of anybody in the world, of the Viceroy of India and the Prime Minister of Great Britain, and that he could chat and joke without diffidence and embarrassment among the high and mighty as well as his intimate friends." He could also hit back, as is shown by a conversation that took place in 1907 between him and Archbold, who was MAO's principal at the time. At Muhammad Ali's suggestion MAO students had invited Gokhale, the Congress leader, to address them. Disliking this, Archbold declared the College out of bounds for Muhammad Ali, who refused to heed the order and was seen by Archbold near the College mosque.

Archbold:	"Don't you know that the College is out of bounds for you?"
Muhammad Ali:	"The College is my own. Who are you to impose any ban on my entry? Besides, I am standing at the door of God's house."
Archbold:	"Remember, it will take me only ten days to return to England."
Muhammad Ali:	"It will take the same period for another Englishman to come out to India on the same salary."[26]

Hamdard's editor, Qazi Abdul Ghaffar, has provided another picture of the Muhammad Ali temperament:

> Once I saw a proof copy of an article of his. Some mistakes remained uncorrected. When Muhammad Ali saw the article in print he walked into my office and gave me a dressing down. I sent in my resignation and came away. The next day Shaukat Ali came to my house and told me that Muhammad Ali had not eaten since I left the office. When I went back Muhammad Ali hugged me and wept bitterly.[27]

The "yawning gap" of which Muhammad Ali had spoken was there for all to see when at the royal durbar of 1911 the 1905 partition of Bengal was declared annulled. Congress had opposed the partition; a few individuals had opposed it with bombs. Hindus welcomed the annulment as a halt to divide-and-rule but Muslims were hurt at the dissolution of East Bengal, which had an unassailable Muslim majority. Khaliquzzaman speaks of it as "the greatest shock of their lives to the Muslims of India."[28] Some Muslims accused the Raj of surrendering to terrorism. Muhammad Ali did not like the annulment but advised India's Muslims to come to terms with it.

His stance, and that of *The Comrade* and *Hamdard*, was simultaneously "communal" and "patriotic." He would defend and also regret separate electorates. They were, he said in 1912, "a hateful necessity — like divorce, which was accepted by Islam as a hateful necessity."[29] As inter-communal relations improved, separate electorates could be phased out and job quotas for Muslims in government departments could also be phased out.[30] At two League sessions, in 1909 and 1912, Muhammad Ali praised "the tough fight," as he put it in 1912, "of the Indians in South Africa against racial distinctions"; that fight was an Indian rather than a Muslim affair.[31] He was at his most Islamic or "communal" when speaking about the conditions, at the time, of Turkey, to which we shall soon turn; in the next breath he would be unambiguously patriotic, successfully urging the Muslim League to adopt as one of its chief aims "the attainment of a system of self-government suitable to India."[32]

* * *

The period we have arrived at is one in which, to many an Indian Muslim, Turkey and Islam were interchangeable terms. Turkey was the globe's premier Muslim state. Islam's sacred places were under its jurisdiction. Its ruler was the khalifa, or caliph, of the Sunni Muslims of the world. India's Muslims saw any threat to Turkey as a threat to Islam and therefore to themselves; they discounted the bid, led by some Turks themselves, to eliminate Islamic traditions from their land. In the view of India's Muslim leaders, Turkey's attempt to Westernize itself had failed. Aping the West, simultaneously introducing Russian uniforms, Belgian rifles, Turkish headgear, Hungarian saddles, English swords and French drill, the Turkish army had become a grotesque parody of Europe. Turkey's future was with Islam, as her past had been; and the future of India's Muslims was intimately connected with the security of the Turkey of the Crescent. Muhammad Ali, for one, felt that a Turkish town threatened by non-Muslims "flashed across the dividing land and sea the never-changing message: 'I am Islam — the Unity of your Allah, the Truth of His Messenger. I am a signal. I wait.' "[33]

So when in 1911 Italy attacked Tripoli in what is now Libya but was then a Turkish possession, and the British told the Turks that they could not pass through Egypt to Tripoli, *The Comrade* attacked the British, and MAO students held daily protest meetings. The loss of Tripoli was followed by the Balkan wars of 1912-13, in which Bulgars, Serbs and Greeks, Turkey's subjects for centuries, routed the premier Muslim state. India's Muslim's felt shattered. Muhammad Ali has recalled the effect on him:

> My feelings during the disastrous war in the Balkans were so overpowering that I must confess I even contemplated suicide.... The latest message of Reuter that had reached me was that the Bulgarians were only 25 miles from the walls of Constantinople — a name that had for five centuries been sacred to every Muslim as the centre of his highest hopes....
>
> I was saved a trial of my courage as well as cowardice by the unexpected appearance of a Muslim friend who had graduated from Oxford not long before and was on this occasion accompanied by an English fellow-graduate of that university who was his guest and had expressed a desire to see an Indian *nautch*.
>
> My friend insisted on my company, and hard as I pleaded the excuse of a busy editor and still harder the state of my feelings after that last message of Reuter, my friend would not take any denial and almost bodily lifted me from the editorial sanctum and carried me by force to the private *nautch* party.... Thus it was that instead of being a

horror of broken bones and bleeding body I was "assisting" at the "orgy" that had been arranged to satisfy the curiosity of a brother Oxonian.[34]

Brother Shaukat too was affected. Resigning his government job to help the *qaum*, he raised money for MAO and assisted pilgrims to Mecca stranded in Bombay. In Muhammad Ali's words:

> From a smart, half-Europeanised fashionably dressed officer of Government who used to be a famous captain of Aligarh cricketers and prided himself on his pretty taste in silk shirts, [Shaukat] became a poorly, not to say shabbily, dressed Bombaywalla in a loose long green coat of queer cut. On the erstwhile smooth cheeks and chin was now to be a seen a shaggy beard which was his protest against Europe and Christendom.[35]

The Comrade asked for money for Turkish relief. Aligarh students saved on food and subscribed. Women parted with ornaments. Approached by Muhammad Ali, the Viceroy facilitated the transfer of relief funds. A medical mission led by Dr. Mukhtar Ahmed Ansari and including eight doctors went to Turkey to help wounded soldiers; the Sultan of Turkey thanked Dr. Ansari "with tears in his eyes."[36] Muhammad Ali, to whose organizing energy the mission owed much, suggested to the Viceroy that its members be decorated.

Lord Hardinge did not act on Muhammad Ali's advice. This was not surprising, for shortly after farewelling Dr. Ansari and his group Muhammad Ali had made an intemperate anti-British speech. Appearing before a Lahore audience in the uniform of the medical mission, he had said that "Indian republicanism" would smash "the heads of the British" if Britain joined others in hurting Turkey.[37]

As Mujeeb says, Muhammad Ali possessed "an intensity that made him at times completely irresponsible."[38] This was one of those times, and it weakened Muhammad Ali's hands when he visited England in the autumn of 1913. He made the journey, along with a League colleague, Wazir Hussain, because of an incident over a Kanpur mosque. Despite Muslim objections, part of the mosque had been pulled down to create a more convenient road alignment. The town's Muslims converged on the site and tried to rebuild the demolished portion. When they disobeyed orders to disperse, the police opened fire, killing several. Muhammad Ali felt obliged to complain in person to H.M.G. in London; he also helped to let the English know of Muslim India's feelings about Turkey.

While Muhammad Ali and Hussain were away, Hardinge persuaded the U.P. Governor, Sir James Meston, to reconstruct the damaged section of the mosque. Also, Hardinge advised Crewe, Secretary of State for India in London, not to encourage Muhammad Ali, who was described as a "clever" and "mischievous agitator."[39] This was not how India's Muslims saw him. According to Khaliquzzaman, the *qaum*, at this juncture, thought of Muhammad Ali as one whose "reputation as a strong, honest and able leader had been well established."[40] All the same, Hardinge's communication closed all ministerial doors in London to Muhammad Ali.

Another Indian who was in England at the time was M.A. Jinnah. After talking with Muhammad Ali and Wazir Hussain, Jinnah, then a prominent Congress figure, decided to join the Muslim League, while clarifying that he was not giving up his Congress links. Jinnah's step was an indication of the strength of the Turkey-related ferment among India's Muslims.

* * *

August 1914 saw the start of the First World War. Muhammad Ali at once said that he had "closed the chapter of controversy" with the British and that the reforms India was asking for could await "a more seasonable occasion."[41] The supplies that remained with the medical mission were given to the Raj as a mark of support. But what if the Turks joined Germany? The possibility was real. Muhammad Ali and Ansari sent a joint cable to Talat Bey, Turkery's interior minister: "We entreat you think a thousand times before launching into war. In case of war between Turkey and England, our condition also will be extremely sad."[42] At Muhammad Ali's instance, his spiritual advisor, Maulana Abdul Bari, head of Lucknow's famed Firangi Mahal, appealed to the Sultan: "We respectfully urge upon your majesty either to support Britain or to keep neutral."[43]

The Times of London had written an editorial that seemd to imply that the Turks had to join the allies or be regarded as enemies. Muhammad Ali answered in *The Comrade*. Under a title *The Times* had used, "The Choice of the Turks," he gave a long list of the wrongs Turkey had suffered at British hands; nonetheless he urged the land of the Crescent not to ally with England's enemies. However, Turkey joined Germany in November.

Like most Indian Muslims, Muhammad Ali was torn. "Although Turkey had thrown in its lot with Germany we could not forsake it."[44] The words are Khaliquzzaman's but they describe the reaction of many, including the Ali brothers. Khaliquzzaman, who was an Aligarh student at the time and had served with the medical mission in Turkey, recalls:

> One night in December the Ali brothers entered my room and whispered to me that it was time that we started sounding our strength

to defy the British should they ever intend to finish Turkey and the Khilafat, and suggested that we should find some way to explore the conditions of the arms factories in the Tribal Area (of the North West Frontier).[45]

Following this conversation Khaliquzzaman and his friends went to the semi-autonomous Tribal Area, as did the Ali brothers. The students were able to inspect some rifles but the Ali brothers, though fraternizing, as Khaliquzzaman puts it, with "ferocious-looking Pathans," made no progress "as all through they were surrounded by the C.I.D."[46]

Turkey's entry into the war had made it impossible for persons like Muhammad Ali to view the war as the average Englishman viewed it. "Muslims," wrote Khaliquzzaman, "were passing through great agony which proceeded from the bottom of their heart."[47] Muhammad Ali claimed with some truth that his Oxford spell, when he "enjoyed participation in the lusty activities of my comrades at my own college and at many others," had given him a "bias . . . entirely in favour of the British people."[48] But his romance with Islam ruled out his supporting a war against Turkey. "The ruler of Turkey," said Muhammad Ali, "was the Khalifa or successor of the Prophet and chief of the faithful, and the Khilafat was as essentially our religious concern as the Qur'an."[49]

Obeying its compulsions, the Raj confined the Ali brothers. First they were interned in Rampur, then in Mehrauli near Delhi and next in Lansdowne in the hills of the U.P. When it was found that some of the "disloyal" were meeting the Ali brothers in Lansdowne, the two were moved to remote Chhindwara in the Central Provinces. The final six months were spent in Betul prison, also in the C.P. Except during the Betul period, their families were allowed to stay with the brothers. The security of *The Comrade* was forfeited; the weekly and *Hamdard* ceased to be. The Raj's maintenance allowance could not cover the brothers' expenses; they were forced to sell the estate that the Raj had given to their grandfather in appreciation of his support in 1857.

In his four-year detention, Muhammad Ali turned to the Qur'an. He read it slowly, memorized it, loved it. He wrote:

> How often have we not felt as if the passages we happened to be reading on a particular day were revealed only that instant in response to our own prayer or to settle some point about which we happened to be undecided and uneasy. My brother would call out to me from his room and recite to me a verse, or I would do the same, pointing out how apposite it was . . .[50]

Romance grows into something like a fire of faith. Now he feels not the equal of kings and emperors and viceroys but their superior: he has the pearl they lack, Islam, which he describes as "the last word in human salvation."[51] He finds himself bursting with joy, and with poetry too — he writes quotable verse — and also with an urge to preach to Europe what it needs, an answer to the narrow nationalism that has produced the war.

* * *

It was shortly before his internment that Muhammad Ali had met Gandhi for the first time; he had previously drawn attention to the struggle of Indians in South Africa that Gandhi had led. "It was a question of love at first sight between us," the Mahatma was to say later.[52] Khaliquzzaman, who was among those who had met the Ali brothers in Lansdowne, writes:

> The Ali brothers thought very highly of Gandhiji and asked us to contact him as early as possible. They gave the opinion that "he alone can be our man." The incident which impressed them very greatly about Gandhiji's views was his address to Calcutta students in which he said, "If I were for sedition I would speak out for sedition and take the consequences."[53]

Gandhi urged the Viceroy to release the brothers, as did Congress, the League and other voices. In a 1918 letter to the Viceroy's secretary, the Mahatma gave his reasons:

(a) If they are kept interned in order that they may not do anything hostile to the Government, the idea is frustrated because they do correspond with, and otherwise send messages to, whomsoever they choose.

(b) Their detention only increases their influence.

(c) Their detention deepens discontent.

(d) Moulana Abdul Bari Saheb is a man wielding tremendous power over thousands of Mussalmans. He is their spiritual adviser and the Government would make him theirs by releasing the brothers.

(e) The brothers are, so far as I am aware, men with a strong will, of noble birth, men of culture and learning, possessing great influence over the educated Mohamedans, open-minded and straightforward. . . . Surely, the Government have every need of such men on their side.[54]

Also, Gandhi advised the brothers to tone down their language. Receiving, in 1919, the draft of a letter that Muhammad Ali proposed to sent to the viceroy, the Mahatma told Muhammad Ali:

> Your language was inflammatory and too full of declamation. . . . Your
> statement of the Mohammadan claim instead of representing an ir-
> reducible minimum was an exaggeration. . . . I would omit all mention
> of personal suffering. It stands as a living record speaking for itself.
> If you adopt my proposal, I would love to revise your draft.[55]

Muhammad Ali had said that if Turkey, now defeated, was not treated
properly by the British and their allies, Indian Muslims would have to
choose between *jehad* (holy war) against the Raj and *hijrat* (migration) from
an India that had turned unholy. Ruled by a power that had attacked
Islam's sanctity, India had become unfit for Muslims to live in. The notion
of *hijrat* was linked to the Prophet's migration to Medina when Mecca
was under the control of Islam's enemies. Argued Gandhi: "The circumstances that attended the Prophet's flight were totally different. . . . He
took with him the whole of the Mohammadans to Medina Sharif. It was
his *satyagraha* (struggle of truth) against the unbelievers of Mecca Sharif."[56]

The brothers' letter to the Viceroy went in its original form and delayed
their release. However, in it they called Gandhi "our guide, philospher
and friend."[57] Another influence on them was their mother, Bi Amman.
Once, according to Muhammad Ali's biographer, Bi Amman, "disregarding the requirements of *purdah*," came into the room where the Deputy
Superintendent of Police was discussing with the brothers a proposal for
their release, and spoke as follows:

> I understand that the Government desires at last to do justice to my
> sons. . . . Naturally I rejoice at this. . . . But I understand that Gov-
> ernment now requires them to given an understanding of some sort.
> Well, they are old enough to understand what is to their advantage,
> and what is not, what is right and what is wrong. . . .
>
> But I want Government to know that if in order to escape from their
> sufferings they will promise anything in the least contrary to the
> dictates of their faith, or the interests of their country, God will, I
> feel sure, give enough strength to my mother's heart, and these palsied
> hands, to throttle them that instant, dear as they are to me. . . . For
> the rest, they have always been law-abiding subjects of the King-
> Emperor, and in your presence I order them to remain so.[58]

This incident took place in 1917, but it was not until December 1919
that the Ali brothers were released. Halfway through their incarceration,
in 1916, Congress and the League had reached agreement on the Muslim
share in Indian self-government. The following year Muhammad Ali was
elected president in absentia of the Muslim League. Bi Amman sat on the

dais in Calcutta and a portrait of Muhammad Ali occupied the presidential chair.

Along with Germany, Turkey was beaten in the war and India's Muslims agonized over what would happen to the Sultan and the Khilafat. Passed early in 1919, the Rowlatt Act threatened personal freedom in India and drew mounting opposition, with Gandhi at its head. And in April 1919 Jallianwalla had occurred, the killing by the Raj's troops of Hindus, Muslims and Sikhs, about 400 in all, in an enclosed area in Amritsar.

Congress and the League were both meeting in Amritsar toward the close of 1919 when, on their release, the Ali brothers arrived there. They had been mobbed at every station en route. At the Congress session Muhammad Ali said for the first time what thousands of Indian activists for freedom would say in the future: "I have come from prison — with a return ticket."[59]

We are now in the memorable era in which India's multitudes, Muslim and Hindu, strove together for India's liberty and Islam's honour. There was glory in their struggle, but also tragedy; truth, but also error; unity, but also suspicion. What made the struggle possible was the simultaneity of Muslim and Hindu dissatisfaction.

Dismayed by what had happened to Turkey, India's Muslims feared that the war's non-Muslim victors would control Islam's sacred places that the Sultan of Turkey had been administering, an abhorrent thought. Indians, as a whole, Hindus, Muslims, Sikhs and others, disliked the Rowlatt Act. They had been shocked by Jallianwalla and even more by what had followed: a decree that Indians passing along the Amrtisar street where an Englishwoman had been assaulted should crawl; another requiring Indians on vehicles or horses in the area to dismount at the sight of a British officer; and the flogging of violators. Almost everyone was unhappy or indignant but also aware that the Raj had the skill to cope with petitions and the strength to cope with home-made bombs.

At this stage Gandhi emerged and said to Muslims and Hindus that there was a third way: non-violent non-cooperation. The Raj would listen or leave if Indians withdrew their cooperation and snapped their links with the Raj's inducements and rewards, its titles, councils, jobs. These had allured and enfeebled Indians.

He had been implying this for some time, and, as we have seen, Muhammad Ali for one had noted Gandhi's candour about sedition. Early in 1919 Gandhi obtained pledges from several leading Indians that they would rather violate the Rowlatt Act and go to prison than submit to it.

Defiance was in the air, along with Gandhi's insistence on peaceful behaviour. Now Gandhi prescribed non-cooperation to Muslims agonizing over the Khilafat; and he asked Hindus to make the Muslim cause their own.

Not everyone warmed to the proposal. Many politicians, Hindu and Muslim, had hoped to enter the reformed councils that a 1919 Act had initiated. These councils possessed nominal or poor powers but offered a tempting platform. Others, however, Muslims and Hindus, humiliated over Rowlatt, the Punjab and Khilafat, saw in non-cooperation a weapon to match the hour. Muhammad Ali, hailed on his release by an Iqbal poem, was not quite the first to embrace the new weapon. But he became its most eloquent proponent, criss-crossing India in the Mahatma's company and rousing thousands to action with his peppery speeches.

First, however, he led a deputation to London, to persuade H.M.G. not to sever the holy areas from Turkish influence. "Loving domesticity," as he put it, but fated to abjure it, Muhammad Ali had not been free for more than a month before he was out on the high seas.[60] In that interval he had travelled widely and given only three or four days to Rampur, where his family was. Yet even that period had been filled with visitors, and in the first letter he received after reaching England his daughters complained that they had not had a single meal with him after his release. "I knew what baggage I was taking," he recalled later, "only when my old servant, who had been my companion since my childhood, gave me the keys of the boxes and a list of the things he thought I would need in Europe."[61]

His reflections while in internment, the sadness over Khilafat, and the simplicity stressed by Gandhi had changed Muhammad Ali's appearance. The man "admired for his keen sartorial sense" had switched to "baggy trousers of coarse cotton" and "a cap which carried the crescent and the star."[62] In England he switched again and became "the debonair gentleman, perfectly dressed."[63]

The most important meeting there was with Lloyd George, the Premier, who referred to Arab desires for freedom from Turkish control. Claiming that he could reconcile the Arabs to Turkey, Muhammad Ali said that Islam demanded Muslim control over its holy places. Turks and Arabs, both Muslims, could work out how the holy areas would be looked after; non-Muslim European powers should stay out completely.

Lloyd George also mentioned the allegations of Turkish massacres of Armenians. Commented Muhammad Ali: "If the Turks really have been guilty of these attrocities and horrible crimes, we will wash our hands of the Turks. To us it is much more important that not a single stain should remain on the fair name of Islam."[64] The Premier's response to the deputation's plea was clear:

> Turkey slammed the gates in the face of an old ally who had always stood by her.... I do not understand Muhammad Ali to claim indulgence for Turkey. He claims justice and justice she will get.... I do not want any Muslim in India to imagine that we are applying one principle to Christian countries and another to a Muslim country. Austria has had justice. Germany has had justice, pretty terrible justice. Why should Turkey escape?[65]

Lloyd George had not understood. India's Muslims did not want Turkey to be treated on a par with the war's other losers. They desired recognition of Turkey's status in Islam, and fulfilment of an earlier Lloyd George word that the allies were not "fighting to deprive Turkey of the rich and renowned lands of Asia Minor."[66] This assurance had helped swell the ranks of Indian Muslims soldiering for the empire against Turkey.

Montagu, Secretary of State for India, found Muhammad Ali "vain," "loquacious," "personally quite honest" and possessing "some power of debate."[67] But the Indian visitor had not lost his capacity for indiscretion and hyperbole. At a meeting in a London mosque he told a group of Indian Muslims that in any war again between Britain and Turkey, Indians would fight for Turkey. On another occasion, referring to the role of Indian troops on the side of the allies, he claimed that "it was the Indian soldiers who beat the Turks."[68]

Success was not on the cards. The Turks were not popular in England, and Armenians and Arabs in England had criticized the deputation for its Turkish sympathies. Equating Islam with Turkey and interpreting "Arab independence" as a slogan inspired by anti-Turk Europeans, Muhammad Ali and the great majority of Indian Muslims of his time ignored the Arab-Turk conflict. This conflict may have suited the European powers, but it was not their invention.

In May 1920 the final terms for Turkey were announced. She lost all her colonies and the Greek-majority areas she once controlled. Hejaz (later Saudi Arabia) was recognized as a free and independent state under Faisal, who had seized power. Palestine and Iraq, the former containing Jerusalem and the latter Karbala, places almost as sacred as Mecca and Medina, were placed under British guardianship, while France was authorized to "advise and assist" Syria.

To Indian Muslims this was a betrayal and an affront. That Faisal was a Muslim was not good enough; suzerainty over Mecca and Medina belonged to none but the Khalifa. Unless they fought to restore the Khilafat, India's Muslims too would be betrayers.

A year earlier, writing to the Viceroy from prison, Muhammad Ali had said that India's Muslims might have to choose between holy war and migration. Now, in the middle of 1920, thousands of Muslims, mostly from the North West Frontier but including some from Punjab, sold their land and chattels and emigrated to Afghanistan, convinced that it was anti-Islamic to stay any longer under the British flag.

They had heard that the Amir of Afghanistan wanted to look after them, but this word was belied. After some weeks the Amir closed the gates. Unwelcome and disillusioned, most of the emigrants returned to India but some died in Afghanistan.

The Hunter Commission's report on the Punjab events was also released in May 1920. It confirmed the grim facts but exonerated the Punjab Governor. Then the House of Lords passed a resolution condoning Dyer's Jallianwalla action, and a group in Britain presented him with a sword and 20,000 pounds. The Raj had managed to outrage all of India, Muslim and non-Muslim.

Returning to India after these events, Muhammad Ali threw himself into the Khilafat and non-cooperation movements and became Gandhi's chief lieutenant. The national body formed to fight for the Khilafat was the first to accept non-cooperation. Congressmen seemed to hesitate but the public's mood was unmistakable, and before the end of 1920 Congress and the Muslim League joined the Khilafat body in asking India's Hindus and Muslims to join hands and cease cooperating with the Raj.

Gandhi secured from Muslim and Hindu leaders a commitment to non-violence. Observed in town after town, a "Khilafat Day" on which Indians prayed, protested and pledged themselves to non-violence was, in the words of a Pakistani scholar, "a great success."[69] "We are subscribing to non-violence as a policy, not as a lifetime principle," clarified many, including Muhammad Ali. The Mahatma said that he would sever himself from the movement if he saw any sign of violence. He had asked Congress, when it condemned Jallianwalla, also to condemn what he called "the Indian excesses." The Raj went mad, he said, but "we went mad also." A Congess resolution admitted this, but only because Gandhi was insistent.[70]

Portraits of Lord Hardinge, the previous Viceroy, and Lady Hardinge were unveiled when Gandhi opened a national medical college that Hakim Ajmal Khan, eminent physician and another of Gandhi's close colleagues, had started. "This," said Gandhi, "shows that non-cooperation is not anti-

British and that good deeds done by anyone, English or Indian, are treasured in our memory."[71]

Muhammad Ali asked MAO to forgo the Raj's grant. When the trustees refused, he spoke directly to the students. They left MAO in droves to join a "national Muslim university" that he and others started in tents and houses outside the MAO campus. This was the origin of Jamia Millia Islamia, transferred in a few years to Delhi. In time the Jamia would receive "the fostering care of Hakim Ajmal Khan, Dr. Ansari and Dr. Zakir Hussain" and grow into "a flowering institution with its own individuality and usefulness" — the phrases are from Ikram, the Pakistani historian.[72] In 1921 Muhammad Ali and Gandhi invited Iqbal to take it over. "The Muslim National University calls you," Gandhi said to the poet, but Iqbal declined and Muhammad Ali became the first rector.[73]

In a letter written in January 1921 Muhammad Ali described his public and family life:

> Gandhi and my brother never spend more than two nights a week in bed, travelling night and day propagating their views, collecting funds and sleeping when they can in railway trains. . . .
>
> I was supposed to be chained to the National Muslim University but had nevertheless to wander all over India dragging my chain along with me. . . . At the end of a month I [had] addressed hundreds of thousands.
>
> At the end of November I managed to marry away two of my daughters so as to be relieved of them! Yet on account of the fear of this Government the Nawab of Rampur turned us out of our home, besides imprisoning for 20 years without trial a cousin and a nephew of ours. We could not have the wedding there. I had to bring the brides and bridegrooms to a neighbouring town.
>
> I was too busy to attend to anything, so my wife looked after everything as best as she could and I just came in as a wedding guest![74]

What were Gandhi and the Ali brothers and their co-workers saying? They asked lawyers to withdraw from the Raj's courts, the aristocracy to give up their titles, politicians to leave the councils, and everyone to wear *khadi* or *khaddar*, the handspun cloth that, to Gandhi, spelt self-reliance and affinity with the deprived. To others it was, simply, "the livery of freedom." Muhammad Ali donned *khaddar*, as did Bi Amman, and learned to spin yarn for it. The climax, said Gandhi, would be a refusal to pay taxes.

Top lawyers ceased their practice, among them Chitta Ranjan Das in Calcutta, Motilal and Jawaharlal Nehru in the U.P., Vallabhbhai Patel in Ahmedabad, Rajagopalachari in Madras and Rajendra Prasad in Patna, little knowing that power or popularity lay in their future. Hundreds of others joined them. Among Muslims in the U.P. who left the courts of the Raj was Khaliquzzaman. Thousands of bright young men walked out of their classrooms, objecting to links with the Raj's funds. Some entered newly opened national colleges like Jamia, others gave themselves to the spreading of *khaddar* or of Hindustani, the elevation of untouchables, a campaign against alcohol, or for Hindu-Muslim unity or for the Khilafat's restoration. To the joy of some and the regret of others, "the platform of Khilafat [became] almost indistinguishable from the platform of the Congress," as Muhammad Ali's biographer puts it.

Villagers learned to settle their cases out of court. The talk against liquor hurt the Raj's treasury. "The preaching of non-cooperation and the picketing of liquor shops have contributed largely to the result," said a Raj official in Madras, reporting "a failure in the sales of toddy shops."[75] It was not to be expected that poor folk would resign their jobs, but fear of the alien ruler seemed to vanish. Congress became a people's movement instead of a debating society. And the Raj shrank, even if it did not leave India. Indians seemed to give allegiance to a growing and unofficial Indian establishment rather than to the Raj. The Khilafat was not restored, but the Viceroy felt compelled periodically to appeal to HMG for "reasonable concessions to the Turks[76]; and it seems fair to assume that the Indian stir prevented the imposition of even harsher terms on Turkey.*

Hindus and Muslims fraternized in unprecedented ways. Orthodox Brahmins asked Muslims to meals in their homes. Swami Shraddhanand, prominent in efforts for Hindu revival, was invited to address Muslims from the pulpit of Delhi's Great Mosque. Gandhi spoke at Bombay mosques. This was not really surprising, for Muhammad Ali was to say toward the end of 1921: "After the Prophet, on whom be peace, I consider it my duty to carry out the commands of Gandhiji."[78]

As a gesture toward Hindus, and to show gratitude for their support over Khilafat, Muhammad Ali stopped eating beef; he and his spiritual teacher, Maulana Abdul Bari, urged the Muslim community to do likewise. For the first time Id was celebrated without beef in numerous Muslim homes. Watching the events, the Viceroy, Lord Reading, wrote to his son of "the bridge over the gulf between Hindu and Muslim" that had been created.[79]

Temptations and suspicions were, however, weakening the bridge. Inevitably, there were some who lacked the strength to implement the

---

*In their meeting in London, Lloyd George told the deputation led by Muhammad Ali that the settlement with Turkey "was largely affected by the opinion of India and especially the Muslims of India."[77]

pledges of non-cooperation they had made; their human failure was at times seen in a communal light. Hindu voices whispered that Muslims were mouthing non-cooperation but retaining their positions or links with the Raj; a corresponding feeling about Hindus was entertained by some Muslims. The element of suspicion and rivalry that existed during the struggle is indicated in Ikram's remark relating to the *fatwa*, or official opinion, of some Muslim divines that Muslims should leave the Raj's police and army:

> The *fatwa* was widely hailed by the Hindu newspapers of the Punjab, who had complained of the Muslim preponderance in the police and the army, but it had no serious results, as very few soldiers and policemen obeyed it.[80]

Still, the verdict of Muhammad Ali's biographer remains valid:

> For the first time India witnessed a mass movement which shook the country and nearly paralysed the British rule. For the first time India realised a new pride and discovered a sense of unity.... For the first and last time, in a rare manifestation of amity and accord, Hindus and Muslims drank from the same cup...[81]

* * * *

Non-violence was not the dominant note in every utterance of the Ali brothers. In March 1921 Muhammad Ali perturbed Hindu friends and gave the Raj a handle by announcing that he would "assist an army invading India from Afghanistan."[82] His qualification that he would do this only if the Afghans came in order to free India and return was not noticed. Gandhi urged Hindus to understand what Muhammad Ali really meant and to dismiss "the bogey of an Afghan invasion."[83] But some Hindus were disposed to believe in the bogey. To allay Hindu anxieties, and also to safeguard the movement's non-violent character, Gandhi asked the Ali brothers to express regret "for the unnecessary heat" of some of their remarks. Gandhi also told the Viceroy, when Reading complained to him about "the violent speeches" of the Ali brothers, that he would obtain regrets from them or dissociate himself from the remarks. The brothers heeded Gandhi and publicly announced their regrets.

Montagu, the Secretary of State, thought that "the recantation of the Ali brothers must detract from their political force." To the Viceroy he wrote:

> I can only believe they made the recantation because Gandhi insisted. If they had not there would have been a breach between them and

Gandhi. They avoided it by their recantation but it must have left very unpleasant thoughts in their minds which are all to the good.[84]

The Raj's intelligence agents reported that while some Indians had viewed the apology as an "unfortunate defeat," others thought it "heroic" or "astute." Like Montagu, Reading too wondered about "trouble coming between the Ali brothers and Gandhi," but the alliance survived. Muhammad Ali wrote to a friend that he had expressed regrets because "we had made up our minds to bring about a complete entente between Hindus and Muslims," and in order to remove "the unwarranted suspicion" of some Hindus — and also "to prove to Gandhi that we have enough respect for our colleague and leader's advice." Praising their step, Gandhi wrote in *Young India*:

> The Ali brothers carry a big burden on their shoulders. The prestige
> of Islam, in so far as they are responsible for it, will be measured by
> the credit they acquire for the most scrupulous regard for honesty in
> their dealings, . . . and courage of the highest order in their bearing.[85]

The Hindu-Muslim entente received a knock in August 1921. Enraged by alleged insults to their religious leaders, the Moplahs of Malabar, Muslims descended from Arab immigrants, rose in rebellion, first against the Government and then against Hindu landlords. An "independent Muslim state" was declared, arson and murder took place, and some Hindus were forcibly converted. The Raj moved thousands of troops into the area. In the full-scale military action that ensued, 2,339 were killed and 24,167 convicted of rebellion or lesser crimes, figures withheld till much later.

The star of the Sultan of Turkey, the man India's Muslims were ready to die for, was not on the ascendant. Emerging as Turkey's man of destiny, Mustafa Kamal derided the Sultan and his government; the government sentenced Mustafa Kamal to death. For some time India's Khilafat activists seemed unaware of Turkey's internal divisions, but in February 1921 a Khilafat conference attended by Muhammad Ali and Gandhi appealed to the Sultan to enlist the partnership of Mustafa Kamal, who had set up a separate government and was winning battles against British-supported Greeks. Mustafa Kamal's run of successes continued and India's Khilafat committee congratulated "Mustafa Kamal and the Government of Angora for their brilliant victories and heroic efforts for the preservation of the Islamic Empire."[87]

But was Kamal striving for "the preservation of the Islamic Empire"?

Did he see any merit in the Khilafat? Before long the questions would be answered. For the moment India's leaders, thrilled by Kamal's feats, banked on a Sultan-Kamal rapprochement. Meeting in Karachi in July, they considered the likelihood of the British Government "resuming hostilities against the Government of Angora" and gave their verdict that "in the present circumstances the Holy Shariat forbids every Muslim to serve or enlist himself in the British Army." The possibility of "the Indian Muslims [resorting], in cooperation with Congress, to civil disobedience" was mentioned, and "the establishment of an Indian Republic" was not ruled out.[88]

The limit had been crossed. What is more, it had been crossed barely four months before the Prince of Wales was due to visit India. "It would be inconvenient," Reading wrote to the Secretary of State with admirable poise, "for a republic to be proclaimed while the Prince was here, I think."[89]

Muhammad Ali was arrested on September 14 at Waltair in South India while he and Gandhi were on their way to Malabar, which they wanted to visit because of the Moplah outbreak. Shaukat Ali was also arrested. Gandhi described the Waltair scene:

> The train halted at Waltair for over 25 minutes. Maulana Muhammad Ali and I were going outside the station to address a meeting. Hardly had we gone a few paces from the entrance when I heard the Maulana shouting to me and reading the notice given to him. I was a few paces in front of him. Two white men and half a dozen Indian police comprised the party of arrest. The officer in charge would not let the Maulana finish reading the notice but grasped his arm and took him away. With a smile on his lips he waved goodbye. I understood the meaning. I was to keep the flag flying.

Added Gandhi:

> The Ali brothers were charged with having tampered with the loyalty of the sepoy and with having uttered sedition. . . . But sedition has become the creed of the Congress. . . . Every non-cooperator is pledged to preach disaffection towards the Government. . . . But this is no new discovery. Lord Chelmsford knew it. Lord Reading knows it. We ask for no quarter; we expect none from Government. . . . We must spread disaffection openly and systematically till it pleases the Government to arrest us.[90]

At his trial Muhammad Ali argued that his conduct was commanded by the Qur'an; he *had* to choose the Khilafat over the King: "I have not a word to say against the King (as a person) — not a word against the

Royal family. But we do not recognize the King who denies our right to be loyal to God." When he concluded his two-day defence, "his voice was choked, tears rolled down his cheeks and he sat down completely overcome."[91]

Shaukat and Muhammad Ali were sentenced to two years rigorous imprisonment. Gandhi's reply was to announce, early in November, that he would lead mass civil disobedience in the Bardoli taluk of Surat district in Gujarat. The people of Bardoli would simply refuse to pay taxes. Said Gandhi:

> When the Swaraj flag floats victoriously at Bardoli, then the people of the taluk next to Bardoli . . . should seek to plant the flag of swaraj in their midst. Thus, district by district . . . throughout the length and breadth of India, should the Swaraj flag be hoisted.[92]

The Prince of Wales arrived on November 17. India observed a *hartal* (suspension of business) that day, but violence in Bombay smeared its success. Rowdy elements attacked those staging a welcome for the Prince. In the riots 58 were killed. Saying, "This Swaraj stinks in my nostrils," Gandhi postponed the Bardoli rebellion.[93]

The Raj curbed the press and banned political meetings. Thousands openly disobeyed the bans and filled the Raj's prisons. By the end of January 1922, 30,000 had courted arrest; the terror of imprisonment had vanished. "Our movement is chiefly to be measured," Muhammad Ali had said shortly before his arrest,

> . . . by the amount of fear it has succeeded in removing. It was fear that had made 320 millions of our people the slaves of a hundred thousand Englishmen. That fear, thank God, is fast disappearing. India's thraldom is sure to disappear after that.[94]

Among the 30,000 were hundreds of the well-to-do, barristers, doctors, professors and the like, including the Ali brothers, the Nehrus, father and son, Das, Vallabhbhai Patel, Rajagopalachari, and Abul Kalam Azad, the leading theoretician of the Khilafat cause. Before his arrest Azad had declared that Islam enjoined Hindu-Muslim unity.[95]

On January 29, 4,000 *khadi*-clad Bardoli residents pledged their readiness to stop paying taxes and "to face imprisonment and even death without resentment."[96] Some of them were veterans of the South African struggles that Gandhi had led. A nod from him and the climax would commence. On February 1 the Mahatma sent Reading an ultimatum: if in seven days there was no declaration that prisoners would be released and the press freed, the tax-strike would start. Reading replied that the Government would stand firm. Gandhi sent a rejoinder, and India was agog.

Then, suddenly, Gandhi called off the struggle. Twenty-two policemen had been hacked to pieces in a place called Chauri Chaura in eastern U.P. by a mob of men who called themselves non-cooperators. The news hit Gandhi with tremendous force; he felt that a halt was the only possible response. After announcing the suspension Gandhi wrote that a voice had tempted him to press on, despite the gruesome deed: " 'Surely it is cowardly,' spoke the voice of Satan, 'to withdraw the next day after pompous threat to the Government.' It was the bitterest cup of humiliation to drink. Satan's invitation was to deny truth."[97]

For fear of uncontrollable unrest, the Raj had not touched Gandhi thus far. His abrupt suspension disconcerted Khilafat and Congress activists. Some voiced doubts about non-cooperation; a few withdrew loyalty from the Mahatma and offered it to the Raj. Emboldened by the weakening in nationalist ranks, the Raj arrested Gandhi in March. Pleading guilty, he said that preaching sedition had become his creed and duty. He was sentenced for six years. Shortly before his arrest he had counselled Congressmen "not to rush to civil disobedience but to settle down to the quiet work of constructon."[98] Chauri Chaura had proved to him that Indians needed more training before they could embark on mass disobedience for the sake of India's freedom or Islam's honour.

The Governor of Bombay at the time, Lord Lloyd, would say: "He gave us a scare. Gandhi's colossal experiment came within an inch of succeeding."[99]Afzal Iqbalwrites: "Thus the movement ended in apparent failure. But things were never the same again. These events formed a psychological watershed in the development of modern India. The colonial mentality had been thrown off."[100]

Lodged in Bijapur jail, Muhammad Ali too was baffled by the suspension. It seemed "synonymous with surrender."[101] Food in prison was meagre and unhygienic, and life often humiliating. Shaukat Ali was asked to remove his clothes, raise his hands and open his mouth to show that he possessed no weapon. When he refused to obey he was forcibly searched and confined to a solitary cell. Muhammad Ali protested, prayed, reflected on Islam and the Prophet, and wrote poetry. Shortly after commencing his term he had heard that his favorite daughter Aminah was seriously ill with tuberculosis. He wrote:

I am helpless but Allah is Almighty
I may be away from you but He is not...

I long for your health;
But if He will it not, I submit to His will.

Then he implored God:

Your bounty, O Lord, is no less than Your power;
It would be but a mercy if Aminah too be spared.

Another verse he wrote in jail says:

All days are days of solitude, All nights nights of loneliness;
Now have begun the meetings with Him in complete privacy;
Every moment there is peace; every moment there is calm.
In my prostrations is the sensation of Ascension,
Such miracles are granted to a mere sinner!
Poor and humble though we are, He might still send for us,
For we too have made presents of a few prayers.[102]

He thought of writing a life of the Prophet and tried to obtain books
that could help. One was *Life of Mahomet* by Professor Margoliouth, who
had taught Arabic to Muhammad Ali at Oxford. Offended by what he
felt were his old professor's distortions, Muhammad Ali struck out, in his
copy, the letters "outh" from the author's name. What remained was
"Margoli" — "Shoot him" in Urdu or Hindustani.[103] The impish schoolboy had not ceased to be.

It was in Bijapur that Muhammad Ali wrote the pages that were published after his death as *My Life: A Fragment*. They describe some phases
of his life and seek to establish his credentials for attempting the Prophet's
life. Muhammad Ali had not started on the biography when his term
ended and he was released.

* * *

Neither India nor Turkey offered cheer. In October 1923, a month
after Muhammad Ali's release, Mustafa Kamal turned Turkey into a republic, himself into its president and the Sultan into a non-entity. When
"the Khalifa of the Muslims of the world" asked for more funds for his
"court," Kamal responded by firing the courtiers, secretaries and councillors. In March 1924 he formally abolished the Khilafat and expelled
the Sultan from Turkey. In the words of Mujeeb, Muhammad Ali tried
"to conceal his mortification by sending telegrams to Mustafa Kamal and
proposing to discuss the question of the Khilafat with him."[104] Kamal,

who had no intention of reversing his position, ignored Muhammad Ali's pleas.

The dynamic and picturesque leader of India's Muslims, who had exhorted them to give money and if necessary their lives for the Khilafat, did not know where to look. And then, eight days, after the abolition, Aminah died, the daughter for whom he had fervently prayed in jail. "National calamities have swallowed my personal afflictions like the staff of Moses swallowed the snakes of the sorcerers," said Muhammad Ali in a letter to a friend.[105]

It was a humiliating and painful season. There was talk, not altogether baseless, of misuse of the funds raised by the Khilafat committee. "Those who had given their all, in terms of sentiment, jewellery and cash, to the Khilafat movement were disillusioned and embittered," writes Mujeeb.[106] The Ali brothers were in prison when the impropriety took place, but the Raj did not miss the opportunity for discrediting and dividing its opponents. Said the Home Member in the Viceroy's council, while the Ali brothers were still in prison:

> When I think of the unfortunate *Muhajirin* (the migrating) whose white bones are strewn up the Khyber, who were induced to migrate by these two gentlemen and their followers, men who never themselves did a Hijrat further than Paris and London, when I think of the money extracted from poor Muhammadans in this country much of which has been squandered in various ways, when I think lastly of the many Hindus dishonoured and killed in Malabar and of the thousands of Moplahs misled and driven to death and ruin by the incitements of Mohamed Ali, Shaukat Ali and those who think like them, then, Sir, I marvel at the simplicty and crass folly of the Muslim population that submits to such treatment and accepts such men as leaders.[101]

Though they had spoken of Hijrat, the Ali brothers were not its principal proponents. As for Malabar's rebelling Moplahs, they had never seen or heard the Ali brothers, and the Khilafat stir in the rest of India was by no means the sole, or even the main, impulse driving them to their folly. But all is fair in war.

The Home Member's reference to "the Hindus dishonoured and killed in Malabar" was not calculated to strengthen Hindu-Muslim relations. Knowing what he was doing, he had put his finger on an episode that had injured trust. Accounts of forced conversions in Malabar had spread all over India, and movements for strengthening the Hindu community and for re-conversion to Hinduism were launched. Called *Sangathan* ("Organisation") and *Shuddhi* ("Purification"), these movements in turn caused

disquiet among Muslims who answered with the *Tabligh* ("Preaching")
and *Tanzim* ("Discipline") campaigns.

Before the abolition, some Muslims had spoken of Hindu "coldness
towards Khilafat."[108] Now Khilafat was gone for ever but Swaraj was still
a possibility. Not all Muslims felt excited about it. Maulana Abdul Bari,
the Ali brothers' adviser, wrote to a friend: "Hindus will succeed in
attaining Swaraj and that Swaraj will not in any way be beneficial to
us."[109] Hindus, on their part, were worried about forcible conversions
and about Pan-Islam. Some of them asked if India could retain the loyalty
of Muslims whose holy areas lay elsewhere. Shocked by the deterioration
in Hindu-Muslim relations, Muhammad Ali said he believed as before in
"Muslim cooperation in an Indian nationality" but added that Pan-Islam
could not be given up. It was "nothing more and nothing less than Islam
itself."[110]

Buoyed by Muhammad Ali's return to their midst, Congressmen chose
him as their president for 1923-1924. One of those he named as secretaries
was Jawaharlal Nehru. To Jawaharlal, who was organizing a Congress
meeting in Kashi (Benares), Muhammad Ali wrote:

> Let the [meeting] send from the sacred soil of Kashi the message of
> the greater and more solid *Sanghatan* of the National Congress which
> should aim at the union of all down-trodden and oppressed humanity.
> ...And let us go forth from this conference truly *Shuddh* [Pure],
> purged of all narrowness, bigotry and intolerance in order to free our
> motherland ...[111]

At Congress's annual session, held in Coconada, Muhammad Ali spoke
like a statesman: "Each community remembers only that which it has itself
suffered, retaining in its memory no record of the sufferings it had itself
caused others."

Referring to Muslim and Hindu attempts at conversion and re-conversion,
which at times involved the scheduled castes, he said:

> Let us befriend the oppressed classes for their own injured sakes and
> not for the sake of injuring others or even avenging our own injuries.
> ...Both sides are working with an eye much more on the next de-
> cennial Census than on heaven itself.

But fondness for the clever but risky phrase had not left him. He was
not wise when he said that, irritated by Hindu-Muslim disputes, he was

inclined to "sigh for the days when our forefathers settled things by cutting heads rather than counting them."[112]

Congress, most of its members freed, was no longer united. The Raj's councils attracted growing numbers. They had been willing to boycott the councils while struggling to overthrow the Raj, but abstention without struggle was tasteless. Das and Motilal Nehru headed the effort to change Congress policy: their opponents, the council-boycotting faithful, were led by Rajagopalachari, Patel and Prasad. Muhammad Ali, Abul Kalam Azad and Jawaharlal strove for a compromise; but, some of his utterances notwithstanding, Muhammad Ali shared the dominant Muslim feeling that Swaraj would be a Hindu prize. If non-cooperation was given up, Muslims would need to battle for their rightful share of the spoils of self-government or developing Swaraj.

With the disappearance of the Khilafat cause, Hindus became rivals instead of partners. True, unlike the Swarajists, as the group led by Das and Motilal Nehru came to be called, Gandhi and those loyal to non-cooperation seemed indifferent to the spoils of office. But how vital was even Gandhi to Muslims now? He was useful, even indispensable, over Khilafat, but loyalty to him now would serve no Muslim purpose; in fact it could even evoke hostility. Toward the end of 1923, some Muslims charged that Muhammad Ali, who had said after his release that "it is Gandhi, Gandhi, Gandhi that has to be dinned into the people's ears because he means Hindu-Muslim unity and non-cooperation," was "a follower of Mahatma Gandhi in his religious principles."[113]

Another man in his position might have contented himself with the dismissal of the accusation as baseless and absurd, but Muhammad Ali did not believe in brevity. Explaining at length and answering questions that had not been asked, he said:

> I profess the same beliefs as any other true Mussulman and am a follower of the Prophet Muhammad (on him be peace) and not of Gandhiji. And further, since I hold Islam to be the highest gift of God, I am impelled by the love I bear for Mahatmaji to pray to God that He might illumine his soul with the true light of Islam.

> I deeply revere my own mother.... Similarly, I regard Maulana Abdul Bari as my religious guide. His loving kindness holds me in bondage.... But in spite of all this I make bold to say that I have not yet found any person who in actual character is entitled to a higher place than Mahatma Gandhi.

> But between belief and actual character is a wide difference. As a follower of Islam I am bound to regard the creed of even a fallen and degraded Mussalman [as] entitled to a higher place than that of

any other non-Muslim irrespective of his high character, even though the person in question be Mahatma Gandhi himself.*

There was an uproar and some demanded the Congress president's resignation. "A molehill was made into a mountain," commented Gandhi after his release, which came in February 1924, four years before it was due, because he was acutely ill. Muhammad Ali had made the statement, added Gandhi, only to prove "the purity of his faith in his own religion."[115] This was doubtless one of the incidents in Mujeeb's mind when he wrote that Muhammad Ali "seemed to be wanting to forget, as often as he could, the need to be tactful, in order that he might assert with even greater vehemence the fact that he was a sincere believer in Islam."[116]

To probe, and perhaps to discourage, the likelihood of a Gandhi-Ali brothers alliance, Sir Muhammad Shafi, a member of the Viceroy's council, spent three hours with the brothers and Maulana Abdul Bari in February 1924. Afterwards he recorded in his diary:

> I spoke frankly to them and told them something about what Lord Reading had done during the Turkish crisis and emphasised the danger to Islam because of *Shuddhi* and *sanghatan* movements. . . . They promised me they would not oppose the organising of the Muslim community for the purpose of defending and promoting Muslim interests in India.[117]

When Muhammad Ali and Gandhi met in Juhu, where the latter was recuperating, they discussed not Swaraj but "the Hindu-Muslim tension," as Muhammad Ali described it. Gandhi had been troubled by a sequence of communal disturbances in which Hindus appeared to be the main sufferers. Saying that "there is a Muslim side too," Muhammad Ali complained to the Mahatma about the "anti-Muslim" attitude of men like Madan Mohan Malaviya, an eminent Hindu figure maintaining close links with the Raj. Gandhi said his assessment of Malaviya was different. To Jawaharlal Muhammad Ali wrote:

> If Bapu believes all that he says about him (Malaviya), then I must despair of the near future at any rate. . . . Your father largely agreed with me that Malaviyaji was out to defeat Gandhism and to become the leader of the Hindus only since he could not be the leader of Muslims as well as Hindus, and that Hindu-Muslim unity was not

---

*Several centuries earlier, asked what would happen in the next world to a non-Muslim of excellent character, Nizamuddin Aulia, the sufi saint, had answered: "This is a matter for God to decide in his mercy; you cannot decide the matter for Him."[114]

his ideal. . . . My dear Jawahar, God knows that the Mussulmans too have their Malaviyas and there is no love lost between them and me.[118]

Then Gandhi made a controversial statement. "There is no doubt in my mind," he said, referring to the recent clashes, "that in the majority of quarrels the Hindus came out the second best. My own experiences but confirm the opinion that the Mussulman as a rule is a bully, and the Hindu a coward. Where there are cowards, there will always be bullies."[119] The remark was a response to Hindus complaining of Muslim violence, but the Mahatma did not confine himself to asking Hindus to shed fear; he made a generalization that Muslims found sweeping and unfair. Discretion was difficult even for a Mahatma.

Learning of a fresh communal riot, this time in Kohat in the N.W.F.P., the Mahatma decided to go on a 21-day purificatory fast. He had been, he argued, "instrumental in bringing into being the vast energy of the people." Now that it had turned "self-destructive," he had to do penance. Significantly, the conviction that he should fast came to him when he was staying in Muhammad Ali's home in Delhi as a guest.[120]

Muhammad Ali criticized the fast. If Gandhi did not survive it, he said, Hindus would wreak vengeance on Muslims. He complained that his right to be consulted — as the Mahatma's host and as president of Congress — had been denied him. He quoted to Gandhi a verse from the Qur'an which said that God would forgive one withdrawing an oath thoughtlessly made. From her sickbed Bi Amman, who had taken to *khaddar*, implored Gandhi to change his mind. But Gandhi was unmoved. To Bi Amman he said that if he had the power to obey his own mother in the matter, he would have carried out her command, but now it was a question of a call from God.

Shaukat Ali journeyed from Bombay to dissuade the Mahatma. "O for Shaukat Ali," Gandhi had said when the Ali brothers were in prison and he was free, " I have felt the gravest need of Maulana Shaukat Ali by my side. I can wield no influence over the Mussulmans except through a Mussulman . . . No Mussulman knows me through and through as Shaukat Ali does."[121] But Shaukat's pleas too were of no avail. India presented to Gandhi a picture where, in his words, "to revile one another's religion, to break the heads of innocent men and to desecrate temples or mosques" was the order of the day; he had to respond by fasting.[122] Eight days after starting the fast, Gandhi said:

It is in the fitness of things that this fast should be taken up and completed in a Mussalman house. . . . I have never received warmer or better treatment than under Muhammad Ali's roof. Every want of mine is anticipated. The dominant thought of every one of his household is to make me and mine happy and comfortable.[123]

The whole household turned vegetarian during Gandhi's stay. On the fast's final day, Muhammad Ali purchased a cow from a butcher so that it could live in a *pinjrapole* or cow-home. Deeply touched, Gandhi wrote him a letter: "What love has prompted the act! May the bond between you twins and me fructify into an indissoluble bond between Hindus and Mussulmans."[124]

Why did Gandhi feel that it was "in the fitness of things" for the fast to take place in Muhammad Ali's home? There was drama in a Hindu fasting in a Muslim home but a deeper reason is suggested in a comment made by Rajagopalachari, who was at Gandhi's side during the fast. One of the Mahatma's closest associates. Rajagopalachari described what he saw as "the psychology of the fast" in a letter to Devadas, one of Gandhi's sons. This was "that Bapu is in deepest grief over the ingratitude of the Mussalmans and the sufferings of the Hindus and the indifference and heartlessness of the Mussulman leaders . . ." Rajagopalachari added that the psychology had not been "realised the least bit" by "the Mussalman leaders."[125] The Ali brothers took excellent care of Gandhi during the fast, and appealed to his heart at its end, but the fast did not increase their consciousness of Hindu suffering. It did not because the issue was not, in their perception, so one-sided.

The following month Bi Amman died. She was 81. In *The Comrade*, which had been restarted, Muhammad Ali wrote three articles about Bi Amman entitled, simply, "Mother." Gandhi, who hurried to her beside when he heard that the end was near, described the scene: "I heard no sobbing, though I noticed tears trickling down Maulana Muhammad Ali's cheeks. The Big Brother restrained himself with difficulty. . . . They were all chanting the name of Allah."[126]

The alliance too was near its end. Gandhi and Shaukat Ali went to investigate the Kohat riot and came to different conclusions. "I tremble to publish ours statements," Gandhi said to Shaukat. "A wide gulf separates us in the affair." Both accounts were printed in *Young India*. "We still love one another," said the Mahatma. But everyone could see that the united front had come apart.[127]

Muhammad Ali's presidentship had ended at the close of 1924. A Unity Committee formed during the Gandhi fast could achieve nothing. Speaking increasingly of Muslim fears and Muslim rights, Muhammad Ali felt that Hindu communalism was gaining ground in Congress. He hoped that Gandhi would stamp it down, but the Mahatma thought that he had lost his hold on Hindus and Muslims alike. Despairing of Hindu-Muslim reconciliation, and disappointed by the Swarajists' tenderness for the Raj's councils, Gandhi withdrew from the political arena. When a Muslim friend complained about his silence, the Mahatma replied:

> Since I am unable to bring about a compromise, what is the good of my writing? I cannot acept that Malaviyaji and others are enemies of Muslims. Nor can I agree to calling Mohamed Ali an enemy of the Hindus. I can never agree to the rule of blood for blood and temple for a mosque. But who listens to me?[128]

* * *

We should sum up. The Turks, emasculating and abolishing the Khilafat, killed the Indian movement. The movement's Indian leaders contributed by failing to read Turkish events or Arab attitudes. They were unrealistic too in imagining that the Allies would be indulgent toward Turkey, and, later, Mustafa Kamal toward the Sultan: this is not how victors behave toward the vanquished. There seemed an error, moreover, in their understanding of Islam. Shortly after Lloyd George's meeting with the deputation led by Muhammad Ali, a British civil servant named J.W. Hore pointed out to the Raj that "there is no canon which lays down that the Sultan of Turkey is and always must remain the Khalifa."[129] Hore was right and those Indian Khilafatists who claimed the opposite were wrong. No matter how hoary, a custom was not a canon of Islam, a truth confirmed when, with the Sultan's expulsion, the custom was destroyed and no Indian Muslim felt that his Muslimness had been diminished.

If there was a flaw in their reading of Islam, there was another, surely, in their view of Islam's honour. They did not see that in the end Islam's honour depended as much on Muslim performance as on non-Muslim treatment of Islamic customs or institutions. Stressing but rarely the need for good Muslims in India, and highlighting offences and threats from non-Muslims in Europe, they spread religious heat rather than true Islam. The note they struck was more accusatory than redemptive.

As for the means of their struggle, non-cooperation no doubt baffled and disturbed the Raj for a while and enhanced Muslim, Hindu and, generally speaking, Indian self-respect. Yet its impact was reduced by the unwillingness of many to make the sacrifice it called for. Finally, as Gandhi, the author of non-violent non-cooperation, admitted, the masses were not trained to keep their non-cooperation peaceful. Many human lives were lost and the struggle was called off. Gandhi's decision to suspend it was disliked by several Muslims, as it was by several Hindus, for "victory" was perceived to be close; but it is hard to see how the struggle's continuance would have saved the Muslim cause. It could not have influenced Turkish developments in the least; and in India the fruits of any "victory" would have largely gone to Hindus.

Uniting against white wrongs did not unite for long. Hindu-Muslim unity did not last because it was not the primary goal of either side. Hindus wanted it for Swaraj's sake, Muslims for the Khilafat. As the latter faded out on the western horizon, Muslim need for Hindu backing also evaporated. Hindus still needed Muslim support for Swaraj, but Muslims would offer it only if their fears of Hindu dominance were removed. The Sayyid Ahmed Khan outlook had returned.

In 1919-1923, the Khilafat question coincided with the Punjab wrongs, Muslims marched with Hindus and solidarity was conveyed. But Hindu-Muslim unity was not the natural state. Unity would not survive if it was merely a means to another goal, even one as inspiring as Indian independence. Yet subordinating Swaraj to the ideal of Hindu-Muslim unity was difficult for Congressmen. They could not see how anything could be more important than Swaraj, or ending alien rule. They would reach it with Muslims if possible, without Muslims if necessary. After the collapse of Khilafat, the Muslim goal was the *qaum*'s security, with Swaraj if possible, without it if necessary.

Yet there was a positive side, too, to the movement of non-cooperation. It banished debasing fear. It involved the masses. At times they lost their self-control, yet often they showed a remarkable discipline; and they were receptive to the view that injustices, and not human being, should be hated. All these were unprecedented developments. Finally, the movement provided an experience of widespread Hindu-Muslim partnership; if brief, this experience was also, in the phrase of Muhammad Ali's biographer, one of "overpowering beauty."[130]

Once the Khilafat vanished, no school of Swaraj could win Muslim confidence. Men like Malaviya, Lajpat Rai and Swami Shraddhanand did not even try to win it; they were content to appeal to Hindu sentiments. Those Congressmen who were keen on entering the Raj's councils made Muslims apprehensive. Gandhi was not trusted either, despite his role over Khilafat. Muslims recalled his interventions — the apology he had asked the Ali brothers to make, the Chauri Chaura suspension, the fast in Muhammad Ali's home — and found them unpleasant and of alien design.

They had accepted as tactical what Gandhi saw as integral; now, looking back, they were not so sure that the tactics had been right. He had described his fast as penance; some Muslims called it coercive. "Be prepared to fill the jails at the bidding of Gandhi." "Follow Mahatma Gandhi unflinchingly." In early 1922, these were two of the exhortations eminent Muslim leaders addressed to their *qaum*. Now, in 1925 and the years following, he was seen as a leader of and for Hindus. Not, to be sure, by all Muslims. Men like Hakim Ajmal Khan, M.A. Ansari and Abul Kalam Azad continued at his side; and they continued to fight unqualifiedly for Swaraj. But the Ali brothers drifted away, as did a majority of the *qaum*.

* * *

Muhammad Ali broke, too, with his preceptor, Maulana Abdul Bari. A conflict in Hejaz (later Saudi Arabia) divided them. Bari opposed Ibn Saud, who was battling to oust Sharif Husain, in view of Ibn Saud's puritanical "dome-destruction." A follower of the rigorous Abdul Wahhab, Ibn Saud felt that it was idolatrous to have domes over tombs, even if Islam's heroes were buried in them. Muhammad Ali supported Ibn Saud not because he sympathized with "dome-destruction" but because he believed stories that Ibn Saud would establish a republic in Hejaz and cooperate in the election by the Muslim world of a new Khalifa.

An unconfirmed report that Ibn Saud's troops had damaged the tomb of the Prophet at Medina turned Indian Muslims against Saud. Maulana Abdul Bari led a campaign that denounced and lampooned the Arab chieftain; his followers attacked Muhammad Ali as a dome-desecrator and a Wahhabi. "The abuse that was hurled at Muhammad Ali during the controversy passed all bounds of decency," says Afzal.[131] Ibn Saud defeated Sharif Husain but Abdul Bari could not forgive him. In January 1926, in an article in *Hamdard*, which had been re-started along with *The Comrade*, Muhammad Ali formally renounced his allegiance to the Maulana. Four days later Abdul Bari suffered a stroke; after two days he died. Muhammad Ali rushed to Lucknow and wept bitter tears at the Maulana's grave.

His grief was doubled because Ibn Saud had declared himself "King of Saudi Arabia" on the day Muhammad Ali's article renouncing allegiance to Bari appeared! Like the Turks, Ibn Saud too had betrayed Muhammad Ali.

Writing long into the night for the journals, pressing his hospitality on visitors, talking to different people on different subjects at the same time, expending his energy on long and repetitious arguments with those around him and, through the journals, with his antagonists, willing to enter any controversy, constantly on the move, eating rich food knowing that it was poison to him, Muhammad Ali was ruining his health. Diabetes had undermined it anyway. He looked and felt much older than his age. In January 1926, when he was 47, he was forced to close down *The Comrade*.

The Ibn Saud affair was not the only question that found Muhammad

Ali at odds with his *qaum*. When, in 1925, two members of the Ahmadi sect were found guilty of apostasy and stoned to death in Afghanistan, Muhammad Ali protested. Apostasy could not be eliminated by eliminating apostates, he held; but, in Afzal's words, "the entire Muslim press and almost all Muslim religious leaders [had] endorsed the action."[132] Two years later Muslims were indignant when the Punjab High Court failed to punish the author of a pamphlet called *Rangila Rasul* in which the Prophet had been slandered. Muhammad Ali wrote in *Hamdard* that the fault lay in the law, not in the judges. This drew fresh Muslim fire, but Muhammad Ali had the last laugh, for his draft of a law that made outraging religious feelings an offence was accepted by all sides; the Raj incorporated it in the Indian Penal Code.

The positions he had taken had hurt *Hamdard*. He was losing money but, proud that he was, he rejected as "charity" a modest allowance that some friends had arranged. Then, in May 1928, *Hamdard* died. Arrears of rent for his house piled up, and the national hero of yesteryear, now ill, humiliated and in debt, had to vacate his house.

The Hindu Maharaja of Alwar, an admirer of Muhammad Ali's verses, said he would send him to Europe for treatment. Shaukat and Dr. Ansari insisted that Muhammad Ali accept the offer. He went to England and regained some health; apart from other things, it was difficult there to eat deep-fried dinners. He had not lost his flair for the dramatic. Once, while at the visitor's gallery of the House of Commons, he rolled out his prayer mat and went down on his knees; to his delight (though not, one imagines, to his surprise), the papers next morning described the scene.

On his return, unpredictable as ever, he demanded that Muslims be excluded from the operation of the Sarda Act, which sought to prohibit child marriages. According to Mujeeb, Muhammad Ali "was aware" that the Act "fulfilled the intentions of the *shariah*," but he opposed it because the letter of the *shariah* "had left early and late marriages a matter of choice." Forgoing food and sleep, Muhammad Ali sat up for 24-hours and typed out a 25-page memorandum for the Viceroy against the measures. Mujeeb sees Muhammad Ali's attitude as tragic, for in his view, " . . . the vicious custom of child marriages and their dangerously early consummation was — and still is — followed almost universally by Muslims in rural areas and also by the lower classes in the towns."[133]

* * *

Hindu-Muslim relations were not improved when a Muslim assassinated Swami Shraddhanand in 1926. Communal riots were growing in frequency. There had been 11 in 1923, 18 in 1924, 35 in 1926 and 31 by November in 1927. Yet attempts for a constitutional settlement continued.

The terms of the Lucknow Accord of 1916 had ceased to satisfy Hindus or Muslims. Under it Hindus and Sikhs had agreed to separate Muslim electorates and to weightage for Muslims in Hindu-majority provinces; in return the Muslims had agreed to equality between Muslims and non-Muslims in the council of Punjab, which had a Muslim majority, and to something like a minority status in Bengal, which too had a Muslim majority. In Khaliquzzaman's opinion, "the seeds of partition of India were duly laid there in Lucknow when due to their inexperience the Muslims agreed to have equality in the Punjab and a minority in Bengal."[134]

By 1927 the Muslims of Punjab and Bengal were restive for a Muslim majority in the councils of their provinces. Also, there was a widespread Muslim sentiment in favour of the separation of Sind from Bombay, and in favour of the North West Frontier and Baluchistan receiving some self-governing powers: these steps would yield three new Muslim-majority provinces. On the Hindu side opposition to separate Muslim electorates had grown; these were seen as denying nationhood. Was it impossible to strike a deal whereby the Muslims gave up separate electorates and in exchange received the three new provinces and majorities in the Punjab and Bengal councils?

Such a deal was spelt out in the so-called Delhi Proposals, sponsored by Muslims led by Jinnah and Muhammad Ali, which also recommended a one-third Muslim representation in the Central Assembly. Influential Hindu, Muslim and Sikh voices opposed the package. Punjab's Hindus and Sikhs spoke of their fears of Muslim domination in their province and there was a general Hindu objection to a one-third Muslim share at the centre, when the Muslim population in the country as a whole was 25 percent. On the Muslim side, "mass opinion," in Khaliquzzaman's words, "was definitely against the acceptance of joint electorates."[135]

The League split, with Sir Muhammad Shafi leading the group against joint electorates. Shafi opposed Muhammad Ali and Jinnah for another reason as well. They had accepted Congress's position that Indians should boycott the Raj's Simon Commission, which arrived in India in 1928 to prepare a constitution for the future. Muhammad Ali and Jinnah canvassed the Delhi Proposals, which to begin with seemed to elicit Congress's sympathy. Before long, however, Congress threw its weight behind the scheme of the Nehru Report, so called because it was drafted by a committee headed by Motilal Nehru. This scheme abolished separate electorates and weightage for minorities everywhere, including in Punjab and

Bengal; and it endorsed the three new provinces; but it gave Muslims a quarter of the national seats, not a third. Also, the Nehru Report envisioned a fairly strong central authority.

On their part Muhammad Ali and Jinnah, too, stiffened their terms. By the end of 1928 their position was that joint electorates would be accepted only after Sind, N.W.F.P. and Baluchistan were actually separated or elevated. They said, in addition, that weightage for minorities should remain, except in Punjab and Bengal, where Muslim majorities should be ensured by statute* — and that the constitution should be federal, with strong provinces.

The alternative proposals were discussed in December 1928 at an All Parties convention held in Calcutta. Muhammad Ali, just back from his European sojourn, argued with passion for his views. So did Jinnah.

Muhammad Ali's speech, in Khaliquzzaman's words, "was like the burst of a crater, emitting lava, smoke and dust, full of hard hits, insinuations and threats."[136] Some in the audience jeered him. Though describing Jinnah as a "spoilt child," Tej Bahadur Sapru, eminent Indian jurist and an ex-member of the Viceroy's council, asked the convention to accept the Jinnah-Muhammad Ali offer. He was opposed by M.R. Jayakar, representing the Hindu Mahasabha. Jayakar's stand was that Hindu groups that had "with great difficulty" accepted the Nehru Report would urge "violent and arrogant claims" if the issue was reopened. According to Khaliquzzaman, "the fate of the country was sealed after these four speeches."[137] The Jinnah-Muhammad Ali proposals were turned down; all that was possible, said Motilal Nehru, was that the Muslim share at the centre could be increased from 25 percent to 27 percent.

Khaliquzzaman thinks that "the sad chapter of disharmony" would have been "closed" if "the few amendments" to the Nehru Report proposed by Muhammad Ali and Jinnah had been accepted by Congress, the strongest body at the convention.[138] He simplifies. Judging from Khaliquzzaman's own description of Muhammad Ali's speech, it does not appear as if Muhammad Ali expected agreement.

Congress did not accept the Jinnah-Muhammad Ali terms partly because of Hindu and Sikh opposition but also because it did not think that an agreement with the two would amount to an agreement with Muslims in general. Influenced by the fact that the Shafi faction of the Muslim League had denounced joint electorates, Congressmen seemed resigned to Hindu-Muslim disagreement.

---

*Behind this demand was the fear that poverty and lack of education would prevent Muslim numbers from being reflected in elections.

Another reason for Congress's attitude was its preoccupation with a fight against the Raj. Congressmen were impatient for it and also divided on how to conduct it. Led by Jawaharlal Nehru and Subhas Bose, younger Congressmen wanted a struggle for "complete independence," whereas Motilal Nehru and other senior figures thought that Dominion status was an adequate, and also more prudent, goal. Returning to the scene after a three-year gap, Gandhi seemed more interested in uniting Congressmen for a battle against the Raj than in a Hindu-Muslim agreement, which to him appeared unrealistic anyway.

Led by Azad and Ansari, some Muslims backed the Nehru Report and awaited the start of a struggle against the Raj. But the bulk of the *qaum* did not. They demanded Muslim unity, which was soon obtained, with Muhammad Ali, Jinnah, Shafi and the rest joining hands and giving up joint electorates. Also, they decided not to support Congress in its anti-Raj bid.

In a conversation with Motilal Nehru in April 1926, Muhammad Ali had condemned "all Congressmen, with the exception of Gandhi, Motilal and Jawaharlal, as open enemies of Muslims."[139] Now, as 1928 ended, Muhammad Ali charged that Motilal Nehru had first accepted the Delhi Proposals and then abandoned them, and that Gandhi, instead of using his influence for a compromise, was "giving free rein to the communalism of the majority."[140]

The Delhi Report, in part his baby, had been consigned to the waste-paper basket. An indignant Muhammad Ali formally left Congress and exhorted Muslims to stay away from its meetings.

* * *

His health was failing. An eye collapsed, a consequence of his diabetes. His feet were swollen; the hands trembled when he wrote. His gestures lost some of their animation but jokes and Urdu and Persian poetry continued to pour out of the wasting frame. He missed the crowds. Never again would he be their darling. The Muslim cause he was now espousing was not unpopular but it lacked the appeal that Khilafat had evoked; moreover, it had other advocates as well, healthier and more fortunate than Muhammad Ali.

Luck frowned on him. In 1929 he went to Burma for a break but a cable about a communal riot brought him back in less than a fortnight. An invitation came from Indians in South Africa; he was keen to go but cancelled the trip in the absence of an assurance against discriminatory treatment. Another of his daughters died and also a grandson, who lived in the state of Rampur. The Nawab's externment order was still in force, and Muhammad Ali could not go to see the boy's body.

Enemies in the *qaum* slandered him. He will accept a job with the Raj, whispered some. Others referred to his proverty and said he was ready to accept any job. When he read an attack he would issue a stinging retort and also risk bursting a vessel, but he did not read everything said against him; his poor sight was a blessing.

Led by Gandhi, Congress launched a mass disobedience campaign in 1930, selecting the salt laws as the ones to defy in the first instance. Thousands illegally collected salt in the coastal areas and entered the Raj's prisons. Many women were among them. It was a remarkable story. But, except in the frontier, where Ghaffar Khan and his followers mounted a memorable bid, Muslim participation was small. His bitterness enduring, Muhammad Ali alleged that Gandhi aimed not at independence but at making "70 million Muslims dependents of the Hindu Mahasabha."[141]

Muhammad Ali's condition worsened and the Raj gave him a room in a Simla hospital. The Viceroy, Lord Irwin, sent his personal physician to look at the former seditionist. There was a slight recovery, and Irwin invited Muhammad Ali to take part in a London conference on India's future. Congesss was boycotting the talks; as part of its struggle, it had withdrawn all its legislators from the Raj's councils. But the non-cooperating hero of 1921-1922 decided to accept the invitation. For the first time, his wife accompanied him to Europe. "I am to beg or borrow some three to four thousand rupees," he had written to a friend, "in order to take my wife along. She has been my companion in all the stages of life and I wish that she should be present while I embark on my last journey."[142]

He had to be carried to his cabin on a stretcher. One of his Khilafat colleagues, Zafar Ali Khan, wrote sarcastic lines in *Zamindar*: "We pray to God that the Maulana should be restored to health so that the desire which has led him in his old age to prostrate himself at the threshold of his British masters is fulfilled."[143]

With Congress staying away, the London conference was not expected to produce much. Muhammad Ali's weeks in England were distinguished by continuing illness and by some quotable utterances. Addressing the British, he said: "I would prefer to die in a foreign country so long as it is a free country, and if you do not give us freedom in India you will have to give me a grave here." "The Hindu-Muslim problem is of your creation. But not altogether. It is the old maxim of 'divide and rule.' But there is a division of labour. *We* divide and *you* rule." Earlier, in a letter to one of his daughters, he had written:

> May God grant both Hindus and Muslims an opportunity of mutual justice, fairplay and tolerance, and may they become so thoroughly

disgusted with slavery that they should not tolerate to become the slaves of any one nor should they seek to make any one their slaves.

His words in London about the position of an Indian Muslim have gone into history:

> I belong to two circles of equal size, but which are not concentric. One is India, and the other is the Muslim world. . . . We as Indian Muslims belong to these two circles, each of more than 300 millions, and we can leave neither.

Muhammad Ali said that Indian Muslims would reject any unitary form of government. Only a federation would do. They would also want, he added, assurance of Muslim rule in Muslim-majority provinces: "That gives us our safeguard, for we demand hostages as we have willingly given hostages to Hindus in the other provinces where they form huge majorities."[144]

On January 3, 1931, he dictated a long letter to Ramsay MacDonald, the British Prime Minister. In the evening he suffered a stroke; the following morning he died. He was 52. His rulers, whose overlordship he had hated, called on his widow and on the Big Brother, and paid tributes to the ex-rebel. In India Iqbal and even Zafar Ali, melting before death, wrote poems in his honour.

The grave in which he rests is neither in Britain nor in India. Muhammad Ali was buried, by the choice of his relatives, friends and admirers, in Jerusalem, the place from where, Muslims believe, the Prophet ascended to heaven. Silent and grieving, sheltering his brother until the end, Shaukat had accompanied Muhammad Ali to the grave near the Dome of the Rock. "Here lies al-Sayyid Muhammad Ali al-Hindi," says the inscription on the grave.

Muhammad Ali left behind no will, property or bank balance. Stoking the fires of Pan-Islam, he burnt his own skin. After a short exhilarating spell, thorns pricked him when he flung himself into what he thought was the garden of Hindu-Muslim friendship. Tragedy continued to stalk him long after his death, and his grave passed into Israel's control. Yet it is not hard to experience a measure of fondness while recalling the memory of the bitter-sad, knocked about, irrepressible Muhammad Ali, who "laid his heart open, cried and raised laughter, and believed in God's mercy."[145] The memories of the Big Brother and Bi Amman evoke a similar reaction.

CHAPTER 5

MUHAMMAD ALI JINNAH *(1876–1948)*

He seemed on the way to leading India; he founded Pakistan instead. For much of his life he championed Hindu-Muslim unity; later he demanded, obtained, and, for a year, ran a separate Muslim homeland. Neither Sunni nor mainstream Shi-ite, his family belonged to the small Khoja or Ismaili community led by the Aga Khan; yet Muhammad Ali Jinnah was in the end *the* leader of India's Muslims. Anglicized and aloof in manner, incapable of oratory in an Indian tongue, keeping his distance from mosques, opposed to the mixing of religion and politics, he yet became inseparable, in that final phase, from the cry of Islam in danger.

He was born in old Karachi on Christmas day, 1876. His father, Jinnabhoy Poonja, was a modestly wealthy hide merchant of Hindu stock; Poonja's father, a Gujarati from Kathiawar, had become a Muslim. Poonja's wife had a name given to many Hindu women in Gujarat, Mithubai. Even as a boy Jinnah was single-minded and self-confident. After spells in different schools in Karachi and Bombay and marrying at age 15 to a Khoja girl called Amai Bai, he went to England to study law. "I did not know a soul," he later recalled, "and the fogs and winter in London upset me a great deal, but I soon settled down and was quite happy."[1] That a fresco at Lincoln's Inn, where he was enrolled, described the Prophet as one of the world's great law-givers gladdened him, but religion did not draw the 16-year-old Jinnah. Neither did art or literature or history. Only two things did, the need to learn his law and an urge to prepare himself for a political career.

A stimulus for the latter was Dadabhai Naoroji's bid for a House of Commons seat, which took place within months of Jinnah's arrival in England. Standing on the Liberal ticket, Naoroji won by three votes and became the first Indian to enter the House; Jinnah would assist him as a secretary 14 years later. At age 18 Jinnah had passed his exams but he had to stay on for another two years to fulfill Lincoln Inn's formal requirements; it was his belief that he was "the youngest Indian student ever to be called to the Bar."[2]

Once, on an Oxford and Cambridge Boat Race night, he and two friends were picked up by the police for disorderly behavior — they were pushing one another up and down a street on a hardcart they had found. "But I am afraid," Jinnah was to recall later, "we were not imprisoned; we were let off with a caution."[3] Also, there was a brief tour with a Shakespeare company. Evidently Jinnah played Romeo once and did some prompting. This and the street incident were diversions. Jinnah's main interests in England were his law books — and debates in the House of Commons. As Hector Bolitho, one of his biographers, puts it, "He did not dissipate his energies with hobbies, nor his stength in dalliance."[4]

He was not quite 20 when he returned to India, eager to make his fortune at the Bar and, when the time was ripe, enter the stage of Indian politics. The London years had made a difference. Now he was, and would always remain, Mr. Jinnah, not Jinnabhoy. His clothes would be English and not Indian. He had taken to the political philosophy of Liberalism. Also, he had acquired a monocle, and a mannerism: shaking his forefinger at his listener, he would say, "My dear fellow, you don't understand." Both would remain life-long habits.[5]

Karachi too had changed. His mother was dead. So was his child wife. His father had become poor. Jinnah left for the city that lured the bold, Bombay. Among its attractions was the High Court. For three hard years this metropolis tested young Jinnah's faith in himself as he trudged briefless between the humble locality when he lived and the courts. In the future he would refer to "the dark distress" of this period. It ended when, following a sudden impulse, he had the temerity, at age 23, to go up "straight to the office of Sir Charles Ollivant, the then Member in Charge of the Judicial Department" and offer himself for a vacancy for a temporary Presidency Magistrate.[6]

He obtained the job, his monetary battles ceased and he moved to a better flat; but he never lost his memory of the harsh days. This memory did not tempt Jinnah — as it might have tempted another in his place — to deviousness, but it contributed to the wariness and sense of loneliness that would always mark him.

There was one person, and one alone, on whom Jinnah would wholly rely, his sister Fatima, his parents' youngest daughter. He had three brothers and two other sisters, but they do not feature in accounts of his life. Fatima alone does. On becoming temporary Presidency Magistrate Jinnah sent for his sister in Karachi and had her admitted as a boarder in a Catholic convent in Bandra. Later the care was reciprocated. Until his death Fatima would be a loyal and encouraging presence at Jinnah's side.

* * *

He was in demand as a lawyer after his short term as a magistrate. Tall, slim as a reed and handsome, the young advocate was expensive but more than worth his fees. He spent long hours at his briefs, thought with clarity, smelt the opposition's weaknesses, and drove his points home with cold logic and a slow, merciless delivery. According to a contemporary, he exuded strength "when he stood up in Court, slowly looking towards the judge, [and placed] his monocle in his eye, with the sense of timing you would expect from an actor."[7] His talent also overcame the effects of an abrasive manner that offended clients, judges and other lawyers. He was called insolent and imperious but not shunned. Not always witty, his rebukes were effective:

Judge: Mr. Jinnah, remember that you are not addressing a third-class magistrate.
Jinnah: My Lord, allow me to warn you that you are not addressing a third-class pleader.[8]

If some of his hits sounded brutal, all of them were open. When others thought he was being arrogant, Jinnah felt he was being frank. Affirming that Jinnah's "apparent rudeness was linked with his deep honesty," one of Jinnah's contemporaries told Bolitho the following story.

> A well-known businessman, Haji Abdul Karim, who had to appear in Court on a serious charge, went to Jinnah and asked him how much it would cost to take up the case. Jinnah answered him bluntly, "Five hundred rupees a day."
>
> The businessman was cautious and asked, "How long will the case go on? I have five thousand rupees with me. Will you accept this to cover the whole of the fees?"
>
> Jinnah answered: "Five hundred rupees a day is my fee. You must engage me on these terms or find another lawyer." Abdul Karim accepted the terms and Jinnah won the case, in three days. He accepted his fee of fifteen hundred rupees with good grace.

Jinnah's candour was also recalled by another of his colleagues at the Bar:

> I was collecting for a relief fund. I went up to him in the Bar Library and handed him the subscription list. He took it, placed his monocle in his eye, read the list, handed it back to me and said, "I'm not interested."[10]

Clients that Jinnah defended for gratis were not numerous but if, after success, they offered money, it was meticulously returned by him. And when a client pleased with Jinnah made a bigger payment than had been agreed, Jinnah returned the excess with a terse note: "You paid me [so much]. The fee was [so much]. The balance [so much] is enclosed."[11]

The suggestion of a proud personality that is neither weakened by sentimentality nor corrupted by greed is confirmed by the assessment of one who was close to him at the time, Sarojini Naidu. A student at Cambridge shortly after Jinnah had left England and later a distinguished poetess and fighter for India's freedom, Sarojini Naidu appears to have been in love with Jinnah in the early years of this century. Her feelings were not returned. Spending his evenings with his briefs, devoted single-mindedly to his career, he remained indifferent. Still, the eye of affection sees what others can miss. In a "biographical appreciation" published in 1917, Sarojini wrote that though Jinnah was "pre-eminently practical and dispassionate in his estimate and acceptance of life, . .a shy and splendid idealism" lay underneath his "calm hauteur."[12]

This idealism, combined with his feeling, dating back to the London days, that there was a role for him on India's political stage, led him to join the Indian National Congress in 1906 and, three years later, to make a bid, which proved successful, to enter the Imperial Legislative Council as the nominee of the Muslims of Bombay. At Congress's 1906 session, Jinnah acted as private secretary to the president, Dadabhai Naoroji. It was a landmark session: for the first time Congress asked, through its president, for "Swaraj," using the Hindi word for self-rule. Later, when Bal Gangadhar Tilak of Poona, famed for his assertion, "Swaraj is my birthright and I shall have it," was prosecuted by the Raj, Jinnah served as one of the Brahmin defendant's lawyers.

And his first act in the Imperial Council was to support a resolution sympathizing with the struggle that Indians in South Africa were waging under the leadership of another London-educated barrister, Mohandas K. Gandhi, seven years older than Jinnah and born, like Jinnah, to Kathiawari parents.

In the Council Jinnah spoke of the "indignation and horror" of "all classes in this country . . . at the harsh and cruel treatment that is meted out to Indians in South Africa." The Viceroy, Lord Minto, who was presiding, interrupted:

> I must call the Honourable gentleman to order. I think that is rather too strong a word, "cruelty." The Honourable Member must remember that he is talking of a friendly part of the Empire, and he really must adapt his language to the circumstances.[13]

Minto found out, as other custodians of the Raj would also find out, that Jinnah was more than a meek listener. He replied:

> Well, my Lord, I should feel inclined to use much stronger language, but I am fully aware of the constitution of this Council, and I do not wish to trespass for one single moment; but I do say this, that the treatment that is meted out to Indians is the harshest that can possibly be imagined, and, as I said before, the feeling is unamimous.[14]

Another link between Jinnah and Gandhi was a person they had both come to know, like and respect, Gopal Krishna Gokhale, who had taught in Poona for twenty years, taking only a nominal salary, and then served on the platforms of Congress and of the Imperial Council. Indians loved Gokhale for his selfless patriotism; figures of the Raj admired him for his skill and moderation. After observing Gandhi's work in South Africa, Gokhale commented that Gandhi had the qualities India needed. Of Jinnah he said: "He has true stuff in him, and that freedom from all sectarian prejudice which will make him the best ambassador of Hindu-Muslim unity."[15] For his part Jinnah said that it was his "one ambition to become the Muslim Gokhale."[16] When, in 1912, Gokhale moved his Elementary Education Bill in the Congress, Jinnah supported him with passion: "Now, Sir, this is a very, very old story that you have no money. All I can say is this — Find money! Find money! I ask, is it such an insurmountable difficulty to get three crores of rupees . . . ?"[17]

A year later Gokhale and Jinnah travelled together to Europe. For eight months they gave each other company, on the continent, in England and on board ships and trains, but, alas, no record exists of what they discussed, or saw, or thought. While in England Jinnah made a significant decision. After talking with Muhammad Ali and Wazir Hussain, who were also visiting Britain, he agreed to join the Muslim League founded in 1906. His step showed Jinnah's recognition of the growing Muslim ferment, a ferment linked, as we saw in the last chapter, to Turkey's conflicts with its non-Muslim neighbours. It is clear that much cogitation lay behind it. Jinnah obviously felt that he should enter the Muslim mainstream; but not only did he not want to lose his foothold on the soil of India-as-a-whole, he wanted it clearly understood that he was not abandoning it.

In Sarojini Naidu's words, Muhammad Ali and Wazir Hussain were required, before Jinnah would agree to join the League, "to make a solemn preliminary covenant that loyalty to the Muslim League and the Muslim interest would in no way and at no time imply even the shadow of disloyalty to the larger national cause to which his life was dedicated."[18]

Not that prior to 1913 Jinnah had been indifferent to the Muslim cause. Two years earlier he had introduced the Wakf Validating Bill, designed to safeguard beneficiaries of Muslim family trusts against the folly of any one member of a family. It received the Viceroy's assent shortly before Gokhale and Jinnah left for Europe. The Bill's passage enhanced Jinnah's status among Muslims and doubtless explains Muhammad Ali's keenness to induct him into the League.

* * *

Either luck or astuteness in judgment or a combination had brought the still-young Jinnah to a position of significance in Congress, the League and the Council alike. When Gokhale and Pherozeshah Mehta, another Congress stalwart, died in 1915, Jinnah's importance increased. Tilak was in prison in Mandalay; among those who remained on the scene, few could rival Jinnah in talent or breadth of influence. His position was further strengthened when, in 1915, Congress and the League agreed, largely at his initiative, to hold their end-of-the-year rallies in the same place and at the same time.

Some Muslims of Bombay, where the sessions took place, tried to disrupt the League's meetings, to which a few Hindu leaders had been invited. When, on one occasion, the Raj's police failed to control the disturbers, Jinnah alleged "connivance."[19] In the future many in Congress would follow the Jinnah of 1915 and accuse the Raj's police of "connivance" with elements that sought to prevent Hindu-Muslim understanding.

The following year, in a speech in Ahmedabad, Jinnah was openly idealistic. In words that remain relevant to this day he said:

> For a real New India to arise, all petty and small things must be given up. To be redeemed, all Indians must offer to sacrifice not only their good things, but all those evil things they cling to blindly — their hates and their divisions, their pride in what they should be thor-

oughly ashamed of, their quarrels and misunderstandings. These are
a sacrifice God would love.

The end of 1916 saw Jinnah at a peak. Sessions of the Congress, which
was now reinforced by Tilak's release and return, and the League, over
with Jinnah presided, produced a Congress-League agreement on a scheme
of self-government, the Lucknow pact. Though some opposed its terms,
there was general acclamation for the Lucknow pact and its main archi-
tects, Jinnah, Tilak and Annie Besant, the Irishwoman who had made
India her home and Indian Home Rule her passion.

When Annie Besant was arrested the following summer and confined
to the Nilgiri Hills, the country's best-known leaders, the old and ailing
Tilak among them, met in the home of one who looked likely to emerge
at their head, Jinnah. They decided to voice a strong protest — and to
reject, after a minute's consideration, a proposal sent by Gandhi that Mrs.
Besant's arrest should be answered by a non-violent march to the Nilgiris.[21]

Gandhi had returned from South Africa in 1915. At a Bombay meeting
Jinnah had welcomed him back; and Gandhi was one of the Hindu leaders
Jinnah had invited to the 1915 League session. Yet he seemed, as Jawaharlal Nehru was afterwards to put it, "very distant and different and
apolitical," and the group assembled in Jinnah's home had no difficulty
in turning down his odd suggestion. None of them guessed, in that 1917
summer, that the man behind the queer idea would upset their plans for
the future.

Indian troops had been fighting for the Empire in the War. Their
endurance in the winter battles of 1914–15 in France and Flanders had
been praised. Within India, however, those wanting to widen political
rights were hamstrung by the Defence of India Rules, a provision of which
had been used to arrest Mrs. Besant. Their hopes rose when Edwin
Montagu, made Secretary of State for India in July 1917, declared on
behalf of H.M.G. that "substantial steps" would be taken toward "the
progressive relisation of responsible government in India."[23] The racial
bar excluding Indians from the King's Commission in the Army was
withdrawn; Mrs. Besant was freed; and Montagu arrived in India in November 1917 to discuss posible reforms.

Touring and receiving on a prodigious scale, he decribed some of the
people he met in a diary published thirteen years later. Mrs. Besant was
"very impressive" and possessed "the most beautiful voice" he had ever
heard. Montagu referred to "the renowned" Gandhi, calling him a "social
reformer" who "dresses like a coolie" and "lives practically on the air."

Jinnah was "perfectly mannered," "a very clever man," "impressive-looking" and "armed to the teeth with dialectics."[24]

"It is of course an outrage," added Montagu, "that such a man should have no chance of running the affairs of his own country." Also, Montagu found Jinnah obdurate. Pressing the Lucknow scheme of self-government on the Secretary of State, Jinnah was, wrote Montagu in his diary, "insistent upon the whole of his scheme . . . Nothing else would satisfy them. They would rather have nothing if they could not get the whole lot."[25]

"At the root of Jinnah's activities is ambition. He believes that when Mrs Besant and Tilak have disappeared he will be the leader." So said Walker, correspondent of the *Manchester Guardian*, to Montagu.[26]

* * *

The Raj's "Montford" reforms — so called because they were jointly proposed by Montagu and Lord Chelmsford, the Viceroy — were announced in June 1918. Provinces would have partial self-government, worked by elected legislatures and "cabinets" of Indian Ministers, but vital subjects would be "reserved" for the Governor to administer with the help of an Executive Council he nominated. Members of a Council would be far more influential than Ministers of a cabinet. At the centre powers would not be shared at all. The former Viceroy, Lord Curzon, H.M.G.'s new Foreign Secretary, called the proposals "rash and reactionary" and Montagu thought that they were a leap, but Indians could not make up their minds. Soon, pushing the reforms into the background, the Rowlatt Act, the Punjab tragedies and the Khilafat question would absorb their emotions.

Meanwhile, for the first and last time in his life, a girl had absorbed Jinnah's emotions. He, 40 in 1917, fastidious bachelor, living for some time now in a large but sombre Malabar Hill house, bowing to ladies and praising their saris but otherwise keeping his distance from them, fell in love with Ruttenbai, or Ruttie, the 17-year-old daughter of one of Bombay's eminent Parsis, Sir Dinshaw Petit. They had met in the home of the Petits, where Jinnah occasionally dined, and also in Poona and in the hill station of Darjeeling. Lively, spontaneous and enchanting, Ruttie touched a hunger that the aloof advocate had concealed well and for long. When he learned that his daughter and Jinnah wanted to marry each other, Sir Dinshaw took out an injunction that prevented Jinnah from seeing her.

Jinnah and Ruttie waited a year; in April 1918, when she was eighteen, she became a Muslim and they were married. "So Jinnah has at last plucked the Blue Flower of his desire," commented Sarajini Naidu in a letter to a friend, adding, "The child has made far bigger sacrifices than she yet realizes."[27]

Joy and laughter entered Jinnah's life. The Malabar Hill house became brighter. A girl, Dina, was born in August 1919. Alas, the happiness was not destined to last; Sarojini's veiled prediction of trouble came true. Ruttie grew tired of Jinnah's single-mindedness. She did not like his unending talks with politicians; at his age he could not summon a sudden fondness for art, or music, or dancing.

For two years or so, however, they seemed enthusiastic about their partnership. Each appeared to encourage the other in standing up to the Viceroy, Lord Chelmsford, and to Lord Willingdon, who was Governor of Bombay at the time. There are several stories, all unverified, of sharp replies and walk-outs. What is beyond doubt is that in June 1918, at a Bombay meeting at which Jinnah was present, Lord Willingdon publicly questioned the sincerity of the support for the War expressed by "a certain number of gentlemen, some of whom have considerable influence with the public, many of them members of the political organisation called the Home Rule League."[28] Jinnah, who belonged to the League, which was headed by Mrs Besant and Tilak, felt insulted.

His retort came at the end of the year. Willingdon was relinquishing the Governorship, and a meeting of "the citizens of Bombay" was convened to appreciate his services. But Bombay's residents were not really enamoured of the retiring Governor. Jinnah and Ruttie took a large number of them to the Town Hall to oppose the appreciation. There was a struggle for seats and shouting; finally, before any resolution in praise of Willingdon could be heard, the Raj's police used force to clear the hall.

Jinnah was assaulted in the process, but, with Ruttie beside him, he spoke to his supporters outside the Town Hall: "Gentlemen, you are the citizens of Bombay. You have today scored a great victory for democracy. Today, December 11, is a red-letter day in the history of Bombay. Go and rejoice."[29]

The episode made Jinnah a hero. His admirers contributed thirty thousand rupees in his honour, which were used to construct Jinnah Hall, a name that has survived the bitterness of following decades. On a wall a plaque refers to "the historic triumph" of Bombay's citizens, "under the brave and brilliant leadership of Mohamad Ali Jinnah."[30]

* * *

Nationally, however, he had slipped off his 1916–17 peak. After her release Annie Besant had stolen the Congress stage and become president for 1917–18; and the 1917-end League rally was dominated by the picture of its president, Muhammad Ali, who was in jail. At the end of 1918, the war over, the "nationalists," as they called themselves, attacked the shortcomings of the Montford reforms and captured the Congress platform. Less critical of the reforms, Jinnah found himself in a minority, but he did not join the Liberal party formed by Congressmen who approved of Montford: he hoped that the tide would turn.

It turned, but not in his favour. In January 1919 the anti-sedition Rowlatt Bill was introduced in the Imperial Council. Appealing to the Viceroy for its withdrawal, but also announcing that he would refuse to obey it if it became law, Gandhi caught the nation's eye. Following his lead, Vallabhbhai Patel and Sarojini Naidu and a number of others made similar declarations; simultaneously, they pledged themselves against violence. In the Council Jinnah, a member since 1909, sternly opposed the Bill. "It is my duty to tell you that if these measures are passed, you will create in the country from one end to the other a discontent and agitation the like of which you have not witnessed."[31]

The Raj did not heed Jinnah's warning or respond to Gandhi's plea. Its Council, in effect a nominated House, passed the Bill. On March 22 the Viceroy signed it into law. The next day Gandhi asked "all the people of India to suspend business"[32] on April 6, and to observe the day "as one of fasting and prayer." Five days later Jinnah resigned from the Council as a protest against what he called "this Black Act."[33]

The step was neither ordinary nor without cost to Jinnah, who liked the Council and shone in it. But it lacked the stirring power of Gandhi's call. Wishing to move beyond protests to defiance, India responded to Gandhi and hailed him as a Mahatma, or great soul. In what was India's first nation-wide strike, business was suspended everywhere on April 6. In the last chapter we saw that this was followed by acts of nobility and courage on the part of many Indians, and also by folly, Indian and the Raj's. What we should note here is Gandhi's sudden ascendance.

The spot that he had filled was one that Jinnah had felt capable of filling all along, sighted for some time and almost reached in 1916–17. It does not really matter how it is put, whether it is said that the prize that Jinnah seemed to deserve and for which he had laboured with skill and patience had eluded him, or that he was cheated of his destiny. The point is that Gandhi was where Jinnah might have been.

* * *

The two cooperated for a while. Sued by the Raj for contempt of court, Gandhi sought Jinnah's help. While vacationing in England, with Ruttie, Jinnah received a letter from Gandhi in which the latter expressed the hope that Mrs. Jinnah would join a hand-spinning class on their return and that Jinnah would learn Gujarati and Hindi "as soon as possible."[34] This was in the summer of 1919. At the end of the year, at Congress's annual session, held in Amritsar, Jinnah backed Gandhi's stand on the Montford reforms, now translated into the Act of 1919; in his speech Jinnah referred to "Mahatma Gandhi."[35] On their urging, and despite the attacks of the nationalists, who were led by Calcutta's Chitta Ranjan Das, Congress agreed to work the reforms; but Amritsar also made it plain that any Congress-Raj cooperation would depend on Britain's response over Punjab and Khilafat.

The Khilafat Conference and the League also met at Amritsar, the former being, at this stage, by far the larger of the two Muslim organizations. In what they asked of the Raj, the League, the Khilafat and Congress were at one.

We saw in the last chapter that the Raj's response disappointed Indians and hurt their feelings, and that Gandhi proposed non-cooperation. While the Khilafat body at once accepted his proposal, Congress's stalwarts were lukewarm or even hostile. In September 1920 Congress and the League gathered in special sessions in Calcutta to discuss the Gandhi scheme. Jinnah was met off his train at Howrah station by Motilal Nehru, who hoped to coordinate strategies for defeating Gandhi.[36] Tilak, who might have lent them his influential support, had died on August 1, 1920. Men like Das, Bipin Pal, Lajpat Rai and Malaviya were cool toward non-cooperation, but younger figures like Vallabhbhai Patel, Rajagopalachari, Rajendra Prasad and Jawaharlal Nehru were with Gandhi, as were virtually all the Muslim leaders. Reflecting popular feeling, the rank and file solidly backed Gandhi. First in Calcutta and then, in December, in Nagpur, both Congress and the League resolved in favour of non-cooperation — boycott of the Raj's councils and ceremonials, surrender of titles and a gradual boycott of the Raj's courts and colleges. One by one, all the stalwarts changed their minds and boarded the Gandhi vehicle — all except Jinnah, Annie Besant and the Hindu leader, Malaviya.

Actually, Jinnah took some time to define his position. Presiding at the League's special session in Calcutta, Jinnah did not commit himself. He said:

> First came the Rowlatt Bill, accompanied by the Punjab atrocities, and then came the spoliation of the Ottoman empire and the Khilafat, a matter of life and death.
>
> India's blood and India's gold was sought and unfortunately given — given to break Turkey and buy the fetters of the Rowlatt legislation.
>
> Mr. Gandhi has placed his programme of non-cooperation before the

country. It is now for you to consider whether or not you approve of its principle; and approving of its principle, whether or not you approve of its details. I would still ask the Government not to drive the people of India to desperation, or else there is no other course left open to the people except to inaugurate the policy of non-cooperation, though not necessarily the programme of Mr. Gandhi."[37]

At the parallel Congress meeting, Jinnah spoke in favour of Bipin Pal's unsuccessful resolution that accepted the principle of non-cooperation but wanted a committee to spell out "suitable" methods of implementing it. What Jinnah said is not recorded, but it angered Shaukat Ali. According to the Governor of Bengal, who sent reports of the proceedings to the Secretary of State, Shaukat Ali " . . . threatened to lay violent hands upon Jinnah for disagreeing with him and was only prevented from doing so by the physical intervention of other delegates."[38]

A month later Jinnah and Gandhi had their first direct clash. It was over the Home Rule League, of which Gandhi had been made president in April. In October, at Gandhi's instance, the body changed its name to *Swarajya Sabha* (Hindi for Home Rule League); it also altered its constitution, so that its aim now was not "self-government within the empire" but, simply, the securing of Swaraj. The changes were achieved by a vote of 42 for and 19 against. Jinnah, long associated with the body, was one of the 19. He wanted the reference to the empire retained; moreover, he charged that the meeting was not competent to change the constitution. Gandhi disagreed. Alleging that Gandhi was acting dictatorially, Jinnah resigned, as did the rest of the 19. Stating that the resignations had "pained" him, Gandhi wrote Jinnah requesting him to reconsider his resignation and inviting him to "take your share in the new life that has opened up before the country."[39]

The notion that he had to be offered a role did not go down well with Jinnah. He replied:

I thank you for your kind suggestion offering me "to take my share in the new life that has opened up before the country." If by "new life" you mean your methods and your programme, I am afraid I cannot accept them, for I am fully convinced that it must lead to disaster.[40]

Viewing as a streamroller what others described as the chariot of deliverance, Jinnah dissented again in December when Congress and the League met in Nagpur to ratify the non-cooperating decision. At Nagpur Chitta Ranjan Das proposed at the Congress what he had assailed three months earlier in Calcutta; other opponents of Gandhi's programme also spoke in its defence; the Congress gave itself over to Gandhi. Annie Besant, her popularity considerably below its 1917 height, did not attend, but Malaviya expressed his disagreement, and Jinnah defied the assembly's roars. In addition to deciding upon non-cooperation, Congress altered its goal, as the Home Rule League had done. Now it would be "Swaraj"; the phrase "within the empire" was deleted.

Jinnah objected strongly to this removal. At first, Das and Pal joined Jinnah and Malaviya in support of "within the empire" while the Ali brothers tried to push through proposals for "complete independence" and a "republic." Gandhi's compromise proposal that mentioned neither the empire nor "complete independence" but only "Swaraj" was accepted by Das and Pal and the Ali brothers. He did not wish to sever the link with Britain, said Gandhi, if that link was useful; he would end it only if it was "inconsistent with our national self-respect."[41] Opposing him, Jinnah asserted that the new goal implied an unconstitutional bid for complete independence, whatever Gandhi said to the contrary.

When he referred to "Mr. Gandhi" and "Mr. Muhammad Ali, "many shouted, "Say Mahatma Gandhi" and "Say Maulana Muhammad Ali," but Jinnah did not oblige them.[42] Standing his ground, he defended "the constitutional way" as the only "right way." At this — according to one of Jinnah's friends, Diwan Chaman Lall — Muhammad Ali "leapt up" and ridiculed Jinnah with an anecdote about a preacher who always spoke of "the right way." Jinnah, Chaman Lall continues, "sat down, with a hurt look on his face. He just lapsed into silence."[43] Later that evening, the session not yet over, Jinnah boarded a train and left for Bombay. His fourteen-year connection with Congress was over. It was over because Congress had become Gandhi's. After Jinnah's departure, an ill Malaviya sent a message, which was read out, opposing both the new creed and the non-cooperation resolution, but it influenced no one. When non-cooperation was put to vote, only two persons voiced dissent, one from Sind and another from U.P. Their names are not recorded.[44]

Their London training in law and Gujarati backgrounds were not the only things in common between Jinnah and Gandhi. Both wanted Hindu-Muslim unity and self-government. Yet, to note some of their differences, while Gandhi demonstrated his religious beliefs, Jinnah never spoke of them. Gandhi embraced and advocated poverty; Jinnah made his pile and urged other able men to make theirs. Wearing the best-tailored suits, Jinnah lived in an opulent house on Malabar Hill; Gandhi wore a peasant's clothes and lived in a hut in an arid village. Almost everyone found Gandhi warm; very few knew that Jinnah could be warm. Gandhi was cheerful in austere surroundings, Jinnah austere in cheerful surroundings. If Gandhi cultivated humility, there were times when Jinnah seemed to cultivate arrogance. Gandhi sought to enlist the common man; Jinnah was content, if we leave out the incident involving Lord Willingdon, to be an elitist. The list of contrasts is long.

Two months after his Nagpur walkout, Jinnah referred, in a Bombay speech, to his "continuing respect and admiration" for Gandhi; but he also said that Gandhi was taking the people into the "wrong channel," and expressed the fear that "violence would result from popular movements because the Indian people were human beings and not saints."[45] Also, in the words of his biographer, Jinnah entertained "a deep, instinctive dislike for the Mahatma's mind." Bolitho does not say when Jinnah first felt this dislike; according to him, it was "finally revealed" over the Home Rule League episode.[46] Different in personality and life-style, differing over the path of self-government, competing for the loyalties of Congress and of India at large, Gandhi and Jinnah were bound, despite their common desire for Indian freedom and Hindu-Muslim partnership, to separate. "In future years," to quote Bolitho again, "Jinnah was to share many talks with Gandhi, but the cleavage remained."[47]

* * *

After Nagpur Jinnah seemed to withdraw from politics. Though he retained his association with the League, that body, its members offended over Khilafat, had little use, in 1921 and for a while thereafter, for Jinnah. For three years he did not attend its meetings. Still, it is noteworthy that he did not leave the League, which had also, in December 1920, ratified non-cooperation and deleted the reference to the empire from the statement of its goals.

Needing a political foot-hold, Jinnah could have joined the Liberals, who had left Congress in 1917–18 and formed a party of their own; they were moderates and attacked non-cooperation. He did not; their moderation may not have appealed to him; perhaps, too, he was influenced by the fact that the Liberal party, while "Indian" rather than communal in its goals, was, in the main, led by Hindu Brahmins. He thought of a new "broad-based" party but dropped the idea.[48] Perhaps his instincts told him that his future lay with the Muslim *qaum*, not in a composite party. In any case, he knew that he had represented, and might want to represent again, a Muslim constituency in the Council in New Delhi. Rejecting radicalism, and facing a choice between liberalism and the *qaum*, he chose, or was obliged to choose, the *qaum*. He would still strive for Hindu-Muslim unity but, henceforth, only from the Muslim shore and no longer from an all-India boat.

In January 1922 Jinnah briefly left the wings for the stage and tried, along with a few other "neutrals," to reconcile Gandhi, whose movement was then at its crest, and the Raj. The attempt was not successful but, as we saw in the previous chapter, Chauri Chaura occurred in February, Gandhi called off his movement, and the Raj arrested him. A year later Jinnah entered the New Delhi legislature again, now, following the Montford reforms, called the Central Assembly and somewhat more influential than the old Imperial Council. As before, he occupied the seat reserved for a Bombay Muslim. In May the following year, after the Turks had abolished Khilafat, the Muslim League, which did not know what to do, invited Jinnah to preside over the Lahore session. He stressed the need for Hindu-Muslim trust: "I am almost inclined to say," observed Jinnah, "that India will get Dominion Responsible Government the day the Hindus and Muslims are united."⁴⁹ Gandhi, just released, commented: "I agree with Mr. Jinnah that Hindu-Muslim unity means Swaraj."⁵⁰ However, as we saw earlier, 1924, 1925, and 1926 saw an increase rather than a diminution of Hindu-Muslim suspicion and bitterness. Gandhi and Jinnah met each other and sat together at a unity conference, but nothing tangible resulted.

An incomplete though not false picture of the Jinnah of 1925 — and of later years — emerges from the recollection of a British military officer, Captain Gracey, later to become General Sir Douglas Gracey, Commander-in-Chief of the army in Pakistan. Gracey had accompanied Jinnah and some other members of the Central Assembly to Sandhurst; they belonged to a committee which was to advise the Raj on the setting up of a military training college in India. Recalls Gracey:

> Jinnah's behaviour with the officers who gave evidence before the deputation was so arrogant; it was as if he were dealing with hostile witnesses before a judge. I had to protest and point out that the officers were giving evidence voluntarily, with the object of helping him, and that they had a right to be treated with courtesy. . . . He calmed down immediately. . . . That was something I always liked about him: once he was challenged, he became reasonable, and he would never bear malice afterwards.

* * *

We should next examine Jinnah's attempts in 1927 and 1928 for a Hindu-Muslim settlement. The stage for him was cleared by Gandhi's decision at the end of 1924 to concentrate on fighting the demons of untouchability, poverty and liquor, leaving Congress's politics to the politicians. The latter, men like Malaviya, Motilal Nehru and Srinivasa Iyengar, Congress's president for 1926–27, entered the Central Assembly. (Before his unexpected death in 1925, Das was set to join the Bengal legislature.) Like Jinnah, these men enjoyed the Raj's councils but found them powerless. Realizing that a Hindu-Muslim front could extract more powers from the Raj, Jinnah, supported by Muhammad Ali and some other Muslims, and Congress's politicians — the Swarajists, as they were called — probed a pact during much of 1927 and 1928.

We saw in the last chapter that the bid did not succeed, and we tried to discover why. Here we should note Jinnah's zealous efforts to obtain Congress's acceptance of the Delhi Proposals, as they came to be called, a package of which joint electorates were a part. It was a high-risk, high-gain exercise. By conceding joint electorates Jinnah would alienate a large Muslim section. Yet Congress acceptance of the package would produce a joint front; it would also restore his 1916 position. Jinnah, who said on the Assembly floor in 1925, "I am a nationalist first, a nationalist second and a nationalist last,"[52] tried hard.

It was an uphill task from the start. According to Ghazanfar Ali Khan, at the time a Jinnah ally in the Central Assembly, the attempt began with a private talk, early in 1927, between Motilal Nehru and Jinnah. By the end of March the Delhi Proposals had been formulated, but the Shafi revolt followed immediately, poet Iqbal back Shafi, and Punjab's Muslims insisted on separate electorates. Led by Lala Lajpat Rai, Punjab's Hindus opposed the idea of an assured Muslim majority in the province; the Sikhs backed the Hindus. But Jinnah did not give up hope: Congress was still weighing the proposals.

He was not in India when Congress' reply, the Nehru Report, was released. We have seen that this did not give Muslims the one-third strength at the centre they had asked for. While it did away with weightage for non-Muslims in Punjab and Bengal, the Report turned down the Delhi proposal for guaranteed Muslim majorities in the legislatures of these two provinces; it argued that adult franchise would produce these majorities anyway. And it did not empower provinces vis-a-vis the centre the way Jinnah would have liked.

All the same, Jinnah seemed open to it when he returned from Europe. The Report, he said, had "made a serious effort to meet the Delhi Muslim Proposals"; and he appealed to Muslims disagreeing with it "not to rebel but to keep calm and organise themselves with a view to pressing their point of view."[53]

His supporters and followers did not rebel, but neither did they authorize him to accept the Nehru Report. Two months after his return, Jinnah went to Calcutta urge Congress to amend the Report and accept the Delhi package. "Majorities are apt to be oppressive and tyrannical," he said, "and minorities always dread and fear that their interests and rights, unless clearly and definitely safeguarded by statutory provisions, would suffer." And he warned that the alternative to a settlement might be "revolution and civil war."[54]

According to K.M. Munshi, who in 1920 had left the Home Rule League along with Jinnah, Jinnah arrived in Calcutta "with the air of a conquering hero" and "in a truculent mood."[55] Calling Jinnah "a spoilt child, a naughty child," Sapru, the Hindu liberal, nonetheless asked Congress to give him what he wanted "and be finished with it."[56] However, Congress was not minded to do so; it feared a Hindu backlash, and it was not sure that a pact with Jinnah would be a pact with the Muslims as a whole.

The occasion has been recalled by one of Jinnah's friends, a Parsi called Jamshed Nusserwanjee, who later became mayor of Karachi:

> Mr Jinnah stood up, wearing the fashionable clothes he had brought back from England, and he pleaded. . . . His demands were rejected. One man said that Mr Jinnah had no right to speak on behalf of the Muslims — that he did not represent them. He was sadly humbled, and he went back to his hotel.
>
> Next morning he left Calcutta by train, and I went to see him off. He was standing at the door of his first-class coupe compartment, and he took my hand. He had tears in his eyes as he said "Jamshed, this is the parting of the ways."[57]

His hurt was understandable. He had imagined that his exertions had brought him close to reenacting his 1916 Lucknow triumph, forging a Hindu-Muslim pact and occupying a spot from which he could steer not just the *qaum* but India-as-a-whole. Calcutta shattered this picture, and Jinnah knew that he would not look at it again.

Confirming Nusserwanjee's account, some have spoken of Calcutta 1928 as a watershed. There, according to Khaliquzzaman, "the fate of the country was sealed." "The shortsightedness of Hindu politicians," he adds, "could not be surpassed."[58] Even at the time Sapru said that failure to agree would lead to "a great damage from which India would not recover for a quarter of a century."[59] It is a fact that after Calcutta no Muslim outside Congress spoke again of joint electorates. Yet, audacious as Jinnah's 1927–28 bid was, it was not realistic. In Punjab, Muslims, Hindus and Sikhs had all, for different reasons, strongly opposed the Delhi Proposals. In India as a whole, the politicians' hands were tied. Muslim sentiment prevented Jinnah from modifying the Delhi package* and isolated men

---

*Left to himself, Jinnah might have agreed to the Nehru Report. He said in Calcutta: "Would you be content if I were to say, I am with you?"[60]

like Ansari and Azad, who accepted the Nehru Report. An opposite feeling restrained Congress's leaders from going beyond the Nehru Report, for which, with some difficulty, they had obtained the agreement of Punjab's Sikhs and Hindus.[61] Telling Jinnah that he was prepared personally to "concede the Muslim demand," Gandhi, who was present in Calcutta, pointed out that the Sikhs had declared that they would back out if additions were made to the Nehru Report.[62]

* * *

The Calcutta disappointment hit Jinnah when another wound was still fresh, the failure of his marriage. Early in 1928 Ruttie had moved from the Mount Pleasant Road house to a room in the Taj Mahal Hotel. Jinnah told a Parsi friend who tried to reconcile him and Ruttie: "We both need some sort of understanding we cannot give."[63] Then Ruttie left for Europe, with her parents. Jinnah followed later, in April 1928. While visiting Ireland he learned that Ruttie was seriously ill in Paris. He went to Paris. Emerging from her hospital room, he told Chaman Lall, who was also in Paris: "I think we can save her. We will change the doctor and take her to another hospital." Chaman Lall has recalled:

> Ruttie Jinnah recovered, and I left Paris soon afterwards, believing they were reconciled. Some weeks passed and I was in Paris again. I spent a day with Jinnah, wondering why he was alone. In the evening I said to Jinnah, "Where is Ruttie?" He answered, "We quarrelled: she has gone back to Bombay." He said it with such finality that I dared not ask any more questions.

When Jinnah was in Calcutta, urging Congress to accept the Delhi Proposals, Ruttie was dangerously ill again, in the Taj room in Bombay. Two months later, her separated husband not in town, the 28-year-old Ruttie died. Jinnah came back for the burial in a Muslim cemetery. During the service he talked "of his political worries" with another of his Hindu friends, Kanji Dwarkadas. When, says Dwakadas, the body was lowered into the grave, Jinnah, 52 at the time, "bowed his head and sobbed."[65]

Then Jinnah recalled his will-power. When an old friend called on him, intending to describe Ruttie's last hours, he saw that Jinnah had ensured that he would not weaken again. "Every photograph, every souvenir of the desperate years was removed." On Jinnah's sleeve was the correct black band of mourning, on his face a resolve not to talk about Ruttie. The friend did not refer to her last hours.[66]

Another picture is painted by Muhammad Azad, Jinnah's chauffeur. According to Azad:

> You know, servants in a household come to know everything. . . .
> Sometimes, more than twelve years after Begum Jinnah's death, the
> boss would order at dead of night a huge ancient wooden chest to be
> opened, in which were stored clothes of his dead wife. . . . He would
> gaze at them for long. . . . Then his eyes would moisten . . . [67]

* * *

As we noted in the Muhammad Ali chapter, Muslim terms were stiffer
after Calcutta: now they comprised the Delhi Proposals plus separate
electorates. Gandhi conferred twice with Jinnah in 1929; there was no
agreement. Different Muslim groups met in Delhi and spelt out the *qaum*'s
position. The initiative behind the convention was Muhammad Shafi's,
the chairman the Aga Khan. Jinnah did not attend; he had not forgiven
Shafi for splitting the League. But the sulk was brief. Returning to the
qaum's mainstream, Jinnah reduced the decisions of the Delhi convention
to fourteen precise demands. Soon they became known as "Jinnah's 14
points."

Congress, meanwhile, was preparing its second major offensive against
the Raj. The Mahatma was back at its helm, calling for "salt" marches
and a campaign of peaceful disobedience. Muslims in the North West
Frontier, led by Abdul Ghaffar Khan and his brother Dr. Khan Sahib,
backed him, as did Ansari, Abul Kalam Azad and some other Muslims
elsewhere, and it was a notable episode. But the *qaum*, on the whole,
stayed out.

In the autumn of 1930, when Gandhi and thousands of others were in
the Raj's prisons, prominent Muslims, princes, Sikhs, Hindu Mahasabha-
ites and Liberals, all believers in the constitutional path to self-government,
conferred with H.M.G. in London. Jinnah, one of several Indians asking
for such a "round-table" conference, was a Muslim invitee. Of him, Irwin,
the Viceroy, had written Baldwin, the Premier, that he had "met very
few Indians with a more acute intellect or a more independent outlook."[68]

The meeting failed. The Indian dignitaries, led, on the Muslim side,
by the Aga Khan, did not agree with Britain or with one another. A
depressed Jinnah chose not to return to India. He would practise law in
England, where the Privy Council had to deal with a number of Indian
cases. He told a Muslim student in Oxford:

> The Hindus are short-sighted and I think incorrigible. The Muslim
> camp is full of spineless people who will consult the Deputy Com-
> missioner about what they should do. Where, between these two
> groups, is any place for a man like me?[69]

Some years later Jinnah would recall: "I felt so disappointed that I
decided to settle down in London. Not that I did not love India, but I

felt so utterly helpless."[70] A factor behind the feeling of helplessness was that in 1930, as in 1920, Congress had placed itself in Gandhi's hands.

A year later Jinnah took part in the second round-table conference, again held in London. This time Gandhi, released by Irwin, the retiring Viceroy, also attended. However, Gandhi's request for a place at the table for Ansari, who headed the Nationalist Muslim group, was turned down by Willingdon, who had succeeded Irwin.

Gandhi said in London that Congress, backed by Muslims like Azad and Ansari, was Indian, not Hindu. This was not so, said the Aga Khan and Jinnah. Gandhi said that Swaraj had to come first. "The iceberg of communal differences will melt," he claimed, "under the warmth of the sun of freedom."[71] His opponents, Muslim, princely and untouchable, replied that agreement among different Indian groups had to precede freedom; otherwise, they argued, Swaraj would oppress minorities. It was, once more, a deadlock.

By this time Jinnah had taken possession of a three-storied villa in Hampstead. His sister Fatima had joined him and was running the house. His thirteen-year-old daughter Dina, entered in an English boarding school, spent her holidays with them. He had given her *Grey Wolf*, a life of Mustafa Kamal, saying, "Read this, it is good." She would say, "Come on, Grey Wolf, take me to a pantomime." Nobody else had ever teased him; nobody else would do so in the future.

His practice was flourishing. At week-ends he walked amidst pretty scenery. Life was more orderly than in India, and calmer. But he had not snapped his links with India. He went there shortly before the second round-table conference and tried, without success, to persuade Congress's Muslims to join a united Muslim front. Also, he stressed the fourteen points, though he added that he "would personally prefer" joint elector-ates.[73] And he warned: if "the British Government gave the Hindus a constitution in accordance with their desire, naturally Muslims would resort to every means to destroy and wreck that constitution."[74] He had not used strong language like this before — not, at any rate, on the Hindu-Muslim question.

Back in Hampstead, he saw something of poet Iqbal, who visited England in 1931 and 1932; it is not improbable that they discussed Iqbal's 1930 idea of a separate Muslim state. If, as sometimes happened, Indian Muslims asked for his advice, Jinnah would cable it. Its essence usually was that Muslims needed to watch both Congress and the Raj with care.

Still, he was something of an exile, and when in 1932 a third round-table conference was held in London, Jinnah was not invited. Gandhi would not be there either; once more he was in prison. Did Jinnah fear that he would fade out? There were times when he looked "most un-happy."[75] But there was no danger of the *qaum* leaving him alone. It felt the absence of a hand at its helm. The Aga Khan was trying to do the impossible, leading Muslim masses in India from France and Switzerland. Muhammad Ali had died. So had Muhammad Shafi, Jinnah's only rival in the League. The League had shrunk in size and discipline. Its finances were misused; functionaries were refusing to resign despite votes of no-confidence. As for Congress, Willingdon had crushed a campaign of dis-obedience it launched in 1932. In 1933 Gandhi seemed much less dominant then he had been the previous three years.

In July 1933 a 37-year-old man, in Europe on his honeymoon, called, with his bride, at the Hampstead house. His name was Liaqat Ali Khan; he would be Pakistan's first Prime Minister. According to Begum Liaqat Ali Khan, her husband "had the belief that Jinnah was the one man who could save the League, and the Muslims." He, and the Begum, pressed Jin-nah to return. Jinnah spoke of his "contentment at Hampstead." Liaqat re-peated his convictions. At the end of a long dinner, during which Begum Liaqat Ali felt that "nothing could move" Jinnah from England, Jinnah said, "You go back and survey the situation. Test the feelings of all parts of the country. If you say, 'Come back,' I will give up my life here and return."[76]

Liaqat did as he was told. He took soundings. Finally he sent the message, "Return." Jinnah sold the villa, disposed of his furnishings and, Fatima beside him, came back. In the view of some of his Hampstead neighbours, he bore the stamp of a man going on a great mission.

In April 1934 the League unanimously made Jinnah its permanent president. Six months later he entered the Central Assembly again, from his old Bombay seat, and became the leader of an independent group of 22 members, of whom 18 were Muslim. Sixty-odd members were Con-gressmen or their allies; Congress had suspended its three-year phase of defiance and re-entered the legislature, a switch in strategy accompanied by Gandhi's withdrawal from Congress's stage. The Raj, too, could count on sixty-odd votes in the Assembly of officials, nominated members and some loyalists. This balance gave Jinnah decisive influence. His group was often on the winning side, voting either with the government against a Congress resolution, or with Congress against an official bill. Since the Viceroy could override the Assembly, the government's defeats did not affect the laws of the land. But they were good for the people's morale.

If Jinnah performed with skill on the assembly floor, he was also trav-elling to towns all across India, enlisting members for the League, and striving to raise it to the status of the *qaum*'s unquestioned voice. Its popularity was tested in the 1937 elections to the provincial assemblies.

These were held under the Act of 1935, which gave substantial powers to provincial assemblies and provided for separate electorates and reserved seats for Muslims, Sikhs and Christians. H.M.G. had rejected Congress's plea for joint electorates.

Congress and the League produced similar manifestos. They saw provincial pro-British parties, and not each other, as rivals. In many a Muslim seat the League candidate was not opposed by Congress, which thought that it might need the League's goodwill after the elections. "Before and even during the elections," says Ikram, "Congress leaders were friendly to the Muslim League."[77]

Congress's victories were bigger than it or anyone else expected. As Ikram puts it, they were the result of the "magic name of a Mahatma," "the whirlwind tours of Jawaharlal Nehru" — who was Congress's president in 1936 and 1937 — and "the organising ability" of Vallabhbhai Patel, who, following the death in 1936 of Dr. Ansari, had become the chairman of Congress's parliamentary board.[78] Congress won overwhelmingly in all the Hindu-majority provinces and also, in partnership with the Khan brothers, in the North West Frontier.

The League captured many Muslim seats in the Hindu-majority provinces, especially in the U.P. and Bombay, but it was humbled in the Punjab, where the provincial Unionist party won handsomely and the League had to be content with only two seats. In Bengal the League was able to claim a ministry but only by offering the Premiership, and a place in the League, to Fazlul Huq, whose Krishak Praja party had defeated many League candidates in the elections.

The lesson was clear: the *qaum* was supporting the League in provinces where it felt insecure, but not where Muslims outnumbered Hindus. Jinnah saw the lesson in a flash and, as we shall see, played his cards with great skill. For the moment let us only note that his pride, his refusal to be ignored, succoured his *qaum* just when, for reasons to which we shall soon refer, its morale was shaken. Jinnah had shown this pride, or defiance, even before the elections. Responding in January 1937 to Jawaharlal Nehru, who had said that India had to choose between Congress and the British, Jinnah shot back: "I refuse to line up. There is a third party — the Muslims. We are not going to be dictated to by anybody."[79] Disregarding the size of Congress's majorities, Jinnah maintained this posture with vehemence and without ceasing, until everyone realized that there would be no settlement in India that left the League and Jinnah out.

* * *

In May 1937, when it was plain that Congress had scored huge victories but not yet clear that it was going to accept office, Jinnah sent a private verbal message to Gandhi, who, despite his withdrawal, was Congress's guide. Conveyed by B.G. Kher, who had been elected leader of Congress's triumphant group in the Bombay assembly, the communication urged Gandhi to take the lead in forging "Hindu–Muslim unity." No more is known about the message but its timing, the choice of Kher and subsequent developments suggest that Jinnah had in mind a Congress-League settlement involving, among other things, power-sharing in the provinces. Gandhi's written reply, which must have seemed a rebuff to Jinnah, was: "Kher has given me your message. I wish I could do something but I am utterly helpless. My faith in unity is bright as ever; only I see no daylight . . . "[81]

In July, after long negotiations with the Raj on the freedom of action of provincial ministries, Congress decided to accept office. This was followed, at least in two provinces, Bombay and the U.P., by Congress-League discussions on power-sharing. Jinnah and Kher talked briefly and informally in Bombay; in the U.P., Abul Kalam Azad, asked by Congress to supervise the formation of ministries in northern India, talked with the U.P. League leader, Khaliquzzaman.

The Bombay negotiations collapsed because of the apparent insistence of Patel, whose approval Kher needed, that League legislators should merge with Congress before becoming ministers, whereas Jinnah would only accept a coalition between two separate parties. The "coalition versus merger" issue also appears to have figured in the U.P. talks, which were disliked by Jinnah because they were initiated without reference to him. In his memoirs Khaliquzzaman speaks of the wish of Congressmen in 1937 to see "the League . . . wind itself up."[81] Azad, however, has given another explanation for the breakdown of the U.P. talks: an unexpected intervention by Nehru, who, according to Azad, reduced Congress's offer of two seats in the ministry to one.[82]

Be that as it may, in the U.P., in Bombay and in five other provinces where Congress was in a majority, ministries were formed without the League. While Congressmen hailed "self-government" and "progress towards Swaraj," others cried, "Hindu rule" and were believed by many in the *qaum*, for it could not be denied or concealed that most Congressmen were Hindus. Ikram simplifies but does not distort when he says that "over the greater part of the country, where the Congress ministries held sway, the Muslims felt that the Hindu Raj had come."[83]

It is the view of many, scholars and public figures alike, that Congress's failure in 1937 to share power with the League turned the *qaum* in the direction of Pakistan. Thus Pyarelal, Gandhi's secretary and biographer, calls it "a tactical error of the first magnitude" — and says that the "decision of the Congress High Command" to exclude the League was "taken against Gandhiji's best judgment."[84]

According to Frank Moraes: "Had the Congress handled the League more tactfully after the (1937) elections, Pakistan might never have come into being."[85] Penderel Moon, a Briton who served with the I.C.S. before and after independence, describes Congress's failure to cooperate with the League in 1937 as "the prime cause of the creation of Pakistan."[86]

We can fairly accuse the Congress of 1937 of being stingy and haughty. It could have openly invited the League as a partner and disproved allegations that it sought Hindu rule. Yet it would be an error to conclude that Congress rejected partnership with Jinnah merely because of miserliness or because success had turned its head; it did so also in the interest of cohesion. Nehru, Patel and Azad believed that Jinnah would be a difficult partner. The thought of having to obtain his concurrence for every measure of the new ministries did not appeal to them or to other Congressmen.* It is evident also that Gandhi was unwilling to provide Jinnah with a say that would have undercut the influence of Nehru, Patel and Azad and reduced the discretion of Congress's chief ministers. Though Gandhi's "best judgment" was in favour of coalitions with the League, it is noteworthy that he was unresponsive when Jinnah sent that private message to him via Kher.

Despite their differences, Gandhi, Nehru, Patel and Azad had learned to work together; they were not sure that a similar teamwork was possible with Jinnah. Yet it was more than a question of personalities that were incompatible, or appeared to be. There were crucial ideological differences as well. Gandhi, Nehru, Patel and Azad could not accept Jinnah's view that Congress was to Hindus what the League was to Muslims. It was not until 1938 that this view became Jinnah's formal pre-condition for any League-Congress settlement, but he had been asserting it from 1931 onwards. He would probably have insisted on its acceptance had Gandhi or Nehru or Patel negotiated with him in 1937.

More generosity or wisdom in Congress might not have produced a pact with Jinnah, but, partially at least, it could have allayed the *qaum*'s fears; and it could have enlisted some sections of the League. Though the Unionist Premier of Punjab, Sir Sikander Hyat, had a comfortable majority, he offered a ministerial berth to the Hindu Mahasabha; similar gestures from Congress to the League in the Hindu-majority provinces

---

*Thus K.M. Munshi, who became Bombay's home minister, felt that Muslim League ministers accepted on Jinnah's terms would have been "at the disposal of Jinnah to obstruct, defy, sabotage, and blackmail the Congress."[87]

would have made it more difficult for Jinnah to convince the *qaum* that Congress was its enemy.

Let us cease speculating and turn to facts. While Congress fumbled its opportunity, Jinnah seized his. Within months of Congress assuming power, he said: "All along the countryside, many of the ten thousand Congress committees and even some of the Hindu officials are behaving as if Hindu Raj had already been established."[88] He said the *qaum* had to unite; it united. Congress argued, truthfully, that a few Muslims, elected on the Congress ticket, were in its ministries; the League called them stooges. When it saw how the *qaum* was beginning to think, Congress took some Muslims elected as independents into its ministries — and was promptly accused of "corrupting a few ambitious, unprincipled Muslims."[89] Now it was not merely communal but evil as well.

Often ill, Jinnah ignored his ailments. His cards were not strong, but he ignored their face value. Soon the determination encased in the thin coughing frame fetched stronger cards. The most prestigious was the presence at the League's Lucknow session in October 1937 of the Muslim Premiers of the Punjab and Bengal, Hyat and Huq. As Ikram puts it, "after having decisively defeated the League in the elections, Hyat and Huq came to terms with Jinnah and agreed to abide by the decisions of the League in all-India matters."[90]

Pressed from one side by Congress, and restrained from the opposite side by the Raj, these regional leaders saw a valuable national ally in Jinnah's League. Conscious also that Muslims in their provinces were sympathetic to the *qaum*'s solidarity, Hyat and Huq were willing to place their provinces in Jinnah's column. Astutely, Jinnah offered an assurance, enshrined in a Jinnah-Hyat pact, that the Punjab unit of the League would not challenge Hyat's position.

Jinnah's strategy was wiser than the one poet Iqbal was urging on him at this juncture. To strengthen the League vis-a-vis the Unionists, Iqbal wanted Jinnah to hold the League's 1937 session in Punjab, but Jinnah shrewdly chose to woo rather than alienate Hyat. Iqbal thought he needed Jinnah for the sake of Punjab; Jinnah knew that he needed Hyat for the sake of the *qaum* as a whole. Also, as we have already noted, Jinnah instinctively realized that his main strength would come from Muslims in Hindu-majority provinces. He therefore chose Lucknow as the venue for the session that would mark the birth of the new Jinnah, transforming the "ambassador of Hindu-Muslim unity" into the advocate of Muslim separation — the Lucknow where, in 1916, Jinnah had architected the League-Congress pact.

At the session Jinnah charged that Congress was pursuing a policy "which is exclusively Hindu"[91] and that "the majority community have clearly shown their hand that Hindustan is for the Hindus."[92] The man who had sought bridges seemed now, for the first time, to have a stake in gulfs; the man who had come close to assuming the leadership of India seemed content now, for the first time, to limit himself to the *qaum*. Mr. Jinnah had become Janab Jinnah and would soon be the Quaid-i-Azam, "the great leader." At Lucknow, for the first time, Jinnah appeared in the long coat and loose trousers of the Indian Muslim, not in one of his well-cut European suits.

Hardening toward Congress, the League did not soften toward the Raj. At Lucknow it affirmed, as Congress had done eight years earlier, that its goal was "full independence." We see an interesting side of Jinnah in the recollection of Khaliquzzaman, who had moved the resolution in favor of "complete independence":

> To my great surprise Mr. Jinnah started opposing this change. . . . I sincerely felt that Congress would utilize this difference in creed to our great disadvantage. Ultimately I made a last appeal to Mr. Jinnah not to be a party to the finishing of the Muslim League. . . . Thereafter he stood up rather excitedly and said: "Well, I say, 'full independence' and not 'complete independence'." This was Mr. Jinnah. . . . He would never accept defeat but would convert it into victory by a supreme nonchalance.[93]

* * *

Never again would Jinnah approach Gandhi or anyone in Congress. That message of May 1937 was his last initiative. The new Jinnah would wait for Congress to come to him, confident that it would have to; Congress had to have an answer to the Raj's question, "Are the Muslims with you?" As Ikram puts its, "Jinnah was not going to lower his flag to come to terms with the Congress. Far from his accepting conditions . . . it would be he who would impose conditions!"[94] It was a posture the *qaum* loved.

Immediately after Lucknow Gandhi wrote him: "I carefully went through your speech. . . . As I read it, [it] is a declaration of war." Replied Jinnah: "I am sorry you think my speech at Lucknow is a declaration of war. It is purely in self-defence." Gandhi wrote again: "You seem to deny that your speech was a declaration of war, but your later pronouncements too confirm the first impression. In your speeches I miss the old nationalist. . . . Are you still the same Mr. Jinnah?" Jinnah hit back:

> Evidently you are not acquainted with what is going on in the Congress press — the amount of vilification, misrepresentation and falsehood that is daily spread about me — otherwise I am sure you would not blame me.

You say that in my speeches you miss the old nationalist. . . . I would not like to say what people spoke of you in 1915 and what they speak of and think of you today.

At Lucknow Jinnah had publicly attacked Gandhi for failing to respond to his approach in May. After their correspondence, Gandhi agreed to call on Jinnah in Bombay. He had wondered about Jinnah visiting him in Wardha, but Jinnah replied that that would not suit him. Gandhi wanted to bring Azad along, but Jinnah wired: "I would prefer to see you alone." In the end Subhas Bose, who had succeeded Nehru as Congress president, joined the Gandhi-Jinnah talks. Congress seemed ready now to discuss coalitions with the League, but the meeting failed. The issue on which they diverged was spelt out by Jinnah in a letter to Gandhi:

We have reached a stage when no doubt should be left that you recognize the Muslim League as the one authoritative and representative organisation of the Muslims of India and, on the other hand, you represent the Congress and other Hindus throughout the country. Only on that basis we can proceed further . . . [95]

Referring to this demand, the scholar Merriam has observed that "Jinnah asked for an exclusive recognition which Congress could not grant and which was, in fact, unjustified by the political situation in India."[96] The League did not represent all Muslims at the time. Congress, in Merriam's words, "did enjoy the support of many Muslims"[97]; and other significant Muslim bodies were also in the field. The claim did not accord with the facts; yet, before long, facts would accord with the claim. Part of the reason why they would do so was Jinnah's resolve — steadfastness to some, obstinacy to others.

Pursuing his line, Jinnah, in April 1938, even asked Congress not to appoint any Muslims to its central committee. Bose replied that Congress could not reject its creed or spurn its Muslim supporters.[98] The ideological gap was unbridgable; and facts too were perceived differently.

* * *

Jinnah could be rude and sharp if he smelled or imagined condescension, as is shown in the correspondence he had with Nehru in 1938.

Nehru to Jinnah, Feb. 25, '38: I am afraid I must confess that I do not yet know what the fundamental points of dispute are. It is for this reason that I have been asking you to clarify them.

Jinnah to Nehru, March 3, '38: I am only amazed at your ignorance. . . .

Nehru to Jinnah, Apr. 6, '38: Obviously, the Muslim League is an important communal organisation and we deal with it as such. But we have to deal with all organizations and individuals that come within our ken. . . . We do not determine the measure of importance or distinction they possess. Importance does not come from outside recognition but from inherent strength.

Jinnah to Nehru, Apr. 10, '38: Your tone and language again display the same arrogance and militant spirit, as if the Congress is the sovereign power. Unless the Congress recognises the Muslim League on a footing of complete equality. . . . we shall have to depend upon our "inherent strength" which will "determine the measure of importance or distinction" it possesses."

His dislike of Gandhi not leaving him, he singled him out, in December 1938, as "the one man responsible for turning the Congress into an instrument for the revival of Hinduism and for the establishment of Hindu Raj in India."[100] Yet he also had the ability to accept a rebuke, at least from those he liked. Bolitho tells of a conversation between Jinnah and a young man called Ibrahim Habibullah, who had heard both Jinnah and Jawaharlal speak at a public meeting:

Habibullah walked away from the hall with Jinnah, who said, "Don't you think that Nehru was talking nonsense?"

"No," answered Habibullah, "I agree with all his views."

Jinnah then said, referring to some points in Nehru's speech, "The laws of the jungle must always prevail. Unless you understand that, you are a madcap."

Habibullah replied, "We call ourselves human beings because we have emancipated ourselves from the jungle. If you do not appreciate that, then, sir, you are the madcap."

Jinnah was delighted with this challenge from someone less than half his age. He said."Oh, I need young men like you. Come and join me."[101]

His private joys were scarce. His daughter Dina was now staying more with her mother's relatives than with Jinnah. Eventually, against Jinnah's wishes, she would marry a Christian; for a while she would be estranged from her father. Though he had Fatima's constant affection, Jinnah would on occasion disclose some of his unsatisfied longings, as when he talked at length to young students about his boyhood and said, "I wish that I had a son,"[102] or when he would take time out, during a political tour, to find a toy–shop and buy a rocking–horse for the little son of his hostess.

* * *

Less than a year after the 1937 elections, the League's membership rose from "tens of thousands" to "hundreds of thousands."[103] Jinnah had shed his inhibitions and could say at a public meeting, "If for uplifting the social, economic and political standards of the Mussalmans of India, I am branded a communalist, I assure you, gentlemen, that I am proud to be a communalist."[104] Now he would frequently champion the Arab cause and assert that Britain had "thrown her friends to the wolves"; and he would liken the Muslims of India to the Sudeten Germans, "who had been forced under the heels of the majority of Czechoslovakia, who oppressed them, suppressed them, maltreated them."[105]

All over India spokesmen of the League charged that Congress ministries were denying jobs to Muslims, forcing Sanskritized Hindi on them, and compelling Muslim schoolchildren to revere Gandhi's portrait and sing lines that were contrary to Islamic beliefs. The loud and long disputes that took place on the correctness or falsehood of the charges are irrelevant before the great truth that the *qaum* seemed to accept the charges as valid.

The Second World War gave Jinnah his second great chance. It destroyed Congress's pact with the Raj. Congress was willing to support and implement the war effort if steps were taken towards freedom; the Raj was unwilling to take the steps. Why was the Raj unwilling? Partly because the idea of a "bargain" in a time of war was disliked; partly because some Britons had been hurt by the intemperate language of Congress extremists over the years; partly because some of them genuinely thought that minorities would be unsafe under Indian self–rule; and, finally, also because some of them were unreconciled to the idea of Indian independence. Its demands rejected, Congress asked its ministries to resign. Hindsight might suggest that this was foolish in the extreme, yet, given the popular thirst for independence at the time, Congress had little choice. It would have been called a toady party had it continued in office without some progress in the direction of liberty.

Once more, Jinnah played his cards with skill. He indicated to the Raj that the League, and India's Muslims, would support the war effort if — but only if — Muslim interests were protected to its satisfaction in any future Indian constitution; and he did not demand immediate steps toward independence. Unlike Congress, he could afford to wait for independence; his constituency, the *qaum*, now looked upon the Hindu and not the Briton as the primary enemy.

The Raj, too, saw its chance, as is apparent from a letter from the Viceroy, Lord Linlithgow, to the King:

As soon as I realised that I was to be subjected to heavy and sustained pressure designed to force from us major political concessions as the price of Congress's co–operation in the war effort, I summoned representatives of all the more important interests and communities in India, including the Chancellor of the Chamber of Princes and Mr. Jinnah ... and interviewed them one by one ... a heavy and trying task, but well worth the trouble.[106]

Jinnah thought that the Viceroy's invitation to him had "shocked Gandhi and the Congress,"[107] The League and the Raj cooperated to foil Congress, but Congress's leaders knew that this was tactics, not an abandonment by Jinnah of his goal of liberty. As Rajagopalachari, Premier of Madras, said shortly after the Jinnah–Linlithgow meeting: "Do I not know Mr. Jinnah? Do I not know the innermost ambition of his heart that India should be free?" However, conveying Congress's frustration, Rajagopalachari added: "We could have had Swaraj in the palm of our hand if the League had played the game. But knowingly [it had gone] from one wrong step to another . . . . The League is puncturing the tyre and stopping the progress of the Indian car."[108]

When the Congress ministries resigned, Jinnah asked the *qaum* to celebrate a Day of Deliverance, release from the "tyranny" of the "Hindu" ministries. Congress's leaders were outraged; justifiably or not, they thought that they had been fair to Muslims. But the bulk of the *qaum* did observe Deliverance Day.

Sentiment in the *qaum* was flowing fast from "Muslim by religion, Indian by nationality" to "Muslim by religion, Muslim by nationality." Gandhi tried hard to arrest the tide. At his suggestions Congress chose Abul Kalam Azad as its president for 1940. In a letter written in 1940 Gandhi addressed Jinnah as "Dear Quaid–i–Azam." In an article in his journal "Harijan," he encouraged Jinnah, whom he called "my old comrade," to lead all the non–Congress forces in the country, including the followers of Ambedkar, the untouchable hero, and Ramaswami Naicker, who had mobilized many Tamils against Congress. Gandhi clearly hoped that Jinnah might make Muslim separatism secondary to an all–India fight against Congress; this fight would hurt Congress, but it would keep the *qaum* linked to India. Jinnah did not bite the bait. "I have no illusions in the matter," he replied. "India is not a nation, nor a country. It is a subcontinent composed of nationalities." He would gladly fight Congress, but from now on he would also, and above all, fight the notion of one India. In fact, he would encourage men like Ambedkar and Naicker also to fight the notion.[109]

In March 1940 the great decision was formally made. At a session in Lahore, in a resolution moved by Fazlul Huq, the League said it would accept nothing short of "separate and sovereign Muslim states, comprising geographically contiguous units, . . . in which the Muslims are numerically in a majority, as in the North–Western and Eastern zones of India."[110] Iqbal had urged Jinnah in 1937 to adopt something like this as the League's goal; the poet, in fact, had called for a separate Muslim state as far back as 1930. Iqbal did not refer to "Pakistan"; neither did the Lahore resolution. The name first occurred, some time in the early thirties, to a man called Khwaja Abdur Rahim. Meaning "Land of the pure," it was also, in English, a combination derived from P(unjab), A(fghania = NWFP), K(ashmir), S(ind) and (Baluchis)TAN. Rahmat Ali, then a student at Cambridge, was the first man to use the expression in print and give it some currency. This was in 1933, seven years before Jinnah's conversion to the idea for which it stood. Needing a name for the independent state (or states) that the Lahore resolution called for, the Press spoke of "Pakistan." After a while the League adopted the term.

It should be noted that the Lahore resolution did not define the boundaries of the new state(s). The reason for this was supplied during the Lahore session by Liaqat Ali Khan, the League's secretary. Fearing that the resolution's wording might be used to justify the partition of Punjab and Bengal, a delegate proposed that "the names of the provinces should be unambiguously indicated." Liaqat replied:

> If we say Punjab that would mean that the boundary of our state would be Gurgaon, whereas we want to include in our proposed dominion Delhi and Aligarh which are centres of our culture. . . . Rest assured that we will [not] have to give away any part of the Punjab.[111]

The passion with which Jinnah advocated a Muslim homeland in 1940 and later caused many to forget his earlier hesitation over it. He was slow to champion the step because it would contradict his long years of struggle for Hindu-Muslim unity. Linlithgow observed, at the end of 1939, that when he told Jinnah that a separate state was the logical implication of his latest position, Jinnah "blushed."[112] He was compelled to champion a Muslim state because of the *qaum*'s growing separatism, and because of his decision, made in the thirties, to limit himself to the *qaum*. Of course, the *qaum*'s growing separatism had been encouraged by him; he and the *qaum* had fuelled each other. Yet the background for this growing separatism was Congress's 1937 success. In the long view, as India strode toward independence, the *qaum* turned toward Pakistan.

* * *

At Lahore Jinnah declared that Hindus and Muslims could "never evolve a common nationality," and that "to yoke together two such nations under a single state, one as a numerical minority and the other as a majority, must lead to . . . final destruction of any fabric [of] government of such a state."[113] Asked what he would do if he did not succeed in obtaining a Muslim state, Jinnah replied, "I will give my life to achieve it." "Prolonged cheering almost drowned" this sentence, the *Times* of London reported.[114]

Gandhi responded in the very next issue of *Harijan*. Congress, he insisted, was not a Hindu body: it had a Muslim president and four Muslims on its 15-member working committee. He asserted, too, that Hindus and Muslims did not belong to two nations. They could not: conversion to Islam had not, he held, changed the nationality of India's Muslims. Speaking of Jinnah, Gandhi said that " . . . his [sur]name could be that of any Hindu . . . . His Indian nationality was written in his face and manner."

Jinnah replied to Gandhi. "Surely today," he claimed, "India is divided and partitioned by nature . . . . I fail to see why there is this hue and cry. Where is the country which is being divided?" "I believe with my whole soul," said Gandhi, "that the God of the Qur'an is also the God of the Gita." Also invoking religious phraseology, the seemingly secular Jinnah called himself "a humble and proud follower of my faith" and claimed that the "sacred duty" of "the servants of Islam" was to fight for Pakistan. This was so because "Hindus and Muslims . . . belong to two different civilisations which are based mainly on conflicting ideas and conceptions."[115]

The confrontation would continue for seven years. That it contained a personal element was obvious from remarks in Jinnah's Lahore speech: "Up to the time of the declaration of war the Viceroy never thought of an important party in the legislature . . . . The Viceroy never thought of me."[116]

After Lahore Jinnah seldom spoke of the personal factor. He was content to refer to Hindu–Muslim incompatibility. In 1942 he made what Merriam justly calls a "stylistically forceful statement":[117]

> The difference between Hindus and the Muslims is deep–rooted and ineradicable. We are a nation with our own distinctive culture and civilisation, language and literature, art and architecture, names and nomenclature, sense of value and proportion, legal laws and moral codes, customs and calendar, history and traditions, aptitudes and ambitions.[118]

Congress persisted in asking H.M.G. for a "national government," a cabinet that represented the Indian people. As the body's president, Abul Kalam Azad sought Jinnah's cooperation, assuring him that Congress wanted "a composite cabinet not limited to any single party." Azad's communication was couched in courteous terms. Jinnah's impolite and sharp reply reflected his passionate commitment to his position and his antipathy towards Azad, as well as his anger at Azad's alliance with Gandhi. Said Jinnah:

> I refuse to discuss with you, by correspondence or otherwise....
> Can't you realise you are made a Muslim "show-boy" Congress Pres-
> ident?...The Congress is a Hindu body. If you have self-respect
> resign at once. You have done your worst against the League so far.
> You know you have hopelessly failed. Give it up.[119]

If Congress attempted to split the *qaum*, Jinnah would help those who wished to split India. A year after the Lahore resolution Jinnah went to Madras and addressed his remarks to the followers of Ramaswami Naicker, who was exhorting the south's Dravidians to oppose Aryan domination: "This land is really Dravidistan.... I shall do all I can to support you to establish Dravidistan."[120]

He had to tread more carefully in New Delhi. He needed an assurance that Britain would not hand over power to Congress, but he could not afford to create an impression of an alliance with the Raj. That would hurt the League; after all, the *qaum* had not forgotten that British rule had ended Muslim rule. Antagonized by Congress's struggles over the years, the Raj's custodians were by no means eager to leave India to Congress. Still, many Britons were uneasy about their country's contin-uing presence in India. Among them were the leaders of the Labour party, now part of Churchill's coalition government.

Jinnah decided he would bid for British sympathy by offering the League's support for the war, provided H.M.G. did not yield to Congress, but also leave no doubt that the *qaum* would revolt if Congress was pla-cated. The strategy was successful. In August 1940 H.M.G. authorized the Viceroy to state that Britain would "not contemplate transfer of their present responsibilities to any system of government whose authority is directly denied by large and powerful elements in India's national life."[121] To remove any ambiguity, Leopold Amery, the Secretary of State, told Parliament that "the foremost among these elements stands the great Mus-lim community of ninety million, constituting a majority both in North–Western and North–Eastern India."[122] Jinnah had gained a powerful card. Congress called it a veto on progress.

It is instructive to contrast Jinnah's approach to the British with Con-gress's. When the war started, Gandhi told Linlithgow that he wanted Congress to offer unconditional support to Britain. This, however, Congress did not do. Influenced by popular sentiment, Congress asked for progress toward independence as its price for supporting the war effort. We have seen that Linlithgow disliked what he called Congress's "heavy and sustained pressure"; his reaction was shared by others administering the Raj. Jinnah, too, imposed his conditions, but, at the time, Britain found it easier, and also more congenial, to delay a transfer of power than to advance it. Merriam refers to "a temporary affinity" shared by Britain and Jinnah, who, as Merriam notes, "undoubtedly disliked British rule."[123] In enjoying the "temporary affinity," Jinnah was helped by Congress's inability to make the unconditional offer contemplated by Gandhi.

Jinnah's keenness to stay abreast of Gandhi's moves emerges from a story told by Mohammed Noman, the first secretary of the All-India Muslims Students Federation:

> One day I went to see Jinnah, early in the morning. He was sitting up in bed, reading a speech that Gandhi had made—it was some time in January or February 1940. Jinnah said to me, "You know, I have not slept a wink, trying to find out exactly what is in his mind."[124]

Another man on Jinnah's mind was Fazlul Huq, the Bengal Premier. Huq had preferred the League's umbrella to that of Congress, but he was not without local backing. Also, he was independent and ingenious. In the middle of 1941 Huq accepted, without any reference to Jinnah, the Viceroy's offer of a seat on the National Defence Council. Though Huq had been invited as Bengal's Premier and not as a League leader, his conduct displeased Jinnah and was censured by the League. Directed by the League to resign from the Defence Council, Huq obeyed, but he also chose to break with Jinnah and seek other allies. A League bid to oust him as Premier failed; Huq successfully formed a new ministry and Bengal left Jinnah's column. Jinnah called Huq "treacherous" and his new ministry "wretched"; Huq accused Jinnah of "authoritarianism."[125]

Following Pearl Harbor, Britain met with reverses in Asia. Hongkong, Malaya and Singapore were surrendered to Japan. In March 1942, soon after the fall of Rangoon, new proposals were brought to India by Sir Stafford Cripps, Labour member of the British cabinet and, like Jinnah, a brilliant advocate. On behalf of H.M.G., Cripps offered India full dominion status after the war, with the right to leave the Commonwealth; a constituent assembly, also post–war, elected by provincial legislatures, except for a proportion nominated by India's princes; and, immediately, a national government composed of representatives of the leading parties. These items, barring the power accorded to the princes, appealed to

Congress. To obtain Jinnah's acceptance of his package, Cripps gave every province the right to secede from the dominion, once the latter had come into being.

However, the League and Congress both turned down the proposals. Britain's readiness to divide India offended Gandhi; Azad and Nehru, Congress's negotiators, rejected the package because the proposed national government would be subject to the Viceroy's veto. Jinnah welcomed the secession clause as a "recognition of Pakistan by implication," but rejected the scheme because it gave provinces and not the "Muslim nation" the right to separate.[126]

He did not quite spell out this objection; later it would become apparent that the League wanted secession to be decided by a vote of all the Muslims of a Muslim-majority province, rather than by a vote of its entire adult population.

The inclusion of the secession clause in a formal H.M.G. proposal gave Jinnah an additional card of value. Yet he was disturbed by the willingness Cripps had shown to go some distance to satisfy Congress. Cripps would have gone farther, but Churchill, to whom Linlithgow and Wavell, the Commander-in-Chief in India, had signalled their support, restrained him.

Gandhi was more disturbed. He saw Jinnah, veto in hand, barring his path to the *qaum*. He saw a pencil to divide India in Churchill's hand. On the faces of Indians he saw growing hatred for Britain, in their hearts a secret but growing admiration for Japan, and a not-so-secret admiration for Subhas Bose, who, escaping from confinement in India, had organized an Indian National Army to win Indian independence with the gun and with the help of Japan.

To these prospects, adding up to a complete denial of all that he had hoped or stood for, Gandhi responded with the idea of Quit India. He would simply ask the British to leave, and back his demand with non-violent mass action. If the Japanese invaded India, he thought, the British would leave anyway. "If they are overwhelmed," he said, "the British will retire from India every man, woman and child, even as they retired from Singapore, Malaya and Burma. India is not the home of the British people."

But he would ask them to leave before the Japanese came—and before they, the British, could divide India. "Orderly British withdrawal," he claimed, would "turn the hatred [for Britain] into affection" and pull "the whole of India's mind away from Japan."[127] Even if the British did not leave, the Quit India call would restore the Indian mind to him and his way.

The masses—the bulk of the *qaum* apart—responded at once but some leaders hesitated. Nehru was afraid that Quit India would hurt the defence of China and Russia against Axis attacks. Soon, however, the nationalist in him triumphed. "If India perishes," he said, "it does not do me any good if other nations survive."[128] Azad thought that the British would kill the movement before it could take off.[129] Rajagopalachari said that Britain would not, and should not, leave. "She cannot," said the former Madras Premier, "add to her crimes the crowning offence of leaving the country in chaos to become a certain prey to foreign ambition."[130]

Gandhi answered that Japan would be fought if they tried to fill Britain's place, non-violently by him and by others believing in non-violence, with arms by the rest. A free India, he clarified, would formally join the Allies and offer her soil to allied troops fighting against Japan. On August 8, 1942 Congress embraced Quit India, Nehru moving the fateful resolution. Azad, too, acquiesced. Rajagopalachari was the lone dissenter.

With the *qaum* if possible, without the *qaum* is necessary. Once more this was how Gandhi and Congress viewed the journey to independence. While admitting that "for the moment" the League had prevented him from reaching the Muslim mind, Gandhi added that thinking Indians could no longer "idle away their time."[131] At Quit India's launching Gandhi referred to Jinnah:

> Jinnah Sahib has been a Congressman in the past.... I pray for long life for him and wish that he may survive me. A day will certainly come when he will realize that I have never wronged him or the Muslims.... I cannot wait till Jinnah Sahib is converted for the immediate consummation of Indian freedom.[132]

Jinnah was outraged by Gandhi's decision to go ahead without settling with the League, and by Gandhi's assumption that he could deal with the world on India's behalf. As for Quit India, Jinnah saw it not as a drive toward freedom but as "the culminating point in the policy and programme of Mr. Gandhi and his Hindu Congress of blackmailing and coercing the British to transfer power to a Hindu raj immediately."[133]

The Raj's war-time regime took no chances. Gandhi, Azad, Nehru, Patel and hundreds of their colleagues were arrested within hours of Congress acclaiming Quit India. And Congress was banned. For some days India, barring the bulk of the *qaum*, seemed to explode. Here and there pockets declared themselves free. Protesters streamed out into the streets. A hundred thousand Indian nationalists were placed behind bars. In the first few days of the August Movement, as it came to be called, at least six hundred Indian demonstrators were killed by the Raj's defenders.

However, by September the back of the rebellion was broken. It had been the gravest threat to British rule since the 1857 Rising.

For a while Jinnah seemed affected by it. Visiting him at the end of August 1942, when the movement was in full swing, his friend Kanji Dwarkadas found Jinnah "extremely weak and shaky" and also lonely. Gandhi and Congress were in the headlines and in everyone's talk. Jinnah felt isolated.[134] As the Raj regained control, and Congress went behind bars or underground, Jinnah realized that his position was strengthening. In Bengal, for instance, Huq was forced to resign; he was replaced by Khwaja Nazimuddin of the League, a man on whom Jinnah could rely. Elsewhere, too, the League emerged as one of the Raj's likely successors, filling some of the vacuum created by Congress's withdrawal and rebellion. A revived Jinnah "roamed India, preaching Muslim nationalism."[135]

By 1944 Jinnah could savour solid success. The League now claimed two million members, compared with only 1,330 seventeen years earlier. Between 1937 and 1943 there were contests, in provincial by-elections, for 61 Muslim seats. Of these the League won 47, independent Muslims 10 and Congress Muslims only 4.

Nonetheless, a small group of Muslims hated him, calling him traitorous for not forging an anti-British front of the League and Congress. In July 1943 a young man called Rafiq Sabir walked up to Jinnah's Malabar Hill house and, as luck would have it, found Jinnah in a room near the entrance, talking to an assistant. As Jinnah turned to go back to his desk in another room, where he had been working on his letters, Sabir attacked him. Jinnah described what happened during Sabir's subsequent trial:

> My whole mind was on my correspondence and, just as I was about to leave the room, in the twinkling of an eye the accused sprang at me and gave me a blow with his clenched fist on my left jaw. I naturally reeled back a bit, when he pulled out a knife from his waist.

Sabir raised his knife but the 66-year old Jinnah was alert and supple. He caught the assailant's hand and softened the blow before others, including Jinnah's chauffeur, overpowered Sabir. There were cuts on Jinnah's chin and hand. A doctor came and, helped by Fatima, bandaged them. Then Jinnah phoned his daughter, still estranged, told her what had happened and added, "I am all right."[136]

* * *

His strategy was simple. He would insist on the Hindu-Muslim divide; and he would insist that the imprisoned Gandhi was no more than the leader of the Hindus. "There is nothing in life," Jinnah told the British writer, Beverley Nichols, in December 1943, "which links [Hindus and Muslims] together."[137] Recalling a 1924 Gandhi statement that "every fibre of my being is Hindu," Jinnah ridiculed his adversary's refusal to speak only for the Hindus.[138]

Jinnah's strategy had another component: an unwillingness to define his Pakistan. He knew that spelling it out in detail would invite disputes within the *qaum* and even within the League. By keeping the goal vague, he enabled different Muslim groups to see what they wanted to see. In the words of Merriam:

> Muslim businessmen foresaw new markets free from Hindu competition. Landlords hoped for a perpetuation of the zamindari system. Intellectuals envisioned a cultural rebirth free from the British and Hindus. To the orthodox, Pakistan promised a religious state. . . . To officials and bureaucrats a new nation offered a short-cut to seniority. In this way, the very vagueness of the Pakistan demand facilitated Jinnah's task as a persuader.[139]

Jinnah could not have anticipated all these reactions. Yet he sensed instinctively that vagueness would suit him. As we saw earlier, he was deliberately imprecise even about the boundaries of the new nation. In April 1944, however, he was obliged to be more specific about this, for Rajagopalachari, the only Congress leader not in prison, called on him and claimed that Gandhi, whom he had seen in jail, was ready to discuss separation.

Gandhi had endorsed a Rajagopalachari formula that called for a joint League-Congress demand for a national government tied to an understanding that "contiguous Muslim-majority districts" could secede following independence, if separation was the preference of their adult populations. "In the event of separation," the formula added, "mutual agreements shall be entered into for safeguarding defence, communications, etc." Jinnah called this a "maimed, mutilated and moth-eaten" Pakistan; cool to it for more than one reason, he disclosed that his Pakistan included all of the Punjab and Bengal, apart from Sind, NWFP and Baluchistan.[140] This was significant, for it meant a Jinnah claim to eastern Punjab and western Bengal, large areas with a Hindu majority.

A month after the Jinnah-Rajagopalachari meeting Gandhi was unexpectedly released. He had had a near-fatal attack of malaria, and the Raj did not want a martyr-death in prison. After conferring with the Mahatma, Rajagopalachari wired Jinnah that Gandhi was still positive toward his formula, which, he said, he now wished to release to the press. He would also announce, added Rajagopalachari, that Jinnah had rejected it. Did

Jinnah mind? Jinnah wired back that it was wrong to say that he had rejected the scheme. If Gandhi dealt with him direct, said the Quaid, he would refer the formula to the League.

On July 17, two and a half months after the British had freed him, Gandhi sent Jinnah a letter—in Gujarati, with a copy in English. Opening with "Brother Jinnah," Gandhi continued: "I have not written to you since my release. But today my heart says that I should write to you. We will meet whenever you choose. Don't regard me as the enemy of Islam or of the Muslims of this country . . . . . . Your brother, M. K. Gandhi."[141]

Jinnah's reply, sent from Kashmir, where he had been resting, was less cordial, but it was polite. Written in English—"the only languge in which I can make no mistake"[142]—it said: "Dear Mr. Gandhi. . . . I shall be glad to receive you at my house in Bombay on my return. . . . By that time I hope that you will have recuperated your health fully. . . . I would like to say nothing more till we meet."[143]

Gandhi, a month under 75, and Jinnah, close to 68, were both ill, but whereas the former was slowly recapturing his health, the frail Jinnah had just learned that there was "unresolved pneumonia in the base of his lungs."[144] Calcium injections, tonics and short-wave diathermy had helped him; still, pneumonia in the India of the mid-forties was a disease to dread.

The two met fourteen times in Jinnah's Malabar Hill house in September and recorded their conversations in a series of letters. Congress leaders in jail were uneasy; Azad, for one, thought the "Gandhiji was making a great mistake."[145] However, photographs in the press showed the two leaders smiling; many in the land prayed; that the protagonists were meeting day after day aroused hopes. Even Wavell, who had succeeded Linlithgow as Viceroy, expected the two to agree. In his diary he wrote that he was "sure that the G-J meeting will result in a demand for the release of the working committee."[146] However, the talks failed, and Jinnah rejected Gandhi's proposal that "a third party" be brought in to arbitrate between them.

Jinnah was not satisfied with the Pakistan that Gandhi was conceding. He did not find it large enough—it excluded the Hindu-majority districts of Bengal and Punjab—, or sovereign enough—Gandhi wanted "bonds of alliance between Hindustan and Pakistan." Also, while Jinnah sought "self-determination for the Muslims," Gandhi made separation dependent on the vote of all the adult inhabitants of the Muslim-majority territory. Finally, whereas Gandhi saw "a separate state as soon as possible after India is free," Jinnah wanted partition to precede freedom: he did not trust a Congress-ruled India to implement a Pakistan promise.[147]

To this Gandhi would not agree. Brother separating from brother could be countenanced. But he was not willing to see Britain dividing India before leaving. The gap between the two was wide.

In the course of their encounter, Jinnah urged Gandhi to "clothe himself" with "representative authority" from Congress, instead of negotiating as an individual. This procedure was neither feasible—Congress's leaders were in jail—nor really necessary. Gandhi's influence with Congress was not in dispute; Jinnah himself, in his reply to Rajagopalachari, had invited a proposal from him. Nonetheless, Jinnah underlined Gandhi's unofficial status, claiming that it resulted in a "great disadvantage to me." He explained that "whereas . . . any agreement . . . would be binding upon me as the president of the League . . . you would as an individual only recommend it."[148]

Perhaps Jinnah feared that Congress might repudiate a Jinnah-Gandhi pact. However, it is also likely, as Merriam puts it, that Jinnah may have "gained some sub-conscious revenge, for in 1928 he had been humiliated by Hindus for his lack of representative authority."[149] Also noteworthy was Jinnah's rejection of a request Gandhi made for an opportunity to talk to the council of the League. Jinnah said that only delegates could go to the council's meetings. Did he perhaps also remember the Nagpur Congress of 1920, when the excited audience was unwilling to listen to Jinnah's case?

After the talks Jinnah said that Gandhi had been "very frank" with him.[150] Gandhi called Jinnah "a good man."[151] But "frankness" and "goodness" yielded nothing, except an increase in Jinnah's prestige and a clearer understanding of what he meant by Pakistan. The fact that Gandhi had gone fourteen times to Jinnah's house spoke of the Quaid's importance; in the opinion of many, it added to his Muslim following, which was already enormous.

* * *

Three years after the Bombay talks Jinnah would obtain a Pakistan of unabridged sovereignty, and obtain it from the British rather than from a free India. Yet this Pakistan would be, in area, almost exactly what Gandhi had offered. Both Jinnah and Gandhi had to swallow the unacceptable. Commenting on the Bombay talks, Khaliquzzaman, who presided over the League in Pakistan after Jinnah's death, says:

> If it was the intention of Mr. Jinnah to agree to a truncated Pakistan, he might have discussed the difficulties which stood in the way by further negotiation . . . Unfortunately, Mr. Jinnah did not call a meeting of the working committee of the Muslim League before breaking up talks.[152]

We can question the legitimacy of Jinnah's demand for the Hindu-majority portions of the Punjab and Bengal. As for self-determination, as Merriam points out, the claim is "normally advanced in the name of all inhabitants in a given territory."[153] In Khaliquzzaman's stronger words, "The right of self-determination of an area with the vote of one community alone formed a demand without parallel in world history."[154] His passion for the *qaum*'s rights had led Jinnah to this extreme position.

Over the timing of partition, however, Jinnah was not unreasonable. Fearing that a Congress-ruled India might renege on division, he asked Britain to divide India first and then quit. Like Gandhi a nationalist of the East, though his nationalism now bore the "Muslim" rather than the "Indian" prefix, Jinnah desired, as he said to Gandhi at the time, "a complete settlement of our own immediately."[155] But he wanted Britain rather than Congress to execute the settlement. Gandhi would not have lost materially by agreeing to this. We do not know whether such a concession would have led to a settlement; what we do know is that Gandhi's nationalist passion prevented him from making it. In his talks with Jinnah, argument had clashed with argument, and emotion with emotion.

* * *

The scene shifts to the Viceroy's lodge in Simla. Convinced that Gandhi and Jinnah had large backing for their wish to sever the British connection, and convinced too that post-war British opinion would favour Indian independence, Wavell sought Churchill's approval for a new offer to India. "You must have mercy on us," replied Churchill,[156] but Wavell's persistence was successful. With H.M.G.'s consent, he declared that Congress's leaders would be freed, and that there would be talks in Simla, not about independence or partition, but about a new Executive Council "representative of organized political opinion."[157]

In the summer of 1945 Jinnah and Gandhi climbed to the mountain town, the latter to advise rather than lead the Congress team, which was captained by Azad, the released president. True to his convictions, Jinnah ignored Azad. With Wavell he was unyielding. He asked for parity on the new "national government" between Muslims and Hindus. Wavell and Congress agreed. Then he insisted that he, as the League's president, would select all the Muslim members. Wavell and Congress disagreed. To the Congress's disappointment and the League's advantage, Wavell refused to arbitrate. He merely announced that the talks had failed and that the status quo would continue.

Several of the Raj's Governors had urged Wavell to go ahead and form a new council, keep vacant a decent number of seats for Jinnah to fill if he changed his mind; but this would have meant a Congress-dominated Council, to which Wavell was opposed. As the Viceroy said a year later in a letter to the King, he could "never entirely rid my mind of the recollection" of what Quit India had done to the war effort when he was Commander-in-Chief.[158]

Jinnah's firmness, or inflexibility, had paid dividends. After Simla the *qaum* knew that power lay with Jinnah. In vital Punjab, the Unionist Premier, Khizr Hyat, lost ground to the Quaid.

Intensifying his campaign, Jinnah charged that in Congress's "Hindu Raj" Muslims would suffer "a fate similar to the Jews in Germany." At the end of 1945, his words were more impassioned than ever: "I shall never allow Muslims to become slaves of Hindus." "When the time comes I shall not hesitate and shall not retrace a single step." "Mr. Gandhi and Congress tried their best to crush us, but . . . no man on earth can crush the Muslim League." "When the time for suffering comes, I will be the first to get bullet shots in my chest."[159]

His personality cast a spell over the *qaum*. The secret behind this was an amalgam of honesty, single-mindedness and consistency. The *qaum* knew that the Quaid meant what he said; that he never lost sight of his goal; and that he kept to one route. Aware of his power, Jinnah enhanced it with mannerisms. Begum Liaqat Ali has recalled:

> I have seen him shake his finger at someone and say, "You are talking nonsense: you don't know what you are talking about." They always subsided into silence. Even with [a great audience] he would use his monocle; put it to his eye, remove it and speak. All this power was asserted in spite of the barrier of language. He spoke to them in English—but they listened, bewitched.[160]

When he displayed aloofness the *qaum* called him independent and admired him; another acting like him would have been called rude and shunned. Begum Liaqat has related a story of a Jinnah visit to Baluchistan, where he had to meet hundreds of people at a garden party: "An old chieftain advanced towards Jinnah and held out his hand. Jinnah, in a sudden mood of aloofness, said, 'If I shake hands with you, I would have to shake hands with all the people here, and for that there is no time'."[161]

Not that he was indifferent to what the party activist or the common man thought. Addressing League workers in Calcutta in March 1946, he said: "I am an old man. God has given me enough. . . . Why should I turn my blood into water, run about and take so much trouble? Not for capitalists, but for you, the poor people."[162] He personally signed every receipt for a contribution to the League. "When I sign a receipt, I know that I have gained one more sympathiser for our cause," he would say.[163] In conservative areas he would make sure that his sister, who did not wear the veil, was not seated with him on the dais. And he founded a daily newspaper to assist the cause, *Dawn*. He was a shrewd and careful campaigner who realized that he did not have to curb his trait of personal aloofness: it added to his charisma.

The Quaid had few recreations. Occasionally he sought relaxation at a billiard table in his house or in a game of cards. That was all. As Bolitho puts it: "The edges of his desk were his horizon, for most of the day and night—except when he went out on speaking tours."[164] Ignoring the disease in his lungs, saying to his friends, "There is nothing serious the matter with me,"[165] toiling away hour after hour, Jinnah was consumed by his cause. It was prospering in the world outside, but inside his large house the lonely Jinnah must have felt a scarcity of intimate faces mirroring the joys of success. Mercifully, the devoted Fatima was there. The butler in the house, we may note in passing, was a Hindu.

* * *

The war was over. In London Attlee had replaced Churchill and ordered elections in India in January 1946. The results were a dramatic triumph for Jinnah. The League won all 30 Muslim seats in the Central Assembly and 427 of the 507 Muslim seats in the provincial legislatures. Nine years earlier it had been routed at the polls; nine years prior to that Jinnah had been told that he could not speak for India's Muslims. Now it was his hour of glory. There was only one place where the *qaum* had not listened to him: the North-West Frontier, where a Congress-Red Shirt alliance was once more in power. Everywhere else Jinnah, and the Pakistan call, commanded the Muslim vote. Enjoying a comparable triumph, Congress won 56 general seats in the General Assembly and 930 in the provinces, and formed eight provincial ministries. The League headed coalition governments in Bengal and Sind, where it was the largest single party. Though it had a similar position in Punjab, the League could not form a ministry there. Abul Kalam Azad, still Congress's president, succeeded in installing a Unionist-Congress-Akali coalition under the leadership of Khizr Hyat.

Attlee now announced that a Cabinet Mission would visit India to see how the New Delhi government too could become Indian. What he said next pleased the Congress ear: "We are very mindful of the rights of minorities. On the other hand, we cannot allow a minority to place a veto on the advance of the majority."[166]

Three wise men arrived on March 24: Lord Pethick-Lawrence, Secretary of State for India, a pacifist who sympathized with Indian aspirations;

Sir Stafford Cripps, President of the Board of Trade, brilliant as before but with a hazardous confidence in what Wavell would call his "ability to make both black and white appear a neutral and acceptable grey"; and A. V. Alexander, First Lord of the Admiralty.

The Mission had two aims: to convert the Viceroy's executive council into a temporary national government, and to devise a long-term constitutional solution, which meant facing the Pakistan demand. Co-opting Wavell into their team, the wise men offered Jinnah the "truncated" Pakistan of the Rajagopalachari formula, clarifying that it could be entirely sovereign and received direct from the British. The Quaid turned it down. They then proposed to him, as an alternative, autonomy within a loose Indian Union for the Pakistan that Jinnah had claimed: all of Bengal and Punjab, Assam, the North-West Frontier, Sind and Baluchistan.

Jinnah entered his objections. There should be no centre. If there had to be one, it should be composed of two bodies of equal size, one sent by the Muslim group and the other by what he called the Hindu group; and its powers should be minimal. The Muslim group should have the right to secede after five to ten years.

Congress, represented by Azad, whose hand Jinnah refused to shake, Nehru and Patel, assailed the idea of the Group's secession and of a powerless centre. Also, it pressed for a province's right to stay out of the "Pakistan" group. Congress was thinking of Assam, which had a clear Hindu majority, and the North-West Frontier, where the League had been defeated in an election in which Pakistan was a major issue. In Congress's view, these two provinces deserved the right not to join the "Pakistan" group. Jinnah fought for their "compulsory grouping." "There is no other way of fitting Assam in anywhere except in Pakistan," he said.[168] As for the North-West Frontier province, it was a Muslim province and could be nowhere else.

When it was obvious, after long weeks of talks in Simla and Delhi, that agreement was impossible, the wise men presented their brilliant—and fatally inconsistent—award. Announced on May 16, it envisaged a Union with restricted but important functions (foreign affairs, defence and communications), provinces with substantial powers, and Groups with substantial powers. It said clearly that partition was not a sound idea and proposed a Constituent Assembly elected by existing provincial legislatures. What it failed to state clearly was whether it was mandatory for Assam and the NWFP to join the "Pakistan" group. In its paragraph 15 the award said the "provinces *should be free* to form groups with executives and legislatures"; in paragraph 19 it said that representatives from the groups "*shall* proceed to settle provincial constitutions" and "*shall* also decide whether any group constitution shall be set up for those provinces."[169] The inconsistency, as we shall see, would cause great resentments.

Jinnah and the League were far from satisfied. Still, on June 6 the League accepted the scheme, though it simultaneously claimed that "the foundation of Pakistan" was "inherent" in what it saw as the plan of "compulsory grouping,' reiterated that "complete sovereign Pakistan" remained its "unalterable objective" and asserted that the plan,' "by implication," gave the Muslim Group "the opportunity and the right of secession."[170] The Raj's records disclose that Woodrow Wyatt, an aide to the Cabinet Mission, advised Jinnah that despite its dislike the League could accept the scheme "as the first step on the road to Pakistan."[171]

Congress was in two minds. It liked the award's explicit rejection of Pakistan and it also liked paragraph 15. But it was upset by a Mission statement on May 25 that Congress's interpretation of grouping did "not accord with the Delegation's intention."[172] Congress's eventual decision was influenced by another Raj statement, this time regarding the new "national government."

The Viceroy announced, on June 16, that he was inviting 14 individuals to constitute it: Jinnah and four of his League colleagues; Nehru, who had succceeded Azad as Congress president, and five additional Hindu Congressmen, of whom one was a Harijan; and three others, a Sikh, a Parsi and a Christian. What if either Congress or the League or both did not join the new government? In that case, said the Viceroy, and this was significant, the new cabinet would be "as representative as possible of those willing to accept" the constitutional award. This clause was Cripps's proposal, inserted to induce Congress and the League to accept the award.*

Jinnah did not like the proposal for the new government. Apart from the fact that Congress was being offered six places to the League's five, the Sikh, Parsi and Christian invited seemed pro-Congress. Yet he had been satisfied on a crucial point: all Muslims invited were from the League. He did not reject the proposal; he would wait for Congress's moves. He knew, as did Wavell and everyone else, that Congress would not say yes to Wavell. The exclusion of a non-League Muslim made this a certainty. If Congress did reject the Wavell proposition, and Jinnah did not, might he not lead the new government, the first Indian government following British rule?

Pethick-Lawrence and Cripps found it impossible to contemplate a

---

*The clause read: "In the event of the two major parties or either of them proving unwilling to join in the setting up of a coalition on the above lines, it is the intention of the Viceroy to proceed with the formation of an Interim Government which will be as representative as possible of those willing to accept the Statement of May 16th."[173]

transfer of authority only to the League. Without informing or consulting Alexander and Wavell, they advised ("instigated,"[174] in Wavell's word) Patel, Nehru and Azad to say yes to the constitutional scheme. Congress's leaders were told that if, while rejecting the Viceroy's cabinet proposal, they accepted the constitutional award, Cripps's clause would not only entitle them to representation in the cabinet; it would give them freedom to choose their representatives.

To let the League possess the government was more than what Congress's leaders could accept. They accepted the award instead. But, and this was crucial, they accepted it with their own interpretation, insisting that paragraph 15 gave provinces the option to stay out of the "Pakistan" group. As far as Congress was concerned, the Mission's May 25 description of what it intended was of no consequence; what mattered was the wording of paragraph 15. Gandhi, who was frontally opposed to Assam and NWFP being placed, without their prior approval, in the "Pakistan" area, had advised Congress to turn down the award. But ministerial office was beckoning; they rejected his advice.

This was on the morning of June 25. Later that day Congress's rejection of the Wavell proposal and its acceptance of the Mission's long-term award were conveyed to the Raj and to Jinnah. The Quaid's instant counter-move was to announce that the League would accept Wavell's terms and join the government he had proposed. Simultaneously, he urged the Raj to disregard Congress's "insincere" acceptance of the long-term award. He was thus asking for, and fully expecting, the installation of a Jinnah government.

It was too late. Like Jinnah, Wavell also felt that the "Congress letter of acceptance is really a dishonest acceptance." Still, the Viceroy thought that "it had to be regarded as an acceptance."[175] Once it was so regarded, Congress aquired the right, by virtue of Cripps's clause, to reopen talks with Wavell on the composition of the new government. Wavell's June 16 proposal was scrapped.

Jinnah was bitterly disappointed. Despite his worsening health, he had displayed remarkable vigilance and courage. He had subjected every item in every proposal to a searching scrutiny. He had demanded and obtained a series of commitments from Wavell and the wise men that had strengthened the League's position. Then he had climbed down and accepted the Raj's proposals. True, he held that a "complete sovereign Pakistan" was still his goal; but the fact remained that for the first time he had said yes to a proposal that did not provide for Pakistan. His switch in tactics, combined with Congress's attitude, had brought him within an inch of a great prize. Then, at the last second, the prize vanished.

He was furious. He accused Congress of dishonesty, Pethick-Lawrence and Cripps of treachery, and Wavell of betrayal. He felt that, following his acceptance of both schemes and Congress's rejection of the Wavell proposal, the Viceroy was "in honour bound" to ask Jinnah to form a government.[176] Here Jinnah was in error, as is the Pakistani writer J. Ahmad, who says, "Sir Stafford Cripps put a wrong interpretation on paragraph 8." Ahmad claims that "the plain meaning" of this paragraph—Cripps's clause—called for a League government.[177] Given the wording of Cripps's clause, however, Congress's acceptance of the constitutional award forced Wavell's hands and killed the prospect of a League government.

For all his vigilance, Jinnah had not foreseen the implications of Cripps's clause. In his resentment Jinnah charged that Cripps had "debased his talents" and placed "a fantastic and dishonest construction" on the clause.[178] This was not so, yet Jinnah was right when he accused Congress of dishonesty over the Mission scheme and he was right too in accusing Pethick-Lawrence and Cripps of collusion with Congress. Once the Mission had said that they intended compulsory grouping, Congress should have either rejected their award or accepted compulsory grouping.

The Raj could not dismiss Congress's acceptance as insincere because paragraph 15 was in fact so worded as to support the Congress position. The construction of paragraph 19, on the other hand, supported the League's position. This inconsistentcy was deliberate and was followed up, we saw, by word separately passed to both Congress and the League that acceptance did not have to be genuine. The Mission resorted to this course in order to obtain the "agreement" of both sides; they were eager to report to Attlee and the House of Commons that an Indian government was taking over in New Delhi. In fact, however, this clever attempt "to make both black and white appear a neutral and acceptable grey" did nothing to narrow the Congress-League divergence; it merely made it more bitter. Jinnah's charges of Congress's insincerity were countered by the accusation that it was Jinnah who had not accepted the Mission's scheme. Hadn't he openly indicated that he would use it as a stepping-stone to a Greater Pakistan?

Nehru now made an aggressive statement. He declared that the Union would be much stronger than the Mission seemed to envisage, that the grouping scheme would probably never come to fruition, and that the Constituent Assembly that was being formed in accordance with the Mission's scheme would have the power to alter its provisions.

Some expected Jinnah to wilt. Meeting the Quaid at this time, one of his followers thought that his "old leader seemed old indeed." "The glass shook in [Jinnah's] hand," the follower recalled later. "For the first time in all the years I had known him, he seemed subdued, as if, at last, his burdens were too much."[179]

But the follower was mistaken. Jinnah took to arms at Nehru's remarks. The League rescinded its acceptance of the Mission's award and decided upon "direct action to achieve Pakistan."[180] Muslims were asked to renounce British titles and observe a Direct Action Day. Said the Quaid:

> What we have done today is the most historic act in our history. This day we bid good-bye to constitutional methods. Throughout . . . the British and the Congress held a pistol in their hand, the one of authority and arms and the other of mass struggle and non-cooperation. Today we have also forged a pistol and we are in a position to use it.[181]

While announcing "direct action," Jinnah claimed that the League, "moved by a sense of fair play, [had] sacrificed the full sovereign state of Pakistan at the altar of the Congress for securing the independence of the whole of India."[182] This had been repaid, he said, "with defiance and contempt."

Jinnah had not defied any law but, almost for the first time in his life, he had spoken the language of disobedience. He told a League rally that he was willing to go to jail, and apparently thought that he would be arrested. A 75-year-old man rose and cried: "Quaid-i-Azam shall not go to jail. We shall offer our lives first. I offer myself to be the first to be fired on by the police, on my bare chest."[183] There is no indication, however, that the Raj intended to place Jinnah behind bars.

Direct Action day proved momentous. There was murder, arson, rape and looting in Calcutta, the capital of Bengal, where Suhrawardy led the League-dominated coalition ministry. The *Statesman*, which had defended Jinnah in his dispute with Wavell and was not inimical to the League, wrote: "The origin of the appalling carnage—we believe the worst communal riot in India's history—was a political demonstration by the Muslim League."[184] If the League ignited the killing, Hindu groups soon gained ascendancy in it. Vallabhbhai Patel wrote in a letter to Rajagopalachari: "This (the Calcutta killing) will be a good lesson for the League, because I hear that the proportion of Muslims who have suffered death is much larger."[185]

Wavell, meanwhile, had asked Nehru to bring a team into the interim ministry. Early in September, Congress's nominees, among them a Congress Muslim and two independent Muslims, were sworn in. Following an initiative of the Nawab of Bhopal, who was friendly with both Jinnah and Gandhi, the two adversaries conferred together in October 1946, their first meeting in two years. Gandhi conceded that only the League had "the unquestionable right to represent the Muslims of India"; and Jinnah finally agreed that Congressmen could have "such representatives as they think proper" in a Congress-League coalition.[186] But hearts had not really met: the two did not agree on Pakistan or on grouping.

Wavell too was discussing a coalition with the Quaid. Jinnah said the League would join, and he did not walk out when Wavell told him that the removal of Congress Muslims was not feasible—the Quaid was prepared to pay a price for power. But he sprang his surprise: among the League's nominees was Jogendra Nath Mandal, a (Hindu) Harijan from East Bengal. If Congress, as Jinnah alleged, divided the Muslims, he would split the Harijans.

Jinnah kept himself out. He would not function under Nehru. And he made it plain that joining a coalition did not mean acceptance of a Union in the long-run or a dilution of the Pakistan demand. Ispahani, Jinnah's "personal envoy" in America said: "The League's participation only means that the struggle for Pakistan will now be carried on within as well as without the government."[187] Acting as a parallel body, the League's members ignored Nehru's status as Vice-President of the Council and de facto Prime Minister. Jinnah said in a public statement: "If he (Nehru) can only come down to earth and think coolly and calmly, he must understand that he is neither the Prime Minister nor is it a Nehru government; he is only the Member for the External Affairs and Commonwealth Department."[188] From its first day the coalition government was a house at war.

* * *

December 1946. Congress insisting on the League's acceptance of a Union in the future and the League in turn pressing for compulsory grouping, H.M.G., still hoping for a compromise, invited Jinnah, Nehru and Wavell for talks in London. Conversation on the aircraft that took the three was limited but courteous. In London the talks were candid but led to no agreement. In the British cabinet, Cripps and Pethick-Lawrence seemed to support Congress's attitude; Alexander and Wavell backed the League's position. Attlee tilted the scales in Jinnah's favour. H.M.G.'s award was that provinces *had* to join their groups and abide by the constitutions that groups made for them. As Patel put it, "Jawaharlal returned almost heartbroken."[189] Patel himself was enraged. He wrote Cripps:

You know when Gandhiji was strongly against our settlement, I threw my weight in favour of it. . . . There has been a betrayal. . . . [HMG's]

interpretation means that Bengal Muslims can draw up the constitution of Assam. . . . Do you think that such a monstruous proposition
can be accepted by the Hindus of Assam?[190]

When Congress declared that, despite H.M.G.'s ruling, Assam and
NWFP were "free to act as they saw fit,"[191] Jinnah demanded the scrapping
of the Mission plan, the dissolution of the Constituent Assembly—and
Pakistan.

Ill and fatigued, he went through a nervous breakdown; for a while he
was not permitted even to listen to the news on the radio. His health
returned shortly after H.M.G. made a major move. On February 20,
1947 Attlee announced that Britain would "transfer power into responsible
Indian hands by a date not later than June 1948." He added that H.M.G.
"will have to consider to whom the powers of British India should be
handed over, on the due date, whether as a whole to some form of Central
Government or in some areas to existing provincial governments or in
such other way as may seem most reasonable.[192] Wavell would leave, said
Attlee. Lord Louis Mountbatten, cousin to the King, would be Wavell's
successor.

"This may lead to Pakistan for those provinces or portions which may
want it," said Gandhi in a letter to Nehru.[193] If Britain seemed ready to
contemplate partition, Congress's will to resist it had all but gone. Its
experience of coalition was frustrating. Congress ministers could not fill
a post or transfer an official without League opposition. Food was short
in the land and strikes were frequent, yet polarization in the cabinet and
in the bureaucracy blocked remedies. Nehru and Patel concluded that a
smaller India in which they could act freely was preferable to a "united"
India that had tied their hands. Three days before the Attlee announcement, Patel told Wavell that "he was quite prepared to let the Muslims
have the Western Punjab, and Sind and NWFP if they wished to join,
and Eastern Bengal."[194]

Attlee's word that independence might be given to the provinces trig-
gered a struggle for their control. Already running Bengal and Sind, and
able to count on Baluchistan, the League was determined to obtain the
Punjab and NWFP. An attempt it made to bring down Assam's Congress
ministry failed, but in the Muslim provinces the slogans of "Pakistan!"
and "Islam in danger," jointly raised, evoked an irresistible response. A
League-led civil disobedience campaign undermined Dr. Khan Sahib's
Red Shirt-Congress ministry in NWFP, and a similar campaign in Punjab
achieved more tangible results.

Unwilling any longer to be called a traitor to Islam, Khizr Hyat resigned on March 2. The next day the League leader in the Punjab Assembly, the Khan of Mamdot, was asked to form a ministry. The Sikhs, who had supported the Khizr ministry, regarded this as the start of oppression; their leader Master Tara Singh called for action from Sikh youths; but the Muslim guards were also ready. Killings took place in Lahore, Amritsar, Rawalpindi and Multan, futher weakening Congress's opposition to partition.

The Calcutta killing of August 1946 had been followed by the loss of Hindu lives in Noakhali in East Bengal and of Muslim lives in Bihar and U.P. Terrible brutalities marked the deaths. It looked as if the price of a united India might be a civil war. On March 5, almost three weeks before the arrival of Mountbatten, Congress's working committee, meeting without inviting or consulting Gandhi, specifically proposed the partition of Punjab and hinted at the partition of Bengal; and it clarified that the constitution that the Constituent Assembly was framing "would only apply to the areas which accept it."[195] In effect, Congress was finally conceding Pakistan.

Yet it was not the Pakistan that Jinnah was asking for. He vehemently attacked the suggestion that Punjab and Bengal be divided. Gandhi too had disliked the suggestion; he still hugged the notion of one India. He would soon see it shattered; and Jinnah too would see the splintering of the "complete" Pakistan on which he had set his heart. They met once again, not long after Mountbatten's arrival, in Jinnah's Delhi home. Their talk lasted nearly three hours and was friendly. Patel had opposed the meeting, claiming it would only enhance Jinnah's prestige. Gandhi countered that he would willingly plead "seventy times seven" if necessary.[196] Agreeing to disagree on partition, they also reiterated an appeal for peace they had jointly made earlier. The contrast in style had not lessened. Jinnah signed the appeal in English, Gandhi in Urdu, Hindi and English.

Gandhi now made a last throw to avert Pakistan. He proposed to Mountbatten that he dismiss the interim ministry and ask Jinnah to form a new one, with full freedom to choose his team and work for Pakistan. Ten years earlier he was unwilling to provide Jinnah with a say at the expense of Nehru and Patel. Now he was prepared to think of sacrificing them. Congress, said Gandhi, would pledge not to use its majority in the Central Assembly to block a Jinnah-led government, as long as Mountbatten thought that the latter was acting in India's interests.

A Jinnah-Mountbatten duumvirate was not what Congress's leaders were willing to accept. According to Azad, "both Jawaharlal and Patel opposed (the suggestion) vehemently (and) in fact forced Gandhiji to withdraw (it)."[197] Would Jinnah, who never trusted Congress's assurances, have accepted the proposal? Chaudhri Muhammad Ali thinks not; but Stanley Wolpert, Jinnah's recent biographer, speaks of Gandhi's "singularly generous offer" and says: "It might just have worked; surely this was a King Solomon solution."[198] It was not, in any case, put to Jinnah.

We need not go here into the well-known details of the Mountbatten Plan that was finally accepted by all parties. Jinnah denounced a truncated Pakistan but settled for it. He asked for "a corridor to link East and West Pakistan"; the demand was turned down.[199] (He did get all the Muslim-majority areas, including NWFP, where a referendum went in Pakistan's favour.) "Better a moth-eaten Pakistan than no Pakistan," he would say.[200] Mountbatten had frankly told the Quaid that "the only alternative was to keep India completely united."[201] According to Chaudhri Muhammad Ali, Prime Minister of Pakistan from 1955 to 1956, Mountbatten's diplomatic skill also played a part. Jinnah and Liaqat Ali, and Congress's leaders, says Chaudhri Muhammad Ali, were "captivated by this glamorous scion of royalty."[202] Adds Chaudhri Muhammad Ali:

> Even a man with the cold dignity and reserve of Jinnah spoke in unusually warm terms about Mountbatten. . . . Mountbatten did not reciprocate Jinnah's sentiments . . . but Jinnah was unaware of it. . . . [Mountbatten] won the confidence of both the leaders of Congress and the Muslim League by denouncing the one to the other. At the very time when he was wooing Congress leaders day and night, he was portraying them to Jinnah as unreasonable men.[203]

Jinnah accepted a truncated Pakistan because he could do nothing else; the arguments with which the League demanded Pakistan were the very ones that clinched the division of Punjab and Bengal. Still, the Quaid refused to give his consent in writing.

He was not going to abandon his "intransigent and unbending posture"—to use the phrase of Chaudhri Muhammad Ali, who lauds the attitude as having been crucial to "the battle for Pakistan."[204] Jinnah did not yield even when Mountbatten, desirous of his signature, rubbed in the warning that in a "completely united India" Muslims would be "at the mercy of the Hindus."[205] Jinnah's reaction to this menacing picture has been recorded by Mountbatten's press attache, Alan Campbell-Johnson: "Jinnah [was] very calm and said simply that he could not stop such a step in any event. . . . The *ballon d'essai* had gone up and come down again, providing only the evidence that Jinnah has a very steady nerve."[206] Jinnah did not sign but, as we all know, his nod sufficed.

On August 7, 1947 Jinnah flew from Delhi to Karachi, the temporary capital of the nation he had created. Before stepping into the plane, he looked back toward the city where he had debated, negotiated and battled for over three decades, the city from where sons of the *qaum* had ruled India for centuries, and reflected aloud: "I suppose this is the last time I'll be looking at Delhi." As the aircraft taxied out, he said, "That's the end of that."[207] On the plane he was silent. When the Dakota descended from the Karachi skies, Jinnah saw that tens of thousands were waiting for him and he "suddenly became buoyant and quite young." He and Fatima drove past great and jubilant crowds. Walking up the steps of Karachi's Government House—he had decided to accept the role of the new Dominion's Governor-General—he said to an A.D.C.: "Do you know, I never expected to see Pakistan in my lifetime. We have to be very grateful to God for what we have achieved."[208]

A note of surprise, not unmixed with regret, is conveyed by more than one Pakistani account of these dramatic events. Chaudhri Muhammad Ali follows up a reference to Congress's March 1947 resolution in favour of dividing Punjab and Bengal with the comment: "The die was cast; the partition of India had become inevitable."[209] Ikram, the Pakistani historian who was a senior civil servant at the time of partition, speaks of Congress's attitude to the Cabinet Mission's award and says: "Those who were in touch with the Quaid state that it was this behaviour which clinched the issue of Pakistan."[210] According to Ikram, Attlee's selection of Mountbatten as Wavell's successor was "a master-stroke for the achievement of the Congress-Labour objectives."[211] The suggestion is that August 1947 saw the fulfillment of Congress's goals, not the League's. Chaudhri Muhammad Ali calls Jinnah's acceptance of the Mission's plan a "courageous and far-reaching decision." With this decision, according to Chaudhri Muhammad Ali, "it appeared that the Hindu-Muslim difference had been amicably solved."[212]

Jinnah's own statement, quoted earlier, that in accepting the Mission plan he had "sacrificed the full sovereign state of Pakistan" out of a "sense of fair play," suggests something similar. Such views imply that, the Lahore resolution notwithstanding, Pakistan was not Jinnah's inflexible aim; and also that if Congress had been statesmanlike over the Mission's plan, Pakistan would not and need not have come into being. Thus Sharif Al Mujahid, the Pakistani scholar, asserts that "had (Congress) accepted unreservedly the Cabinet Mission plan, the Pakistan demand might have, in all probability, lost its force and fury."[213]

In the opinion of Chaudhri Muhammad Ali, Congress "quibbled" over the Cabinet Mission plan because "Hindu leaders" could not show even "a little generosity of spirit" and were not "ready to live in partnership with Muslims without grasping for total power."[214] While acknowledging the Mahatma's "humanitarian impulse," Chaudhri Muhammad Ali accuses him of desiring Hindu rule over the whole sub-continent." He speaks, too, of Gandhi's "strategy aimed at reducing the territories of Pakistan," and of his "endeavours to clothe Hindu ambition in terms of love and unity."[215] Making a similar point, Jinnah told Mountbatten that the Hindus always wanted "seventeen annas in the rupee."[216]

Whether or not Hindu rule was Gandhi's aim, and Congress's, is outside the scope of this study. It should suffice here to note that the charge was denied. What is indisputable is that Gandhi and Congress were opposed to the compulsory grouping of NWFP and Assam in the "Pakistan" area of the Mission plan, and that this opposition, along with Nehru's provocative remarks, killed the plan.

Chaudhri Muhammad Ali thinks that this stand was an outcome of a "passion for rule by the Hindu majority over the whole sub-continent."[217] However, there is another explanation. Congress feared that compulsory grouping would not be the end of the long and unhappy story. It suspected that the League would treat compulsory grouping as a half-way house to "complete sovereign Pakistan." The League had said as much when it first accepted the Mission plan. Mindful of the possible secession of the Pakistan area, Congress opposed the placing of Assam and NWFP in it. As Patel said in his letter to Cripps after H.M.G.'s decision in favour of compulsory grouping: "Jinnah swears by Pakistan and everything conceded to him is to be used as a lever to that end."[218]

Jinnah had a case when he argued, though not in so many words, that Pakistan had to be large enough if it was not going to be sovereign. Referring to this, Abul Kalam Azad conceded, "There was force in Mr. Jinnah's contention."[219] What Jinnah did not do was to persuade Congress that compulsory grouping would be the last chapter. He did not even try. With him personally, given his age and the state of his health, compulsory grouping was doubtless going to be the end of the story: *his* claim of sacrifice was honest. But the League's statement that "complete sovereign Pakistan" remained its ultimate goal made Congress suspicious.

All three parties, the Raj, Congress and the League, were guilty of a lack of frankness. The Raj seemed to want compulsory grouping but did not say so clearly. Congress said it "accepted" the Mission's plan while rejecting what seemed essential to it. The League was willing to settle for something less than Pakistan, but said the opposite. It is noteworthy that no one, whether from the Raj or an Indian side, directly asked Jinnah, in the presence of Gandhi or Nehru, whether he would give up a sovereign Pakistan if he received a "Pakistan zone" composed of all the provinces he wanted; and noteworthy, likewise, that no one directly asked Gandhi or Nehru, in Jinnah's presence, if Congress would let Assam and NWFP go to a "Pakistan zone" if Jinnah yielded a sovereign Pakistan.

* * *

The Jinnah-Congress contest for territory was not always governed by the two-nation principle. Congress, on its part, had never accepted the principle; all it had finally conceded was that Muslim-majority areas could form Pakistan if they wanted to. As for the Quaid, he did not believe that Pakistan had to be confined to Muslim-majority areas. H.M.G. having left the choice of independence or merger to either dominion to the rulers of princely states, Jinnah tried to persuade some rulers of Hindu-majority states bordering Punjab and Sind to join Pakistan. He was unsuccessful. The Sikh ruler of Patiala has stated that Jinnah also sought Sikh support.[220] In Chaudhri Muhammad Ali's words, "Jinnah time and again assured the Sikhs that their rights would be fully safeguarded and their claims dealt with generously."[221] According to J. Ahmad, "In the final stages of negotiations for the transfer of power, the Muslim League leadership went all out to placate the Sikhs and accommodate their wishes." As Ahmad says, "There was no response from the Sikhs."[222]

The stretch of 1947 that began with the last days of June and ended with the end of September—and took in the independence of India and the birth of Pakistan—pains anyone touching it. Khaliquzzaman calls it "the blackest period in Indian history."[223] Man became fiendish. Neighbours slaughtered one another. Children and pregnant women were pitilessly done to death. Multitudes left their homes and crossed the new Indo-Pak border. Muslims went one way; Hindus and Sikhs the other way.

Bolitho has described Jinnah's condition at the time. "He was still in his house in Delhi when the reports of slaughter were brought to him. But he was helpless, exhausted by the long struggle of words, already emaciated by his stealthy disease, and unable to lessen the agony."[224] According to Khaliquzzaman, who met Jinnah in Delhi on August 1, the Quaid was "disconcerted as never before" and unable to answer "questions concerning the Muslims who would be left over in India."[225] A month after Pakistan's emergence, Suhrawardy, who had lost Bengal's Premiership following the province's partition, felt that "the Muslims in the Indian Union have been left high and dry."[226]

At least once, however, Jinnah's helplessness gave way to a smile. On August 15, on the first morning following the creation of Pakistan, an A.D.C. saw the "the Quaid went to the balcony, where he could not be seen, to look at the members of the cabinet (who had gathered to be sworn in) and the crowds beyond." Then, adds the A.D.C., "he smiled." It was the first time that the A.D.C. had "seen a look of happiness on [Jinnah's] face." It was the smile of triumph, and it was deserved. However, the Quaid quickly suppressed it and "went through the ceremony without showing any emotion."[227]

Four days earlier, in an address Pakistan's Constituent Assembly as its first president, Jinnah had made a remarkable utterance:

> If you change your past and work together in the spirit that every one of you, no matter to what community he belongs, is first, second and last a citizen of this state with equal rights . . . there will be no end to the progress you will make. . . . I cannot emphasize it too much. We should begin to work in that spirit and in [the] course of time all these angularities of the majority and minority communities, the Hindu community and the Muslim community . . . will vanish. We should keep that in front of us as our ideal and you will find that in [the] course of time Hindus would cease to be Hindus and Muslims will cease to be Muslims, not in the religious sense, because that is the personal faith of each individual, but in the political sense as citizens of the state.[228]

Bolitho calls this "the greatest speech of his life."[229] Yet it contradicted Jinnah's words in Lahore when the League first asked for a Muslim homeland. "It is a dream," Jinnah had said, "that the Hindus and Muslims can ever evolve a common nationality."[230] According to Khaliquzzaman, Jinnah "bade goodbye to his two-nation theory" with his August 11 speech.[231] Agreeing, Naim asserts that Jinnah "negated" the two-nation theory "in no uncertain terms" with the speech.[232] In Merriam's words: "The preservation of national unity, which had been one of Gandhi's primary goals before Partition, became a major objective for Jinnah after Partition." Adds Merriam: "Once in power, Jinnah made an about-face in his approach to Hindu-Muslim relations"[233] M.S.M. Sharma, a Karachi-based Hindu journalist who did not leave Pakistan until a year after its creation, has recorded a conversation with Jinnah:

> The long and short of his lecture to me was just this. Now that he had got Pakistan, he had no longer any grudge against the Hindus. In fact he was anxious to revert to his old and familiar role of "Ambassador of Hindu-Muslim unity." "Now, my dear fellow," he roared, "I am going to constitute myself the Protector-General of the Hindu-minority in Pakistan."[234]

His confidence in himself—in his ability, among other things, to protect Pakistan's Hindus and Sikhs—had taken precedence over the Jinnah trait of unyielding consistency. Of Jinnah's reaction to a riot in Karachi in which Hindus suffered, Sharma writes: "In fairness to Jinnah I must record that he was the most shocked individual. . . . He visited the Hindu refugee camps and at least at one of them the iron man lost his nerve and shed a few tears."[235]

Karachi's mayor at the time, a Parsi who was one of Jinnah's friends, had accompanied the Quaid to the camp. He has recalled: "When he saw their (the Hindus') misery, he wept. I saw tears on his cheek."[236] The exodus of Sind's Hindus made him unhappy. He was unable to arrest it but that he had hoped that Hindus and Sikhs would stay on in Pakistan is of significance.

So is the effort Jinnah evidently made, some months after Pakistan's birth, to "convert the Muslim League," of which he continued to be President, into a "non-communal and national organization whose membership would be thrown open to all citizens regardless of religion."[237] Though the words are Sharma's, we should note that Ikram believes his account to be "substantially correct."[238] And in December 1947, *Dawn*, which went with Jinnah to Karachi, quoted the Quaid as saying: "The decision to form a purely Muslim organisation in Pakistan is not irrevocable. It may be altered as and when necessary."[239]

He also appeared to melt a little towards Gandhi. According to Sharma, he told the League council "that Mr. Gandhi was a true friend of the Muslims and that the Muslims of India should stand solidly by him."[240]

In his talks with Jinnah after Pakistan's birth, Sharma glimpsed the idealism that Sarojini Naidu had sensed thirty years earlier. "Jinnah's highest ambition in life," Sharma felt, "was a hazy notion that he must be hailed as a born deliverer of men from bondage."[241] The idealism needed the glow of pre-eminence. When the lamps faded, the idealist in Jinnah withdrew. When Pakistan came into being and the light shone on its unquestioned leader, the idealist found his voice.

* * *

We have seen that in his new nation—the fifth most populous in the world and the biggest Muslim state—Jinnah headed the state, the legislature (the Constituent Assembly was Pakistan's first parliament) and the ruling party. Also, he personally chose the first Prime Minister (Liaqat Ali) and the rest of the cabinet; and he reserved for himself the affairs of Kashmir, over which a bitter and costly Indo-Pak dispute would soon begin, and of the sensitive Frontier areas. As a Pakistani scholar, Saleem Qureshi, puts it, "Not only did the conventions of parliamentary government not apply to Jinnah, the Constituent Assembly further expanded the powers of the Governor-General."[242] We should note, in passing, that the Constituent Assembly formally resolved that he should be addressed as "Quaid-i-Azam" in all official acts, documents, letters and correspondence.[243]

Yet, as Qureshi correctly adds, "This concentration and personalization of authority need not be attributed to lust for power or glory, for as the Quaid-i-Azam of Muslim India, Jinnah had both."[244] No one objected to Jinnah's powers; they seemed to flow naturally from his status. The immediate past set the style. To quote Qureshi again:

> The need for Muslims to speak with one voice and the confrontational nature of the politics of the League, whether in dealing with the British or Congress, had necessitated the subordination of many views to the one authoritative view, expressed always, and only, by Jinnah himself. . . . Jinnah conducted the affairs of the government of Pakistan as he had been accustomed to conducting those of the Muslim League.[245]

As Chaudhri Muhammad Ali says, "Even if Jinnah had not occupied any official position in Pakistan, those in authority would have turned to him for guidance."[246] Jinnah and the League had rejected a proposal that Mountbatten should serve as Pakistan's and India's common Governor-General. There were three reasons. A common Governor-General would dilute the sense of separation. Secondly, Jinnah had begun to lose faith in Mountbatten's impartiality. Finally, the League could not see the Quaid taking the second place in the warrant of precedence; that Jinnah's writ would run was not enough.

Often he presided over cabinet meetings, where he would listen, decide and explain. Occasionally he exploded at stupidity. Chaudhri Muhammad Ali, who headed Pakistan's bureaucracy at the time, found that Jinnah "carefully and conscientiously read every paper submitted to him" and that "not detail escaped him."[247] He set high norms of industry and integrity but had neither the time nor the energy to sketch out a constitution for the land he had created. However, he did leave behind some significant thoughts:

> I do not know what the ultimate shape of [our] constitution is going to be, but I am sure it will be of a democratic type, embodying the essential principles of Islam. Islam and its idealism have taught us demmocracy. . . . In any case, Pakistan is not going to be a theocratic state—to be ruled by priests with a divine mission. We have many non-Muslims—Hindus, Christians and Parsis—but they are all Pakistanis. They will enjoy the same rights and privileges as any other citizen.[248]

In 1941 Jinnah had said in Madras, "Thank God Hindi did not go very far here."[249] However, feeling that his new nation's unity depended on a national language, he urged East Pakistan to accept Urdu. Bengali had its place in the prorvince but only Urdu "embodying the best . . . in Islamic culture,"[250] could be the common language of the two wings. The stand provoked oppostion: "We are Muslims, we are Pakistanis," stressed the Quaid; he warned of "Indian propagandists and their agents in our midst,"[251] but the resistance did not disappear, and Jinnah saw the ominous face of Bangla dissent before he died.

* * *

We must now touch on beautiful Kashmir, 80 percent Muslim, ruled by a Hindu prince, bordering both Pakistan and India, the source of important rivers. Jawaharlal Nehru, descended from Kashmiri Brahmins, loved the region. Sheikh Muhammed Abdullah, Kashmir's popular leader, liked Nehru and was pro-India. Jinnah, on his part, was sure of "Kashmir's accession to Pakistan because of its Muslim population and geographical situtation."[252] According to Chaudhri Muhammad Ali, Jinnah used to say, "Kashmir will fall into our laps like a ripe fruit."[253]

H.M.G. had left the choice to the ruler, Maharaja Hari Singh, who vacillated. He was not pro-India. Indians feared he would opt for indepenence or Pakistan; Pakistanis were afraid that being a Hindu he might join India. "The Quaid-i-Azam himself," recalls Chaudhri Muhammad Ali, "wanted to go to Kashmir about the middle of September; he hoped to have a friendly talk with the Maharaja, but the Maharaja did not want him to come."[254]

On October 24, 1947, five thousand guerrillas from Pakistan's tribal areas crossed the Pakistan-Kashmir border. India later alleged that Pakistan had planned the attack. The charge was denied, but Chaudhri Muhammad Ali has admitted that Pakistani authorities knew of the assault before it took place. He writes:

> On October 21, Liaquat Ali Khan told me in a state of unusual excitement that a tribal lashkar, some thousands strong, was on the way to Kashmir. I asked him if he had informed the Quaid-i-Azam and he said, "Not yet," as he had just received the report.

Chaudhri Muhammad Ali adds: "There was nothing the Pakistani government could do about it." Chaudhri Muhammad Ali's account of what followed is also of interest:

> The tribal lashkar . . . quickly overpowered the state forces, and by October 26 had reached the vicinity of Srinagar, the capital of Kash-

mir. The previous night the Maharaja fled from Srinagar to Jammu. Had the tribal lashkar been more disciplined, and had it not indulged in plunder on its way, it would have been in occupation of the Kashmir valley on October 26.[255]

The tribesmen's arrival ended Hari Singh's indecision. Acceding to India, he asked for Indian troops, which flew into the valley and pushed back the tribesmen.

From Lahore, where he was at the time, Jinnah ordered General Gracey, acting Commander-in-Chief of the Pakistan army, to send troops into Kashmir. Gracey contacted Field-Marshal Sir Claude Auchinleck, who had stayed on to oversee the partition of the Indian Army and was in charge of all the British officers that had remained, whether on the Indian or the Pakistani side. Auchinleck told Gracey that the presence of Indian troops in Kashmir was justified, since the Maharaja had accceded. Any action by the Pakistani army, added Auchinleck, would force him to withdraw all British officers. Jinnah abandoned the move for the time being, but in April 1948 he sent regular troops into Kashmir. "The turn of events in Kashmir had an adverse effect on the Quaid-i-Azam's health," writes Chaudhri Muhammad Ali. "His earlier optimism gave way to a deep disappointment. 'We have been put on the wrong bus,' he remarked."[256]

* * *

He was in bed in Lahore for much of November. In Karachi Colonel Birnie, a British officer who was Jinnah's military secretary, referred, in his diary, to Jinnah's illness and added: "Everything is at a standstill . . . . Even the Ministers are devastated as they can get no decisions on anything."[257] When Jinnah returned to Karachi, Birnie was "definitely shocked" at the Quaid's appearance. He observed: "Jinnah left here looking sixty years of age. Now he looks well over eighty."[258]

However, the spirit inside had continued to fight. Jinnah had proposed to Mountbatten that the two Governors-General "should be vested with full powers to restore peace" in Kashmir and to arrange the plebiscite that Nehru had promised.[259] Nehru did not agree, but early in January 1948 he took the Kashmir dispute to the United Nations, complaining of Pakistani support to the attacking tribesmen. Jinnah lodged a comprehensive counter-complaint.

In the middle of January Gandhi went on a fast to obtain redress for wrongs suffered by the Muslims of Delhi at Hindu and Sikh hands. When he learned that the Government of India was withholding payment of fifty-five crore rupees due to Pakistan, the Mahatma said that the sum had to be transferred. The Indian cabinet and Delhi's Hindu and Sikh leaders met Gandhi's terms. He ended the fast on its sixth day. Twelve days later, on January 30, 1948, Gandhi was assassinated by a member of an extremist Hindu group.

Publicly Jinnah spoke of Gandhi as "one of the greatest men produced by the Hindu community," but in private he also "acknowledged how great was the loss for the Moslems."[260] The assassination affected his opposition to a proposal Colonel Birnie had been making for some time. The military secretary wanted a high wall that would screen the portion of Karachi's Government House that the Quaid used. "No harm would come to me," Jinnah had always said, adding, "Anyhow, it is a waste of money." On the evening of January 30, after hearing the Gandhi news, Jinnah said to Birnie: "About that wall—you can start building it immediately."[261]

*   *   *

"Jinnah was very careful with his money, some would say miserly, for he seldom parted with his own money except in personal pursuits," says Saleem Qureshi.[262] Ispahani, Pakistan's ambassador to the United States and one who often saw Jinnah at close quarters, found that "throughout his life the investments [Jinnah] made were . . . shrewd" and profitable. Adds Ispahani: "It is true that he was not too generous with his money in his lifetime."[263] We saw above that he was frugal with public money as well. Many have referred to this trait, including Ispahani, who was struck by the fact that Jinnah was constantly "switching off unwanted lights in the Governor-General's house.[264] Yet, as was revealed after his death, the thrifty Quaid was not without a sense of duty to others. In Ispahani's words, "He had bequeathed a large sum of his hard-earned money [to] several eduational and other institutions."[265] Among the beneficiaries was Aligarh Muslim University.

"Sentiment had to give way to discipline." As Ispahani notes, this was a Jinnah motto. The Quaid's remorseless adherence to it at times left his admirers "rudely shocked and tongue-tied." An instance was Jinnah's response to a suggestion that he visit a prominent League figure who had been hospitalized. If he took to visiting the sick and ailing, said Jinnah, he would be doing little else. "After uttering these words," writes Ispahani, "Jinnah switched his attention back to the pile of papers."[266]

"He never, if he could help it, compromised," observed Sir Francis Mudie, Governor of Punjab after Pakistan's creation and, as such, Jinnah's host when the Governor-General was in Lahore. Still, Mudie could say: "Jinnah impressed me more, I think, than anyone else I have ever met, and I was very fond of him."[267]

R. A. Casey, Governor of Bengal in the mid-forties, offered this assessment: "He holds his cards very close to the chest. He is not a 'warm' man . . . . He is dogmatic and sure of himself; I would believe that it does not ever occur to him that he might be wrong." Casey added, however, that "there is something in his eye that hints at a sense of humour."[268] Jinnah's "iron discipline"—Casey's phrase[269]—kept this sense buried most of the time. Roger Hicks, an Englishman associated wtih Moral Re-Armament who saw something of Jinnah in London in December 1946, twice glimpsed it. Witnessing a meeting of the House of Commons, Jinnah smiled when an M.P. cracked a joke against himself. The second occasion was at a play, "The Forgotten Factor." A character on the stage, holding a newspaper, read a headline aloud: " 'WILL NOT BUDGE'." The Quaid laughed.[270]

When Wavell was asked for his opinion of Jinnah, the former Viceroy sighed and said, "He was a very difficult man to deal with."[271] Also finding him hard, Mountbatten did, however, once say to his Press Attache, "You know, I like the old boy, really."[272] A man like Auchinleck "admired" Jinnah's "inexorable determination."[273] This determination thwarted Gandhi's one-India bid, yet the Mahatma called the Quaid "a good man" in 1944 and "a great Indian" in 1946.[274] Earlier, in the late twenties, Gandhi had described Jinnah and Sir Tej Bahadur Sapru as "the two cleverest lawyers of India."[275]

The *qaum* loved him and was proud of him. Because of him Muslims inherited a part of the subcontinent. It looked as if even a light push would topple the thin old man. In reality his spirit had the strength and stability of granite, and his mind the sharp edge of a razor. He did not budge, no matter what the threat, fear or inducement; and he did not let adversaries get the better of him in argument or negotiation.

That he was a Shia in a *qaum* with a large Sunni majority did not hurt him. He and the League successfully used the slogan of "One God, one Book, one Prophet." The formula that removed the *qaum's* misgivings in this regard was one that has been used in all ages and places: "We will side with brothers against cousins, and with cousins against outsiders."

Jinnah did not break bread or crack jokes with the common man, yet neither did he shame Muslim masses with accusations of backwardness. Sayyid Ahmad Khan, the reformer, had done that, to his cost. Jinnah did not exhort them to alter their ways; he only asked for their support for political aims. Aware that his unbending posture strengthened the League, the Muslim masses, as we have seen, not only forgave the posture, they admired him for it.

He was not a religious or social reformer, or a religious or social thinker, but Saleem Qureshi exaggerates when he says that "Jinnah seems to have altogether lacked an inner life."[276] We know that Sarojini Naidu had recognized Jinnah's interior idealistic impulse when he was in his late thirties; and we have seen that it was never extinguished. Let us look, at this stage, at two additional instances where the impulse showed itself.

In March 1948, when bitterness over Kashmir was fresh, Jinnah was asked by Eric Streiff of the *Neue Zurcher Zeitung* if Pakistan and India would cooperate against any outside aggression. Replied Jinnah:

> Personally, I have no doubt in my mind that it . . . is of vital importance to Pakistan and India as independent sovereign states to collaborate in a friendly way jointly to defend their frontiers.

> But this depends entirely on whether Pakistan and India can resolve their own differences in the first instance . . . . If we can put our own house in order internally, we may be able to play a very great part externally in all international affairs.[277]

The other instance is a radio broadcast he made on Eid Day in November 1939. Said Jinnah:

> If we have faith in love and toleration towards God's children, to whatever community they may belong, we must act upon that faith in the daily round of our simple duties . . . . No injunction is considered by our Holy Prophet more imperative or divinely binding than the devout but supreme realisation of our duty of love and toleration toward all other human beings.[278]

* * *

In the early months of 1948 Jinnah permitted himself a few long-denied luxuries. He would sit in the garden of Government House, contemplate, and even enjoy a short nap in the open. Or he would bend down and pick a flower. But he was not avoiding work. Callers found him "surrounded by mounds of files."[279] He minutely examined every Bill requiring his signature. Often he would return it, demanding clearer language.

In April 1948 he was too ill to work at his desk. He would lie on the sofa in his Government Houe suite, reading newspapers, official documents, and yards of teleprinter tape. The following month he moved to the hill town of Ziarat, seventy-odd miles from Quetta. But it was not a holiday. Black despatch-boxes, the initials M.A.J. stamped on them, arrived daily, and the Quaid studied their contents. An A.D.C., who was in Ziarat said afterwards: "My clearest memory of him is of his slim hands, busy with papers."[280] Another aide remembers that Jinnah could be sharp-tempered but also willing to apologize. "I am old and weak and sometimes I am impatient," he would say. "I hope you will forgive my bad manners."[281]

Toward the end of July the doctor that Fatima had summoned, Colonel Ilahi Baksh, found that the Quaid's lungs were dangerously diseased. He gave Jinnah and his sister "the grave news" but the Government was not immediately informed. When Liaqat Ali Khan came to Ziarat and asked the doctor what he suspected, Baksh avoided a clear answer. Next morning Jinnah said to Baksh: "What did the Prime Minister ask you about me?" When Baksh answered that he had told the Premier nothing, Jinnah said: "Congratulations. I, as head of state, will tell the nation about the nature and gravity of my illness when I think proper."[282]

On July 29 the Nursing Superintendent of Quetta's Civil Hospital, an Englishwoman called Phyllis Dunham, arrived to nurse Jinnah. The Quaid did not like the idea but gave in. On August 9 he was shifted from Ziarat's risky altitude to Quetta. At one point it looked as if he was improving, but on August 29 he said to Dr. Baksh. "You know, when you first came to Ziarat, I wanted to live. Now, however, it does not matter whether I live or die."[283] The doctor saw that there were tears in the Quaid's eyes as he spoke.

On September 11 the Governor-General's Viking arrived in Quetta to take him to Karachi. To avoid alarm the journey was kept secret; the Prime Minister was informed but asked not to come to the airport.

Karachi, where Jinnah was born some 72 years earlier, went about its business as the Viking landed and the Quaid was carried out on a stretcher and into an army ambulance. On its way into town, shortly after passing a crowded refugee settlement, the vehicle broke down. Sixty minutes went by before another ambulance arrived from Karachi.

During that hour the Governor-General, whom everyone called the Great Leader and honoured as the Father of the Nation, lay as helpless as any dying refugee in the slum his ambulance had just driven past. Flies attacked him. Sister Dunham found a piece of cardboard and fanned Jinnah's face to keep the flies away. After some minutes, Jinnah lifted a hand and placed it on Sister Dunham's arm. He did not speak but "there was such a look of gratitude in his eyes," as Sister Dunham was afterward to say.[284] The second ambulance took him to Government House where, finally, he was put on his bed. At 10:20 that night he breathed his last.

CHAPTER 6

FAZLUL HUQ

(1873–1962)

Writing in 1937 to Linlithgow, the Viceroy, the Governor of Bengal, Sir John Anderson, said that Fazlul Huq was "the most uncertain quantity in Muslim politics, completely devoid of principle and trusted by nobody."[1] In 1940 Huq moved the League's crucial resolution at Lahore; two years later Jinnah attacked him as a "treacherous person doing incalculable harm to the Muslims of Bengal."[2] Others, however, have hailed Huq as the toiler's friend and Bengal's tiger; he has been called "a giant of the sub-continent,"[3] "a wizard politician"[4] and an "eagle-eyed statesman."[5]

Abul Kasem Fazlul Huq was born on October 26 1873 in his mother's village, Saturia, in Barisal district in what is now Bangladesh. For much of the 19th century, most Bengali Muslims stayed out, or were kept out, of the Raj's schools, colleges and offices. Their poverty and conservatism and the Raj's distrust came in the way. Thus, no Muslim name occurs in the Bengal government's lists of the 1845–52 period of persons qualified for its jobs.[6]

However, Huq's immediate forebears were neither poor nor conservative. His father Muhammad Wazid, a resident of Barisal district's Chakhar village, was given an "English" education; he became Bengal's third Muslim graduate and the second Muslim in the province to obtain a law degree. The Raj made Wazid a government pleader in Barisal town, a position in which he thrived, and in due course he was elected vice-chairman of the district board "by the joint votes of the Hindu and Muslim members."[7]

Wazid's son, the subject of our study, received Arabic, Persian and Urdu lessons at home and went to school in Barisal before he was sent to Calcutta, where he read mathematics and law and evidently helped found the Mohammedan Sporting football club. His academic performance was exceptional and he was made an M.A. (Math.) examiner. But he chose law as his profession and was articled to the eminent educator and jurist, Sir Asutosh Mookerjee.

Wazid's death in 1901 took Huq back to Barisal, where he managed the properties his father had left, practised law, joined the municipal committee, started a journal for the youth, taught mathematics part-time, and raised a family. His wife Khurshid Begum, a wealthy landowner's daughter, bore him two girls. One of Khurshid Begum's brothers was Syed Hussain, who assisted Motilal Nehru as private secretary and after independence became India's ambassador to Egypt. A sister of Khurshid Begum married Sir Hasan Suhrawardy, the first Muslim vice-chancellor of Calcutta University; Sir Hasan's nephew, H.S. Suhrawardy, would enter Huq's later years as, alternately, a foe and an ally.

Huq was made for politics and oratory. Possessing a rich voice, fluent in Bengali, English and Urdu and cultivating a rhythmic delivery, he backed the call for Bengal's partition, a Muslim demand for which Sir Salimullah, the Nawab of Dacca, was the chief spokesman. In 1905 the demand was conceded, and Dacca became the capital of the new province of East Bengal and Assam.

Barisal was too small for Huq. In 1906 he went to Dacca for the launching of the Muslim League, at which he was asked to help write the body's constitution. In Dacca Sir Bampfylde Fuller, Governor of the new province, offered him a deputy Magistrate's post; Huq took it and served in Dacca, Jamalpur and Madaripur. Following Congress's vigorous campaign against it, Bengal's partition was annulled by the Raj in 1911. Resenting the annulment, and resenting also the appointment of another to a position he had coveted, Huq quite the Raj's service and went to Calcutta. Mookerjee welcomed him back to the Bar, where Huq's progress was rapid.

* * *

He also ascended the political ladder. In 1913 he won the Dacca division seat in the Bengal Provincial Council, where his speaking prowess was immediately noted, and was also elected general secretary of the Bengal Muslim League. A university in Dacca was one of the things he and the Bengal League were asking for; it would be founded in 1921. Salimullah died in 1914 and Huq found himself the Bengal League's president. In

his presidential address he defended the separate Muslim electorate that
the Raj had provided for.[8] But he added:

> The principles inculcated by the League are gradually losing their
> sectarian character and are becoming less and less the creed of a party
> and more and more the faith of a united Indian nation.[9]

In essence the speech was a warning to the Raj not to take Muslims for
granted. Recalling the annulment of Bengal's partition, Huq said that "the
feelings of an entire community had been trampled under foot" and that
the Muslims had been treated "like valueless pawns on the political chess-
board, to be mercilessly sacrificed for the requirements of political expediency."[10] Claiming that "the absence of our community from the political
platform" had thus far been "the sheet anchor of the official defence . . .
from the onslaughts of the Indian National Congress,"[11] Huq hinted that
the League would join hands with Congress if the Raj was not responsive
to Muslim pleas.

The threat was implemented in two years. Events involving Turkey
had turned India's Muslims against Britain. At the end of 1916, Huq
playing an important part, Congress and the League entered into the
Lucknow pact. Congress accepted the separate Muslim electorate and
weightage for Muslims in the Hindu-majority provinces; in exchange the
League agreed to weightage for Hindus and Sikhs in Punjab and for
Hindus in Bengal, and the two bodies decided jointly to press India's
claims.

We saw earlier that the premier Muslim figure in Lucknow was Jinnah,
the League's president for the year, but Huq's role should not be under-
estimated. As Bengal's leading Muslim he had much to lose in conceding
weightage to the province's Hindus. Still, he took the difficult step. Influenced in part by his example, Punjab's Muslim delegates in Lucknow
also accepted weightage for their province's Hindus and Sikhs. Huq had
gambled: he hoped to gain on an all-India stage the place he was consciously risking in Bengal. In Lucknow he spoke as an Indian rather than
as a Muslim or a Bengali, and he exuded optimism:

> Hindus and Muslims should stand united and use every constitutional
> and legitimate means to effect the transfer of power . . . to democracy.
> India has, I believe, turned a corner. . . . The promised land is within
> sight.[12]

It looked as if the gamble was paying off. In 1918 Huq became the
League's president. Joining Congress as well, something that many Mus-

lims did at this time, he was made that body's general secretary. The following year he chaired a session of the Bengal Congress and was appointed a member of Congress's committee inquiring into the Jallianwalla tragedy.

* * *

Enviably, he had found niches of importance in Congress, the League and a council of the Raj. Jinnah, who was three years younger, had done likewise. Both were successful lawyers but there was a difference. Unlike Jinnah, who chose not to mix with the masses, Huq cultivated Bengal's peasants, speaking their language and opposing Bengal's landlords on their behalf. This activity had led to the emergence, in 1917, of a Calcutta Agricultural Association.[13]

In 1919 this difference between Jinnah and Huq did not seem significant. That year both looked like candidates for national leadership. We have seen that the events of 1920—the ascendance of Gandhi and the pressures of the Khilafat movement—diverted Jinnah to the *qaum*. Their effect on Huq was to confine him to Bengal. The Ali brothers, closely allied to Gandhi at this juncture, and Azad took the centre of the Khilafat stage, which in 1920 was India's principal Muslim platform. Huq backed the Khilafat cause and thundered before mass audiences in Bengal but despite his capacity for Urdu oratory he could not rival the all-India position of the Ali brothers and Azad. Also, he was unable to be enthusiastic about the non-cooperation that Gandhi had proposed. His instincts told him that the exercise would be resisted by many who enjoyed the councils, courts and colleges of the Raj; and his head told him that boycotting colleges would hurt Bengal's Muslim youth. Moreover, he was angered by what he called the "taunts and insults" with which "so-called delegates" of Congress were shouting down "those who differ from them."[14]

Huq voted for non-cooperation when Congress discussed it in Calcutta in September 1920 but in February 1921 he denounced the programme in a letter to Sarat Bose, one of Bengal's leading Congress figures, who had sought Huq's presence at a non-cooperation conference in Barisal:

> You have adopted an ideal in the Congress to which I cannot subscribe. . . . I refuse to sit on the same platform with a set of politicians who have behaved towards me in the meanest way possible. . . . I have never believed in the programme of non-cooperation but I allowed myself to fall in with people with whom I never agreed. . . . My policy will be non-cooperation with your conference.[15]

Snapping his links with Congress, Huq nurtured his role in the legislature. In 1918 he had attacked the reforms that had given some additional powers to the Raj's councils as "a hoax."[16] But he re-entered the Bengal council in 1921. His victories there, earned in teamwork with Hindu and Muslim members, included a successful resolution against the large salaries the Raj was giving to its officials and another objecting to "the annual exodus of the Government of Bengal to Darjeeling."[17] Such resolutions were not binding on the government but they were good for the public's morale.

In the 1924 council Huq moved up: he became a Minister. Though real power lay with the Executive Members that the Governor appointed rather than with ministers, Huq was able, as education minister, to create a fund for deserving Muslim students, to ease the emergence of Islamia College in Calcutta and to name an Indian, B.M. Sen, as principal of Presidency College.[18] In six months, however, the ministers lost the council's confidence and had to resign.

* * *

Having decided that Bengal rather than all-India would be his field, Huq now chafed at the weightage given to Bengal's Hindus by the Lucknow pact, which the Raj had enforced. He was prepared now to accept joint electorates as a quid pro quo for the removal of the weightage. This was the proposal of the Motilal Nehru Report, which Huq supported, along with Muslims such as Azad and Ansari.* The man who had had a part in architecting the Lucknow pact now commented:

> I think the less said about the Lucknow pact the better. . . . So far as Muslims are concerned, every Muslim leader of any importance has since then seen that the Pact resulted in grave injustice to Muslims in Punjab and Bengal and they have repudiated it.[19]

Huq's sympathy for the peasantry was in evidence when in August 1928 the Bengal council discussed the Bengal Tenancy (Amendment) Bill. Officially introduced, supported by all the councillors, whether Hindu or Muslim, who represented seats reserved for landlords, and backed also by the large European contingent, the Bill was on balance a pro-landowner measure, though it was presented as pro-tenant. Huq opposed it spiritedly, as did Nausher Ali of Jessore and many other Muslim legislators. They were ably supported by two Hindus, J.L. Bannerji and Naresh Sen Gupta, but the other Hindus on the council, many of whom were identified with Congress, including the Bose brothers, Sarat and Subhas, backed the Bill, which was passed.

---

*As we saw in earlier chapters, Jinnah and Muhammad Ali and a majority of India's Muslims were not willing to accept the Nehru Report.

Pro-tenant amendments advocated by Huq, Nausher Ali, Bannerji and Sen Gupta were thrown out. The discussion and voting on the Bill and the amendments did not exactly endear Congress to Bengal's peasants, a large majority of whom were Muslim; they were now inclined to view Congress as, simultaneously, pro-landlord and anti-Muslim. *Jambeer*, a Muslim weekly hitherto friendly to Congress, wrote that the episode "has made us change our opinion," while the Muslim League, sensing the peasantry's mood, attacked the new measure as "extremely detrimental to the interest of the rural population."[20]

Following the episode, many Muslims left Congress in Bengal. Early in 1929, Huq, who "from the very inception of his public life had perceived that the edifice of his political base had to be in the countryside,"[21] took the initiative to launch the *Nikhil Proja Samity*, or the All-Bengal People's Committee. The new body's charter members were largely but by no means wholly Muslim: Huq desired "a peasant-oriented political organisation" rather than a community party.[22] The contacts Huq had kept with the peasantry helped and the body grew; it was strongest in the rural region of eastern Bengal.[23]

* * *

Yet Huq had no intention of disappearing into the countryside. Though Bengal's villagers found him a sympathetic listener and a champion of their rights, he was not going to cut himself off from the honours that capital cities bestow on the fortunate. Invited by the Raj for round table discussions on India's future, he went to London in 1930 and 1931. Few details of his days in England seem to be available. If his admiring biographer Abdur Rab is to be believed, Huq took time out during the second of these conferences to address an election rally.

"His speech was a brilliant piece of oratory which enchanted and captivated the entire audience numbering more than ten thousand. . . . He gave a lurid picture of the misrule and oppression of the Britishers. . . . The candidate in whose favour he spoke was a supporter of the Indian cause and he won an easy victory over his rival."[24]

Abdur Rab does not say who the candidate was, or where and when the meeting took place. The account is an obvious exaggeration, but the notion of Huq sounding forth at an election rally in Britain is entirely believable. What Huq said at the round table talks was, of course, recorded. It is of interest that he spoke for and about Bengal, rather than about India as a whole. He spoke, too, as a Muslim, and assailed Congress's practice of distinguishing between "nationalist" and "communal" Muslims:

My friend has said that there is a body of Muslims whom he called the "nationalist Muslims". . . . I have heard that expression used and I for one wish to testify that to me that expression is meaningless. Every Muslim is a nationalist; there cannot be a division of Muslims into nationalists and non-nationalists, any more than they can be divided into tall or short and fat or lean.[25]

He attacked the "special interests" seats that the Raj had provided for in its Indian councils:

There is the Association of Money-lenders—"Mahajana Sabha". Two hundred and thirteen of them have the privilege of returning one member to the legislature, whereas I have a constituency of 21,000 voters. That is not only a disparity but it is rank injustice to the people to foist on the electorate a special representation of this kind.[26]

He admitted that Indian troubles were not entirely a British creation:

The round table conference . . . has dispelled the wild calumny that the British Parliament wants to put obstacles in the way of Indian constitutional advance. There is not a single delegate here who can say that he has not been deeply impressed by the fervour, the ardour, the single-minded devotion of the attempt that has been made here in order to help us solve our own difficulties.[27]

The spokesman of the rural masses unsuccessfully sought, in 1934, the mayoralty of India's largest city. The following year he tried again and won the prize, thanks to an agreement among the Hindus and Muslims elected to the Calcutta corporation. A moved Huq said:

There are those who think that Muslims and Hindus in India live only to quarrel and cut one another's throats. They say that the future of India is doomed. . . . Here to my right (*Huq pointed to the Deputy Mayor*) I find a Hindu of Hindus. . . . May I say that this combination of Hindus and Muslims in one common endeavour is something like the hand of Providence working out some good for our common motherland.

If in a moment of forgetfulness or on any occasion I give offence to anybody I sincerely hope you will pardon me because I have also got shortcomings and I must not be judged by too high a standard.[28]

* * *

Huq continued to climb. The peak he had chosen was the Premiership of Bengal. The Government of India Act of 1935 had abolished "Executive

Members" and made the Premiership a post of power. Elections were due early in 1937. In April 1936 Huq and his friends converted the People's Committee into the Krishak Praja Party (K.P.P.), the Peasants and People's Party.

Huq, who was elected the party's president, knew that the K.P.P. was not going to capture power on its own. Allies were needed. Huq hoped that Congress would team up with him, and some at least in the Bengal Congress reciprocated the wish. Such a partnership would not have been unnatural: the K.P.P.'s goals were couched in secular terms, and Congress's pronouncements were no longer pro-landlord

But the marriage did not take place. Congressmen's attacks on the Communal Award of the British Government, which provided for a separate Muslim electorate, made the largely-Muslim K.P.P. wary of a Congress embrace. Aware of the Muslim sentiment, the All-India Congress had avoided rejecting the Communal Award, though it could not, given its ideology, accept it either. This neutral position was not good enough for Bengal's Congressmen. Condemning the Communal Award, they alienated Muslims who were ready to move towards them.

Hindus not belonging to Congress were stronger in their denunciation of the Award. 120 prominent Hindus of Bengal, led by the poet Tagore, urged H.M.G. in June 1936 to annul the Award and to enable more Hindus to enter the Bengal legislature. Their memorial to H.M.G. was followed by meetings all over Bengal against the Award. While these rallies did not influence the Raj, they made it difficult for K.P.P. Muslims to espouse an alliance with Congress.[29]

A charge that the Calcutta corporation had failed to recruit enough Muslims also damaged the prospects of a Congress-K.P.P. understanding. Muslims living in Calcutta believed the allegation; feeling in the *qaum* was so strong that, one member apart, all Muslim corporators, including Huq himself, the previous year's Mayor, resigned their places.[30]

Huq wanted the Premiership. Jinnah wanted Bengal. The League had empowered Jinnah, its president, to induct Muslim leaders from the provinces into a central parliamentary board (CPB) as a step towards "unifying the Muslim community" for the 1937 elections.[31] Knowing Huq's popularity, Jinnah named the Bengal leader to the CPB; it is not clear whether he consulted Huq before doing so.

The League's Bengal unit was lifeless. Huq's Muslim rivals in Bengal belonged not to the League but to the United Muslim Party (U.M.P.), which was hurriedly assembled in May 1936. The U.M.P.'s leaders were Nawab Habibullah of Dacca, Sir Khwaja Nazimuddin, H.S. Suhrawardy, A.R. Siddiqui and M.A.H. Ispahani, all men with landed or commercial interests.* Their slogan was Muslim unity under Islam.

Arriving in Calcutta, Jinnah tried to bring both the K.P.P. and the U.M.P. under the League umbrella. To begin with both demurred. Jinnah's terms—the K.P.P.'s merger with the League and a dilution of the K.P.P.'s stand against the *Zamindari* or land-owning system—were unacceptable to Huq. Huq said, moreover, that merging with the League would be "unfair" to the Hindus who belonged to or supported his party.[32]

Desiring independence from Jinnah's supervision, the U.M.P. leaders too were reluctant to merge with the League. But staying out would have invited the charge of obstructing the *qaum's* unity; they accepted the Jinnah terms. On the eve of Jinnah's departure from Calcutta it was announced that the U.M.P. was going into voluntary liquidation and entering the League, and that a Bengal parliamentary board of the League (BPB) would be set up. Chaired by the Nawab of Dacca, the BPB would have 15 U.M.P. members, 7 from the Bengal League and 11 others, including 4 that Jinnah would nominate. The K.P.P. was told that it could send 15 of its men to the BPB if it accepted the Jinnah terms.[33]

When Huq declined the offer, Jinnah removed him from the League's central board, saying that Huq was "guilty of breach of the Bengal agreement." In the words of the Bangladeshi writer, Enayetur Rahim, "Huq was removed from a body to which he never belonged by his own consent, and was held responsible for breach of an agreement into which he had never entered."[34] Hitting back, Huq accused Jinnah of "autocratic behaviour."[35]

* * *

The election was fiercely fought. Huq dramatized the contest by challenging Sir Khwaja Nazimuddin in his seat. Nazimuddin was a leading *Zamindar*, a polished politician, first cousin to the Nawab of Dacca and an Executive Member. Though he did not lack for resources or workers, several League activists came from afar to assist him. Huq, according to his biographer, "was a Machiavelli and a demagogue and a past master in the art of electioneering." With more cunning than truthfulness he told the voters that "he came from a family having no resources." He claimed, too, that "by the grace of God" he would abolish Zamindari "within the shortest possible time," and that "the peasantry of Bengal were dearest to his heart."[36]

He defeated Sir Khwaja. In a house of 250 Congress won 60 seats, the

*Nazimuddin and Suhrawardy were later to assume Pakistan's Premiership.

League 40, the K.P.P. 35, independent Muslims 41, a scheduled castes grouping 23, the Europeans 25. The independent Muslims joined the League or the K.P.P., so that the League ended up with 60 seats and the K.P.P. with 58.

Any two of the three more or less equal forces, Congress, the League and the K.P.P., could form a government by joining hands. It did not look as if the League and the K.P.P. would, not after the bitter Huq-Nazimuddin clash. A K.P.P.-Congress coalition seemed more likely. In the opinion of the writer Gautam Chattopadhyay, "Almost all K.P.P. leaders were keen to form a ministry with Congress support."[37]

This hope was not fulfilled. There were two difficulties, one theoretical and the other practical. The theoretical hitch was that Congress's central board had ruled out a ministerial role by Congressmen in provinces where they were not a majority. Principles of this kind seldom prevent "exploratory discussions." If such discussions yield tangible results, principles can be modified, or re-interpreted.

Discussions took place. They led to what looked like an agreement. Huq would be the Premier, Congress would have its share of posts, and the K.P.P. and Congress would jointly initiate political and economic reforms. A dinner was arranged at a Congress M.L.A.'s house; it was to be followed by both sides signing the deal. Over dinner the K.P.P. men said that the new ministry should first enact laws to relieve tenants and debt-burdened peasants. The Congress side said that while such measures were called for, they could only follow the release of pro-Congress freedom-fighters arrested by the outgoing government. The K.P.P. men argued that such an order of events would destroy their party. The British Governor would obstruct the release, the ministry would be forced to resign and in any fresh elections the Muslim League would "successfully paint the K.P.P. as the B team of the Congress." The League would also ridicule the K.P.P.'s failure to help the peasantry. According to one of the K.P.P. men present, Abul Mansur Ahmed,

> The Congress leaders refused to budge. They passionately declared that in the far off Andaman islands hundreds of sons of Bengal were on hunger strike, their lives were at stake and hence this issue must get priority over the demands of the impoverished peasants. At one o'clock that night the unity talks broke down and all of us left Mr. Gupta's residence down-hearted and depressed.[38]

The Congress ministries that were formed in other provinces were able to release imprisoned Congress supporters; their British Governors found the step distasteful but did not block it. But how was the K.P.P. to know that the Raj would yield on this score?

While Congress "missed a golden opportunity," as Niharendu Dutta-Mazumdar, a Congress M.L.A. at the time, has said, [39] Jinnah did not allow the memory of his dispute with Huq to blind him to his opening. He instructed the Bengal League to offer Huq the leadership of a League-K.P.P. ministry. Huq got what he had desired. And Jinnah made progress towards his goal. There were four from the League in Huq's ministry of eleven men, including Suhrawardy and Nazimuddin, who won a by-election. The K.P.P. had two, Huq and Nausher Ali. To give the ministry stability, and also to assure Bengal's Hindus that they would not be victimized, five non-Congress Hindus were included, including two belonging to the scheduled castes.

A role in the K.P.P.-League understanding was played by Calcutta's Muslim students and journalists, who demanded the *qaum's* unity and charged Congress with "trying to divide the Muslim camp."[40] As Anderson, the Bengal Governor, reported to the Viceroy, Lord Linlithgow, the course of events was influenced by "the feeling among Muslims generally that somehow or other their leaders must hold together."[41]

It felt good to be Premier but survival in that role was not simple. Five Hindu ministers were too many, complained the League. Muslim rallies deplored Huq's failure to "give the government a definitely Muslim colour."[42] The K.P.P.'s left wing attacked Huq's compromise over the abolition of Zamindari: he had named a committee to study abolition instead of doing away with Zamindari "in the shortest possible time." Yet without the compromise Huq would have lost the League's support, as well as the support of at least two of his Hindu ministers. He would have lost, in other words, his Premiership. One of these Hindu ministers, B.P. Singha Roy, "glorified the Zamindari system and advocated its perpetuation" at a conference of landholders.[43] Yet he held the revenue portfolio and was to handle any Zamindari abolition that Huq's committee might recommend.

Huq had denounced the Raj's high emoluments and promised lower ministerial salaries, but his coalition partners insisted on the Rs. 3,000 a month that the Raj had granted. Yielding to them, Huq accepted Rs. 3,600 a month for himself. Ministers in Congress-ruled provinces were taking Rs. 500 a month, and the K.P.P. radicals were up in arms. They left Huq and joined the Congress-led opposition, forcing Huq to lean more and more on the League.

He physically embraced Jinnah at Lucknow in October 1937, signed the League pledge and announced that he would advise all coalition members to join the League. The Quaid had obtained Bengal. In 1916 Jinnah and Huq had helped produce the Lucknow pact between Congress and the League. Now they stood together again in Lucknow, censuring Congress.

Huq asked Muslims to keep themselves at arm's length from the "selfish, deceptive and hypocritical Congressmen" and unite under the banner of Islam. "If Muslims were ill-treated in Congress-governed provinces," he warned, "the Bengal ministry would retaliate."[44] However, his Hindu friends in Bengal "knew that Huq was not the kind of person to carry his threats into practice."[45] "The strongest impulse of the moment has governed all my actions," Huq would say in the future.[46] After yielding to his impulse in Lucknow, he returned to Calcutta, found himself before an audience of Hindus and told them that "as long as he was in power they had nothing to be afraid of."[47] Then, addressing a Bengal Muslim Conference, he sought to undo some of the effects of his Lucknow utterance:

> Power has come into the hands of the Muslims because they constitute the single biggest group in the assembly. But when power is in your hands do not be selfish. You have to look to the Hindu interest also and you have to be impartial.[48]

Huq's Lucknow decision brought over to the League the Muslim masses of eastern Bengal, to whom he now spoke on the League's behalf and as its Bengal president, a position that Jinnah was willing to concede to Huq, along with a place in the central League's working committee. Huq did not confine himself to Bengal in his new role as the League's promoter; talks by him in Assam, Orissa, Bihar and elsewhere added to the League's popularity in a wide area.

The League's gain was the K.P.P.'s loss. Huq had resisted pressures in Lucknow for the K.P.P.'s dissolution. But he couldn't prevent its disintegration. K.P.P. factions loyal to him became auxiliaries of the League; the party's left wing and its Hindus drifted to Congress. A valuable bi-communal force had crumbled.

He himself didn't bang the door on Congressmen coming to woo him, but neither did he deny himself the profitable role of an exposer of Congress designs. Thus he declared:

> The Congress is even outdoing Satan himself in Bengal in creating division amongst Muslim ranks and setting brother against brother. But if the Muslims of India unite and organize under the Muslim League they can easily frustrate all the machinations of their enemies.[49]

There were desertions from the Huq-led ranks. The scheduled caste M.L.A.s crossed over to Congress's side. Nausher Ali, barring Huq the only K.P.P. minister, also joined the opposition. The votes of the 25-member European group saved Huq when, in August 1938, he faced a no-confidence motion. It was rejected by 130 votes to 111. After this close shave Huq won back two K.P.P. M.L.A.s who had left him by offering them ministerships, but at the end of 1939 he lost Nalini Ranjan Sarkar, his finance minister. Sarkar, a former Congressman, was a prominent Hindu whose presence in the Huq cabinet had served to soften Hindu hostility to it. He resigned shortly after the start of the Second World War, which, as we have seen in earlier chapters, widened the Congress-League gulf. Sarkar's standing among Hindus would have shrunk to nothing had he remained a League ally thereafter. After his exit no Hindu M.L.A. was prepared to accept a berth in Huq's cabinet.

Sarkar's departure came on the heels of a belligerent exchange in the assembly between Huq and the Hindu Mahasabha leader, Shyama Prasad Mookerjee, son of Sir Ashutosh Mookerjee, to whom advocate Huq had once been articled. Opposing a government Bill to create, for the first time, a special Muslim electorate for voting to the Calcutta corporation, Mookerjee said:

> There are dark and ominous clouds today. . . . The choice between peace and conflict is to be made by the government. . . . If you fight, we will also fight for our lives, our rights and our liberties.[50]

Huq defended the Bill, which was passed, and added:

> Dr. Shyama Prasad Mookerjee has challenged to a mortal combat not merely the Muslim members of the coalition party but practically the 30 million Muslims of Bengal. Somehow or other, I may tell him frankly, he has earned the reputation of being one of the most communally-minded men in Bengal.[51]

* * *

The polarization in the Bengal assembly was not, alas, an isolated event. We noted in previous chapters that, rightly or wrongly, the Muslim masses in the provinces that Congress ministries governed had come to see these ministries as agencies of Hindu hegemony; and we saw too that when, following the start of the War, these ministries resigned, a great many Muslims rejoiced.

Huq did not merely adjust to the reality of polarization; he adjusted with fervour. He was more than willing, when the League met in Lahore in March 1940, to sponsor the resolution asking for the separation of India's Muslim-majority regions. Before moving the resolution he said, "amidst thunderous applause":

> We assumed power on behalf of Muslims and other people in Bengal in 1937. We have been given an opportunity by the Almighty to serve our people after a couple of centuries and we are not going to barter away the power and the opportunity to an imaginary and unknown central authority.... I am a Muslim first and Bengalee afterwards. ... It was in Bengal in the year 1906 that the flag of the Muslim League was unfurled and it is now my privilege as the leader of Bengal to move the resolution for the homeland of the Muslims from the self-same platform of the Muslim League.[52]

Huq spoke of "homeland" in the singular in the remarks just quoted, but the resolution he moved and which the League passed said that "geographically contiguous units ... in which the Muslims are numerically in a majority as in the North-Western and Eastern zones of India should be grouped to constitute independent *states*." Not many noticed at the time, but the Bangladesh of the future was provided for in the League's first "Pakistan" resolution.

Though Huq and Jinnah were heroes together at Lahore and shared power in Bengal, they had not grown to like each other. Convinced for years that he was Bengal's natural leader, Huq resented his dependence on Jinnah and on League factions in Bengal loyal to Jinnah; on his part Jinnah remembered Huq's refusal to fall in line during the 1937 elections and feared the possibility of an understanding between Huq and Bengal's Hindus.

Notwithstanding his Lahore remarks, Huq, as Jinnah well knew, was very much a Bengali. Since he had confined his ambition to Bengal's leadership, he had a stake in Hindu-Muslim harmony. The fact that Hindus made up 43.8 per cent of Bengal's population (the Muslim percentage was 54)[53] meant that no Muslim ruler could feel secure without some Hindu support. This political reality was reinforced by cultural and economic considerations. The cultural one is described by Rahim: "Fazlul Huq and his men were conscious of their Bengali identity and heritage and fondly shared the unique Bengali ethos."[54] Economically, Huq sought a better-off peasantry and knew that religious rallying cries were insufficient for reaching that goal.

Just three weeks before Huq moved the League's Lahore resolution he had spoken in Calcutta of "my countrymen of all castes and creeds" and of "this common motherland of ours."[55] Before the Lahore meeting and following it, he issued emotional appeals for communal harmony and a month after Lahore he expressed his readiness to talk with Azad, the Congress president, on the communal and constitutional questions.[56] This came close to defying Jinnah, whose dislike of Azad was well known and who, moreover, had ruled out negotiations with Congress until it recognized the League as Muslim India's sole voice. Jinnah's Calcutta friends warned Huq against approaching Congress "over the head of the Muslim League," and in January 1941 Jinnah himself accused Huq of dividing the Muslim camp.[57]

When Tagore died in August 1941 Huq called himself a "proud member" of the "great Bengalee race" while paying a tribute to the poet on the assembly floor. Said Huq:

> It is not enough to say that Rabindranath was great. He was great as a poet. He was great as a philosopher. He was great as an educationist. He was great as a humanitarian. . . . I hope that (my) words will be taken to be indicative of our deep sense of sorrow . . . as members of the great Bengalee race who are proud today that we had in our midst one like Rabindranath. . . .[58]

* * *

By this time Huq had decided to break with Jinnah. The issue that led to a rupture was Huq's acceptance, in July 1941, of the Viceroy's offer of a place on a National Defence Council that the Raj was setting up. Terming Huq's act "highly objectionable,"[59] Jinnah ruled that as a League member Huq should have sought the party's permission before saying yes to the Viceroy. Huq and the League Premiers of Punjab and Assam, guilty of the same "breach", were directed by the League to resign from the Defence Council. Sikander Hyat and Saadullah, the Premier, respectively, of Punjab and Assam, complied at once and Huq after a long delay, but Huq also resigned from the League's working committee and, in a letter addressed to Liaqat Ali Khan, the League's general secretary, called Jinnah "a single individual who seeks to rule as an omnipotent authority even over the destiny of 33 million Muslims in the province of Bengal."[60]

At the heart of the conflict was Huq's assertion of his, and Bengal's, autonomy vis-a-vis Jinnah and the central League. In his letter to Liaqat he said:

> For my part , I will never allow the interests of 33 millions of the Muslims of Bengal to be put under the domination of any outside authority, however eminent it may be.

His words were sharp and unprecedented, but Huq took care not to announce a divorce until he was sure of a welcome elsewhere. He used every weapon to buy time. First he explained his action, arguing, with some justice, that he had been taken on the Defence Council as a Premier, not as a League member. Then, while maintaining that he had done no wrong, he resigned from the Defence Council and claimed that his resignation proved his discipline. Shortly after his attack on Jinnah he even extended a half-apology for it.

Simultaneously—and secretly—he probed the minds of Bengal's Hindu politicians. They were willing to help him. In November Huq, Sarat Chandra Bose, Shyama Prasad Mookerjee and some other M.L.A.:s, Hindu and Muslim, met at the home of J.C. Gupta, the Congress M.L.A. who had hosted the abortive 1937 dinner. This time the parleys were fruitful.

Two days later League M.L.A.s "raised angry questions about the truth of such a meeting and such moves on the floor of the assembly, but Fazlul Huq hotly denied all charges."[62] Realizing that "the fight is on, . . . a life and death struggle,"—to quote from a letter that Ispahani, Jinnah's loyal Calcutta ally, wrote to the Quaid[63]—the League members of Huq's cabinet, including Nazimuddin and Suhrawardy, resigned. Their confident expectation that Sir John Herbert, the Governor, would ask for Huq's resignation as well was fulfilled, but their estimate that Nazimuddin would be asked to form a new ministry was proved wrong.

As soon as the League ministers resigned, Huq announced that a new group, the Progressive Coalition party, had emerged, and that it commanded a majority in the assembly. Congress, K.P.P. dissidents, the scheduled caste bloc and non-Congress caste Hindus had assured Huq and his "official" K.P.P. of their support. It was enough to form a government. Though Congress M.L.A.s in Bengal were divided into two groups at this juncture—a fall-out of the Gandhi-Subhas dispute of 1939—both groups gave Huq their backing, the Bose group joining the coalition and the "official" Congress guaranteeing support on the assembly floor.

A surprised Herbert hesitated before asking Huq to lead a new cabinet and doubtless questioned his principles but the arithmetic of the former mathematics lecturer was hard to fault. After a long and unusual wait—Huq later alleged that Herbert wanted to install Nazimuddin as Premier[64]—Huq was called upon to form his second ministry. This was on December 10. Sarat Bose, leader of the Congress (Subhas) group in the assembly, was to be the deputy Premier in the new cabinet but the Raj arrested him under Defence of India Rules on December 11. The next day Huq announced a cabinet: himself, the Nawab of Dacca and, to everyone's astonishment, Shyama Prasad Mookerjee, whom he had denounced two years earlier as one of Bengal's most communally-minded men. Seven others, three Muslim and four Hindu, were inducted a few days later.

League supporters called Huq a traitor—a "Mir Jafar," recalling the man who had sold himself to the British in the 18th century. Telling Huq that his "conduct amounted to treachery," Jinnah expelled him from the League and barred his return to the party in the future.[65] Seemingly indifferent to such reactions, Huq chose to dwell on the Hindu-Muslim collaboration that produced his new cabinet:

> The formation of this party, bringing together as it does the diverse elements in India's national life, is an event unprecedented in the history of India.[66]

Sarat Bose, too, claimed that the consideration of Hindu-Muslim unity governed his role. While in detention he wrote to Herbert's successor as Governor, Casey:

> I have always been of opinion that the rights and interests of the people of Bengal could be safeguarded and promoted only if the Hindu and Muslim legislators combined to free themselves from the malignant influence of the agents of British Imperialism. With that end in view, I promoted the formation of a coalition party in Bengal in November 1941.[67]

Though apparently successful, the bid was four years too late. Hindu and Muslim legislators should have been combined in 1937. That opportune moment was missed by Bose and others in Congress. The November 1941 exercise did not bring Hindus and Muslims together. Huq's personal popularity notwithstanding, that exercise was seen by Bengal's Muslims as a Hindu maneouvre to remove the League from power. When elections were next held in Bengal (in 1945–46), the province's Muslim votes went solidly in the League's favour.

* * *

Jinnah did not think the new ministry could last. Removing it, he said, would be "as simple as falling off a log."[68] Yet it survived for 16 months. Huq colourfully claimed that "he would be the best defender of Hindu interests and Mookerjee would protect Muslim interests."[69] Renouncing the resolution he had moved in Lahore, Huq said that "the Pakistan scheme could not be applied to Bengal."[70] On his part, Mookerjee helped create places for Muslims in some government departments and at Calcutta University.[71] Though the new ministry did not unite Muslims and Hindus, it successfully prevented communal violence.

Eventually, however, the ministry was crushed by a combination of three major events: the start of the war with Japan, Congress's Quit India movement, and the early days of the Great Bengal Famine. The first two stiffened the Raj and forced Huq into a dilemma: to defend Congress's rebellion during a war would invite dismissal, but to defend the Raj's repression when India's freedom movement appeared to be at its climax would invite the public's censure.

The worst of the Famine would hit the successor ministry, not Huq's. Still, the rice shortage, accentuated by a terrible cyclone and by Japan's capture of Burma, rice from where used to end up on plates in Bengal, also divided the ministers from the Raj. One of the Raj's aims was to deny Bengal's rice to any Japanese invaders. To this end, and also to divert surpluses to deficit areas, the Governor and his permanent officials, British and Indian, enforced measures of procurement and removal that were often ill-prepared and harsh. The Raj's emergence as a buyer pushed up the price of rice. Hastily-recruited buying agents pocketed fat commissions from the rice sellers.

The avoidable and unavoidable stings of the Raj's rice policy hurt the ministers' popularity, even though the rice policy was not wholly, or even largely, theirs. Yet if Premier Huq was to attack the "government's" rice measures, he would look ridiculous, risk dismissal and advertise his impotence.

He stomached the unpopularity and walked a tight-rope. But in the end Governor Herbert ousted him. It was an attack by Mookerjee—in February 1943—on the Raj's repression that put Huq on the spot. Detailing excesses by officials in Midnapore, where large numbers had responded to the Quit India call, Mookerjee said that he could no longer remain a helpless minister. He resigned, Congress M.L.A.s asked for an inquiry into Midnapore, and Huq agreed on the assembly floor that "an enquiry is desirable."[72]

An enquiry into the deeds of the Raj's defenders? An angered Herbert immediately asked for "an explanation tomorrow morning of your conduct." Huq wrote back that while he owed "no explanation whatever," he did "owe a duty to administer a mild warning that indecorous language such has been used in your letter under reply should in future be avoided."[73] A censure motion against Huq, undoubtedly blessed by Herbert, was rejected by just 10 votes. The following day Herbert persuaded, or pressurized, Huq into signing a letter of resignation.

Why Huq signed is not clear. Perhaps he was told that he would be dismissed if he did not resign. All we know is that the following letter, typed out and ready, was given by Herbert to Huq, who signed it:

Dear Sir John:
Understanding that there is a probability of the formation of a Ministry representative of most of the parties in the event of my resignation, I hereby tender my resignation . . . in the sincere hope that this will prove to be in the best interests of the people of Bengal.
Yours sincerely,
A.K. Fazlul Huq.[74]

Promptly "accepting" the resignation he had drafted, Herbert governed Bengal himself for a month and placed curbs on the Press. On April 24 he swore in Nazimuddin as Premier. Nazimuddin had needed the interval to gather sufficient support, an exercise in which he received Herbert's assistance. The Governor, who had refused Huq permission to expand his team of ten ministers and one parliamentary secretary, allowed Nazimuddin 14 ministers, 13 parliamentary secretaries and four whips.

Though Linlithgow, the Viceroy, saw "great advantage in being rid of Huq," he felt "dismayed," as he wrote in a confidential letter to London, at Herbert's "great folly" in "playing politics." The Viceregal remedy, however, was no more than to send the Governor "a pretty stiff letter." Linlithgow told Amery, the Secretary of State for India, that he was convinced of the "necessity for protecting (Herbert's) position and saving his face."[75]

The Governor's manoeuvres had been as successful, and as deplorable, as the ones with which Huq had retained his position in December 1941. A second wrong does not make the first right. The Huq who now breathed indignation on the assembly floor was no innocent, yet he spoke bitingly. He had lost his Premiership but he won a debate:

My memory travels back to the happy days I had spent with four successive Governors before I met Sir John Herbert. . . . While working with these Governors, we all felt that the council of ministers and the Governor formed a team. . . .

For some time Sir John Herbert was to me a considerate friend. . . . Gradually, however, he began to exhibit a tendency to interfere in the details of administration. We felt his interference and obstruction so keenly, that I addressed a letter.

On August 2, 1942 I wrote: "I am convinced that the time has come when I must speak to you quite openly. . . . You are acting as if your Ministers did not exist. . . . In cabinet meetings you monopolise all the discussions and practically force decisions on your ministers, decisions which are in many cases the outcome of advice tendered to you by permanent officials."

In the meantime, the disastrous consequences of the mistaken rice policy began to manifest themselves. . . .

After he had once managed to secure my so-called letter of resignation, the only end Sir John Herbert had in view was somehow to smuggle Sir Nazimuddin into power. He forgot his solemn promise to me that he would . . . try to form a national cabinet. Even the so-called letter of resignation drafted and kept ready by the Governor himself emphasized this point.

Of all the faults of which a Governor can be guilty, the fault of partisanship is most reprehensible. . . . A partisan Governor is no more fit for his high office than a partisan judge.

It is not the votes of the opposition that (the new ministers) should dread, but the tormented cries of the famine-stricken people of Bengal. . . . The ministers will not be saved, unless Providence in His Mercy deems it fit to forgive their sins. . . . Some day, sooner or later, they will be humbled to the dust.[76]

Poor Sir John Herbert died in Calcutta in December 1943.

* * *

What had Huq achieved in his six years as Premier? His first ministry fortified the tenant-peasant against the landlord and the moneylender. This help was neither as prompt nor as large as Huq had promised before he became Premier, and it did not reach the sharecropper, but it was undoubtedly a step forward. The first ministry also started a number of schools, colleges and hostels for Muslim students, and fixed a fifty percent Muslim quota, and a fifteen per cent scheduled caste quota, in new recruitment to government jobs. It could not help the jute-grower of east Bengal, in part because Huq needed the votes of the jute manufacturers represented in the assembly. His second ministry, pre-occupied even more than the first with survival, did not initiate socio-economic reforms.

The Nazimuddin ministry lasted 23 months. It could not cope with the Famine, the scale of which London failed to understand. Wavell, Linlithgow's successor as Viceroy, complained that H.M.G. had "wasted at least two critical months in appointing a Governor" and that the acting Governor, Rutherford, was "only thinking of getting away on leave."[77] In Wavell's view, the Nazimuddin team did not have either the intention or the ability "to get down to things" over the Famine.[78] In Janury 1944 he urged H.M.G. to dismiss the League-controlled ministry and impose direct British rule, but Churchill and Amery vetoed the proposal: they did not want to weaken the League, which had blocked the advance of the seditious Congress.

Hundreds of thousands perished in the Famine. Wavell noted in his diary that "old men, women and children drifted into Calcutta, where there was inadequate provision for giving them food and shelter and they began to die like flies. . . . "[79]

Nazimuddin remained Premier until March 1945, when his ministry lost a snap vote. Huq's claim that he could form a ministry was not tested, H.M.G. deciding that Casey, the new Governor, should rule directly. In September the assembly was dissolved.

Though Huq cabled a plea to Churchill for "justice," he knew that Bengal no longer wanted him. Psychologically it had split into two, and neither the Muslim nor the Hindu half desired Huq's leadership. He was a betrayer to Muslims and, once the assembly was defunct, of no use to the Hindus. The 72-year-old campaigner consulted his instincts. These told him that retirement would be insipid, if not fatal, and told him too that any future still left for him in politics would come via the *qaum*.

Aware that the road to rehabilitation in the *qaum* would be long, winding and rocky, Huq nonetheless planted his feet on it. In October 1945 he claimed that talk of his having given up his belief in the separation of Muslims was false, and that he stood by "the resolution whose wordings I drafted and which I moved in the Lahore session."[80] Those urging Huq to reconcile with Jinnah were asked by him to "write to Mr. Jinnah to remove the ban he has put on me so that I may join the Muslim League."[81] Huq, in other words, was willing.

But Jinnah did not need Huq yet. The League had won all Muslim by-elections held in Bengal following Huq's alliance with Sarat Bose and Mookerjee, and Jinnah was confident that the province would return the League to power in the general elections that Britain's new Labour government had scheduled. Rebuffed, Huq challenged the League with what was left of his K.P.P., but early 1946 was not 1937. Though Huq himself won both the seats he personally contested,—a testimony to his continuing hold on Muslim peasants—, his K.P.P. was routed. The League won 114 seats, the K.P.P. 3. Congress swept the polls in the general seats, winning 86 of them. The architect of the League's Bengal triumph, and the new Chief Minister, was H.S. Suhrawardy.

* * *

Huq's marriage with Khurshid Begum, the mother of his two daughters, was not a success. She left and sued him, winning a house and a monthly allowance of Rs. 500. His second wife was Musammat Jannatunnisa Begum, niece of a prominent Muslim divine of Howrah in west Bengal, the Pir of Furfurah Sharif. He had no children from her. When Premier he married a third time. The bride, Khadija Begum, who came from Meerut in the U.P., bore him a son, Faizul.

There were innumerable cousins, nephews and nieces. Huq did what he could for them. One of his nephews, Yusuf Ali, a matriculate, applied for the post of chief inspector of registration when his uncle was Premier.

Huq requested the inspector-general of registration, a man called M. Mukherjee, "to consider Yusuf Ali's case." Mukherjee considered it but chose a more qualified man. A "wounded" Huq spoke to the Governor, Sir John Anderson, who gave Yusuf Ali a special appointment. "What are Mr Yusuf Ali's qualifications?" an MLA asked in the assembly. "His qualification, sir, is that," Huq, rising from his seat, answered, "he is the nephew of the Premier of Bengal."[82]

"Uprightness" is not the word that leaps to the mind of one seeking Huq's outstanding quality. Neither does "consistency." Huq himself maintained that his "changes of policy" were not "deviations from principle." Policies, he once said, were mere means, and could be likened to an umbrella. The end was to save one's body from the sun and the rain. To do this one had to "hold the umbrella in different directions according to necessity."[83]

Abdur Rab, who quotes this argument, is too respectful to refer to what it implies. The argument suggests that Huq's principle was to save himself from the sun and the rain. Few would deny the success, in this respect, of Huq's flexibility. All the same, as Rab points out, there generally was a limit to it. Huq's quarrels with Congress stopped short of his accepting honours from the Raj; though he let the K.P.P. radicals down , he stopped short of aligning with the Zamindars; and his clash with Jinnah was never enlarged into an anti-Pakistan campaign. For all his about-turns, Huq desisted from sticking a knife into his beliefs.

Though Jinnah and Huq shared the platform at three historic moments, twice in Lucknow and once in Lahore, they were opposites in several ways. Jinnah was upright, meticulous and cold, Huq flexible, casual and warm. Jinnah obeyed his mind, Huq his instincts. Jinnah was aloof, Huq accessible. Jinnah withdrew the hand he had extended to the Baluchi chief because there wasn't time to greet everyone else present; Huq would hug a peasant, whether on a platform before thousands or in his home. Young men from east Bengal stayed in Huq's Calcutta residence; he gave money he did not have to students, widows and shrines. Jinnah was parsimonious, Huq, in Rab's apt phrase, was "the benevolent insolvent."

Jinnah dwelt on the meaning of sentences and clauses, Huq loved the sound of words. Jinnah was absorbed with laws and resolutions, Huq read poetry and religious books. According to the owner of Delhi's leading Islamic book-store, Huq was one of "the two best subscribers of Islamic literature in India."[84] He prayed five times a day and most mornings recited passages from the Qur'an, practices that Jinnah did not follow.

Huq's outstanding quality was sympathy. Like food and freedom, sympathy too was in short supply in the India of his time. When Huq provided it, Bengal's common man responded. Thus, whether in office or out of it, Huq would write letters recommending the case of virtually everyone who approached him. Only rarely were they fruitful: the ease and frequency with which they were issued destroyed much of their value. Yet they were prized by the persons on whose behalf they were written, humble folk unaccustomed even to gestures of concern. Because Huq showed his sympathy to many and for long, he was loved.

If with one hand he was altering the angle of his umbrella, with the other he was drawing a man in need into its shade. That the subcontinent appreciates sympathy is one lesson of Huq's popularity. Like Anderson the Governor, quoted at the start of this chapter, Wavell too thought Huq to be unprincipled. He was appalled when, in the summer of 1946, Nehru proposed a place for Huq in the central government; following Wavell's strong reaction, Nehru dropped Huq's name. Yet, for large numbers, Huq's lack of probity lay dissolved and unnoticeable in his sympathy. We should note Rab's view, even if we may not agree with it, that Huq was, simply, "the greatest son of Bengal."[85]

Other traits and gifts helped him. His vigour was infectious. Always "a robust optimist," as he called himself,[86] he never accepted defeat. His oratory was compelling. And he did not bend his knee before power. No other Indian Premier had administered "a mild warning" to his Governor. His forthrightness was a reason, though not the only one, for the Raj's custodians disliking him, and for the Indian public liking him.

The circle of his Hindu friends was large. They respected his academic record, legal skill and commitment to Indian self-government, and were pleased at his being "thoroughly a Bengali."[87]

* * *

There was no tribute to, or role for, Huq when Pakistan was born in August 1947. Considering his politics in the 1941–45 period, this was hardly surprising. But he had not been idle. Shortly before the partition Huq argued before the Radcliffe Commission for the cession of disputed districts to Pakistan. He sought, too, the inclusion of Calcutta, or of one-half of it, in East Pakistan, maintaining that the "seceding" Hindus of Muslim-majority Bengal could not take its capital away with them. He later claimed, not very fairly, that Jinnah did not fight hard enough for Calcutta. Jinnah did, but he could not change the city's Hindu-Muslim arithmetic.

The truth was that Huq wanted to live in Pakistan and Calcutta both; this was only possible if Calcutta was assigned to Pakistan. The city had given him glory, adulation, love. It was there that he had studied and practised, roared and reigned. He knew its ways and intrigues, its alleys and mansions. He did not want to leave it. But the pull of a future in politics was stronger. He departed for Pakistan but, as "an out-and-out Bengali," for Dacca rather than for Karachi.[88]

Tens of thousands of other Calcutta-based Muslims did the same and competed for Dacca's living space. The tiger and ex-Premier of Bengal was now like them, a mere member of a transferred mass, even though he had found a place in Pakistan's Constituent Assembly. For a year he stayed in a flat vacated for him by an admirer. Then he purchased a house on K.M. Das Lane. After buying it he heard that the government had decided to requisition the house for its use. Huq gave such a loud roar that Nazimuddin—who had beaten Suhrawardy in the race for East Bengal's Chief Ministership—cancelled the requisition.

Huq needed crowds. A public meeting was arranged in Dacca but vandals allied to his political enemies wrecked it. "The furniture brought to the park for the meeting was burnt to ashes."[89]

On Jinnah's death a year after partition, Huq's long-standing rival Nazimuddin became Governor-General. At the end of 1950, Huq, 77 and restless, said in a letter to a friend:

> The gods of Karachi seem convinced that the people of East Bengal are no better than goats and may be slaughtered with impunity. . . . They think that East Bengal contains only milch cows and that the Royal Bengal Tiger is dead. Sher-e-Bangla they think is no more. The time is coming when the Sher-e-Bangla will roar again. I am going to Karachi on the 15th instant and will then decide on my return what to do.[90]

Pakistan's rulers, Liaqat Ali Khan, the Premier, and Nazimuddin, sensed Huq's temper and offered him the post of Advocate-General of East Pakistan. It would appease him and also keep him out of politics. He accepted the job but did not surrender a secret hope.

Meanwhile Liaqat was assassinated and the well-bred Nazimuddin became Pakistan's Prime Minister. Dignified but weak, he was dismissed in a year and a half by Ghulam Mohammed, the Governor-General, who named M.A. Bogra, ambassador to Washington at the time, as the new Premier. Though, like Nazimuddin, Bogra was a Bengali, East Bengal continued to feel that she was Pakistan's neglected half. The foreign exchange she earned was invested in the western wing. Her people had resented Jinnah's declaration that Urdu would be the only state language. The students of Dacca demanded an equal status for Bengali, pointing out that Bengali-speakers easily outnumbered those who spoke Urdu or

Punjabi. The police fired at a student procession, several students were killed, and a movement was born.

The League's habit of terming critics of government anti-national aided the growth of a sentiment of "us" and "them." More and more people in East Bengal believed that "they", ruling from far-off Karachi, had no understanding of "our" situation. The man who seemed to profit most from these tides of opinion was Huq's other rival, Suhrawardy. Supported by Maulana Bhashani, the fiery Muslim socialist, and by a young man called Sheikh Mujibur Rahman, and using the platform of a new party, the Awami League, Suhrawardy was rallying East Bengal's aggrieved populace.

* * *

Once more Huq's instincts guided him to a peak that no one else thought was within his reach. He resigned his official post, revived the K.P.P., altered it to the K.S.P.—the Krishak *Sramik* (Peasants and *Workers*) Party— enlisted Muslim League dissidents and offered his partnership to Suhrawardy, who accepted it. There being no question of the tiger of Bengal accepting a second place, Huq became the united front's leader.

Elections took place in March 1954. "The Muslim League," a West Pakistani army officer posted at the time in Dacca relates, "was hopeful. All the central ministers and League leaders, including Miss Fatima Jinnah, visited Dacca during the election campaign. In the beginning they expected an eighty per cent victory. The figure slowly went on decreasing but never went below fifty per cent."[91]

The battle pumped new life into Huq, who was now 80. He thundered from one end of East Bengal to the other. His oratory and "the superb organizing skill" of Suhrawardy[92] turned East Bengal's unhappiness into a stunning united front victory. It won 223 seats against 10 obtained by the Muslim League. A front student trounced Nurul Amin, the incumbent Chief Minister, who lost his deposit.

Early in April 1954 the tiger was Chief Minister again. Yet in less than two months he was out. His impulsiveness had given his enemies a pretext. The temptation to visit Calcutta as Chief Minister was strong. He yielded to it. Facing audiences there of his old friends, including men who had admired his sense of a Bengali identity, Huq professed unfamiliarity with the distinction between Hindustan and Pakistan. A little later the *New York Times* quoted him as saying that he desired East Bengal's independence; Huq claimed that "he had mentioned autonomy, not independence."[93] Very soon riots between Bengalis and non-Bengalis broke out at the Adamjee Jute Mills. "Instigation!" cried Huq's followers. "Hostility against non-locals!" alleged West Pakistanis. On May 30 the Huq ministry was dismissed and central rule imposed. Bogra went on the air and used a word for Huq that the tiger had heard before, "Traitor!"

Anger and disappointment, if not age, should have killed Huq but there were fruits that the "robust optimist" still hoped to pluck. He looked to the future with the expectancy of a boy out of college, and was rewarded. In 1955 he became Pakistan's Interior Minister. How? First Bogra, his chair shaky, felt obliged to lean on Huq. Central rule was withdrawn from East Bengal and a Huq nominee, Abu Hussain Sarkar, was made Chief Minister. Then, in August 1955, Huq joined forces with Bogra's rival, Chaudhri Muhammad Ali, and helped him become Prime Minister. As a result of the deal, the previous year's "traitor" found himself Pakistan's Interior Minister. Not to be outdone in flexibility, Bogra returned to Washington as ambassador.

What did Huq now think of his Calcutta remark? "In an unguarded moment, perhaps in my exuberance, I said things which I should not have said."[94] He moved to Karachi and helped Chaudhri Muhammad Ali shape Pakistan's first constitution, which appeared to succeed in reconciling the demands of Islam and of a modern nation. Also, Bengali was given, with Urdu, the status of a national language, and Pakistan became a republic.

There was a final fruit Huq plucked. In March 1956 he returned from Karachi and took up residence in Dacca's Government House as East Bengal's Governor, a fit recompense for his exertions in Karachi. However, he smelled danger. Bogra was not the only man foiled by the Muhammad Ali-Huq deal. Suhrawardy, who had hoped to replace Bogra, was another. Bogra had peaceably gone to Washington but Suhrawardy desired revenge. He held some strong cards and his skill was formidable. Huq had watched him in Karachi, and continued to watch him from Government House in Dacca.

The scrutiny was of no avail. First Suhrawardy toppled the East Bengal ministry, even though Huq was the Governor, and installed his ally Ataur Rahman Khan in Sarkar's place. Then, ousting Chaudhri Muhammad Ali, he became Pakistan's Prime Minister. Huq had found it pleasant to think that he was a governor, sitting where men like Anderson and Herbert had sat—mellowing, or perhaps forgetting, he even recalled, in a letter to Ataur Rahman, "my very happy days" with Herbert [95]—but there was another taste in the mouth when he had to go to the airport to receive H.E. Mr H.S. Suhrawardy, Prime Minister of Pakistan.

There are periods when the pendulum of fate, never still, swings fast. After 13 months as Prime Minister, Suhrawardy lost a vote in the Pakistan assembly and had to go. His old rival was still the Governor in the east. However, on March 31, 1958, six months after Suhrawardy's fall, the pendulum finally struck the tiger in the head. President Iskander Mirza dismissed Huq. A mere 85, and hoping to bounce back, he became the K.S.P.'s president again: general elections, after all, were less than a year away. But they were not held. In September 1958 Mirza declared martial law.

* * *

A witness to Huq's popularity, and to his ways, was Major Jilani, A.D.C. to the Governor of East Pakistan. Writes Jilani:

> Governor Huq visited his home village, Chakhar. We went as far as Barisal by steamer, then 20 miles by jeep on a dirt road and covered the last mile on foot. The Governor was carried in a palanquin by the villagers, all of whom seemed eager to take their turn. The love, affection and respect displayed by the villagers for him was very impressive.[96]

At Barisal Huq was confronted with a demand for a medical college. According to Jilani, the Governor "both stunned and amused" the people making the demand "by leading them to an open ground, digging a token foundation and praying that it might soon materialize into a medical college."[97] Actually, a medical college had been an old Huq dream and promise. Herbert had even laid a foundation-stone for it back in 1939. Sarkar's K.S.P. ministry revived the scheme early in 1956 but, as Huq charged, the Ataur government consigned it "into the cold storage of neglect." "I will not take this insult lying down," vowed Huq.[98] When a medical college and hospital finally rose in Barisal, Huq had been six years in his grave.

An example of Huq's letters of recommendation is a communication he sent as Governor to a district official:

> The bearer of this letter, Md. Eshaq Munshi, is now in serious trouble with regard to his properties. He will be ejected and turned into a street beggar.... Kindly give him a very patient hearing and advise him. It will be a very long story, but I hope you will have the patience to hear it.[99]

His musings while at Government House often turned to the past. To a friend at Barisal he wrote about the house he had inherited from his father: "My only object is to have something like marble slabs showing where it was that my mother and my father breathed their last. I have asked Sukhmoy Babu to see you.... I want the memory of my forefathers to be preserved."[100]

Shortly before he was forced out of Government House, Huq thought he should write "my own biography", believing, characteristically, that it would help "in the maintenance of my career in public life." His trouble, he said, was that "I do not remember very much of what I have been or done." Alas, the friends exhorted by him "to collect the history of events of my life" were not able to oblige him in time.[101]

In February 1957, after delivering a convocation address at Dacca University, Governor Huq said:

> I have spoken more than I had intended. My only excuse is that I am an old man and old men are proverbially garrulous.
>
> I am the living history of Bengal and East Pakistan of the last 60 years. I am the last survivor of that band of unselfish and courageous Muslims who fought fearlessly again terrific odds. . . . I am now in the evening of my life and I am licking the wounds which I received in the long fight during the last six decades. I am getting old physically, but my heart is young and my optimism is unimpaired.[102]

The man who called himself "the living history" was also capable of noteworthy modesty. Opening the Dacca Law College in July 1957, Huq—still the Governor—said that he wished "to pay the homage of a grateful heart to the memory of those at whose feet" he had acquired his legal training; and he recalled, "with legitimate and pardonable pride," that "Dr Sir Asutosh Mookerjee, who was very strict in selecting his juniors, . . . had selected me for the coveted honour."[103]

* * *

Four years after he had left Government House Fazlul Huq died in a Dacca hospital. He who in 1943 had wanted to see Nazimuddin and Suhrawardy bite the dust now shares the same stretch of earth with them. All three are buried, side by side, in the grounds of Dacca High Court. For a while two of them were called Prime Minister of Pakistan. Fazlul Huq was not. But only he was spoken of as the royal Bengal tiger.

CHAPTER 7

ABUL KALAM AZAD

(1888–1958)

"He was fifty the day he was born," said Sarojini Naidu, referring to Maulana Abul Kalam Azad's accomplishments as a youth.[1] In his teens he wrote poetry and articles and brought out periodicals. When they first met him, many, including the poet Hali, took him to be the son of the writer they expected to see. Abul Kalam Mohiuddin Ahmed, as he was named, was born in Mecca in 1888. His father, Maulana Khairuddin, was a scholar and divine who had suffered in 1857 at the Raj's hands. Khairuddin spent about thirty years in Arabia, where he helped repair a canal, wrote books in Arabic and married Alia, niece of a learned Arab called Sheikh Muhammad Zahir Vatri. Some of Khairuddin's forebears were sufis. Others had capably served the Mughals in Agra and Delhi. After his Arabian sojourn Khairuddin settled down in Calcutta, where he acquired disciples and a following.

As a boy Azad "would climb a raised platform and ask his sisters to surround him and applaud him and then get down and walk off slowly and deliberately," as Fatima Begum, one of the sisters, recalled.[2] His mother died when he was eleven, his father ten years later. Married at thirteen to a girl called Zuleikha, Azad yielded, around the time of his father's death, to desires and lusts he later spoke of but did not specify. In his *Tazkirah* (written in 1917), Azad describes this phase of his life, which he says lasted for 17 months, in general terms:

> Intoxication filled the cups. Youth's frenzy took me by the hand. The
> yielding heart imagined that the path shown by desire and lust led

to the destination. Though at first taken by surprise, wisdom and awareness too nodded in assent, that this was indeed the right path, and the right time to enjoy life. . . . Wherever I cast my eyes, I found a city populated by love and adoration . . . each idol ravishing one's heart and reason, so beautiful that one felt compelled to offer it one's head; each sight of the loved one like a flash of lightning, consuming one's self-respect and self-control . . . ; each glance annihilating one's resistance.

Every corner in which I sought refuge turned into a prison-house for my reason and sanity. . . . It is better to confess openly. . . . There is no licence and no heresy which I was not fated to experience.[3]

Sayyid Ahmad's advocacy of a modern approach to religion had impressed Azad. Now it conspired with his tempters:

After a few days of agonised thinking, I made up my mind one night and gave up saying my prayers from the next morning. By God, I still remember that night and shall remember it for ever.

Azad does not relate how he returned to faith and sanity but he uses allegorical phrases to describe belief's rebirth:

The shock of unilateral love opened my eyes, as if into a different world. . . . Every leaf was like a letter. Flowers opened their lips. Stones rolled up to point out something. The skies came down to resolve my queries. Angels held me by their arms that I might not falter. The sun came to light my way that I might not stumble. All the veils were taken off.[4]

At the age of sixteen, as a result of instruction at home arranged by his father, who was implacably opposed to European education and to Sayyid Ahmad's path, Abul Kalam had attained high levels in Arabic and Persian and in religious studies. Now a sequence of pleasure, pain and peace seemed to confirm the truth of the faith that his teachers had taught. He embraced it afresh and with new ardour but he retained the *nom de plume* he had given himself when, to use his own words, he had "felt free of all conventional ties"—"*Azad*," or "*Free*."[5]

In 1906 Azad, 18 at the time, had attended the Dacca occasion at which the Muslim League was founded. However, his heart rebelling against the League's philosophy of loyalty to the Raj, he joined one of Bengal's revolutionary groups. Almost without exception, the revolutionaries of this period were Hindus, and Hindus, moreover, who viewed Musims as the Raj's collaborators. Muslim enthusiasm for Bengal's partition had offended them; and their feelings were not softened when East Bengal's Lieutenant-Governor, Fuller, said that "the Government looked upon the Muslim community as its favourite wife."[6] The revolutionaries were surprised by Azad's wish to join them. As he was later to say: "At first they did not fully trust me and tried to keep me outside their inner councils. In the course of time they realized their mistake and I gained their confidence."

Finding that "their activities were confined to Bengal and Bihar," Azad appears to have persuaded the revolutionaries to start "secret societies in several of the important towns of Northern India and Bombay." This is what Azad affirms; a promise he made of "a fuller account" and of "many interesting as well as amusing stories of the way in which organisations were set up and new members recruited" remained unfulfilled at the time of his death.[7]

Haseen—"handsome"—, Azad's only child, a boy, died at the age of four. In 1908, shortly after his "political ideas had turned toward revolutionary activities," Azad visited Iraq, Egypt, Syria and Turkey, where he met men who, in his words, "could not understand why Indian Muslims were mere camp-followers of the British." He returned to India "more convinced than ever that Indian Muslims must cooperate in the work of political liberation of the country.[8] *Al Hilal*—"a brilliant paper, written in a new moving style, amazingly forceful," possessing a "prodigious influence," in the words of W.C. Smith—was a result of this conviction.[9]

The first issue appeared in Calcutta on July 13, 1912. In the opinion of Mushir Haq, a scholar who is sharply critical of some aspects of Azad, "*Al Hilal* became so popular among the Urdu-reading Muslims of India that within a very short time Azad was known from one end of the country to the other."[10] Ikram, the Pakistani historian, says that the journal spoke "the language of a high-souled prophet" and "completely swept [readers] off their feet."[11]

Al Hilal preached pure Islam and Indian independence, simultaneously. Azad did not see a conflict between the two when he started his journal; he would never see it. He claimed that the Qur'an commanded a fight against slavery and sanctioned Muslim-Hindu cooperation to end it. Later he would be countered by the arguments that the Holy Book prescribed obedience to authority, and that it discouraged association with Hindus; those arguing thus would obtain adherents; but few of them would equal Azad's eloquence.

"Demolishing the barriers between journalism and creative literature," as one observer puts it,[12] focussing on struggle but also turning to themes such as Ghalib and Omar Khayyam, *Al Hilal* was prized by its readers.

Three months after its emergence all issues had to be re-printed—every subscriber wanted a complete set. In two years its circulation was in excess of 26,000 and greatly in excess of the readership of other Urdu papers.

The Raj did not like *Al Hilal*'s message. The paper had to pay and forfeit two deposits, one of Rs 2,000 and the other of Rs 10,000. In November 1914 the journal died. A year later it reappeared as *Al Balagh*, but only for six months, for in April 1916 Azad was externed from Calcutta under Defence of India Rules. He went to Ranchi in Bihar. The Raj forbade him from leaving the town; he would stay there, his condition more or less that of a prisoner, until January 1, 1920.

The Raj's attitude to Azad and the popularity of his papers were linked to Turkey. We saw in the chapter on Muhammad Ali how Muslims in India had been embittered by their perceptions of injustices to Turkey in the years preceding and following the First World War. Muhammad Ali's *Comrade* and Azad's *Al Hilal* (and *Al Balagh*) addressed an identical ferment, but, unlike Muhammad Ali, Azad seemed clear, right from the start, that the Turkish question could be used in aid of Indian nationalism. After 1920 Muhammad Ali allied himself with Gandhi and, for a while, allowed Swaraj to intertwine with Khilafat in his heart; but he had entered the Indian stage as a spokesman of the Muslim *qaum*, and he left it, too, in that role. In Azad's case Indian nationalism and Pan-Islam were always inseparable. As early as 1912 he had said, "For the Hindus patriotism might be a secular obligation, but for the Muslims it was a religious duty."[13]

As Mushir Haq points out, while Azad "never asked the Muslims to *follow* the Hindus, he always insisted on cooperation" between the two communities.[14] "As long as we follow Islam," he held, "we do not have to follow the Hindus in politics."[15] But he also said:

> Indian Muslims followed blindly the policy of the British government. . . . [They] broke off all relations with the Hindus who were the real active group in that country. . . . We were warned that the Hindus were a majority and if we went along with them they would crush us. . . . The result was that the government which should otherwise have become the target of the Muslims' spears was saved, and their own neighbours became their mark instead.[16]

Added Azad:

> Let us not be afraid of the Hindus. Only God is to be feared. If you want to live in India you have to embrace your neighbours. . . . If there is any hindrance from their side in cooperating, just ignore it.

... Even if others do not treat you well, you must behave as gentlemen. Older people do not cry when they are teased by youngsters;
they only smile and forgive them.[17]

On another occasion he wrote:

It is certain that a day will come when ... the bonds of slavery would
have been slashed by the winds of freedom. At that time do you
realise what would be written about the Muslims? It would be in-
scribed that there was an ill-fated community that served as a play-
thing in the hands of the covetous rulers, a pack of cards for the
pleasure of the foreigners. ... It would be said that when the bugle
was blown on the battlefield the Muslims went and hid themselves
in the caves.[18]

These passages show that Azad had the blood, and emotions, of a
Mughal aristocrat over whose home, India, the European now ruled.
Sending the foreigner to his home was Azad's primary concern; the Muslim *qaum*'s security in an independent India took second place. He said,
"There will be nothing left with us if we separate politics from religion,"[19]
but he said it to encourage Muslim participation in India's freedom struggle, not to foster Muslim solidarity. If his Islam enjoined patriotic rather
than communal action, it also breathed a universal spirit. *Al Hilal* of
January 1, 1913 has the following significant passage:

Islam does not command narrowmindedness and racial and religious
prejudice. It does not make the recognition of merit and virtue, of
human benevolence, mercy and love dependent upon and subject to
distinctions of religion and race. It teaches us to respect every man
who is good, whatever his religion.[20]

His religious views were courageous, unusual and unorthodox. Even
so a large number of devout Muslims responded to him because of his
eloquence and because purity of faith was suggested by the clarity of his
message. When he said that Islam commanded a fight against oppression,
and said it with fervour, and quoted the Qur'an in aid, his audience felt
they were listening to an authoritative voice. As Mushir Haq puts it, "Not
all of them had necessarily digested Azad's religious ideas, but many were
hypnotized by his writings."[21]

Azad's plan was to enlist and organize a body of dedicated Muslims,
make an agreement with the Hindus, and launch a joint struggle against
the British. In *Al Hilal* he asked, in April 1913, for names and pledges.
Within a week about 800 volunteered. In an article in December 1913

Azad disclosed that he had formed a "Party of God," or *Hizbullah*, through which the committed would strive "to establish a system of government to take care of the people according to the wish of God." "The method and function of the controlling body is a secret," he wrote.[22]

We know that a joint Hindu-Muslim struggle was launched in 1920; and before long we will turn to Azad's role in it. What we should note here is that the *Hizbullah* bid was not successful. Though he had roused many Muslims across the land, the *ulama*, Islam's recognized spokesmen, did not support Azad. He was to say later:

> As far back as in 1914 I had thought that I should remind the *ulama* and the heads of the sufi orders of their duties. I hoped that some of them would rise to meet the challenge of the times. But with the exception of one person, Maulana Mahmudul Hasan of Deoband, all of them regarded my invitation as *fitnah* (temptation) and rejected it.[23]

According to Azad, the *ulama* argued that political involvement might make Muslims neglectful of prescribed prayers, and bring them into "contact with unveiled non-Muslim women, which might create some *fitnah*."[24]

The traditional *ulama* backing away, Azad tried to create a new generation of theologians. An admirer donated land and money for a school and a dormitory, and *Darul-Irshad* (House of Guidance) opened classes in Calcutta in October 1914. Through *Darul-Irshad* Azad hoped to teach the Qur'an as he saw it to graduates of universities or seminaries, but his externment in April 1916 led to the institution's early demise.

Towards the close of 1916, as noted earlier, the Raj interned Azad in Ranchi. He had three restful years. He wrote, reflected on the life of the tribals amidst whom he found himself, and preached in local mosques. His *Tazkirah* was written in Ranchi; it could be published because one of his friends and helpers, Fazluddin Ahmed, took possession of the manuscript.

At Ranchi Azad also worked on his Qur'an translation and commentary. He had begun the labour earlier and translated eight chapters before the government ordered him to leave Calcutta. But the Raj confiscated his text and refused to return it, and at Ranchi Azad "started the translation and commentary anew from the very first chapter."[25] He made progress but the work was incomplete when he was released on January 1, 1920.

* * *

The India he found seemed an answer to prayer. Muslims and Hindus were ready to work together for independence. Events—the Rowlatt Act, the Jallianwalla tragedy and various developments over Khilafat—had succeeded where Azad's exhortations had failed. Within three weeks of his release Azad was in Delhi, where he met Gandhi for the first time. To Azad and other Muslim leaders Gandhi proposed non-violent non-cooperation with the Raj and a Hindu-Muslim alliance. Others wanted time to consider the implications of the Mahatma's proposal but Azad, as he was later to recall, "said without a moment's hesitation that [he] fully accepted the programme." Added Azad:

> As soon as Gandhiji described his proposal I remembered that this was the programme which Tolstoy had outlined many years ago. . . . To indulge in political murder was to sow the dragon's teeth. . . . The proper method to paralyse an oppressive government was to refuse taxes, resign from all services and boycott institutions supporting the government. . . . Such a programme would compel any government to come to terms. I also remembered that I had myself suggested a similar programme in some articles in *Al Hilal*.[26]

Azad had urged a joint Hindu-Muslim struggle in *Al Hilal*, but he had not referred to non-cooperation or non-violence. When Gandhi used the terms, Azad instantly saw their significance and announced himself as Gandhi's ally, the first prominent Muslim to do so in India. Joining Gandhi a little later, the Ali brothers at once appeared on centre-stage, and it became obvious that the lively Muhammad Ali would fascinate crowds more than the somewhat aristocratic Azad. Yet Azad the orator could move an audience almost as effectively as Azad the writer. All over India people heard him, and one of the many his speeches recruited for the national cause was a young man in Bihar called Jayaprakash Narayan.

While taking his place at the Mahatma's side, Azad made it clear that he was adopting non-violence as a policy, not as a principle valid for all periods and situations. The Mahatma and the Maulana clicked with each other from the start, and also understood each other. In 1920 Azad accepted Gandhi's leadership of India's struggle but not all of Gandhi's beliefs. As Mujeeb points out, Azad not only "declared openly that non-violence was for him a matter of policy, not creed," he also "smoked freely and continuously in Mahatma Gandhi's presence, in spite of its being known that Mahatma Gandhi was strongly opposed to such indulgence."[27]

The India of 1920 satisfied Azad in another vital respect. The *ulama* had come round. Their feelings wounded by Britain's attitude to Turkey, the *ulama* were now willing to face the risks of a political struggle and of Muslim-Hindu fraternization. They now held Azad in especial respect; at a Lahore meeting in 1921 about 10,000 of the *ulama* came close to choosing him as *Amirul-Hind* or *Imamul-Hind* (Leader of India), and at least once in 1921 he was called *Quaid-i-Azam*, the title that later came to be associated with Jinnah.[28]

Quoting the Qur'an, Azad had said in 1920 that considerations of unity and discipline required an Imam, or Leader, in India. "Whatever he orders them, provided it is not contrary to the Qur'an and the *sunnah*, must be obeyed," said Azad.[29] There is no doubt that Azad saw himself as the Imam, but there was more than self-regard or vanity in his call for an Imam. Having helped bring religion into India's politics, Azad wanted to control its impact. As he said once in a conversation with Mahadev Desai, Gandhi's secretary:

> The power of religion is limitless. Religion is like a powerful engine of a train, which needs a careful and intelligent driver. In a train accident, it is hard to estimate the casualties. . . . If the power of religion is not handled by the right persons, there will be tremendous harm.[30]

Azad's desire for a grip on religious activity was strengthened by his awareness that he needed an Imam's influence if he wanted the *qaum* to accept his universalist view of Islam. Boldly he said that an Imam was needed; equally boldly he implied that he could be one. Though, as Haq states, referring to the 1920–21 period, "Maulana Azad was commonly known among the Muslims of India as Imamul-Hind,"[31] no Imam was in fact chosen. It is possible that the *ulama* were dissuaded by fears of rivalry for the honour; in any case, Azad's bid failed.

He was without the platform he had hoped for, but he still had his voice and his pen. In 1921 he stated that Hindu-Muslim partnership was sanctioned by the Prophet's own example:

> When the Prophet Muhammad migrated to Medina he prepared a covenant between the Muslims and the Jews of Medina. In the covenant it was mentioned that ultimately the Muslims and non-Muslims would become one nation (*ummah vahidah*).
>
> *Ummah* means a *qaum* or nation; *vahidah* means one. Thus if I say that the Muslims of India cannot perform their duty unless they are united with the Hindus, it is in accordance with the tradition of the Prophet who himself wanted to make a nation of Muslims and non-Muslims. . . .[32]

We should note that in 1921 no Muslim contested Azad's opinion. We should note, too, that though Azad cited the Prophet's example as his authority, his view was based, as Mujeeb points out, "on the deep conviction that such friendship and cooperation was a fundamental injunction of Islam and represented its true spirit."[33]

This "deep conviction" stayed with Azad all his life, but he must have had second thoughts about another statement he made during the Khilafat movement. This was his 1920 *fatwa*, or considered opinion, in which Muslims were told that the Shariah required them to migrate from India, if that was possible, or to assist those who were migrating.[34] Ruled by a power that had attacked the Khilafat, India was no longer a land fit for Muslims to live in. As we saw in the Muhammad Ali chapter, the *fatwa*, supported by others, was obeyed by thousands, who suffered greatly during their trek into, and back from, Afghanistan.

The *fatwa* is out of key with Azad's words and deeds in the 1920s, and it is both unfortunate and odd that Azad should have issued it. It is odd because Azad seemed to take care in his utterances to emphasize the practical and stay clear of the theoretical. Thus, in his presidential address to a Khilafat conference held in Agra in 1921, he said:

> Let us first define the field of our activities. Is the goal somewhere outside India? In fact our goal is not outside India. It is not in Iraq or Syria or Asia Minor. Our objective is to test the power of our belief, determination and action. The goal is in our own country. Unless you succeed in your own country success will not greet you elsewhere. . . . India is the first goal of the Khilafat movement.[35]

Azad's message was that Indians had to be free to be of any use to the Khilafat.

* * *

We will not dwell on the spirit or happenings of 1920 and 1921; they have been covered earlier. We saw that those were years in which Indians were affected in their depths. They caught a whiff of the breath of freedom, felt the thrill and anxieties of sacrifice, sensed, for the first time in decades, their muscle, tasted the honey of Hindu-Muslim partnership and tasted as well the bitter brew of prison life.

If Muhammad Ali was the voice of the *qaum* during this phase, Abul Kalam Azad was its mind. He was the ideologue, familiar with scripture, clear in thought and expression, speaking with the ring of authority. But now his audience extended beyond the *qaum*, for he increasingly found himself on the Congress stage.

He forged a close relationship with several on that stage. The one with Chitta Ranjan Das is perhaps especially noteworthy. As Azad later observed, Das "had a princely practice at the Calcutta Bar . . . and was also noted for his fondness for luxury, but he gave up his practice without a moment's hesitation, donned khaddar and threw himself wholeheartedly into the Congress movement." As keen as Azad on Hindu-Muslim co-operation, Das "shook the Bengal Congress to its very foundation"—Azad's words—by announcing in 1923 that if "Congress secured the reins of power in Bengal, it would reserve 60 percent of all new (governmental) appointments for the Musalmans" until the community obtained its due share of government jobs.[36] Das's death in 1925 deprived Azad of a valuable ally and India of a figure committed to cordiality in Hindu-Muslim relations.

But we should return to 1921. On December 10 that year Mr. Goldie, deputy commissioner of police, arrived at Azad's Calcutta home with a posse of policemen and told him that he was being arrested for instigating a revolt in two speeches he had made in a mosque in the city. That night Azad was removed to a room in Alipore presidency jail where, as he later recalled, he "slept soundly for the first time in two years."[37] He was tried while in detention and sentenced in February 1922 to a year's imprisonment.

Loyal to the principle of boycotting the Raj's courts, Azad had not defended himself. But he submitted a written statement entitled *Qaul-e-faisal*, or The Final Verdict. Described by Gandhi as "the most forceful and truthful statement offered by a satyagrahi,"[38] it deserves to be quoted at some length:

> Certainly I said that the present government is a tyrant. What else could I say? If I am convinced that this government is evil, I cannot pray for its long life.... Whatever attractive things may be done for those in bondage, slavery is after all slavery. I deem it my national, religious and human duty to liberate my country and my people from servitude.
>
> The present government is a negation of the wish and will of millions of people. It justifies the barbarous general massacre of Jallianwalla Bagh. It does not consider it unjust that people should be made to crawl upon their bellies like beasts.... It does not desist from riding rough-shod over the Islamic Caliphate despite persistent pleadings of 300 million human beings.
>
> There is no city where I have not reiterated all the statements included in the two speeches filed against me. In fact, I must admit that the previous speeches were even more definite, clear and categorical. In the speeches filed against me I had declared that the seed of freedom can never be nurtured until it is watered by violence and repression. And the government has started watering it.
>
> When I ponder on the great and significant history of the convicts' dock and find that the honour of standing in that place belongs to me today, my soul becomes steeped in thankfulness and praise of God.[39]

A wire that Zuleikha Begum, Azad's wife, wanted to send to Gandhi was not communicated by the Raj's telegraph office. It said:

> The court announced its decision today in the case of my husband. He has received a sentence of only one year's imprisonment. This is noticeably less than what we were prepared for.... You will agree that injustice has been done to him in this respect.... I would like to inform you that for the vacancy that has been caused in Bengal through his absence I have offered my unworthy services.... From today I shall perform all the tasks of the Bengal Khilafat Committee.[40]

While arresting Azad, the Raj's police had removed most of his papers, including his unfinished Qur'an translation and commentry. At Alipore jail Azad did not take up his pen for the commentary or for anything else. The calm with which he had started his imprisonment was broken by events outside, which were exciting to begin with and then became bewildering. From December to February Azad heard of a mounting struggle outside the walls of his prison and of the imminence of a tax strike, starting in Bardoli in Gujarat.

Then, in the second week of February, when Azad was awarded his twelve-month sentence, he also learned that Gandhi had abruptly called off disobedience because policemen had been killed in Chauri Chaura. Azad was shocked. Not viewing non-violence as an absolute principle, he could not accept that a whole struggle should be halted merely because a mob somewhere in eastern U.P. had lost its sanity. Later he would write: "[The suspension] caused a severe reaction in political circles and demoralized the country."[41] What Azad did not say was that many Muslims resented the fact that Gandhi had called off disobedience without consulting him or the Ali brothers. Not that consultation was possible: Azad and the Ali brothers were in jail. Still, Muslim dissatisfaction was a reality, as was Azad's own unhappiness.

To Jawaharlal Nehru, who, unlike Azad, had conveyed his sense of shock to Gandhi, the Mahatma wrote: "I assure you that if the thing had not been suspended we would have been leading not a non-violent struggle but essentially a violent struggle."[42] As Judith Brown, the British scholar, observes, Gandhi could no longer "lead such a movement and retain his integrity."[43] He saved his integrity but Azad saw a retreat and also something else that was sad, a crack in the edifice of Hindu-Muslim trust.

* * *

Abul Kalam Azad was not fully 35 when he came out of prison in January 1923. The Indian scene was discouraging. Though most of those arrested in the 1920–21 campaign had been released, Gandhi was in prison and expected to be there till 1928. Hindus and Muslims had forgotten their quarrel with the British and started squabbling with each other. Congress was divided, with one group, the "pro-changers," headed by Das and Motilal Nehru, wanting to enter the Raj's councils, and the other group, the "no-changers," who were led by Rajagopalachari, Patel and Rajendra Prasad, keen to continue with the boycott decided upon in 1920.

The fervour of Azad the ideologue was well-known. Now he showed his mediatory skill and helped prevent a split in Congress. As Kripalani, a future Congress president, was to say later, "It was [Azad's] moderating influence that avoided a cleavage at the time between the pro-changers and the no-changers."[44]

Trusted by both groups, Azad was asked to preside when Congress met in September 1923 to decide its future course. No one younger had been, or would be, given the honour. In his address he said:

> As in the case of individuals, the real source of action in a nation lies in the mind. When a struggle advances but haltingly, and there are stoppages on the way, a mood of despondency and weariness overtakes us. Winds of dissension begin to blow and the national struggle has a most trying time. Nevertheless, if the vital parts of the struggle are sound, then [the present will prove to be] but a momentary pause.

Azad was clear on what was vital to, and indeed greater than, the struggle. He said:

> If an angel descends from the heavens today and proclaims from the Qutb Minar that India can attain Swaraj within 24 hours provided I relinquish my demand for Hindu-Muslim unity, I shall retort to it: "No my friend, I shall give up Swaraj, but not Hindu-Muslim unity, for if Swaraj is delayed, it will be a loss for India, but if Hindu-Muslim unity is lost, it will be a loss for the whole of mankind."[45]

* * *

If Jinnah always wore well-cut western-style suits, Azad looked distinguished in his fur cap, long coat and narrow white trousers. Both Azad and Jinnah were tall and erect and early risers. The eyes of both flashed intelligence; the thoughts of both were clear. Both were avid smokers. Unlike the clean-shaven Jinnah, Azad wore a small, trimmed, pointed beard and a long turned-up moustache. Eleven years younger than Jinnah, Azad had stirred the Muslim masses with *Al Hilal* a quarter-century before Jinnah would do so with his Pakistan cry. Both found it tedious to mix with the masses or to listen to the common man's tales of woe, yet both frequently addressed crowds, Jinnah binding them with his resolve and

Azad sweeping them off their feet with his eloquence. Both liked solitude. When alone Jinnah planned his moves of defence or attack; Azad turned to a history or a novel or a poem, in Urdu, Arabic, Persian, Turkish or English, or to his work on the Qur'an. Jinnah was silent or combative in company, except when he was absolutely sure of its loyalty. Azad was refined, cordial and even deferential, and indeed a finished conversationalist; yet he always seemed to want to return to his reading.

Neither found it hard to defy popular currents. Jinnah refused to go along with the Gandhi wave of the early twenties; and Azad presented, as we shall shortly see, an uncommon interpretation of Islam. Both felt at home in a leader's role, but whereas Jinnah was the League's unquestioned guide, Azad, even when Congress's president, was only one of a team of leaders. There were occasions when his views did not prevail in Congress's councils; at all such times Azad accepted the decision of the majority. There were other occasions, such as the one in 1923, when Azad successfully reconciled rivalling points of view. "He never seems to be in want of the right word, and . . . he is at his best in committee meetings," said Mahadev Desai, who edited Gandhi's *Harijan* and observed many a Congress committee in action.[46]

* * *

It was in 1930 that Azad finally finished his *Tarjuman*, a translation of, and commentary on, eighteen of the Qur'an's thirty chapters. In it he concluded that the Qur'an did not ask adherents of other religions to embrace Islam as a wholly new faith. In fact it asked them "to return to the true form of their own religion."[47] Distinguishing between the principle of religion (the *din*) and its forms, Azad found the Qur'anic concept "comprehensive enough to include all forms of monotheism."[48] Hindus too had a place. Though, as Mujeeb puts it, Azad regretted "the fact that Hindus who knew better have been willing to make compromises with forms of belief that were polytheistic or idolatrous," he still regarded cooperation between Hindus who submit themselves to the one God and Muslims as "a fundamental injunction of Islam."[49] In *Tarjuman* Azad quoted what to him was a key Qur'anic passage:

> We have set for each [group] of you a particular code and path. Had God so willed, he could have made you one people, but He tests you by the separate regulations which He has made for you. . . . So [do not lose yourself in these differences but] endeavour to surpass each other through your good deeds.[50]

The message of Azad's *Tarjuman* was bold. In his *Islam and Pakistan*, Freeland Abbott, the American scholar, summarizes it as follows:

The law of man's spiritual fulfilment was the same for all; the greatest error of religious men was to divide themselves into mutually hostile groups. While rituals and customs vary, religion is the same for all—for it consists in being submissive to God and in leading a life of right action.[51]

What lay behind Azad's universalist interpretation? According to Mujeeb, it was the Qur'an itself that moulded Azad's thought:

The Qur'an inspired all his thinking. He did not limit his horizon by accepting traditional interpretations, by deriving his opinions from other sources and using the Qur'anic text as formal proof. He could therefore think more independently than others, and warn and guide with complete self-confidence.[52]

In Mujeeb's opinion, the "full implications" of Azad's interpretation would be "explosive enough to destroy the distinctions created between Muslims and monotheists professing other religions." The Muslims would then "have no justification for confining their thoughts and activities to their particular community," or for regarding the *shariah* as immutable. If Azad is right, then the Qur'an sanctions a review of the validity of an item in the *shariah* if it is found to divide where it should unite.[53]

These implications were not spelt out in so many words by Azad, but they flow inescapably from his conviction that "the mission of Islam was to make believers in one God realize that there was a spiritual bond uniting them all."[54] In any case Azad's deeds and politics were those of Muslim-Hindu cooperation from the start; in the final phase of his life he would also practise cooperation between Indians and Europeans.

In 1921 no Muslim had challenged Azad's religious and political position. A time would come when few Muslims would endorse it. Yet, as Mujeeb has put it, Azad's "faith was so deep-rooted that he could stand alone. And perhaps some day it will be acknowledged by the Indian Muslims that he had in fact discovered a new world of religious thought to redress the balance of the old."[55]

At first sight Azad is not a modernist. As Ikram says, some of *Al Hilal's* pages contain a "revivalist, anti-modern and anti-intellectual" flavour.[56] Functionaries of *Jamaat-i-Islami*, which seeks, for Pakistan, an Islamic state that would conform to the letter of the *shariah*, have at times claimed Azad as "the very first champion" of their objective.[57] But, as we have seen, even in *Al Hilal* Azad's thrust was on Hindu-Muslim cooperation; and if he spoke in that journal of Islam's early days of purity and glory, it was to stir the *qaum* to oppose foreign rule, not to oppose modern institutions.

Azad's father had no doubt "turned foe to everything Western," as Mahadev Desai puts it; this was a consequence of the father's "bitter memories of the Rebellion of 1857." But Azad himself had always felt that the Muslim community would "profit by Western education and sciences."[58] In any case, as Ikram points out, "The author of the *Tarjuman* is not the fiery youth who edited *Al Hilal*."[59]

In 1940 Azad would categorically say that "revivalism in social matters is a denial of progress."[60] The revival he supported was of submission to the one God, the *din* stressed by Prophet Muhammad. If we want to describe Azad's place on a scale of ascending or descending orthodoxy, we cannot do much better than to quote Wilfred Cantwell Smith, the western scholar, who, writing while Azad was alive, said:

> Azad is a thoroughly profound scholar of Islam, his scholarship being liberal in the very best sense. He has a place in the front rank of the classic theologians; he is also among the foremost of the moderns. . . . His Islam is humanitarian.[61]

Mujeeb, finding Azad's conclusions "clear, reasonable and satisfying" and the *Tarjuman* "free of any attempts to read into the Qur'an what is really not there," calls it "perhaps the finest example of the constructive thinking enjoined on the Muslim."[62]

Even those disagreeing with Azad's views have praised the *Tarjuman's* clarity and the learning that produced it. Azad himself commented: "I devoted about 23 years of my life in studying the Qur'an. I have deliberated over every chapter, every verse, every phrase and every word. I can claim to have studied the larger part of all the commentaries. . . . "[63]

* * *

The toil over the *Tarjuman* was proof of political stillness. The years from 1923 to 1930 were punctuated by Hindu-Muslim riots, not by steps toward liberty. Azad supported Gandhi's unsuccessful and intermittent efforts for harmony and on occasion organized relief, finding lorries to remove "sixty to seventy Muslim tailors harboured during a riot by Hindus in a thickly populated Hindu locality" to safety, or rendering a similar service to "Hindus sheltered by a Mussalman in Mussalman localties."[64] When, in 1927, Jinnah and Muhammad Ali made their effort for a Congress-Muslim agreement, Azad backed them. When Congress's Motilal Nehru committee made a similar bid in 1928, Azad backed the committee.

We saw in the last two chapters that Congress did not concede the Jinnah-Muhammad Ali demands. Azad's comment on the disagreement revealed his outlook. He said that the Muslims were fools to make the demands and the Hindus greater fools to refuse them.[65] This was towards the close of 1928, when Congress also warned Britain of a struggle if India was not given dominion status in a year.

Responding to the smell of battle, Azad advised Muslims to abandon their demands, no matter how justified. "The war has started," he said.[66] Rejecting the advice, the bulk of the Muslim League chose instead to avoid the war that commenced when Congress's deadline expired at the end of 1929. By this time Azad, Ansari and their friends had left the League and sponsored the Muslim Nationalist party "to promote broadminded patriotism and oppose communalism,"[67] with Ansari as president and Khaliquzzaman as secretary. Though he did not formally join the new party, it was clear that the fervent scholar and divine had broken with the *qaum*.

Azad played a vigorous role in the 1930 struggle but the *qaum* as a whole did not, except in the North West Frontier, where the Khan brothers brought thousands of their Khudai Khidmatgars—Servants of God— to the field of battle, pledged, at Gandhi's insistence, to non-violence. Even Khaliquzzaman, who had helped form the Muslim Nationalist party, stayed out of the struggle, being, as he recalled later, "firmly of the view that with Muslims sulking, . . . any fight for independence was a colossal blunder."[68]

We need not go into the highlights or ups and downs of this war, except to note that it was followed by a notable Gandhi-Irwin pact, Irwin being the Viceroy at the time, and by an infructuous round table conference in London. Azad spent six months in prison in Meerut before the pact and another six months in Delhi in 1932, after the collapse of the London task. For some days before each imprisonment he had functioned as Congress's "dictator," named to that position by the "dictator" whose arrest had created the vacancy, and naming, on his arrest, a "dictator" to succeed him.

Finding the Raj shaken but still in place, Congress gave up disobedience in 1934 and decided to fight its battles from the floors of the Raj's legislatures. Thus far Congress had either shunned these councils as a trap or, while joining, treated them with disdain. Congress's switch was facilitated by a Bill before the House of Commons, soon to become the Act of 1935, handing over slices of real power to provincial legislatures. Azad became a key member of Congress's parliamentary board, formed to regulate Congress's entry into the legislatures.

How most provinces came under Congress rule in 1937 was seen in the Jinnah chapter. Here we should add that Azad was asked by Congress's working committee to oversee the installation of ministries in the northern provinces. In the U.P. he offered seats in the cabinet to two League members of the Assembly, Khaliquzzaman, who had rejoined the League, and Nawab Ismail Khan. They seemed willing, but Jawaharlal Nehru, Congress's president at the time, decided that only one could be taken; he stuck to his position even when, at Azad's insistence, Gandhi asked Nehru to agree to the inclusion of both. The League group would not settle for one seat, and Azad's effort for a Congress-League alliance in the U.P. failed.

Later Azad was to assert that Nehru's attitude enabled Jinnah to retain the crucial support of the League's U.P. contingent, which "had been on the point of leaving Mr. Jinnah." Added Azad: "Jawaharlal's action gave the Muslim League in the U.P. a new lease of life. All students of Indian politics know that it was from the U.P. that the League was reorganized. Mr. Jinnah took full advantage of the situation and started an offensive which ultimately led to Pakistan."[69]

Khaliquzzaman, in his memoirs, says that Azad "is justified in drawing the conclusion that the foundation for Pakistan was really laid" following the breakdown of the U.P. talks. According to Khaliquzzaman, the talks failed because Congress wanted the League to "agree to wind itself up in the U.P." and not because only one place in the cabinet was offered. Azad himself, claims Khaliquzzaman, was "prevailed upon" by two elements in Congress, one anti-Muslim and the other pro-Communist, to demand the League group's dissolution as the price for places in the ministry. In Khaliquzzaman's view, "things would have perhaps changed" if Azad "had put his foot down" and "threatened to resign" his position as Congress's chief for the northern zone "if he was thwarted in his efforts at settlement." "But," says Khaliquzzaman, "Azad's courage failed."[70]

That men like Khaliquzzaman were disappointed and embittered when the deal fell through is clear. Khaliquzzaman writes of how, following the breakdown, he lost a night's sleep, and chose to oppose Congress in the U.P. Assembly and all over the province, and "finally came to the conclusion that separation would perhaps be the best remedy for both the Hindus and the Muslims."[71]

Early in 1939, before the start of the war and the resignation of Congress's ministries, Khaliquzzaman visited England and proposed partition as a solution to the Secretary of State for India, Lord Zetland. On his return he recommended it to Jinnah, who "carefully heard every word . . . at times asking me to repeat certain words, and assured us that he was not opposed to it." Jinnah added that the question of partition "had to be examined in all its bearings."[72] A year later Jinnah and the League asked for partition.

Seven years later, when Pakistan was a fact and Khaliquzzaman had migrated from the U.P. to the new nation, Vallabhbhai Patel called him, in a speech in Lucknow, "the man responsible for Pakistan."[73] We have seen, however, that Azad thought that Nehru was responsible, and that Khaliquzzaman suggested that Azad was. Chaudhri Muhammad Ali implies, referring to a later episode, that Patel was: "Patel was was psychologically preparted for a parting of the ways and, with his usual determination, promptly set about it."[74] Who speaks the truth? None, and each, and Khaliquzzaman, when, as we have noted before, he says, "Pakistan was our destiny rather than our choice."[75]

Subhas Bose followed Nehru as Congress's president. When Bose's term ended in 1938, the name of Azad "was on every lip," as Mahadev Desai has recorded,[76] and Gandhi asked him to accept the post. However, Bose wanted to serve for another year. This was unusual but not unheard of; Nehru had just presided for two consecutive years. The idea of a contest with Bose not appealing to him, Azad turned down Gandhi's proposal. He did not wish to offend his numerous friends in Bengal, where Bose had become a hero. Bose was re-elected; he defeated Pattabhi Sitaramayya of the Telugu country, despite the fact that Gandhi had publicly blessed Sitaramayya's candidacy.

Azad did not lack a role. Ansari had died in 1936; thereafter no Muslim rivalled Azad's status in Congress. He guided Congress's ministers in the northern provinces and at times eased their path. In Bihar, as a result of his "great tact and power of persuasion"—to use the words of Rajendra Prasad, a Bihari who was India's President from 1950 to 1962[7]—landlords undertook not to challenge new legislation that gave relief to cultivators.

A joint Gandhi-Bose leadership proved impossible. Their personalities and views clashed. Reverting to the Mahatma, Congress asked Bose to appoint his working committee "in accordance with the wishes of Gandhiji."[78] Bose resigned and left Congress and Rajendra Prasad acted as president for the remainder of his term.

At the end of 1939 Gandhi again asked Azad to lead Congress. Agreeing this time, Azad was elected president by 1854 votes as against 183 secured by M.N. Roy, who stood on a leftist platform. Azad had been president once before, at the age of 35. Now he was 52, but facing a world where Hitler's war had begun, and an India where Jinnah and the League seemed suddenly able to block Congress's advance.

Congress met in Rangarh in Bihar in March 1940. Azad's presidential address revealed his frustration at the Raj's success in answering Congress's demands for independence with quotations from Jinnah. It also conveyed Azad's love of Islam and of liberty, his confidence that the *qaum* would be secure in a free India, and his faith in India's oneness. Representing the outlook of the Muslim minority that disagreed with the Pakistan idea, the address is significant. It was, moreover, eloquent. Said Azad:

> India cannot endure the prospect of Nazism and Fascism, but she is even more tired of British imperialism . . .

> The Congress put forward a clear and simple demand, to which no [one] could possibly object. It asked, if India was being invited to participate in this war, for an opportunity for India to feel that she was breathing in a changed atmosphere . . .

> It was not in our remotest thoughts that the communal question would be raised in this connection. . . . The communal problem is undoubtedly with us. To admit its existence, however, does not mean that it should be used as a weapon against India's national freedom.

> Muslims in India are a vast concourse spreading out all over the country. They stand erect, and number between eighty and ninety millions. It is true they number only one-fourth of the total population, but the question is not one of ratio, but of large numbers and the strength behind them. If they are in a minority in seven provinces, they are in a majority in five.

> Do we, Indian Musalmans, view the future of India with suspicion and distrust or with courage and confidence? If we view it with fear and suspicion, then undoubtedly we will have to follow a different path. No present declaration, no promise for the future, no constitutional safeguards can be a remedy for our doubts and fears. We are then forced to tolerate the existence of a third power.

> Every fibre of my being revolted against [this] alternative. I could not conceive it possible for a Musalman to tolerate this, unless he has rooted out the spirit of Islam from every corner of his being.

> I am a Musalman and proud of the fact. Islam's splendid traditions of thirteen hundred years are my inheritance. I am unwilling to lose even the smallest part of this inheritance. In addition, I am proud of being an Indian. I am part of the indivisible unity that is Indian nationality.

> I am indispensable to this noble edifice. Without me this splendid structure of India is incomplete. I am an essential element which has gone to build India. I can never surrender this claim.

> It was India's historic destiny that many human races and cultures and religions shoud flow to her, and that many a caravan should find rest here. . . . One of the last of these caravans was that of the followers of Islam. This came here and settled here for good.

> We brought our treasures with us, and India too was full of the riches of her own precious heritage. We gave her what she needed most, the most precious of gifts from Islam's treasury, the message of human equality. Full eleven centuries have passed by since then. Islam has now as great a claim on the soil of India as Hinduism.

> Everything bears the stamp of our joint endeavour. Our languages were different, but we grew to use a common language. Our manners and customs were dissimilar, but they produced a new synthesis. Our old dress may be seen only in ancient pictures . . .

No fantasy or artificial scheming to separate and divide can break this unity.[79]

* * *

Meeting that same month in Lahore, the Muslim League asked for Pakistan. The *qaum* did not embrace the idea right away. A month after the League's Lahore resolution, seven Muslim organizations opposed it at a joint rally held in Delhi. As the scholar Smith notes, they represented "a majority of India's Muslims" at the time.[80] But Congress's impatience for independence was to play into the hands of Jinnah, who warned Muslims against exhanging white masters for Hindu ones. He also characterized Azad, in a telegram to him, as "a Muslim showboy Congress president." The "not particularly polite" text of the telegram—to use Khaliquzzaman's phrase[81]—was included in the Jinnah chapter. Azad did not hit back, but he countered Jinnah's assertion that Hindus and Muslims had "different civilisations, different epics and different heroes" and that "very often the hero of one is a foe of the other."[82] Said Azad:

> Providence brought us (Hindus and Muslims) together over a thousand years ago. We have fought, but so do blood-brothers fight.... No, it is no use trying to emphasize the differences. For that matter no two human beings are alike. Every lover of peace must emphasize similarities.[83]

Britain not responding to its demands, Congress opened a campaign of disobedience limited to chosen individuals. The idea was to compel Britain's attention without embarrassing her when she was struggling against Germany. As he was to put it later, Azad was for "a more extensive and active anti-war movement" but, in his words, "Gandhiji would not agree to this."[84]

The campaign led to Azad's fifth term of imprisonment. Arrested before he could recite the unlawful statement that Congress had prescribed—"It is wrong to help the British war effort with men or money"—, Azad was sentenced for two years and detained in Naini jail near Allahabad. Jinnah could now preach Pakistan without being controverted by one who was once called *Imamul-Hind* and was still esteemed by the *qaum*. A year later, shortly before Japan's attack on Pearl Harbor, Azad was released. He has recalled:

> I was in a state of mental distress when the order of release reached me. In fact, I felt a sense of humiliation.... I felt keenly that even though the war had been going on for over two years, we had not been able to take an effective steps towards achieving freedom.[85]

One of two things could remove the feeling of humiliation: generosity from the Raj or a struggle against it. Also emerging from prison, Rajagopalachari openly advocated "readiness to come to a settlement" with the British.[86] He thought that Japan's sweep across Asia would oblige Britain to offer better terms to India. Differing, Gandhi said that "nothing is to be expected from the government."[87] Azad supported Rajagopalachari and Congress backed the two. In January 1942, recognizing "the new world situation," it offered cooperation to the allies in the war if India's freedom was declared.[88] Resolved to stop Japan, Roosevelt urged Churchill to make a move to win India's goodwill. Chiang Kai-Shek did the same; in February he visited India and tried to bring the Raj and Congress together. Azad told him that if Britain "assured us about freedom after the war" and agreed that during the war Indian representatives on the Viceroy's Executive Council could work with "a sense of freedom and responsibility," the Congress "would not refuse the offer."[89]

In March Rangoon fell and Churchill's hands were forced. He sent Sir Stafford Cripps, advocate, diplomat and politician, to India with the offer we looked at in the preceding chapter: dominion status after the war and the immediate entry of Congress and the League into the Indian government. To obtain Jinnah's acceptance, Cripps offered every province the right to secede from India, once the latter had become a dominion.

We have seen that Gandhi was strongly opposed to this provision for secession. Azad and Nehru, who were Congress's negotiators, also disliked it and called it "a severe blow to the conception of Indian unity." Yet they seemed ready to accept it: Cripps had argued that "no province would, in fact, demand the right," and Sikandar Hyat, Punjab's Premier, had assured Azad that "the vote of the Punjab Assembly would be on national and not on communal lines."[90]

What Azad could not accept was the Viceroy's veto in the proposed new government. At first, in fact, Cripps had indicated that the veto would be withdrawn; later he pleaded that this could not be done. Azad told Cripps that any reform that retained the Viceroy's veto would be "far removed from all that we have striven for."[91] As he was to say later, while he "preferred the democracies to the fascist powers," he wanted "the democratic principle applied to India's case, . . . if India was to support the war effort."[92] Conferring under Azad's chairmanship, Congress's working committee rejected the Cripps offer.

Struggle now seemed the only option, and Gandhi prescribed it. He asked Congress's leaders to ask Britain, simply, to Quit India. Azad was torn. He felt, as he put it at the time, that "Congress had gone as far as it possibly could" in talks, and that the time for action had come.[93] Yet

Japan was at India's gate and seemed capable of storming through it. Azad argued that in such a situation Britain would act swiftly to suppress any Indian rising. Congress's leaders would be arrested the moment a struggle was announced; bereft of guidance, the masses would either turn violent or submit to repression.

While not disputing all of this, Gandhi thought that passivity or an appeal for patience would isolate Congress and allow extreme, violent and pro-Axis elements to capture the Indian mind. Three different wars were now being fought: Britain against the Axis powers, India against the British, the League against Congress. None felt that its war should or could be postponed. Azad proposed that Congress "should wait upon the course of events,"[94] but the Mahatma did not agree.

For a while Nehru joined Azad in arguing against Quit India, fearing that it would hurt the defence of China and Russia, but in the end the nationalist in him triumphed. Azad, too, fell in line. He and Nehru knew that Gandhi was right when he said that he did not need Congress for his move: the sands of India, he had declared, would throw up a movement larger than Congress if it did not act.

* * *

Zuleikha, Azad's wife, had been ill during much of 1941. By the middle of 1942, aided by a spell in Ranchi, she felt better. Her only child had died at the age of four and she never saw much of her husband. He was in jail in 1941 and travelling without pause after release. As he was to write later, "No sooner than I reached one destination, another place seemed to summon me urgently."[95] On July 31 Azad was back in Calcutta after a three-week tour; on August 3 he left for Bombay. Of the four days at home Azad has written:

> I had to look after so many things that I had hardly time to talk to her. She knew that I did not like to be interrupted. So she too kept quiet. On the 3rd of August, when I was leaving for Bombay, she came as usual to the door to bid me goodbye. I told her that if nothing unexpected happened I should return by August 13. She did not say a word besides *Khuda Hafiz*. But nothing that she could have said would have been more expressive than the silent agonized look on her face. It was the face that cried, not the eyes. I must have parted from her hundreds of times. Yet I had never seen her so sad.

* * *

On August 8, meeting in Bombay, the All India Congress Committee voted overwhelmingly in favour of Quit India. Azad presided. His doubts behind him, Nehru moved the fateful resolution. Gandhi, father of the idea, spoke. But the most potent speech was Patel's:

They will round up the leaders, round up all. Then it will be the duty of every Indian to put forth his utmost effort—within non-violence. No course is to be left untapped; no weapon untried. This is going to be the opportunity of a life-time.[97]

Non-violence not being Azad's immutable creed, he had said the following to Congressmen he had met in the second half of July:

If the Government allow[s] us to function, the movement must develop strictly according to Gandhiji's instructions. If, however, the Government arrest[s] Gandhiji and other Congress leaders, the people [should] be free to adopt any method, violent or non-violent, to oppose the violence of the Government.[98]

On the night of August 8, some hours after the Quit India decision, a relative who had a friend in the Bombay police informed Azad that Congress's leaders would be arrested in the morning. Azad has recalled what happened thereafter:

I told Bhulabhai Desai (Azad's host in Bombay) that if the news was true, I had only a few hours of freedom. It was better that I should have dinner quickly and go to sleep so that I could face the morning better. Soon I lay down to sleep. I got up at 4 a.m. . . . Still very tired, I took two aspirins and began to draft a letter to President Roosevelt but I could not finish it. I felt drowsy and lay down to sleep. I could not have slept for more than fifteen minutes when I felt someone touch my feet. I opened my eyes and found Dhirubhai Desai, son of Bhulabhai, standing with a sheet of paper in his hand.[99]

It was a warrant for Azad's arrest. Gandhi, Nehru, Patel and hundreds of others too were arrested by dawn. And Congress was banned. Gandhi was confined in Poona; Azad, Nehru, Patel and others of the working committee were taken by train and cars to the gate of Ahmednagar Fort, where a police chief handed them over to an army officer. Calling out their names, one by one, the army officer asked them to go inside. Outside, in a thousand places and more, the August Movement exploded—and, in time, was put down.

We know little of what Azad thought and did in his earlier prison terms, but of his time in Ahmednagar Fort he has left an account. His portable radio was seized and not returned until he was freed; he and his colleagues were fed for a while on iron platters; for the first six weeks newspapers and letters were disallowed. At Jawaharlal's initiative, they worked on a garden, watching the plants grow and the flowers bloom. And they wrote.

In "Letters" that he did not intend to post, Azad described what was happening around him and put down his thoughts. Published after his release under the title *Ghubar-i-Khatir*, these letters have been described by Ikram as the "*tour de force* of a literary craftsman."[100] In *Ghubar-i-Khatir* Azad discusses the Almighty, pictures himself playing the sitar under "a marble dome bathed in the moonlight, the silvery waves of the Jumna rippling by," writes charming tales about crows and sparrows, and observes a newborn bird's first flight:

> It had come out of the cover of its nest and stood face to face with the boundless sky but it was not yet unaware of its powers. [Suddenly] it realized in its bones that it was a flying creature. A breath of life ran through the lifeless frame. The drooping wings began to quiver for a take-off. In the twinkling of an eye the urge to fly shook its whole frame and it jumped off as if it had received a shock. The next moment the bird of courage was traversing space like an eagle.[101]

On religion he writes:

> I do not know what is Sunnism and what the Shias believe in. I have full faith in Allah and His Book and I acclaim the Prophet. I have also been bestowed with reason and I go after established facts. What is white remains white, what is black, black ... [102]

Zuleikha passed away in April 1944, a few weeks after the death of Gandhi's wife Kasturba. Detained along with her husband, Kasturba died in Gandhi's lap, but Zuleikha was 1500 miles away from her husbnd. *Ghubar-i-Khatir* contains this "letter" written on April 11, 1944:

> On March 23 I received news of her critical illness, through a telegram. When the newspapers arrived they contained the same news. The superintendent told me that if I wanted to make any representation in this connection he would send it immediately to Bombay. I told him firmly that I wanted to make no request to the government.
>
> The equilibrium of my life was shaken. ... The newspapers arrive here between noon and 1 p.m. My room faces the superintendent's office. The jailor brings the paper from there direct to my room. As soon as he got out of the office and I could hear his footsteps, my heart used to palpitate with the apprehension that the paper may contain some dreadful news. Then I used to check myself with a jerk.
>
> My sofa does not face the door. Until the visitor comes inside he cannot see my face. By the time the jailor arrived, I was able to nod at him with a smile and to indicate that he might leave the paper on the table. Then I used to resume my writing as if I was in no particular

hurry to glance at the paper. I admit that all this was a show put up by my conceited self so that its power of patience and dignity may not be tarnished by over-anxiety.

Finally the poisoned cup of sorrows brimmed over. On April 9 the superintendent handed over to me a telegram conveying the bad news. Thus ended the 36 years of our wedded life. Though my determination did not desert me, it seemed as if my feet had no strength left in them.

There is an old grave in the Fort compound. God knows whose it is, but ever since I arrived here I have seen it hundreds of times. Now when I look at it I seem to have developed a certain affection for it. Last evening I gazed at it for a long time.[103]

Three months after Zuleikha's death, Azad's sister Abru Begum, who lived in Bhopal, passed away.

* * *

He was not happy when he learned that Gandhi, released because of illness, was approaching Jinnah. We have discussed this initiative and its outcome in the Jinnah chapter; here we should note that Azad described it to his colleagues in jail as a blunder. Later Azad would write:

> Large sections of Indian Musalmans were doubtful about Mr. Jinnah and his policy, but when they found that Gandhiji was continually running after him and entreating him, many of them developed a new respect for him. It was Gandhiji who first gave currency to the title of Quaid-i-Azam, or great leader, as applied to Mr. Jinnah.[104]

Rivalry probably played its part in influencing Azad's assessment, yet we should note that Patel and some other Congress leaders also thought that Gandhi's attitude to Jinnah strengthened the latter's position. Not agreeing, Khaliquzzaman has commented: "Muslims in India had started calling him (Jinnah) Quaid-i-Azam, and even if Gandhiji had not addressed him as such Mr. Jinnah would not have suffered in popularity or prestige."[105]

In April 1945, 32 months after his arrest, Azad was moved from Ahmednagar Fort and detained in a two-storey house in Bankura in Bengal, and allowed to listen to the radio. One evening in June he heard that the Viceroy was inviting the presidents of Congress and the League to a conference in Simla. Freed the next day, Azad took a train for Calcutta. Later he wrote:

> The platform and station at Howrah were a welter of humanity. It was with the greatest difficulty that I could get out of my compartment and enter my car. . . . As the car was crossing Howrah bridge, my mind moved back. . . . My wife had come up to the gate of my house

to bid me farewell. I was now returning after three years but she was in her grave and my home was empty.

I told my companions to turn the car, for I wished to visit her grave before I went home. My car was full of garlands. I took one and placed it on her grave and silently read the *Fateha*.[106]

* * *

He had lost forty pounds and was weary and hungry for a holiday. But he and his colleagues had to get together. They assembled in Bombay, where Azad stayed in the room in Bhulabhai Desai's house from where three years earlier he had been removed to prison. "The familiar surroundings and old friends were the same. The same Arabian sea stretched to the far horizon." Azad felt as if "the incidents since August 9, 1942 had never taken place."[107]

But the world was different. The war in Europe was over. And Wavell's invitation seemed to indicate that India's struggle for independence might end too. From Bombay Azad, Gandhi, Nehru, Patel and others of the working committee journeyed to Simla. At the conference table Wavell placed Jinnah to his right and Azad to his left. Loyal to his principle of having no dealings with Azad, Jinnah ignored the Congress president's hand. Wavell and Azad responded warmly to each other, and Congress agreed to the Viceroy's proposal: a new Executive Council filled by representative Indians. Wavell explained that his veto was not likely to be used in the new Council.

It was Wavell's intention to form a Council with five Congress nominees, five from the League and four others representing Sikhs, untouchables and independents; he hoped to include a Muslim from Punjab's Unionist party in the last category. Asked for its names, Congress proposed Azad, Nehru, Patel and two others—a Parsi and an Indian Christian. If Jinnah had named five Muslims, the 14-member Council would have contained seven Muslims and two caste Hindus. But Jinnah named none. He rejected the proposals, objecting to the idea that Congress and the Viceroy could nominate Muslims. As Wavell put it: "[Jinnah] refused even to discuss names unless he could be given the absolute right to select all Muslims. I said that this was entirely unacceptable."[108]

That Congress's list would include the name of Azad, its president, was widely assumed. Thus, in a statement made in London before the Simla conference opened, Leopold Amery, Secretary of State for India, had referred to the likelihood of Azad and Nehru taking office.[109] Jinnah announced in Simla that the League would not join if Azad or indeed any non-League Muslim was included. Wavell could have gone ahead with a new Council without the League, keeping five places vacant for the League to fill if Jinnah changed his mind. This was a course several Governors recommended, but the Viceroy did not adopt it. He merely announced that the talks had failed. Remembering that Quit India had hurt the war effort—he was the allied Commander-in-Chief at the time—, Wavell decided against launching a Congress-dominated government. Azad was deeply disappointed. If a new Council had been formed, he as Congress's head would have become its Vice-President, or *de facto* Prime Minister, the position Jawaharlal Nehru enjoyed between September 1946 and August 1947.

The story of the 1946 elections was told in an earlier chapter. All we need repeat here is that thanks to Azad's efforts Congress found a share in Punjab's coalition ministry headed by the Unionist, Khizr Hyat. The story of the Indian visit of the British Cabinet's three wise men was also told. Here we should note that Azad was one of the few in Congress ready to accept compulsory grouping; even if it seemed unpleasant to some, it was an alternative to partition and hence, to Azad, worth settling for.

Moreover, Azad favoured the wise men's structure of a centre with limited but important powers presiding over substantially autonomous provinces. Unlike Nehru and Patel, he was wary of an all-powerful centre. If provinces controlled everything except defence, foreign affairs and communications, fears that Muslim-majority provinces would be dominated by a Hindu centre would be allayed; yet Azad's preference for strong provinces did not spring only from communal considerations. In his view, "considerations of constitutional propriety and practical administration" in a country of India's size and nature called for "the largest possible measure" of provincial autonomy.[110]

He was unhappy but helpless when Gandhi said that compulsory grouping was not acceptable and, later, when Nehru declared that it was not likely. Congress's letter to the Raj conveying its acceptance of the Cabinet Mission's plan but not of compulsory grouping was signed by Azad as president, but this was no more than party loyalty.

Azad was Congress's president through and beyond the war. The struggles and imprisonments of Congress's leaders had extended a twelve-month term to one of six-and-a-half years. In July 1946 Azad was succeeded by Nehru. The choice was beween Jawaharlal and Patel. Gandhi, to whom the issue went, preferred Nehru and ensured Nehru's leadership of the interim government that was to be formed. Patel was the better administrator of the two, but Nehru was more acceptable among Muslims, had a better international standing and, unlike the rightist Patel, was a bridge between Congress's extremes.

In his memoirs Azad speaks of "a general demand that I should be re-elected president" and of a train journey during which "men assembled in large numbers at almost every station" raising the slogan "that I should continue."[111] However, the sloganeers did not represent anything like a majority in Congress.

Though he had enjoyed a long spell as president, Azad did not find handing over easy. He had conducted Congress's crucial war-time negotiations with Cripps and Wavell and again, after the war, with the Cabinet Mission. The talks had finally yielded fruit and Congress was about to be invited to form a government. That the long-hoped-for invitation would be addressed not to him but to another could not have thrilled Azad, even if he could truthfully say the following about his relationship with the more fortunate man:

> From the very beginning . . . Jawaharlal and I have been the best of friends. We have always seen eye to eye and leaned on one another for support. The question of any rivalry or jealousy between us had never arisen.[112]

At any rate, when, within days of assuming the presidentship, Jawaharlal said that Congress's entry into the Constituent Assembly created under the Mission's plan would be "completely unfettered by agreements," Azad felt that "those who wanted me to continue for at least another year were perhaps in the right."[113] Following Nehru's remark, the League, as we saw in the Jinnah chapter, withdrew from the Cabinet Mission's plan and announced Direct Action for gaining Pakistan. What happened thereafter is, too, a tale that has been told.

Despite urgings from Gandhi, Nehru and Patel, Azad did not join the interim government when it was formed in September 1946. Four months later, when Gandhi said to him, as Azad would recall afterwards, that "whatever might be my opinion or my personal feelings, it was my duty to join the government," and "Jawaharlal was of the same view," Azad became minister of education.[114] Attlee's historic announcement committing Britain to leave India came a month later. Then, in March, Mountbatten replaced Wavell.

The retiring Viceroy had found Azad "really a much truer representative of the Muslims than Jinnah"[115] and had enjoyed talking history and the Arab world with him; Azad, on his part, appreciated Wavell's 1945 initiative that produced Congress's first agreement with the Raj. Jinnah's stand had killed the agreement, but, as he said when he learned that Wavell was leaving, Azad recognized the fact that Wavell had "opened a closed door, in spite of initial opposition" from H.M.G.[116]

Azad tried to stop the partition that Mountbatten canvassed shortly after his arrival. Jinnah also was against it; he thought Mountbatten's Pakistan too small. Azad was opposed to division itself. As an Indian he hated the notion of slicing India into two. As a Muslim he thought, as he said in April 1946, that the millions of Muslims remaining in the Hindu-majority provinces "will awaken overnight and discover that they have become aliens and foreigners, . . . left to the mercies of what then would become an unadulterated Hindu Raj."[117] Moreover, as he would say later, Azad was "not prepared for a moment to give up my right to treat the whole of India as my domain or to content myself with a mere fragment of it."[118]

We have seen, however, that by the end of March 1947 Patel had become keen on division and that Nehru too was reconciled to it. Azad, in his own words, "was surprised and pained" when Patel, frustrated at every step by the polarization in the interim government, told him that "whether we liked it or not, there were two nations in India."[119] Nehru spoke to Azad "in sorrow"; still, as Azad puts it, he "asked me to give up my opposition to partition."[120]

Azad told Jawaharlal that he "could not possibly accept his views." On March 31 he met Gandhi, who had arrived earlier that day from East Bengal and Bihar. According to Azad, Gandhi said to him: "Partition has now become a threat. It seems Vallabhbhai and even Jawaharlal have surrendered. Will you stand by me or have you also changed?"

Azad replied: "Never has my opposition to partition been as strong as it is today. . . . My only hope now is in you. If you acquiesce, I am afraid India is lost."

To this, according to Azad, the Mahatma said: "What a question to ask? If the Congress wishes to accept partition, it will be over my dead body." Yet in two months even Gandhi was resigned to it and gave Azad "the greatest shock of my life" by saying that "partition appears inevitable." Nehru and Patel had "vehemently opposed" Gandhi's suggestion, conceived as a final ploy against partition, that Jinnah be given the opportunity to form an all-India government. Gandhi told Azad that the only question left was the form partition should take.[121]

Azad too acquiesced. In *India Wins Freedom* he has written of his battles to prevent division but at Congress's meetings he did not oppose the Mountbatten plan. Neither the Mahatma nor the Maulana defied Nehru and Patel, who were backed by Rajagopalachari, Rajendra Prasad, Govind Ballabh Pant and many others. These leaders of Congress's establishment were eager for independence and office and were getting old; moreover, they seemed satisfied that rejection of the Mountbatten plan would lead to an unavoidable civil war. "We should accept our defeat," Azad told the A.I.C.C.[122] Gandhi asked Congress not "to disown the leaders [who] have agreed on your behalf," unless it was ready for "a big revolution."[123] In the middle of June the A.I.C.C. and the League voted to accept the independence and partition of the Mountbatten plan.

* * *

Even after nearly forty years it is hard to speak of the cruelties that we, Hindu, Muslim or Sikh, permitted ourselves to inflict in our year of independence. Azad gives a glimpse of how he was affected.

> Many Muslims asked for shelter in my house. Rich and well-known families came to me completely destitute and with no earthly possessions except the clothes they were wearing. My house was soon full and I put up tents in my compound. Men and women, rich and poor, young and old, huddled together in sheer fear of death.[124]

The League's establishment left for Pakistan. So did millions of ordinary Muslims. But not everyone could migrate. What was to be the future of the majority that remained in India? Suspected and disliked because their votes had strengthened the League and won Pakistan, inviting, because they were Muslim, the fury of the Hindus and Sikhs who had been obliged to flee Pakistan and seek shelter and livelihood in India, they felt cheated, helpless, and threatened.

Three months after partition Azad addressed a large crowd of them from the pulpit of Delhi's Jama Masjid. As he faced the *qaum* that had heeded him not, the vessel of his self-restraint burst and his feelings came crashing down in a torrent of eloquence. Hurt, anger, I-told-you-so, pride in Islam and faith in the *qaum*'s future were thrown together in a magnificent rebuke:

> It is nothing new for me to address a vast crowd in the historic mosque built by Shah Jahan. I have addressed you earlier, when your faces shone with confidence, instead of being smudged with anxiety . . .
>
> You remember that I called you and you cut off my tongue, that I took up my pen and you lopped off my hand, that I wanted to walk and move, and you tripped my foot. . . . My lapels cry because your impudent hands have torn them. . . . If you live with fear now, it is just retribution for your past deeds.
>
> I told you that the two-nation theory was the death-knell of a life of faith and belief. . . . Those on whom you relied for support have forsaken you, left you helpless . . .
>
> Behold the minarets of this mosque bend down to ask you where you have mislaid the pages of your history! It was but yesterday that your

caravan alighted on the banks of the Jamuna. . . . How is it that you feel afraid of living here today in this Delhi, which has been nurtured by your blood?

That some faces disappeared from your sight is no cause for alarm. Indeed they have brought you together to make their departure easier. If they snatched their hands away from your hands, it is no bad thing. But beware if they have taken away your hearts.

I am not asking you to obtain certificates of loyalty from the new ruler or to live like camp followers. This country is ours. There are quite a few pages still blank in the history of our country; we can become the heading of these pages.

You are afraid of quakes, when not long ago you were yourself a quake? Today you shiver in the darkness; don't you remember that you were yourself a light? Should you take notice of this water trick-ling down from the skies and hitch up your trousers when your forefathers plunged into the seas, trampled upon the mountains and laughed at the bolts of lightnings? Is you faith breathing its last that you who used to catch hold of kings by their collars are today searching for customers who would buy your collars?

Dear Brethren! I have no new antidote for you, only something that was brought about 1400 years ago. . . .

Do not fear and do not grieve,
And you will indeed gain the upper hand
If you are possessed of true faith.[125]

* * *

Though not, except in the *Al Hilal* and Khilafat phases, a leader in the sense of one with a large following, Azad was and remains a leader in the realm of ideas. The crowds loved Nehru and refreshed him; without them Nehru was home-sick. Azad was nourished by solitude; though possessing the skill to stir or shame the masses, he had to be persuaded to appear before them. As reluctant as Azad to mingle with the multitude, Jinnah cast a spell on the *qaum* by appealing to its fears; his stand ensured a following.

Azad asked the *qaum* to trust Hindus and invited isolation until Pakistan came into being and the bulk of India's Muslims realized that they had to continue in India. The *qaum* looked to him for guidance in independent India, and Hindus admired him for having stood up to Jinnah, but Azad would never attain the popularity of Nehru or Jinnah, or the strength of Patel.

Yet followings evaporate or die more easily than ideas, and Azad's still-relevant conviction about Hindu-Muslim partnership has perpetuated his name. Using scholarly and scriptural arrows, he demolished the notion that Hindu-Muslim partnership was un-Islamic; and he espoused his view with unwavering consistency. While Muhammad Ali called him "stub-born" and Jinnah said he was Congress's "showboy," another observer wrote in 1946 that even Azad's "greatest opponents" had to concede the "stability of his character and immutability of his faith."[126]

The *qaum*'s leadership would have been in the palm of Azad's hand if to his remarkable assets—his *Al Hilal* capital, his link with Mecca, his ancestry, his scholarship and his flair as a writer and orator—he had added but one more ingredient, support for separatism. His integrity came in the way, and he spurned the crown.

Culture went with integrity. As Mujeeb notes, Azad did not, in his *India Wins Freedom*, make "even a passing reference to the invective, the abuse and the gross insults heaped upon him by his Muslim opponents."[127] The same point is made by the Pakistani scholar Ikram, who quotes the testimony of Abdul Majid Daryabadi, "by no means a friend or admirer of Azad."[128] Attending a private gathering in Azad's house some months after Pakistan's creation, Daryabadi found "not a trace of complaint or criticism" in Azad's remarks about "his opponents, particularly the Muslim League."[129]

In political terms, Azad's restraint was a weakness. An admirer complained in 1946 that instead of "rectifying misunderstandings that his opponents create" Azad was "quietly listening to their strongest allegations."[130] A similar criticism is implied in Mujeeb's remark that Azad was "a statesman who would not accept the normal functions of a politician."[131] In 1970, twelve years after Azad's death and 23 years after Pakistan's emergence, the scholar Mushir Haq charged that Azad "sat silent, chewing his fingers" while the soil for Pakistan was being prepared; in Haq's view, Azad had the "clarity of vision, intellectual vigour and political influence to remedy the situation."[132]

He was attacked from both ends. In 1945, a Muslim scholar asked in *Dawn*, the paper Jinnah had founded: "Has the Maulana ever looked into the government offices, where the Muslims are crushed by every possible means by their Hindu superiors?"[133] In Mushir Haq's view, on the other hand, Azad erred in not driving home, as long as he was alive, a point he made posthumously in *India Wins Freedom*:

> It is one of the greatest frauds on the people to suggest that religious affinity can unite areas which are geographically, linguistically and culturally different.... History has proved that after the first few decades Islam was not able to unite all the Muslim countries into one state on the basis of Islam alone.[134]

Adds Haq: "Had Azad emphatically expressed this opinion when it was needed, probably the situation would have become different."[135] Haq suggests that fear of the *ulama*'s reaction inhibited Azad's use of a secular argument against Pakistan. This may be true. A fair section of the *ulama* had stayed with Azad despite the pull of Jinnah's stand, and Azad did not want to lose their backing. Whether a more vigorous Azad would have averted Pakistan is, however, a different question.

In any case, he was not going to be more vigorous, or to argue his case. Abul Kalam Azad was too proud to do that. He would declare his un-conventional views, adhere to them over a lifetime and wait for history's verdict. Anything more would be undignified.

Pride was Azad's failing. We glimpse it in *India Wins Freedom*, not only in its estimable aspect to which Mujeeb refers—Azad's refusal to hit back at detractors—but also in the less attractive form of I-was-wiser-than-the-rest. Indifferent, during the battle for the *qaum*'s mind, to the opinion of his time, Azad is anxious in *India Wins Freedom* to influence the view of history. He refers several times in it to the errors of Gandhi, Nehru and Patel and, not less frequently, to his sounder judgment. "Later events proved that my apprehensions were correct."[136] "Later events proved how justified my apprehensions were."[137] We encounter such sentences a shade too often. The repetition smudges our notion of the refined Abul Kalam Azad but the notion is not a false one. The courageously humble Azad of the *Tazkirah* and of *Ghubar-i-Khatir* was moulded by the reflection that detention enabled. *India Wins Freedom*, by contrast, was written during hours snatched from the demanding schedule of India's Education Minister, and written, moreover, as stated earlier, by one suddenly anxious about what the future would think. The haste and the anxiety, and the fact that he relied principally on his memory, have produced some one-sided judgments and also several simple inaccuracies. While a valuable item for any student of independence and partition, *India Wins Freedom* has to be supplemented, and in places corrected, by other works.

He was not immune from jealousy. Mujeeb, who thinks that Azad's "faith and courage entitles him to a high position among the great men of the world,"[138] notes also that "Maulana Azad did not want Dr. Zakir Husain in a position of influence and authority in Delhi" and "was not too pleased" when, in 1957, Husain was appointed Governor of Bihar.[139] No doubt Azad fell. But he also soared, and was fearless, self-assured and regal while soaring. And also solitary. Yet a time may come when Azad is described as having flown ahead rather than alone.

* * *

In January 1948 Gandhi sent for Azad and told him that he was going on a fast which would end only when the insecurity felt by Delhi's Muslims ended. The fast was a protest, too, at the Indian government's apparent unwillingness to make over Rs 55 crores due to Pakistan. Patel, who was Home Minister, was hurt; speaking to the Mahatma, he charged that the fast was unfair and defamed him and Hindus generally. The government, he said, was doing everything possible to protect Muslims. Azad, sitting at Gandhi's side along with Patel and Nehru, has recorded Gandhi's comment: "I am not in China now but in Delhi. You are asking me not to believe my own eyes and ears."[140]

In Azad's assessment the fast had an "electric" effect. Arms were surrendered. As an act of atonement, Hindu and Sikh leaders helped restore the damaged Muslim shrine of Khwaja Qutbuddin. Thousands of Hindus and Sikhs pledged that they would cease and prevent attacks on Muslims and strive for the resettlement of those who had fled from their homes. On January 18, the sixth day of the fast, after 25 Hindus and Sikh leaders of Delhi repeated the pledge in his presence, Gandhi said he would break the fast. A grand-niece brought a glass of orange juice. Then, as Azad has recalled, "He made a sign that she should hand the glass to me. I held the glass to his lips and Gandhiji broke his fast."[141]

Twelve days later Azad was with the Mahatma for an hour in the afternoon. Realizing, some time after returning home, that a couple of important points had not been covered, he went again to Birla House: "Thousands were standing on the lawn and the crowd had overflowed into the street. Someone said, 'Gandhiji has been shot.' I had a dazed feeling and heard, as if in a dream, 'Gandhiji is dead.'"[142]

* * *

Jinnah died in September that year. The Maulana's attitude "towards Pakistan and her leaders . . . was dignified and statesmanlike," writes Ikram,[143] noting Azad's capacity to leave the past behind, which also struck Chaudhri Muhammad Ali, a future Prime Minister of Pakistan. Visiting New Delhi in 1950 to explore an Indo-Pak agreement, Muhammad Ali, a civil servant at the time, found Azad "keenly interested in a just and equal treatment for the minorities on both sides."[144]

Vallabhbhai Patel died in December 1950. His perspective on the Hindu-Muslim question had differed from the one that Nehru seemed to share with Azad, who continued as Education Minister and, in addition, counselled Nehru on a variety of matters. Yet there were occasions when Azad had to play the reconciler between Nehru, the Prime Minister, and his powerful deputy, Patel. Neither Azad nor Patel liked the influence that V.K. Krishna Menon exercised on Nehru. As Azad would write afterwards: "I did not feel happy about this, as I felt Krishna Menon often gave Jawaharlal wrong advice. Sardar Patel and I did not always see eye to eye, but we were agreed in our judgment about Krishna Menon."[145]

Patel's death made Nehru all-powerful and reduced Azad's importance to him. He was still "companion, friend, colleague and comrade" to Nehru, as the latter would say on Azad's death.[146] In the forties Nehru had written that Azad reminded him of the French encyclopaedists and added, "One is continually astonished at the odd bits of knowledge that come out of him almost unawares."[147] In 1958 Nehru would again say that Azad brought to mind "the encyclopaedists, men of intellect, men of action."[148] Yet, as long as Patel was alive, Azad was also an ally to Nehru and a mediator between Nehru and Patel, roles no longer needed after Patel's death.

Krishna Menon's influence grew and Azad's declined. Badruddin Tyabji, who was in regular touch with both Nehru and Azad in the fifties, writes: "Panditji saw Maulana Sahib less and less, while Mr. Krishna Menon, though not taken into the cabinet, became more and more the *de facto* principal adviser of the Prime Minister, at least in foreign affairs."[149]

We need not, in this study, dwell on Azad's performance as Education Minister. Those who wanted to celebrate independence by banishing English were defied by Azad, even though he himself was a product of traditional schooling in Arabic and Persian. He tried to foster technical, adult and women's education. Many institutions were born while he was at the ministry's helm—a grants commission, a cultural relations council, an *akademi* of literature, an institute of technology, an Arabic quarterly, and more. Some Azad had himself conceived.

Saiyidain, secretary in the Ministry, found him a just chairman in committee but "never interfering in details, not even greatly interested in them."[150] Using less diplomatic language, Mujeeb says that Azad "was so engrossed in principles that he could not become an efficient administrator."[151]

Picking up a Minister's pen, Azad had surrendered the author's. His presence in the cabinet gave the *qaum* a measure of security and enabled dignitaries visiting India to profit from his learning, but, *India Wins Freedom* apart, he wrote nothing between 1945 and 1958. It is a loss.

Abul Kalam Azad died on February 22, 1958, at the age of seventy. A dignified corner in Old Delhi contains his bones. Rajghat, where flames absorbed Gandhi's body, and Shantivana, where, six years after Azad's death, Nehru was cremated, are not far. Also close is the Red Fort, where Azad's ancestors mingled with the Mughal rulers, and the Jama Masjid, where he admonished, and gave heart to, his *qaum*. Zuleikha, his wife, lies a thousand miles to the east.

CHAPTER 8

LIAQAT ALI KHAN

(1895–1951)

Azad and Muhammad Ali occupied Congress's presidential chair, Jinnah was once its rising star and Huq its general secretary. Supporting, though only briefly, Congress's 1920 struggle, Iqbal wrote a poem eulogising Gandhi. Zakir Husain, who features in the chapter to follow, was Congress's candidate for India's Presidency. Of the eight lives studied in this volume, only two—those of Sayyid Ahmed and Liaqat Ali Khan—were wholly free of links with Congress.

We saw, at the start of this book, that Sayyid Ahmed refused, despite strong persuasion, to join Congress, founded 13 years before his death. Twenty-five years after Sayyid Ahmed died, some Congressmen tried to recruit Liaqat but failed. The young Nawabzada, or "the estate-lord's son," followed Sayyid Ahmed's line of thinking twice before aligning with the Raj's opponents.

Liaqat was born in 1895 in Karnal, now in Haryana but then belonging to the large Punjab province. He was the second son of Nawab Rustam Ali Khan, a rich land-owner apparently linked, across the ages, to Nausherwan, the Iranian king. An ancestor of Rustam Ali migrated to India in the fifteenth century. Owning estates around Karnal and also in western U.P., Rustam Ali sent Liaqat to M.A.O. at Aligarh.

In 1919, a year before nationalism and non-cooperation hit the Aligarh campus, Liaqat became a graduate of Allahabad University, to which M.A.O. was affiliated at the time, and went to Oxford. Enrolled there at St. Catherine's, and later at Exeter, he obtained a degree in jurisprudence in 1921. The following year, completing terms at London's Inner Temple, Liaqat was called to the Bar. He missed, therefore, the high Khilafat and non-cooperation tides of 1920–21. When India was struggling to shake herself free of the Briton's rule, Liaqat found himself in the places that fashioned the ruler's mind and might.

But it was possible to speak up for India in Oxford. Liaqat did this in debates and was elected treasurer of the *Majlis*, the platform of Indian students in Oxford. Evidently he had "friends in all communities." An Indian contemporary, K.P.S. Menon, later secretary-general in the foreign ministry, found Liaqat "a good sportsman and a good friend."[1]

Returning to India in 1922, he divided his time between Delhi and the U.P. town of Muzaffarnagar. Govind Ballabh Pant, the future U.P. Premier and Indian home minister, was—it would seem—one of the Congressmen who tried, in 1923, to bring Liaqat into Congress, but the young barrister "refused to subscribe to the Congress creed."[2] Following Gandhi's ascendancy, Congress had adopted as its end "the attainment of Swaraj by peaceful and legitimate means" in place of "the attainment of Swaraj within the empire." What considerations and experiences lay behind Liaqat's attitude is not known. Perhaps it was shaped by family upbringing, or by a class reaction, but there are no facts to enlighten us.

In 1920–21 fervour for Hindu-Muslim partnership was such that the Muslim League, too, had adopted the new creed. By 1923 Hindu-Muslim differences and the Raj's strength were apparent. The League had second thoughts; the empire proviso was re-introduced; and Liaqat joined the League. By no means the country's premier Muslim body, it had only 1,093 all-India members in 1922, 1,097 in 1923 and 1,184 in 1924.[3] The Khilafat committee was stronger but also more anti-Raj and therefore less attractive to Liaqat.

He did not practise law. Politics and education were his chief interests. The involvement with education too was evidence that he possessed the Sayyid Ahmed outlook. Giving and raising money for Muslim education, Liaqat became president of the Muzaffarnagar Madrassa, and held the office till partition.

In 1924 he attended a League session that Jinnah presided over; in 1926 he entered the U.P. legislature from a Muslim seat in western U.P., more as an individual than as a member of the League; and in 1928 he was part of the Jinnah-led Muslim team to the all-parties convention at Calcutta that failed to bridge Congress-League differences. This Calcutta exercise saw the start of a Jinnah-Liaqat partnership that was to make a considerable impact on Indian events.

We saw in the Jinnah chapter that in the late twenties and early thirties he seemed to prefer joint electorates to separate ones. It was a preference that Liaqat shared. He told the U.P. council that separate electorates were "harmful for a minority," apart from the fact under such electorates the Hindu stood "for the Hindus, the Muslim for the Muslims, the Christian for the Christians and the Sikh for the Sikhs."[4]

A statement he made in 1932 acquires significance in the light of the separatist positions that Liaqat took from 1937. Addressing the Muslim Educational Conference, a body that Sayyid Ahmed Khan had launched, Liaqat, while agreeing that Muslims had "a distinct culture of their own" and the right to preserve it, added:

> But the days of rabid communalism in this country are numbered and we shall witness ere long the united Hindu-Muslim India anxious to preserve and maintain all that rich and valuable heritage which the contact of the two great cultures has bequeathed us.[5]

* * *

Liaqat married a second time in 1933. We know little about his first wife or their life together. It is Raana, the second wife, who enters the record books as Liaqat's beautiful and talented partner, as the hostess, after Pakistan was formed, at the Prime Minister's residence, and, after her husband's assassination, as Pakistan's ambassador to Holland. Her forebears, who belonged to the hills of U.P., were called Pant and were Hindus before becoming Christian; Raana, a teacher and an economist, exchanged Christianity for Islam. Her marriage with Liaqat, 37 at the time, was news.

Bespectacled, balding a little and stocky if not stoutish, Liaqat none-theless looked neat in his European-style suits. For Raana and also for others, he had the appeal of a man who was both able and a Nawabzada. Free from the insecurity that besets many a dull Nawabzada, and free too from the pushfulness of the unrecognized, Liaqat could afford to be gentle and relaxed. He was also bright and successful in the U.P. council, where he headed a group of MLAs calling themselves the Democratic party, spoke with clarity, and silenced adversaries with coolly-delivered retorts. What few noticed was Liaqat's discernment of opportunity and capacity for bold action.

His marriage with Raana was followed by a honeymoon in Europe but experiencing Europe's wonders with a radiant-looking bride was not the only thing Liaqat had in mind. He had a plan for turning the Muslim League, starved, in 1933, of members, money and leadership, into a strong and popular party. The plan involved a man who had stayed on in England after attending conferences convened there. To those running into him in

London, Muhammad Ali Jinnah gave the impression that he despaired about India and his place in her future. As Raana was to put it later, "It was believed that Jinnah would never come back and that he was disgusted with his own people."[6]

Liaqat's aim was to rekindle Jinnah's hopes and to enlist him for the League's renewal. Just before he and Raana left for Europe, what remained of the League had split into two at a meeting that Liaqat attended. Convinced, along with some others, that Jinnah was the only answer, Liaqat intended to ask Jinnah to end his pleasant exile.

Meeting Jinnah at a reception in London, Liaqat "immediately began his appeal to Jinnah to return." In Raana's words: "Jinnah listened, but did not answer at first. He talked of his life in England and of his contentment at Hampstead. But Liaqat was not to be denied. He said, 'You must come back. The people need you. You alone can put new life into the League and save it.' "[7]

Jinnah invited Liaqat and Raana to his Hampstead home for dinner. They saw the quiet comfort of his life and Raana "felt that nothing could move him out of that security." However, Liaqat knew of the unfulfilled longings of Jinnah, older than him by 19 years. He gave Jinnah the text of a League resolution "requesting Mr Jinnah to come over to India and give a lead to Moslems in these critical times,"[8] and proceeded to assure him of the potential in his return. In the end Jinnah said: "You go back and survey the situation. I trust your judgement. If you say, 'Come back,' I will give up my life here and return."

As they drove back to London, Raana saw that Liaqat "was a very happy man." Liaqat had hit bull's-eye, and Jinnah had found his ally. The pair that would achieve Pakistan had trusted their future to each other. Neither knew that Pakistan would become their goal. In 1933 their ambitions centred round the 1934 voting to the Central Assembly and the provincial elections expected thereafter. Jinnah correctly sensed that Liaqat would be a superb aide but never a rival; that he meant what he said and did not intend to knife Jinnah after using him; and that he would execute Jinnah's plans rather than undermine them.

Back in India, Liaqat "devoted every day for some months" to the survey that Jinnah had asked for. He asked a hundred intelligent Muslims, living in different parts of India, if they thought Jinnah's return would help. Then he wrote to Jinnah: "Come."[9]

Elected, in his absence, as the League's president, Jinnah returned to India early in 1935. The following year Liaqat was elected the League's secretary but the Jinnah-Liaqat partnership soon ran into trouble. The reasons were political, not personal. Elections were approaching. Anxious to broaden the League's influence, Jinnah opened its doors to a whole range of prominent Muslims who had avoided or left the League. In Bengal he wooed Huq; in the U.P. he sought the support of the *Jamiat-ul-Ulema-i-Hind*, the Indian Ulema party, and of the Muslim Unity Board formed by the raja of Salempur and Choudhry Khaliquzzaman.

Many of the U.P. Muslims whom Jinnah hoped to enlist had previous or continuing links with Congress; a number like Khaliquzzaman were Khilafat veterans ready for a fresh anti-Raj alliance with Congress. Liaqat had differed with them for years. Jinnah was less distant from them: in March 1936 he had told a Lahore gathering that "there has been no change in me, not the slightest, since the days when I joined the Indian National Congress."[10] In exchange for the support of Khaliquzzaman and his friends, Jinnah offered them a majority on the League's parliamentary board for the U.P.

To Liaqat's cost and disappointment a Jinnah-Khaliquzzaman deal was made; the power that should have been his had gone to others. An embittered Liaqat resigned from the League's central and U.P. boards, sailed to England, returned and entered the new U.P. assembly as an independent. In the house he joined the National Agriculturist group formed by his friend the Nawab of Chhatari. He did not sit with the League members because of his belief that Khaliquzzaman and his friends had "a veiled kinship with Congress."[11]

The story of Congress's abortive attempt, in the U.P., to draw the League into its 1937 ministry was told in the Jinnah and Azad chapters. There is a suggestion, hard to confirm, that Pant, the Congress Premier, offered a seat in the U.P. cabinet to Liaqat as well, and that Liaqat turned it down.[12]

The man who had persuaded Jinnah to return to India was nowhere in the picture when, in the summer of 1937, the League gathered in Lucknow, the U.P. capital, to denounce Congress and the Hindu rule that Congress ministers were supposedly establishing. At Lucknow, thanks to the efforts of Khaliquzzaman, the League decided that like Congress it too wanted "full independence" for India; the reference to Dominion status, suggestive of a link with Britain, was dropped. The new goal would enable the League to rebut charges of softness towards Britain; it did not mean that the League was prepared to join hands with Congress.

Not at all. Lucknow, in fact, characterized Congress as the League's number one foe—the Raj was displaced from that rank. Now Liaqat and Khaliquzzaman could work together. Lucknow's success told Liaqat, moreover, that there was no future for him outside the League. Early in 1938 he returned to the all-India League as its secretary and joined the

League group in the U.P. assembly. Khaliquzzaman would concede later that Liaqat was "a forceful speaker and very good at repartee" and that "his admission to our party gave it great advantage."[13]

The shortcomings of Congress, now ruling most Indian provinces, had presented the League with a favourable climate. Exploiting it called for leadership, which Jinnah brilliantly provided, and for organizing skill, which, fortunately for the League, Liaqat was able to supply. He travelled, raised money, selected representatives, opened branches and mediated quarrels. The astute Jinnah, choosing to ignore Liaqat's 1937 sulk, "entrusted him with new responsibilities day after day."[14] In May 1939 Jinnah wrote his will, naming his sister Fatima, Liaqat and a Bombay solicitor as its joint executors, but, as Raana was to say afterwards, "he never told Liaqat of this."[15]

The country saw the League's mutation into a strong, nationwide body. At the League's 1940 rally, held in Lahore, Liaqat's was a crucial if unspectacular role. Jinnah, Huq and Khaliquzzaman made the orations, and Liaqat fielded the delegates' tricky questions on the new Muslim state, or states, that the League was demanding. There were good reasons for keeping Pakistan imprecise: details might divide the *qaum* and also commit the League to vulnerable positions. Liaqat performed skilfully, but one of his replies was unrealistic. Pressed on the leadership's reluctance to claim all of the Punjab for Pakistan, Liaqat said in Lahore that to name a province would imply the exclusion of unnamed areas, and that he did not wish to give up the Muslim claim to Delhi and Aligarh.[16]

* * *

He was moving up. In 1940, leaving the U.P. legislature, where he had spent 13 years, he entered the Central Assembly and became the deputy leader of the League group there. Since Jinnah, who headed the group, was frequently ill or preoccupied elsewhere, Liaqat functioned as the *de facto* leader. But he did not reduce his travelling, which was aimed at consolidating the League. Between August 1942 and April 1943, for instance, he "toured about 14,000 miles and visited each and every province of the sub-continent."[17]

Much of his work was off-stage but not all of it. The Nawabzada spoke to the Muslim masses in Urdu, urging them to unite under the League's banner and trust its concern for the poor. Abid Husain, a Muslim of the Nationalist school and scarcely a League backer, said that the "zealous" Liaqat was "no arm-chair politician" but one "trying to reach the Muslim masses and to understand their needs and desires." In addition, noted Abid Husain, Liaqat persuaded Jinnah "to do what was against his whole nature and temperament" and approach the Muslim in the street.[18]

At the end of 1943 the Quaid, in effect, named Liaqat his successor. Addressing the League, which was meeting in Karachi for its annual session, Jinnah called Liaqat "my right hand." Added Jinnah:

> The Nawabzada has worked day and night, and no one can possibly have an idea of the great work he has shouldered. He commands the universal respect and confidence of the Musalmans. Though a Nawabzada, he is a thorough proletarian, and I hope other Nawabs will follow his example.[19]

A few months after Karachi Liaqat accepted another load: the presidentship of Delhi's Anglo-Arabic College. His election to this office was a recognition of his interest in Muslim education, which politics had not been able to smother; Liaqat had been giving some thought, for instance, to the educational needs of Muslim women.[20] His link with Anglo-Arabic College obliged Liaqat to work with the educator Zakir Husain, who was unabashedly pro-Congress and had been chosen as the college's vice-president. Eye-brows were raised in both camps, but Liaqat and Zakir Husain managed to guide the college without clashing with each other.

* * *

Another "foe" with whom Liaqat was rubbing shoulders was Bhulabhai Desai, brilliant lawyer and leader of Congress's representatives in the Central Assembly. As the *de facto* leader of the League group, Liaqat had frequently crossed swords with Desai on the assembly floor; but there were also times when the captains of the principal opposition teams collaborated to inflict defeats on the Raj. "My Government," wrote Wavell, the Viceroy, "continues to be beaten in the Assembly."[21] These "victories" of the Indian parties did not shake the Raj but they pleased the public, and tended to bring Liaqat and Desai closer to each other.

We are speaking of the 1944–45 period. After two years in detention, a sick Gandhi was released in the middle of 1944, but Nehru, Patel and Azad and the other Congress leaders were still in jail. In September 1944 the abortive Gandhi-Jinnah talks took place. Thereafter Jinnah fell ill, and at least some in the League thought him to be "almost on his deathbed."[22]

It was alleged afterwards that Liaqat was one of them,[23] and also that he thought that "Jinnah and Gandhi, being older men, had so far adopted a rigid attitude."[24] Some Pakistani writers have suggested that these factors led Liaqat to negotiate, behind Jinnah's back, with Desai. Wavell, on the other hand, thought that Jinnah's subsequent statement that he knew nothing of Liaqat's talks with Desai was "an obvious falsehood."[25]

A letter written to Desai by Syed Mahmud, a Congress Muslim, suggests that it was Liaqat rather than Jinnah who prompted the talks. After informing Desai that "news has reached that Nawabzada Liaqat Ali Khan wants to come to terms with the Congress if the formation and the composition of the interim government are settled,"[26] Mahmud, who was staying with Gandhi at the time and writing, as he put it, with Gandhi's authority, went on to ask Desai to probe Liaqat's mind. Shortly afterwards, Gandhi asked Desai, who had begun negotiations with Liaqat, "to see to it" that any agreement had "Jinnah's approval."[27]

Whether or not Liaqat was acting with Jinnah's knowledge may never be clearly established. What is beyond doubt is that Liaqat and Desai signed an agreement, that Gandhi blessed it, and that a recovered Jinnah disowned it. Its text, along with Liaqat's signed initials, appears as an appendix in M. C. Setalvad's biography of Desai.[28]

The pact proposed that Desai and Jinnah be invited to form an interim government at the centre, consisting of five each from Congress and the League and two to represent others. For the provinces, too, it envisaged Congress-League coalitions. It was agreed that, as its first act, the new central government would order the release of Congress's leaders. Long-term questions, such as the Pakistan demand, were not touched.

As V.P. Menon says, the pact's "merit was that it was not unduly ambitious; that it did not try to attack the main points of difference between the main parties; and that it was well-timed."[29] That Wavell, the Viceroy, wanted a settlement of this kind made the timing good.

In January 1945 Desai told Wavell of his pact with Liaqat and of Gandhi's support. He was "confident," he added, that "Jinnah was aware and had approved of what had passed between him and Liaqat Ali Khan." Wavell informed H.M.G. that the plan "afforded an excellent opportunity of making progress in the political sphere."[30] However, when, at Wavell's instance, Colville, the Governor of Bombay, asked Jinnah what "his attitude to the Desai proposals" was, the Quaid, in Wavell's words, "disclaimed all knowledge of Liaqat's talks with Desai."[31] Jinnah also issued a public statement to the same effect.

An undeterred Desai told V.P. Menon, a senior civil servant on Wavell's staff, that "no serious notice need be taken" of Jinnah's disclaimer, which, explained Desai, "had been expressed in very guarded language." Jinnah, added Desai, "might grumble about the food, but . . . . would eat it all the same."[32] Wavell heard that Desai was even "offering portfolios to his friends,"[33] but the Congress leader's confidence was misplaced. On March 26, 1945, no doubt following a decisive word from Jinnah, Liaqat said in the Central Assembly that his alleged pact with Desai was "a cock-and-bull story."[34] Privately he told Desai that "he was obliged to deny [the pact] for political reasons."[35] Desai refrained from contradicting Liaqat in the assembly. Six months later Liaqat explained:

> During my talks with Mr Desai, which were purely of a personal nature, I made it absolutely clear to him that whatever I had said was my personal view and I was not speaking either on behalf of the Muslim League or any one else.[36]

Why did Jinnah reject a pact that gave the League a bigger share in power than was warranted by population ratios? Because it did not bar Congress from nominating a Muslim. Liaqat was less rigid than Jinnah on this score. He was, in the terse words of Jinnah's biographer, Mujahid, "ready to compromise."[37] The Quaid had the intelligence, however, not to penalize his chief lieutenant. He knew that a chastened Liaqat was preferable to a Liaqat estranged.

Not everyone agrees that the Liaqat we have just looked at was acting alone. Thus, implying a Jinnah-Liaqat teamwork, K.M. Munshi thinks that "Bhulabhai Desai walked into the trap laid for him by his friend Liaqat Ali."[38] In this view, Liaqat was able to wrest from Desai the important concession of Congress-League parity in any central government, enabling Jinnah thereafter to take parity as given and demand more. Mujahid, in contrast, accuses Liaqat of "lukewarmness" and of the offence of a "clandestine understanding" with Congress.[39]

These contrary views only reveal the suspicions endemic to the subcontinent. What seems clear is that both Liaqat and Desai were eager for a settlement as well as for office—one seemed impossible without the other—and thought, mistakenly in Liaqat's case, that their principals, if they continued to be around, would endorse the accord.

* * *

The ill-fated Desai-Liaqat pact was followed by the unsuccessful Simla conference convened by Wavell. We have studied this conference in earlier chapters and seen that it broke down on Jinnah's insistence that only the League could name Muslims to an Indian cabinet. Congressmen were not the only ones disappointed by the meet's failure: some from the League, too, had hoped to become ministers. Just before failure was announced, Hossein Imam, leader of the League group in the upper house in New Delhi, urged V.P. Menon, who was one of the conference's secretaries, "even at that late hour to see Liaqat Ali Khan in order to find a way out of the impasse." Recalls Menon:

> I telephoned Liaqat Ali Khan, who readily agreed to meet me . . .
> . . His attitude during our discussion did not strike me as being in any

way other than helpful. Liaqat Ali told me that he would consult Jinnah and let me know his reaction the next day. I never heard from him.[40]

Twelve years earlier Liaqat had pledged himself to assist Jinnah, not to contest him. He would present a dissenting opinion, his own or another's, to the Quaid. Then he would carry out Jinnah's response. He was, as Jinnah had said, the Quaid's right arm, not his mind.

Wavell's views of Liaqat, available to us because the Viceroy kept a journal, are instructive; they tell us something about both men. Wavell emerges as a British general who desires gentleness in Indians and peace in India. He did not like the single-mindedness either of Gandhi or of Jinnah; and he judged Gandhi as hostile and Jinnah as rude. But he took to Liaqat, who, from October 1946, would hold the Finance portfolio in the Congress-League "coalition" ministry. Wavell and Liaqat had met at the Simla conference but did not have a proper talk until January 1946. Wavell's comments after this meeting suggest that Liaqat's early belief in the Sayyid Ahmed outlook had not died:

> Liaqat Ali Khan is rather an attractive person, much pleasanter and easier to talk with than Jinnah..... He said that we should have to stop for many years yet, and that the Muslims were not at all anxious that we should go; India could not stand alone and would only get some worse master. (Jan. 24, '46)[41]

Later Wavell would write:

> He is a gentleman and likeable. (March 8, '46)[42]

> There is Liaqat, solid, pleasant, speaking only occasionally, to echo Jinnah, but quiet and reasonable. (May 6, '46)[43]

> I saw Liaqat and spoke to him of the necessity for the Muslim League to accept the Statement of May 16 forthwith. He referred me to Jinnah. Liaqat seems a sensible level-headed person. (Oct. 29, '46)[44]

> The League members do not show up well in Cabinet discussions, except Liaqat, who always talks good sense. (Jan. 21, '47)[45]

> I have always liked Liaqat and thought him full of common sense, but he has no use for Hindus. Still if he had been in Jinnah's place I think we could have got a solution. (March 8, '47)[46]

There is no need to repeat here the tale of the Cabinet Mission's constitutional plan, the reservations and conflicting interpretations with which Congress and the League accepted it, the League's annulment of its acceptance and its Direct Action call. We may note, however, that when, following the call, many Muslims surrendered the Raj's titles, Liaqat announced that "although the prefix Nawabzada had not been conferred upon him by the alien Government, he wished in future to be addressed as Mr Liaqat Ali Khan."[47]

In October 1946, despite its rejection of the long-term plan, the League was inducted into the government by Wavell, who thought the step would help Hindu-Muslim peace. A month later Wavell, who was being pressed by Congress, told Liaqat that the League could not stay in the cabinet without accepting the long-term plan. Showing a toughness that surprised the Viceroy, Liaqat said that he and his League colleagues would rather resign than accept the plan, unless Congress also accepted the League's interpretation of it. Wavell told H.M.G. that "he had argued with Liaqat for over an hour but failed to move him."[48]

No more was Liaqat an echo. He had found his separate voice. It defended the positions that Jinnah was defending, but it was commanded by Liaqat. To the League it was of immense value. When, in December, Nehru, Jinnah, Liaqat and Baldev Singh were invited to London by Prime Minister Attlee, the League case was argued before H.M.G. by Jinnah and Liaqat both. If we are to go by Wavell's account, Liaqat's alertness in London put Cripps, regarded by the League and by Wavell as pro-Congress, in an awkward spot. [49]

Liaqat had to find the right relationship with Jawaharlal Nehru, technically the Vice-Chairman of the Viceroy's Executive Council but thought of by many as the *de facto* Prime Minister. A U.P. Nawab's courtesy conflicted with, and yielded to, the requirements of politics. The League had joined the government, to quote Mujahid, "in opposition to, and not to coalesce with, the Congress bloc,"[50] and Liaqat asserted that Nehru was "nobody's leader except of the Congress bloc." He added that the Muslim bloc "functioned under its separate leader," namely himself.[51]

Wavell, Nehru and Liaqat sat down together to look at the unusual situation. Wavell's version, the only one we have, is that Nehru "suddenly blew up" and said that to speak of a coalition was absurd, because "the Muslim League members refused to accept him as *de facto* Premier." After Nehru had "calmed down a little," Liaqat, who had remained "very quiet and self-possessed," said that "the Muslim League members were quite prepared to co-operate in the Cabinet but not to recognize Nehru as the head of it."[52] There were other times when Wavell thought that Nehru and Liaqat were not on speaking terms.[53] Yet co-operation and even fellow-feeling showed when the two went together to an area under communal violence.

A Finance Minister's fingers can be long, and, by design, Liaqat's were. He, or the finance secretary, Chaudhri Muhammad Ali, who had offered Liaqat and the League his services,* could always question an item of expenditure and thus delay, even if it was not possible to prevent, a Congress-conceived appointment or project. The man who most resented this was Patel, the Home Minister. Meeting Patel and Liaqat on their return from Bihar, where a frightening riot had taken place, Wavell found them "still on friendly terms,"⁵⁴ but the experience of "coalition" was killing Patel's faith in Indian unity. Some time in December 1946 or January 1947 he, and V.P. Menon, decided that partition was preferable to the "co-operation" they were experiencing.⁵⁵

Then, in February, Liaqat produced a budget that convinced Patel and Menon that their decision was sound. It was a clever budget**: the poor, Muslim and Hindu, hailed it, Congress's rich backers hated it, as did Patel, and Nehru did not know whether to defend or oppose it. The League's financiers disliked it too, but they were not as numerous as the men funding Congress. It was said that Liaqat intended to cause a rift between left and right in Congress and even to "ruin the economic life of the country and then go away to Pakistan."⁵⁷ His supporters recalled that Jinnah had described Liaqat as a "proletarian" in 1943, and Liaqat himself said in the assembly:

> India is a land of glaring contrasts and disparities. . . . .And although
> I am not one of those who consider the abolition of private property
> and the complete equalisation of incomes as the only remedy, ...
> I do believe in the Qur'anic injunction . . . . .against the accumulation
> of wealth in the hands of individuals.⁵⁸

Luckily for the League, what Liaqat felt to be his sincere view, and in accord with Islam, was also astute. Though he modified his proposals in response to urgings from Wavell and from his successor, Mountbatten, there was no doubt that he had won, for himself and the League, a psychological victory.

* * *

Rightly is Jinnah called Pakistan's founder but Liaqat's role in its emergence was not minor. He would never have achieved Pakistan on his own: without Jinnah he may not even have striven for it. Yet it is questionable

---

*V.P. Menon had similarly offered Vallabhbhai Patel his services.
**Among its features were: a commission to study tax evasion; abolition of the salt tax; withdrawal of income tax on the slab at the bottom; a 25 per cent tax on business profits in excess of Rs 100,000; and a tax on capital gains.⁵⁶

whether Jinnah would have returned to India had Liaqat not goaded him in England in 1933; and the cruciality of Liaqat's sweat in the late thirties and early forties is beyond doubt. Without Jinnah there would have been no Pakistan; without Liaqat Jinnah would not have obtained it.

This truth, and the exposure and experience he had gained in the interim cabinet, meant that Liaqat could pick any post he desired in Pakistan save for the one the Quaid wanted. Had Mountbatten functioned as India's and Pakistan's common Governor-General—as we saw earlier, the idea was once considered on all sides—, Jinnah would have been Pakistan's first Prime Minister and Liaqat his number two. But Mountbatten did not, Jinnah deciding against it, and Liaqat found himself owning the rank and title that Jawaharlal acquired in India. Pakistan's first Prime Minister: nobody would ever share that honour with Liaqat.

He had to give up, of course, his large Delhi house; though Prime Minister he was also, like millions on the subcontinent, a refugee. Before leaving New Delhi with Raana and their two sons he coped with other implications of partition. Civil servants, the armed forces, institutes, records, assets and liabilities had to be divided. Along with Jinnah, and assisted by civil servants, Liaqat sat on the Partition Council* and laboured over vital details while hate, revenge and sadism took over in many a town and village, destroying the bodies and crippling the souls of Hindus, Muslims and Sikhs.

Muslim officials migrated to Karachi. Fear and ambition were not the only motivations. Many wanted to lay the new nation's early bricks. A number had come ahead of their families. Then they heard of communal riots in India and agonized. Migrating in the opposite direction, Hindus and Sikhs nursed identical pains. Later Liaqat would recall that some officials, and many records, perished on the trains that were to take them to Pakistan; and he would praise the spirit of Pakistan's first body of civil servants:

> When the flag of independence was unfurled, our offices had neither chair nor pen nor inkstand nor paper..... I wish to make it clear that the successful working of administration in Pakistan owes itself neither to me nor to my ministers but to the industry and devotion of our government servants.[59]

* * *

As long as Jinnah was alive, Liaqat did not have the powers that Nehru enjoyed in India. Jinnah was Pakistan's decision-maker. He headed the

---

*Patel and Rajendra Prasad represented India on the Council.

state, the party and the constitution-making body, which was also the legislature; and he was in direct charge of Kashmir and Frontier affairs. Yet the Quaid was frequently ill; during such periods, as Chaudhri Muhammad Ali observed, Liaqat had to assume complete charge and rely "on his own judgement and initiative."[60]

Resettling the refugees was his first concern even as, in India, it was Nehru's and Patel's. Early in 1949 he said that "seven million refugees have so far come to Pakistan."[61] Five million Hindus and Sikhs, he added, had gone to India. According to V.P. Menon, who gives figures "up to the middle of 1948", 5 1/2 million Muslims left India for Pakistan and 6 3/4 million non-Muslims migrated the other way.[62] It is instructive to compare the descriptions the two give. In a book published in 1957 Menon depicts the 1947 Punjab scene, as viewed from Delhi:

> What started as a trickle very soon developed into a flood.... The uprooted millions were in a terrible mental state. They had been driven from their homes under conditions of indescribable horror. Most had to move out at the shortest possible notice.... They had witnessed their near and dear ones hacked to pieces and their houses ransacked, looted and set on fire.... They had no choice but to seek safety in flight, filled with wrath at what they had seen and full of anguish for missing kinsmen and for their womenfolk who had been abducted.[63]

Liaqat, addressing a League meeting in Karachi in February 1949, said:

> Muslims began to die in thousands. Thousands of women were abducted. Thousands of children were cut to pieces. Millions of refugees arrived in Pakistan. They had heaven above and earth below..... Hungry, naked, ill, infirm, they trekked on for hundreds of miles. On the way they often enquired, "Has Pakistan come?" Told, "Not yet," they plodded on with hearts full of hopes. On reaching the borders, some of them, stating "Thank God," dropped down, never to rise again.....[64]

If, as the League maintained, we were two nations, we were, nonetheless, one in our inhumanity, in our one-sidedness—and in our credulousness. Matching Menon's statement that "while panic-stricken refugees poured into the city of Delhi, the capital buzzed with rumours of a deep-laid, long-prepared Muslim conspiracy to overthrow the new Government of Free India and to seize the capital," and that "such rumours were believed,"[65] Liaqat, in that Karachi speech, referred to "the fear in Lahore that Pakistan might be attacked at any moment and that on the first impact it would go under."[66]

Jinnah did not dismiss the rumour that Pakistan would be attacked. At his instance Liaqat was in Lahore for long spells in the months following Pakistan's birth. "The Quaid-i-Azam had told me," Liaqat would recall, "that Pakistan could be defended from Lahore, not from Karachi."[67]

* * *

Liaqat and Jinnah, the latter's strength steadily waning, gave of themselves to the conflict in Kashmir and the U.N. dispute over Kashmir; to creating army, air and naval academies and a naval dockyard (the Quetta Staff College was the only institute for military training that Pakistan inherited); to the refugees; to the special problems of the tribal regions in Baluchistan and the N.W.F.P.; to the need for a central bank . . .

Liaqat "unreservedly backed" Jinnah in his wish to open the League's doors to non-Muslims, as M.S.M. Sharma, the Karachi-based journalist, found, but all others were opposed and the idea was dropped.[68] The two were again of one mind in wanting non-Muslim officials to stay on and serve in Pakistan. The Hindu and Sikh officials did not think they could. In arguing, as Liaqat did, that "there was no reason why those who could serve a foreign government could not serve their own," Liaqat was questioning the two-nation theory, but most of West Pakistan's Hindus and Sikhs had accepted it.[69]

Jinnah's illness took him to Quetta and Ziarat. As we saw in the Jinnah chapter, the Prime Minister was denied timely or adequate information about Jinnah's condition and left to make his own guesses. It would appear that Fatima Jinnah, the Quaid's sister, was largely responsible for this. Her attachment to her brother was so strong and of such long standing that she did not take kindly to the links that Liaqat and Raana had with Jinnah. Some time after the Quaid died she claimed that, following a visit that Liaqat had made to see Jinnah at Ziarat, Jinnah "told her with trembling voice, 'Do you know why he has come? He wants to know how serious my illness is, how long I will last.' "[70]

As Pakistan's second most important man Liaqat had both a right and a need to know how serious the Quaid's illness was, but either Jinnah was too ill to apppreciate this, or, what is more likely, Fatima gave a coloured account of Jinnah's reaction. It should be said to Liaqat's credit that the coldness and resentment that he encountered around the bedridden Jinnah had not the slightest effect on his dignity. Though naturally different from those of Fatima, his ties with Jinnah were precious. Indeed they had made history. But such realities are not always apparent to a dying ruler's near ones.

Pakistan had been called "the house that Jinnah built,"[71] and when the builder died on September 11, 1948, some wondered whether the house would survive. Writing to Nehru, George Bernard Shaw said that if Jinnah had "no competent successor, you will have to govern the whole peninsula."[72] However, Liaqat was ready. Nazimuddin became Governor-General but power moved to a self-confident Prime Minister whose faith in his country seemed complete. Affirming that the source of his faith was his view that Pakistan was more a gift from Providence than an achievement, Liaqat said in February 1949:

> I assure you, never did I, for a single moment, doubt that Pakistan would survive. For I think, indeed I believe, that we had not done anything to deserve so high a boon as Pakistan, and that God will not deprive us of this boon unless and until we prove ourselves, by our misdeeds, to be unworthy of it.[73]

The words ring true, and their significance is not affected by the fact that he was referring, when he uttered them, to the difficulties that threatened to overwhelm Pakistan in 1947, rather than to the circumstances following the Quaid's death. In any case, Liaqat did not hide his confidence. Within days of Jinnah's death he was displaying it at mass meetings all over Pakistan and declaring, in addition, that, if Pakistan was attacked, "he, his colleagues and all Pakistanis will shed the last drop of their blood in defending every inch of the soil of Pakistan."[74] It is not in Pakistan or India alone that people are stirred by such ringing pledges. All the same, Pakistanis were stirred, and also reassured, by Liaqat's faith. There was another injection of confidence, this time not confined to Pakistanis, when, in the month following Jinnah's death, Liaqat flew to attend a London conference of Prime Ministers. Dining with him, Wavell, now semi-retired in London, found Liaqat "in good form, looking well, and very friendly," and describing the Pakistan cabinet as "not brilliant but honest."[75]

His old Lucknow rival Khaliquzzaman took over the League's presidentship from Jinnah, so that the capital, Karachi, situated in West Pakistan, had a Governor-General from East Bengal and a Prime Minister and a party chief who were from the U.P. Ambitious for Karachi's future, Liaqat hoped it would "before long become the greatest metropolis in Asia."[76]

He saw that Pakistanis identified themselves as Punjabis, or Sindhis, or Bengalis, or whatever, and not just as Muslims. Hoping, like Jinnah, that Urdu would unite the new country's two wings, he made it "a compulsory subject in post-primary schools throughout Pakistan," including

East Bengal. Bengali was made "an optional subject in West Pakistan."[77] This did not strike Bengali-speakers as fair, but Liaqat would not live to see the full extent of East Bengal's alienation.

* * *

Indo-Pak disharmony showed itself when, in September 1949, the pound was devalued. India devalued her rupee in consonance but Pakistan did not; a hundred Pakistani rupees now equalled 150 Indian rupees. An economic war took place; Indian coal did not go to Pakistan and the export to India of Pakistan's jute and cotton was stopped. Liaqat said he would not yield. At a secret meeting of the League in Dacca he said: "We shall drown the jute in the Bay of Bengal but will not give it to India."[78] After 18 months, when India accepted Pakistan's rupee rate, there were understandable cries of "victory" in Pakistan, and praise for Liaqat's firmness.[79]

Battles of this kind do not always inspire across time; we of a later period are apt to note the hardships they produced. Fortunately for Liaqat's name, he has achievements to his credit that are more significant than his "rupee war" success. He strengthened Pakistan's administration. An Indian editor who visited Pakistan in 1949, A.D. Mani, felt that "the devotion of the services to the welfare of the state" was "far more pronounced than in India."[80] Liaqat had contributed to this state of affairs, praising civil servants when praise was due and, more importantly, by "making a suitable selection of key men."[81]

Equally significant was Liaqat's bid to unite Muslim tradition with a modern state's needs. His "objectives resolution," embodying, as he put it, "the main principles on which the constitution of Pakistan is to be based," defined the place that Islam, religious minorities and modern institutions would have in Pakistan.[82] The resolution began in "the name of Allah, the Beneficent, the Merciful," said that "sovereignty over the entire universe belonged to God" and that "authority was a sacred trust," and among other things stated that in Pakistan

> Chosen representatives of the people (would) exercise power and authority.
>
> The principles of democracy, freedom, equality, tolerance and social justice, as enunciated by Islam, shall be fully observed.
>
> The Muslims shall be enabled to order their lives in the individual and collective spheres in accord with the teachings and requirements of Islam as set out in the Holy Qur'an and the Sunna.
>
> Adequate provision shall be made for the minorities freely to profess their religions and develop their cultures (and to) safeguard the legitimate interests of minorities and backward and depressed classes.
>
> The independence of the judiciary shall be fully secured.

It was Liaqat's view that the presentation of the "objectives resolution" before Pakistan's Constituent Assembly was "a most important occasion in the life of this country, next in importance only to the achievement of independence." The speech he gave at the time was almost as significant as the resolution. There being no priesthood in Islam, he said, "the question of theocracy simply does not arise." Still, Islam was "not just a matter of private beliefs and conduct"; it wasn't merely a relationship "between the individual and his God"; it had to "affect the working of the state." The state had to help "bring about a new social order based upon the essential principles of Islam."

He told sects within Islam that the state would not "curb the freedom of any section of Muslims in the matter of their beliefs." And he told Pakistan's Hindus that "it would have been un-Islamic to impinge upon the freedom of the minorities." Repeating an earlier thought, he said it was "Providence which has brought Pakistan into existence." Among his final lines were these:

> It is not every day that great nations come into their own; it is not
> every day that peoples stand on the threshold of renaissance. . . . We
> whom destiny has chosen to play a part, howsoever humble and
> insignificant, in this great drama of national resurrection, are over-
> whelmed . . . with the opportunities before us.[83]

A critic of the government, Mian Iftikharuddin, once a Congressman, called the resolution "beautiful" and the speech "even more beautiful."[84] When a Hindu legislator from East Bengal said that "some Lahore ulema" had told him that "no non-Muslim can be the head of the administration" in a state that respected Islamic teaching, Liaqat repudiated that view as "absolutely wrong." "These so-called ulema who have come to you," said Liaqat, "have misrepresented the whole ideology of Islam."

Liaqat had rejected at least three demands of the hard-line *Jamaat-i-Islami*. The *Jamaat* wanted Pakistan's legislatures not to frame laws but only to interpret divine ordinances, with the help of Islamic scholars. It also desired the phrase "the Islamic state of Pakistan," whereas the resolution spoke of "the sovereign independent state." Finally, the *Jamaat* wanted Pakistan's Muslims to be "compelled" to abide by the Qur'an and the Sunna, but Liaqat was not prepared to go beyond "enabled."[85]

Though a successful Prime Minister, Liaqat lacked Jinnah's independence and authority and was obliged at times to compromise on his convictions. He doubtless spoke from the heart when, during the debate on the "objectives resolution," he said that he wished Pakistan "to be a laboratory where we could practise the Islamic values."[86] But whether, left to himself, he would have gone even as far as he did in the direction of a formal Islamic state, or whether Jinnah, had he continued to live, would have gone as far, is doubtful.

* * *

Rulers and journalists of other lands noted that in discussion Liaqat "never raised his voice, never spoke in bitterness" but also that "his resolution was plain, and what he said, when he put the case of Pakistan, was as strong as words could make it," to quote David Lilienthal, former chief of America's Tennessee Valley Authority.[87] Invited by President Truman, he and Raana enjoyed a successful American visit, during which he took care to explain that Pakistan's Islamic ideals did not "spell out a sectarian, medieval, intolerant society" and to assert that "equality before the law of all citizens, irrespective of race or creed" was an "article of faith with us."[88]

Finding in the west "a tendency", as he put it, "to take Pakistan for granted," he also accepted an invitation to Moscow.[89] However, he died before a Soviet trip could materialize. He defined Pakistan's international stance:

> Pakistan is neither tied to the apron-strings of the Anglo-American
> bloc nor a camp-follower of the Communist bloc. It has steered clear
> of inter-bloc rivalry and has an absolutely independent foreign policy.[90]

He built ties with Muslim lands and urged "unity of thought and action amongst the Muslim states."[91] With Iran he felt a special affinity, partly, no doubt, because of his ancestral links, and he gave the Shah a great welcome in 1950.

Yet India was the main preoccupation. Kashmir was not resolving. How to share river waters was another vital question. Nehru proposed a no-war pact. Liaqat said he would sign it if it also envisaged a machinery for tackling disputes. All disputes might not be amenable to a single procedure, argued Nehru. Liaqat pressed for a procedure for Kashmir, to begin with. It was a political question, not a judicial one, answered Nehru. The correspondence, endless and fruitless, proved the subcontinent's mistrust.[92]

A ruler's resolve to be restrained crumbles when he finds a large audience before him and anticipates its sounds of applause. Liaqat was no exception to this universal truth. At mass meetings he often made telling points aimed at India, but he did not always stop there. At times he would end his speech by raising a clenched fist.

We should note, however, that this happened in the summer of 1951, when growing domestic criticism of his rule coincided with a belief in Pakistan in the likelihood of an Indian attack. A defiant posture towards India seemed the right response to both developments. According to General Ayub Khan, whom Liaqat chose as his country's first Pakistani army chief, Liaqat was tempted in 1951 to "fight it out with India." Ayub claims that Liaqat, who had kept the defence portfolio with himself, said to him, "Let us fight it out. I am tired of these alarums."[93] Mercifully, neither side attacked the other.

There had been talk of war the previous year too. It ended in April 1950 when Liaqat went to Delhi at Nehru's invitation—his first visit since partition—and signed an agreement on the treatment of minorities in the two countries. It would have astonished Delhi-ites to know that some of Liaqat's friends had urged him not to go to Delhi; they thought his life would be unsafe in India. And many in Pakistan were astonished, after the pact was signed, to learn that two Indian cabinet ministers, Shyama Prasad Mookerjee and K.C. Neogy, thought that Hindus were unsafe in East Bengal. Believing that the pact did not do enough to protect them, these two ministers resigned.

Each country was convinced that it defended minorities better than its neighbour. "We claim that we have done so more effectively than Pakistan," Nehru had said to Liaqat in January 1948.[94] Liaqat, on his part, spoke with equal self-satisfaction of "what we have provided here for minorities," adding, "I only wish that India had provided similar concessions and similar safeguards for the minorities in India."[95]

Interestingly enough, Liaqat made a positive impact, during his 1950 trip, on Vallabhbhai Patel. In a broadcast he made from Calcutta, Patel, who generally weighed his words, noted "the clear acceptance of the principles of democracy by the Prime Minister of Pakistan" and said that Liaqat's "earnestness and visible sincerity" had made "a profound impression" on him.[96]

* * *

One day in 1951 Liaqat called Iskander Mirza, the defence secretary, and Ayub, the army chief, and said to them, "Gentlemen, I have bad news for you. There is to be a military coup." I.I. Chundrigar, Governor of the N.W.F.P., had tipped him off. Mirza and Ayub helped Liaqat foil the bid.* Within hours all officers and civilians involved were arrested.[97]

There was open criticism too. Following Khaliquzzaman's resignation in October 1950, Liaqat had become the League's president as well, in-

---

*In 1958, after Mirza, by now President, had imposed President's rule, Ayub deposed him in a successful coup.

viting the accusation of power-lust. An active opponent of his was the Khan of Mamdot, who had been removed from West Punjab's chief ministership on charges of corruption.

Another foe, though she never referred directly to Liaqat, was Fatima Jinnah. Her statements suggesting that Pakistan was going downhill undermined morale and hurt the government. Not surprisingly, she was incensed when parts of a broadcast she made in September 1951, on the anniversary of her brother's death, could not be heard. Explaining, the controller of broadcasting spoke of technical problems. Fatima told him he had an "obliging set of transmitters ready to fail at your convenience."[98]

Liaqat's biggest disappointment was over the constitution. The "basic principles" proposed by a committee of the Constituent Assembly evoked such strong opposition that Liaqat was forced to shelve constitution-making. Ayub's comments on Liaqat's last months and on the Pakistan of 1951 are of interest:

> Politics became regionalized, and the Muslim League was forced to depend more and more on the refugee group.... The affairs of the Muslim League were in a mess. It looked as if Liaqat Ali Khan might prove too slow to regain initiative. His eye-sight was deteriorating. ... The people around him were equally slow and indecisive.[99]

On October 16, 1951 he was assassinated while addressing a Rawalpindi meeting by a man in the audience's first row, fifteen yards away. People at the rally killed the assassin on the spot. Later the government said that his name was Said Akbar and that he was an Afghan national and a hired assassin. Money was found on his person. He had told people at the lodge where he had booked a bed that he was in town "on C.I.D duty."[100] Who hired him was never established. Afterwards, it was Raana's view that "the government did not try hard enough to investigate the assassination and bring the culprits to book."[101]

If Jinnah founded Pakistan, Liaqat, underestimating his own role, felt that he simply found it. Jinnah had the pride of attainment, Liaqat the enthusiasm of obtainment. The spirit of his devotion to Pakistan is conveyed by his remark, "If I can render service to Pakistan as a *chaprasi*, I shall be the proudest man in the country."[102] The Nawab's son, leaving valuable property in India, stayed "landless" in Pakistan, refusing to claim, as compensation, land evacuated by Hindus or Sikhs. But he showed the world that Pakistan was viable.

However, returning on Liaqat's death from the U.K., where he had gone for medical treatment, General Ayub found that none of Pakistan's new leaders "mentioned Liaqat Ali Khan's name" or expressed "a word of sympathy or regret." "Eveyone," says Ayub, "had got himself promoted in one way or another."[103] Pakistan's misfortune was that Liaqat did not have, unlike Jinnah, a Liaqat at his side.

CHAPTER 9

ZAKIR HUSAIN

(1897-1969)

We saw that Abul Kalam Azad was a devout and proud Muslim who early in his life realized his Indianness and proclaimed it without hesitation. Zakir Husain, who, like Azad, had an orthodox Muslim upbringing, did not need to realize it. He just assumed it. Azad, for a while the *qaum*'s guide, found virtue in, and Qur'anic sanction for, Hindu-Muslim partnership. Zakir Husain, President of India from 1967 to 1969, took it for granted that India was his home and Hindus his associates.

Zakir Husain was born in February 1897 in Hyderabad in the south, from where, acknowledging British suzerainty, the Nizams ruled their large state, also called Hyderabad. Fida Husain Khan, Zakir's father, had migrated there from Qaimganj in western U.P. where his ancestors, soldiering Pathans, had settled early in the 18th century, leaving their wild, mountainous and romantic home across the vague India-Afghanistan border. Of the Pathans of Qaimganj, who suffered, as did Pathans settled elsewhere, from endemic tuberculosis, Mujeeb has written:

> [Their] ideal of self-respect was served more often by doing away
> with rivals who gave offence than by acquiring wealth and worldly
> honour. . . . Generally Pathan opinion considered not the nature of a
> crime but the form of provocation that was declared to have led to
> it.[1]

Ghulam Husain Khan, Zakir's grandfather, stabbed a man who continued, despite warnings, to carry away clay from his pond. But he also gave to the poor, shopped for the neighbourhood widows and became the disciple of a Muslim sufi and also of a Hindu called Bans Bihari. His son Fida Husain Khan moved at age 20 to Hyderabad, where he prospered as a printer and publisher of law books and a law reporter. Naznin Begum, Fida Husain's wife, gave birth to seven children, all boys, of whom Zakir Husain was the third; four, including the two oldest, died of tuberculosis.

Zakir Husain was raised on the "Baghdadi Primer," which taught the Arabic alphabet, and on chapters of the Qur'an; some lessons in Persian and, following those, in Urdu were also given. Since his father had become important, Zakir and his brothers had to use a carriage to visit relatives living on their street; going on foot was not proper to their station. But Fida Husain died at 37 and Naznin Begum returned to Qaimganj with her children. Zakir Husain was ten. Four years later Naznin Begum died of plague. She had refused to send for her sons, saying, "It will disturb their studies."

Zakir Husain was in a residential school at Etawah, the Islamia, started by Moulvi Bashiruddin, who hoped to impart English education as well as the Islamic way of life. His version of the latter included compulsory prayers, coarse clothes, hard beds and tasteless food. Zakir Husain survived the regimen, helped no doubt by the attention he received from Bashiruddin and from the school's headmaster, Moulvi Altaf Husain, who, spotting Zakir Husain's talent, often chose him to represent the school in debating or writing competitions or to deliver an address of welcome for an eminent visitor. Bright as well as respectful, Zakir Husain won the confidence of teachers and students alike; a peak of his Islamia phase was reached when, at his persuasion, the management abandoned its practice of depriving a student of a meal for missing a prayer.

The youth's gentle exterior masked a rage. Like Muhammad Ali and Abul Kalam Azad, who were several years older, and like thousands of other Muslims, Zakir Husain, 14 to 16 at the time, saw the Tripolitan and Balkan conflicts of 1911–13 as Europe's aggression against the world's only independent Muslim state, Turkey. He would wait at Etawah's railway station for the arrival of *The Pioneer*, published in Lucknow, and rush back to tell his fellow-students what was happening in Turkey. Also, he would speak about Turkey's plight at the local mosque and pass his cap round for donations to save Islam's honour. His manner was mild but his words were strong: "Your coins will be converted into bullets that will pierce the hearts of the enemies of Islam."[2]

Invited to dinner at Bashiruddin's place, Zakir found the school's founder sitting on a string bed. Bashiruddin made room on the bed for Zakir Husain. When the dinner of meat-and-gravy arrived, Bashiruddin poured water on it. After it had been eaten, Bashiruddin said, "Zakir Husain, don't look for pleasure in life."

From Etawah Zakir Husain, sixteen, tall and getting filled, went to MAO at Aligarh, where he spent seven years. In 1957, delivering the year's Convocation Address at Aligarh, Zakir Husain recalled "that hot mid-day forty-four years ago, when I first arrived at this university":

> Two of my brothers were already here. One of them helped me to buy a pair of shoes, some books and a lantern in the afternoon. We had gone to the city on foot but returned in an *ekka* (*a small horse-drawn carriage*), for it was considered beneath the dignity of gentlemen to carry things in their hands. My brother left me in his hostel room and went off to meet friends, telling me that after sunset, when the bell rang, I should go to the dining hall.
>
> The bell rang somewhat earlier than I had expected. For sixteen years I had eaten without putting on a Turkish cap, a Turkish coat, socks and shoes; donning this uniform caused some delay. I could not put the shoe-lace in the eye-lets. When I put the lace through two eyelets and pulled, I pulled it all out.... And I forgot completely the trick of knotting the shoe-lace that my brother had taught me in the afternoon....
>
> When at last I left the room dressed and ready, it was quite late, and others had already gone to the dining hall. I did not know the way. After a fruitless search I returned to where my room was.

We should suspect the details of this story, for Zakir Husain had a technique of sounding and appearing more helpless than he was. It was his way of putting others at ease: he would act diffident so that others might feel more confident and less envious, and also to attract assistance. But the posture of the lost soul could not survive scrutiny. Within days of arriving at MAO he was nicknamed "Murshid" ("Mentor"). His contemporaries would recall that Zakir Husain was "lethargic," "light-hearted," "irresponsible" and one who "often cut classes"; that his conversation would "enliven the environment"; that he was an an effective debater.[3] He was elected vice-president of the students union; he won prizes including the coveted Iqbal Medal; he stood first in his class in several exams. Failing to act on Bashiruddin's parting advice, he sought pleasure, at least in food. He would ask for "a three-minute start at a dinner party" but his friends would "loudly refuse to allow it," knowing that "he will deprive them of their dinner" if given the opening.[4]

But this picture too is incomplete. It leaves out of account a deeper, if also more troubled, Zakir Husain, who wants to study, who remembers his painful bereavements and shares the Muslim unhappiness over Turkey; and who remembers too his sufi friend and distant relative, Hasan Shah. Going about with "his earthly belongings and his books strung at the two ends of a pole which he carried on a shoulder," Shah timed his wanderings to be at Qaimganj whenever Zakir Husain went home for the vacations. Frequently, responding to a request of the sufi, who was thirsty for knowledge, the supposedly carefree, even careless, Murshid of MAO would copy out a whole book—and copy it out with "such care that he acquired a remarkably fine handwriting."[5] Some of Hasan Shah's sufism and familiarity with Persian also rubbed off on Zakir Husain. It is likely too that Shah's freedom from religious narrowness confirmed Zakir Husain's instincts. It would seem that Shah had purchased this freedom at a price. Rebuked once for prejudice against Hindus, Shah made amends by walking all the way to Peshawar in the North-West Frontier—the home of the Pathans—and back.

Eyeing a medical career, Zakir Husain studied science. A year's illness changed his mind; he switched to a bachelor's course in English, economics and philosophy. Then, in the fall of 1920, when he was 23, an M.A. and law student and a part-time teacher, he made what he later called "the first conscious decision of my life, perhaps the only one I have ever taken, for the rest of my life has but flowed from it."[6] This statement cannot be literally true. Before this he had chosen subjects for his studies and at the age of 18 he had assented to his marriage—to a girl named Shahjehan Begum. But there is no doubt that the course of Zakir Husain's life was being decided when he chose, in October 1920, to "non-cooperate" with institutions aided by the Raj and therefore to leave MAO.

On October 12, Gandhi and Muhammad Ali described their non-cooperation programme to students at the campus. Though Zakir Husain lacked "the urge to give up everything and follow" Gandhi,[7] a part of him had responded to Gandhi's call for a sacrificial struggle. Jallianwalla had stirred his mind, as had Azad's writings in *Al Hilal* and *Al Balagh*. But he had to be in Delhi, where Dr. M.A. Ansari examined him for an illness, when Gandhi and Muhammad Ali spoke to the students. Returning to Aligarh in the evening, Zakir Husain heard derisive comment at the station platform about Gandhi, who had spoken and departed. The coarseness of some of the remarks, which were made by a group of strolling students, and the fact that some of his friends seemed to enjoy them, filled Zakir Husain, as he later told Mujeeb, "with the deepest shame" and with a conviction that atonement was called for.[8]

Muhammad Ali and his brother Shaukat, who were in town still, appeared next day at the students union. With tears in their eyes they told the boys that they had failed in rousing them, that "they had come to bid farewell and were going away broken and beaten."[9] This was a reference to the apparently successful efforts of pro-Raj elements on the campus to frustrate the hopes of Gandhi and the Ali brothers. The disappointment of the brothers was so transparent that many students, including Zakir Husain, also began to weep.

Then Zakir, running a high fever and not intending to speak, rose and announced that he would resign his teaching assignment and forgo a scholarship he was getting. It was clear that others too were willing to take risks; the despondency of the Ali brothers was not justified. Within a few days Zakir Husain was in Delhi, where he assured Ajmal Khan, Ansari and Muhammad Ali that a large number of teachers and students would leave MAO and join a national institution, if one was started. On October 29 the Jamia Millia Islamia—the National Muslim University— was born.

The head of the prestigious Deoband seminary announced Jamia's birth at a meeting in the mosque of MAO. Jamia members continued to stay in MAO's buildings, and for a while it was not clear who belonged to MAO and who to the Jamia. Dr. Ziauddin, MAO's principal, met the situation by declaring the college closed and asking the students to go home. A large number would not, so Ziauddin and his supporters wired the parents to come and rescue their sons. Zakir Husain was offered a government job; he turned it down. Finally, the Raj's police was asked to remove the rebels. They marched out into tents and improvised lodgings. Nationalist newspapers reported their doings, and before long the Jamia band were joined by a number of bright and dedicated young men from different parts of India. Some of them were Hindu Brahmins. Six months earlier, the idea of their teaching in a Muslim institution would not have entered their dreams or the dreams of the Muslims whose lives they were now sharing.

Ajmal Khan was elected Jamia's first Chancellor and Muhammad Ali its first Vice-Chancellor. A.M. Khwaja, one of Jawaharlal Nehru's contemporaries at Cambridge, became the first principal. The Khilafat committee, which, along with Congress, conducted the non-cooperation campaign, financed the new college when it could, and some of its members tried also to run it. The ups and downs of the Khilafat movement directly affected Jamia, as did the self-importance and egotism of some of its leaders. Of some of Jamia's early students, Mujeeb has written: "Their hearts were all fire, their heads were foggy. Thoughtfulness was almost completely lacking, so was balance of mind. It seemed they could do anything when roused, and nothing otherwise."[10]

For a while "studies" meant no more and no less than a part in the Khilafat movement's political campaigns. Many students courted imprisonment. Some were of the highest quality. Mujeeb describes one of them, Shafiqur Rahman Kidwai:

> He was in the final year of his B.A. in 1920, and distinguished by love of comfort. When the change came, he made a bonfire of his foreign clothes and took to coarse *khaddar*. Hitherto shy and silent, he became all at once a master of political rhetoric. His capacity for patient, persistent endeavour stood suddenly revealed. He was a sportsman; he could sing, he could laugh, he could stimulate and console.[11]

An even stronger tribute was paid to Shafiqur Rahman by Rajagopalachari, Mountbatten's successor as Governor-General of India, who had observed him in Vellore jail, where the two were prisoners together in 1921–22. Rajagopalachari called the former Jamia student "a saint in the disguise of a citizen."[12]

Zakir Husain, too, took to *khaddar*, but he did not defy the Raj's laws. He taught—when that was possible—and he translated into Urdu Plato's *Republic* and Cannan's *Political Economy*. And after two years he left for Germany. As President of India Zakir Husain would recall:

> Dr. Hamied took charge of me, of my present and my future. He decided that I should go to Germany for further studies. My objections, difficulties, inertia counted for nothing. He had decided, so I had to go. He booked my passage, he accompanied me to Bombay. And he used the few days we were together in Bombay to teach me the elements of civilised living—how to dress, how to eat with knife and fork and generally how to conduct myself in European countries.[13]

Hamied, later a successful businessman in Bombay, had left Allahabad university to join Jamia. It is clear that he pressed Zakir Husain to go to Germany, where he himself went a few months later, but it is improbable that Zakir Husain's account is the whole truth. The inadequacy portrayed in it was in part a put-on; we can assume that Zakir Husain wanted himself to make the journey. Mujeeb has well described Zakir Husain's style:

> His obviously abundant intellectual energy was balanced by physical lethargy.... An effective means of protecting himself against all avoidable exertion, and prodding others to come to his assistance, was an air of helplessness.... I thought that in spite of his height and dignity he was a man who needed somebody to hold his hand and

lead him around, till I discovered that he had more courage, more
initiative and a greater ability to handle men and situations than many
who openly claim to possess these virtues.[14]

Thanks to Mujeeb, who was also in Germany at the time, we have a
fairly clear picture of Zakir Husain's three years abroad. Living most of
that time in Berlin, Zakir Husain obtained a Ph.D. for a dissertation on
Britain's agrarian policy in India; some of his work for this was done in
London. But the philosophy of education seemed his chief academic interest, and he also did some Arabic. He enjoyed the company of Hamied
and of Luba, the German girl Hamied married not long after arriving in
Europe. Virendranath Chattopadhyaya, or Chatto, Sarojini Naidu's
brother, who was also in Berlin, sought fruitlessly to convert Zakir Husain
to communism; Zakir Husain defended Gandhian non-violence· in discussions with him.

He visited Sweden, where he paid his way by writing an article on
Gandhi for a Stockholm newspaper. But he was not careful with his
money, or that of his friends. Thus he invested the cash he had and what
he could borrow from Mujeeb and another Indian student, Abid Husain,
to produce a pocket edition of Ghalib's *Diwan** in Berlin, because a printing
press there possessed an excellent Persian type, as well as a short book in
German on Gandhi's economic thought written by himself with the help
of a friend from Berlin. As Mujeeb puts it, the publishers of the latter
book "thought that the money given to them to cover costs was a free gift
and Dr. Zakir Husain's courtesy did not allow him to remove this
misunderstanding."

In Mujeeb's view, Zakir Husain's three years in Germany were perhaps
"the happiest in his life." "He had no responsibilities; he was not tied
down to any routine."[17] The Germans he was meeting were eager to know
about India and also companionable; their attention to detail and "ceaseless
intellectual and aesthetic activity" impressed Zakir Husain.[18] But he did
not emulate their sense of order. Says Mujeeb :

> Dr. Zakir Husain had an antipathy towards ordered living, acquired
> probably during his student days at Aligarh, which he could not
> overcome. Though he admired a sense of order in others and as a
> teacher never tired of emphasizing its value, he seemed to regard it
> as an irksome limitation on freedom when applied to himself. He
> could not keep a diary or plan his activities.[19]

---

*Writing in 1971, Mujeeb called this edition "about the best that has so far been produced."[15]

Significantly, Zakir Husain made at least one speech in which he "warned Germans against surrender to the new forces that could undermine their culture."[20]

* * *

Chatto had a sister, Mrs. Nambiar, who used to arrange occasions where Indians and Germans met one another. Then she stopped giving her parties and, in Mujeeb's phrase, "our social life became a blank." One day Zakir Husain, feeling lonely, rang Mrs. Nambiar to ask when her next party was going to be. Her reply is not recorded, but it so annoyed Zakir Husain that he told Mujeeb, "I will show that Mrs. Nambiar is dispensable." This Zakir Husain proceeded to do by phoning a young woman he had met at Mrs. Nambiar's, Gerda Philipsborn. So began, in the words of Mujeeb, "a friendship whose depths no one could fathom and which lasted till Gerda Philipsborn died in the Jamia Millia in 1943."[21]

Belonging to a rich Jewish family of Berlin, Gerda Philipsborn had a large circle of artistic and intellectual friends. Zakir Husain saw concerts, operas, plays and art exhibitions in her company. But "they lived their separate lives," thanks to an apparent resolve by Zakir Husain against a romantic attachment. Since Gerda Philipsborn was only one among the women Zakir Husain met in Germany, Mujeeb would on occasion reel off to him "a list of your girl friends."[22] Depending on his mood, Zakir Husain would, in response, either "frown with disapproval or add a name to the list." Of one of them, Mujeeb writes:

> She was nearer forty than thirty and had a mass of hair and a large head, whose weight seemed to explain her pronounced stoop. Her eyes, too, were large and dark, and told of centuries of suffering and sorrow. . . . She thought all the time of what she could do for Dr. Zakir Husain. She translated his thesis and typed it for him . . . but for her it was obviously not enough.[23]

The combination of Zakir Husain's tall Indian figure, thick black hair, neat beard and intellectual capabilities made him attractive to German women. Zakir Husain did not follow, in Europe, the Muslim tradition that requires a man to avoid the company of women; and he was not immune to the call of spring. Yet he managed to keep to the safe side of a line he had accepted.

* * *

Of those we are looking at, only Fazlul Huq and Azad did not study in Europe. The rest, Sayyid Ahmed Khan, Iqbal, Muhammad Ali, Jinnah, Liaqat and Zakir Husain, all did. Each was greatly influenced. Not unlike

Iqbal, Zakir Husain felt in Europe that India and the world could be remoulded. Iqbal hoped for a creativity better than Europe's, more uniting and less nationalistic, and thought that Islam would bring it about. Zakir Husain's response was at once more modest and less limiting; he only hoped that more Indians would tap their creativity, yet, at the same time, he hoped that all Indians, Muslims, Hindus, Sikhs and the rest, would do so.

But the news from home was bad. Jamia seemed to be disintegrating, a result of the collapse of the Khilafat movement. When, in 1924, the Turks abolished the Caliphate, no reason remained for the Indian Khilafat committee to collect funds to save the Caliph's honour, or for Indian Muslims to contribute to the committee. Since the committee was Jamia's only source of finance, this meant the new college's bankruptcy. Muhammad Ali lost his interest, but Ajmal Khan, who was encouraged by Gandhi's support, Khwaja, the principal, and some teachers and students were not prepared to give up. They brought Jamia to Delhi, where rooms were found in the suburb of Karol Bagh.

Though he seldom spoke about Jamia in Germany, Zakir Husain had not yielded his commitment to it. Mujeeb has recalled a crucial and moving conversation:

> One day, early in 1925, there was serious talk about the Jamia Millia between him and Dr. Abid Husain, with me listening in. Dr. Zakir Husain said that he had decided to work in the Jamia Millia, come what may. Dr. Abid Husain offered to join him. I said I too would join the Jamia Millia. Dr. Zakir Husain looked doubtfully at me and said, "No, you should not." I wanted to know why. He replied that the Jamia Millia was not a proper place for me. I still wanted to know why; if it was the proper place for him, why not for me? He said his case was different; he was already committed.
>
> When I persisted in saying that I would also join, he said with some sharpness, "Look, if I put you in a carriage at Delhi station and take you to an open space and tell you, 'This is the Jamia Millia,' what will you do?" I replied that if he called the open space the Jamia Millia, I would also say it was the Jamia Millia. We had all the while been standing in the middle of the room. In reply to my last remark he hugged me and said, "Very well, you also join us."[24]

The three then sent a telegram to Ajmal Khan and Ansari saying that they would serve the Jamia. They added a request: decisions about Jamia's future should await their return.

A year later Zakir Husain and his two friends sailed to Colombo. A train and a ferry took them to south India, other trains to Delhi. Zakir Husain went straight to Jamia, where those who had refused to bow down welcomed him with enthusiasm. He found that staff and students, about eighty in all, lived, ate and prayed on the first floor of a large commerical building and studied in three houses across the street. A fourth house was the "office." Zakir Husain took charge, acquiring at the age of 29, the title of Vice-Chancellor, or *Shaikhul Jamia*. From eight to four the Ph.D. from Berlin sat cross-legged on the floor, bending over a low writing table or leaning back against a hard *khaddar*-covered bolster. He made brief visits to Qaimganj, and a year after his return from Germany his wife joined him in a rented house in Karol Bagh. Until then the Vice-Chancellor slept in a room adjacent to his office.

Teachers and students piled their hopes, fears and advice on him. He was fund-raiser, accountant, secretary, editor (and generally sole writer) of the Urdu journal *The Jamia*, and the solver of problems that arose. To the annoyance of Mujeeb, who wanted Zakir Husain to be businesslike, up and doing and reaching out to potential donors, the Vice-Chancellor would listen at length to fools and bores. Writes Mujeeb:

> He was expected to have no personal needs, but to be available to anybody at any time, to consider only the wishes and needs of others, to be ready with consolation or advice on all matters, to continue the most idle conversation till the other party or parties had had enough of it.[25]

Zakir Husain's salary was Rs 100 a month. Abid Husain and Mujeeb, owners like him of European degrees, were given Rs 300 each to begin with, but they soon agreed to accept Rs 100, whereupon Zakir Husain reduced his salary to Rs 80. Two years after Zakir Husain's return, a new constitution placed Jamia's governance in the hands of a society whose members pledged themselves to twenty years' service to Jamia on a salary not exceeding Rs 150 a month. Not that these salaries were actually paid. Until 1944, when salaries were at last given in full and debts to teachers began to be cleared, Zakir Husain was receiving Rs 40 a month in cash and Rs 40 in credit. The share she had in her grandfather's estate brought Zakir Husain's wife Rs 10 a month. That was about all. Zakir Husain had property in Qaimganj but the relative managing it kept all its income. It was not unusual, therefore, for Zakir Husain to "stand meekly before his wife and say he wanted money,"[26] or for his wife to send the servant boy to borrow from the *bania* in a nearby shop. Forty years later, when Shahjehan Begum was the first lady, Subba, the bania, received hospitality at Rashtrapati Bhavan.

But, though his clothes were of coarse *khaddar*, Zakir Husain was always neatly dressed, and his bearing was dignified, so that he looked like nothing as much as an aristocrat who had adopted a simple life-style; no one coming to borrow from him could think that Zakir Husain had no money to lend. Since he lacked the courage to return a plain no to a request, Zakir Husain parted with cash and furniture that his family needed. Those wanting comforting words from him also received them, and seekers of interesting conversation were rewarded too. Mujeeb has described "the type of conversation (Zakir Husain) enjoyed best":

> He had a distaste for saying simple things simply, and was clear and direct only if he had to be. He would maintain the opposite of what the others seemed to be agreed upon, or even of what was obviously the reasonable position. His colleagues looked forward to these conversations; they would see that his intellectual positions had nothing to do with his actual practice.[27]

Fund-raising required tact rather than dialectics and Zakir Husain had that as well, though not in the quantity Ajmal Khan possessed. As Jamia's Chancellor, Ajmal Khan helped in the raising of finances, but the time he gave to this was limited by his practice as a physician, which was large, and by the numerous obligations tied to his social and political standing. Now and then, however, he would have Zakir Husain and perhaps Mujeeb speak of Jamia to some of his rich friends. On one such occasion a courtier of the Nawab of Rampur asked Ajmal Khan what the British government thought of Jamia. "Instead of replying to him," Mujeeb recalls, "Hakim Ajmal Khan asked someone present to pull aside the curtains as there was not enough light. This interruption enabled the conversation to be given another direction."[28]

Gandhi helped, discreetly. Zakir Husain agreed with him that the Mahatma's active involvement in raising funds "might have an unfavourable effect on Muslim opinion about the Jamia." The two met for the first time at Gandhi's Ahmedabad ashram in June 1926 and "took to each other instinctively."[29] That a Muslim convinced about Hindu-Muslim unity was in charge of Jamia pleased Gandhi; and Zakir Husain was glad to find that the Mahatma trusted him and offered no advice on how the Jamia should be run.

"This understanding and trust grew with time," as Mujeeb says, but it was not always recognized by others.[30] When Gandhi announced his disobedience campaign in 1930, Zakir Husain had to choose whether Jamia should join the protest and wind up its work, or stay clear of it. He decided unreservedly that Jamia's academic work should continue. Members feeling the call of conscience could, as individuals, take part in the disobedience provided they gave due notice, but Jamia would continue with its normal work. It was a decision that Gandhi understood, but some of his followers did not. Shafiqur Rahman and some others at Jamia—including Devadas Gandhi, the Mahatma's son, who was teaching Hindi at the time—joined the Gandhi-led campaign against the Raj; the rest quietly went on teaching; and Zakir Husain proceeded to Hyderabad to persuade the Nizam to give Jamia money.

This was a bold bid. His position dependent on British goodwill, the Nizam was hardly the man to approach for funds by one who was, or thought to be, an ally of the seditionist Gandhi. But what Mujeeb calls Zakir Husain's "shrewd appraisal of persons, his tact and charm"[31] worked, and the Nizam's council sanctioned a cash grant of Rs 50,000 for a building and a monthly grant of Rs 1000. Zakir Husain announced his success to the Jamia community, to the latter's "immense relief," but a great deal of the pleasure vanished when it became clear that the monthly grant, which could have covered many salaries, would go first to Delhi's British Chief Commissioner, who would decide whether Jamia deserved it.[32] Though Gandhi's campaign was followed by his 1931 pact with Irwin, the Viceroy, Delhi's Chief Commissioner withheld the Nizam's grants from Jamia for four years.

* * *

He could feel progress. Jamia had brought out books for children, including some that Zakir Husain had written himself, and a magazine for children, *Payam-e-Talim*, that was proving popular. In the world of Urdu these were pioneering ventures. A primary school, too, had been started. Thanks to the abilities of the man looking after it, Abdul Ghaffar Mudholi, its young pupils were showing "self-confidence, spontaneity and a cooperative spirit."[33]

One day in 1933, when Zakir Husain was distributing sweets to the boys who had passed a test in the primary school, a peon came and whispered to him that his three-year-old daughter Rehana, described by Mujeeb as "a lovely creature, with rosy cheeks, chestnut hair and large thoughtful eyes," was very ill. Zakir Husain continued to give away the sweets A little later the peon came again and told him, in his ear, that Rehana had died. Zakir Husain turned pale but did not stop what he was doing. Then the campus bell was rung and everyone learned that Dr. Zakir Husain's girl had died. Asked afterwards why he had not left the school at once, Zakir Husain replied that "the children were feeling so happy, he did not like to interrupt it." His wife told Mujeeb later that for several days after the event Zakir Husain's pillow was wet every morning.[34]

* * *

Gerda Philipsborn arrived at Jamia in December 1932. Zakir Husain had asked her not to come but she insisted; there was no question, in any case, of her staying on in Hitler's Germany. As she had had some experience in teaching small children, she was assigned to the primary school. Shortly before she arrived Zakir Husain told his wife how he and Miss Philipsborn had got acquainted, and how the acquaintance had grown into friendship. He had to honour, he added, the lady's affection for him.

After an eleven-year stay, Gerda Philipsborn died at Jamia of cancer. When her disease was diagnosed, she requested Zakir Husain to read the Qur'an to her whenever he had the time and to arrange, on her death, a Muslim burial for her. The wishes were fulfilled. Her years at Jamia were not without tension. Her assumption that she had a right to Zakir Husain's time and attention offended others and did not always please him, but he was too polite to let her know that. Satisfied that there was nothing more to the relationship than what her husband had told her, Shahjehan Begum accepted it. Mujeeb, who was as resentful as anyone else of Gerda Philipsborn's demands on Zakir Husain's time, nevertheless concedes "her deep concern for [Zakir Husain's] personal welfare and the genuineness of her interest in the Jamia."[35]

* * *

Three streams, the traditionalist Muslim, nationalist and modern, seemed to come together at Jamia. Zakir Husain and his colleagues had broken away from MAO, now Aligarh Muslim University, because of the latter's dependence on the alien Raj, which, in that Khilafat phase, they also saw as anti-Muslim. The role played at Jamia's opening by the head of the Deoband seminary symbolized its Islamic character; its respect for Gandhi and his steady friendship for it spoke of its nationalist character.

If Muslims thought at times that Zakir Husain was not loud enough about his Muslimness, some Hindus were disappointed that this quality was not wholly dissolved in his Indianness. They did not like it when, in 1935, he reminded Hindus that Muslims nursed "the deep suspicion that under a national government there would be the fear of the cultural identity of the Muslims being obliterated,"[36] or when he added that this was "a price that Muslims are not willing to pay under any circumstances."[37]

While not ashamed of the fact that, in his words, Jamia was a "Muslim institution with Islamic ideals," he was resolved that "no narrow or false interpretations of these ideals will be allowed to convert Jamia into a breeding-ground of communalism." To him, India was "our own dear country."[38] In that 1935 utterance he also said: "It is out of the earth of this country that we were fashioned and it is to this earth that we shall return."[39]

We should note that Zakir Husain was anxious lest nationalism turned into xenophobia, or love of Muslim culture into opposition to reform. He would speak, therefore, while defining Jamia's aims, of "the nefarious consequences of bigoted patriotism," and argue, too, that Islam's survival depended on its ability to function as a dynamic, creative force. In 1928 he had asserted that "releasing woman from the four walls of an unhygienic house" was an act of saving, not destroying, Islam. His Islam, he said, was

> ... the religion that made believers out of unbelievers, civilized men out of barbarians, that gave woman a status and a place in a society in which she had none before, which recognizes only an aristocracy of character amidst a brotherhood of man.[40]

After the collapse of the Khilafat movement and of the Hindu-Muslim trust that had marked it, "religious intellectuals turned communal and reactionary, and progressive intellectuals turned agnostic," as Wilfred Cantwell Smith puts it.[41] But Jamia's Muslim intellectuals lost neither their religious nor their progressive beliefs. If Zakir Husain, Mujeeb and Abid Husain never yielded their right to be good or even devout Muslims, neither did they give up their faith in Hindu-Muslim friendship and in Muslim reform. Of their attitude to the Hindu-Muslim question we will have much to say in what follows; here let us note their position on reform. Despite orthodox objections, painting was introduced as a subject at Jamia. In other departures from custom, plays were written and produced, and girls sat with boys in the primary school. Moreover, there was freedom and free discussion. As Mujeeb says:

> [Zakir Husain] did not enforce orthodoxy in any form. His practising the tolerance envisaged in the Qur'anic verse, "There is no compulsion in belief," created an atmosphere in which views could be freely expressed and differences of opinion and belief respected. . . . The Jamia Millia has represented Muslim tradition and culture . . . without committing itself to the orthodox.[42]

However, Zakir Husain was spared the kind of attacks from orthodoxy that Sayyid Ahmed had received, forcing the latter to leave religious instruction at Aligarh in conservative hands. Zakir Husain's tact helped him and Jamia. But his nationalism proved a great block. For a long while the Raj did not recognize Jamia's degrees, which meant that enrolment in Jamia's college and secondary school was small. The *qaum* did not want to send its sons to an institution whose degrees would not qualify them for jobs. Some idealists did join, and felt redeemed from the thraldom of careerism; but the growth of Jamia's college and senior school was effectively restricted.

* * *

Another obstacle was Zakir Husain's willingness, in 1937, to join with Gandhi in propagating the concept of *Nai Talim* or New or Basic Education, as it was called. Teaching based on the spinning wheel, or spindle, or another suitable production device, said Gandhi, would be more useful for young pupils than learning-by-rote. Congress ministries had taken office in most provinces, and Gandhi hoped that they would provide every rural child with an education that was free and compulsory and revolved around creative work. Zakir Husain was one of those invited to discuss the concept at Wardha, near Gandhi's new ashram at Sevagram. Rising to speak after the Mahatma had outlined his proposal, he told the gathering that the idea was not original, and he disagreed with a view Gandhi expressed that production by pupils should pay for the schools. "There is a danger," Zakir Husain said, "in over-emphasizing the self-supporting aspect. . . . Teachers may become slave-drivers and exploit the labour of poor boys. . . . If this happens, the spindle will prove even worse than books."[43]

Gandhi saw the spindle providing subsistence to the rural poor. It was cheap, it could be worked in the hut, and by everyone. Zakir Husain agreed, and he agreed, too, when Gandhi said that much could be taught along with the skill of spinning—knowledge of varieties of cotton and soils, arithmetic, history of the decay of crafts and of British rule, and so forth. But he could not accept the spinning wheel as a panacea, and he said so; and he said too that the development of the intellect through handwork should not become a fetish.

Some of the Mahatma's admirers were shocked by Zakir Husain's candour but Gandhi himself was not. He asked Zakir Husain to head a national committee constituted to prepare a scheme of Basic Education. The syllabus this committee recommended impressed many, including agencies of the Raj, as sound, and won Zakir Husain nation-wide recognition. In some schools in Congress-ruled provinces the syllabus was introduced; the experiment would have continued had Congress ministries not resigned in 1939.

Jamia, however, was hurt even as Zakir Husain gained. We saw in the Jinnah chapter that Congress's mistakes and the League's intensive cam-

paign against it alienated many Muslims from Congress in 1937–39. Linked
as it was to Gandhi and Congress, Basic Education was decried in Muslim
circles, and the *qaum* became less willing than before to donate to Jamia.
When Congress's Premier in the Central Provinces, Pandit R.S. Shukla,
gave the name *Vidya Mandir*, or Temple of Knowledge, to the schools
offering Basic Education, he made it easier for Muslim opponents of the
scheme to attack the schools as places of Hindu worship that the *qaum*
could not touch. Jamia suffered from the fall-out, as it also did when
Congress's ministries in U.P., Bihar and C.P. tried to propagate a Sans-
rikitized Hindi.

* * * *

Yet headway was being made. Land had been acquired for a new campus
at Okhla. Hyderabad had given another large grant, this time of a lakh.
And an interest Zakir Husain found and displayed in the work of Maulana
Ilyas and his *Tablighi Jamaat*, which prodded Muslims to understand and
live out Islam, told the *qaum* that fostering New Education had not made
Zakir Husain less of a Muslim. One day in 1943, Mujeeb, holding charge
while Zakir Husain was away and needing money "to meet the daily
requirement," found a large envelope on his desk; it contained Rs 10,000
in notes, sent by a Muslim whose confidence in Jamia had been restored.[44]
Jamia's matriculation degree was recognized, and also the diploma it gave
to those completing its teacher-training course. A new adult education
wing achieved excellent results. The Tata trusts helped "gracefully" toward technical education at Jamia.[45] And in Hyderabad Sir Mirza Ismail,
the Premier, invited Zakir Husain to lunch and presented him with a
cheque for Rs 5 lakhs.

Mujeeb faults Zakir Husain on two scores. One was his inability to
fend off unwanted callers. Until 1957, when he became Governor of Bihar
and found himself with A.D.C.s who regulated visitors, anyone who
wanted to could rob Zakir Husain of his time, energy and money. The
second was Zakir Husain's unwillingness to confine himself to the Jamia.
He allowed himself to be elected to the court of Aligarh Muslim University, agreed to supervise affairs at Delhi's Anglo-Arabic college and at a
Muslim orphanage and worked for the *Tablighi Jamaat* and for Basic Education, flouting the Persian line he habitually quoted to his colleagues
and students: "Hold to one thing and hold to it fast." He loved Jamia and
toiled for it; without him it would have perished. He supplied brilliant
and effective ideas—a new course, a new technique for raising funds, a
new exhibition or booklet to popularize Jamia's work, and he extracted
work from his staff and held them with his affection; but he did not, to
Mujeeb's regret, "devote his time and energy to the practical application

of his ideas even in one institution." In Mujeeb's unprovable view, the results might have been "revolutionary" had Zakir Husain done so.[46]

Basic Education was introduced with enthusiasm in Jamia's primary school but lost its momentum; students of teaching were taught to educate through craft—but not for long. Accomplishment rather than passing exams was announced as the goal at the secondary school but it was not really reached. Writing in 1946, Wilfred Cantwell Smith called Jamia's system "one of the most progressive and one of the best in India,"[47] but it remained an example—a heartening example, to be sure—and did not become a dynamo.

* * *

If, like most, Zakir Husain was several men in one, one of them, surely, was a sufi. He responded to promptings of the spirit and had a mystical concept of knowledge. He would frequently quote Rumi's lines;

> Knock at its body, knowledge is a snake;
> Knock at its heart, it is a friend, your friend.

The sufis spoke a language that appealed alike to the Muslim and the Hindu heart. So did Zakir Husain. "The stringing together of hearts" was his longing, and he would often quote universally valid verses, such as:

> Ask not for water but attain a thirst
> And you'll see waters bubbling on all sides.[48]

He exercised the sufi's freedom. Instead of praying five times a day, he would, often, pray only late at night or early in the morning. There was an element of concealment in his prayer; and he prized the Qur'anic verse that spoke of believers who "wake up at night and weep for their sins."[49] His answers to questions about his beliefs were often incomplete or indirect, leaving hearers to make their own deductions. Once, when colleagues pressed him for his views on the Way to the heart of knowledge, he fixed his gaze on Mujeeb, who was greatly embarrassed, and recited a Rumi verse:

> It's not the Way I talk of, I seek him,
> Who'll walk the Way with me;
> It's been said, first the comrade, then the Way.[50]

Mujeeb did walk with him. At least he carried Jamia's burdens with Zakir Husain, and became the Vice-Chancellor when, in 1948, Zakir Husain went to Aligarh.

A second part of Zakir Husain was the cultured citizen who collected objects of art: bamboo sticks, when he had money for nothing else; pieces of calligraphy; brassware; and, later in his life, fossils, rocks and paintings. Muslim culture gives a high place to good food, regarding it as one of God's blessings to man and enjoining not only its serving but also, to please a host, its appreciative and hearty eating. This etiquette was fully observed by Zakir Husain. Combined with his taste for rich dishes, this contributed to the diabetes and glaucoma from which he suffered.

Though in his mind he planned his speeches and lectures in advance, he hated the task of writing them down. He would put off the chore till the last, at times discovering "work" that enabled him to do so. Engaging his eldest daughter Saeeda in a discussion, he would ask if she knew why he was wasting her time, and add, "It is because I have some urgent writing to do."[51] Once, at Delhi University, he commenced a lecture while a typist was still to type the concluding pages.

When the inescapable moment of writing arrived at night, he would write sitting on his bed, using his pillow as a table. Mujeeb tried "for years" to equip Zakir Husain's office with a writing desk, but Zakir Husain would not agree. One day, when Zakir Husain was not in Delhi, Mujeeb had the low table and bolster removed and a chair and desk substituted. Zakir Husain "did not like the change."[52]

* * *

As we have seen in earlier chapters, three wise men of the British cabinet arrived in India in 1946 to urge Congress and the League to agree on India's future, and on an interim national government. To prove that it was Indian rather than Hindu, Congress wanted, we saw, to name one of its Muslims to the new government. Abul Kalam Azad, Congress's president, was its first choice, but in view of Jinnah's known hostility to Azad's inclusion, Congress thought of Zakir Husain. Though not a politician, he was unquestionably able, and a nationalist. (But not a conformist. He had displeased some Congressmen by cooperating, while overseeing the Anglo-Arabic college, with Liaqat Ali Khan, Jinnah's principal lieutenant, and also by declaring in a speech in Sind that denominational schools had their value.) Zakir Husain said he would be willing, but only if the League also wanted him. He desired, he said, to work for unity, not to cause a fresh disagreement.

Azad and Nehru proposed Zakir Husain's name to Wavell, the Viceroy, who mentioned it to Jinnah. "Zakir Husain?" Jinnah exclaimed. "He is a Quisling. Utterly and entirely unacceptable."⁵³ Though Congress and he were told that Jinnah was against his joining the interim government, Zakir Husain never came to know of the phrase Jinnah used to oppose it, which was not revealed until 1973, four years after Zakir Husain's death, when Wavell's diaries were published. Had Zakir Husain known what we know, his activities in the weeks that followed might have been different.

These activities were linked to Jamia's silver jubilee, which was celebrated with fervour in November 1946, three months after the Great Calcutta Killing. An interim government of Congress and League leaders had just been installed. It included pro-Congress Muslims—Wavell had at last overruled Jinnah's objections—but Zakir Husain was not one of them; he had no wish to join a house-at-war, which is what the new government was.

Responding to an inner prompting, Zakir Husain decided to use the jubilee to bring Jinnah, Jawaharlal, Azad and Liaqat Ali together, and to admonish them together. The Quaid-i-Azam, on whom he called, said bluntly that he was opposed to everything that Congress proposed or supported, and that this applied to Basic Education. Yet Zakir Husain's tact was not without effect. As a result of the interview, Fatima Jinnah, the Quaid's sister, came to see an educational exhibition at Jamia. She must have reported positively to her brother, for word soon came from Jinnah that he would attend the jubilee occasion.

This was the climax of a huge, four-day affair. Food was scarce, and tensions abundant, but Zakir Husain was determined to board and lodge two thousand persons, invited from all over the country, in a part of Delhi that had no water or electricity. The Jamia community laid roads, pipes and cables. Foodgrains, meat and vegetables were somehow procured. The campus heard rumours that dignitaries coming to the jubilee would be stabbed, and true stories of stabbings in the city. Zakir Husain concerned himself with a hundred details, including the placing and seating of the VIPs, to which their admirers, if not the VIPs themselves, were bound to be extremely sensitive. Mercifully, and amazingly, everything went off well, and Zakir Husain, with Nehru, Jinnah, Azad and Liaqat Ali sitting beside him, gave, in Urdu, what Mujeeb calls "the most eloquent and moving speech of his life."⁵⁴

He spoke of Jamia's willingness to suffer destitution for its ideals, of its faith that the Almighty would protect it. He quoted a double affirmative from the Qur'an: "Indeed, every hardship is followed by ease. Every hardship is followed by ease." Then, addressing the VIPs, he said:

You are all stars of the political firmament; there is love and respect for you not only in thousands but millions of hearts. I wish to take advantage of your presence to convey to you with the deepest sorrow the sentiments of those engaged in educational work. The fire of mutual hatred which is ablaze in this country makes our work of laying out and tending gardens appear as sheer madness. This fire is scorching the very earth in which nobility and humanity are bred; how can the flowers of virtuous and balanced personalities grow on it? How shall we save culture when barbarism holds sway everywhere? These words may appear harsh to you, but the harshest words would be too mild to describe the conditions that prevail around us.

An Indian poet has said that every child that is born brings with it the message that God has not altogether despaired of mankind, but has human nature in our country so lost hope in itself that it wants to crush these blossoms even before they have opened? For God's sake, put your heads together and extinguish this fire. This is not the time to investigate and determine who lighted this fire. The fire is blazing; it has to be put out.[55]

* * *

Not only was the fire not put out, it nearly killed Zakir Husain himself. Weary and ill, diabetes squeezing out his strength, he decided, a few days after independence, to have a short break in Kashmir. The papers spoke of killings on trains in Punjab and colleagues urged him not to travel, but, on August 21, accompanied by a servant-boy called Manzoor, Zakir Husain boarded a train for Pathankot. He travelled second-class; a wealthy resident of Jullundur named Fazle Haq sat in a neighbouring first-class compartment. The train's progress was slow and halting; at Ludhiana Zakir Husain went out and asked the station-master if there was a quicker train to Pathankot. He said there wasn't; there was mischief in the eyes of a group who stood nearby.

Zakir Husain returned to his compartment, where he was joined by Fazle Haq, who had been drinking. When the train arrived at Jullundur, where Haq was to get off, the platform looked deserted, with a few Gurkhas strolling on it. It did not look as if the train would proceed further, and Zakir Husain had his luggage taken off too. A big burly man, followed by a crowd of youth, walked up to Zakir Husain and instructed his accomplices to seize his luggage. Haq protested; the burly man repeated his order; Haq slapped him.

"Shoot the two of them," said the burly man to the Gurkhas, who aimed their rifles at Haq and at India's future President. Manzoor jumped and placed himself between a rifle and Zakir Husain. The Gurkhas did not fire, but Zakir Husain's and Haq's luggage was removed. Meanwhile a railway officer called Harbanslal Kapur, who had been travelling on the train taken by Zakir Husain and who had been informed by Manzoor, in answer to his question, that Manzoor's bearded boss was Zakir Husain, told the Jullundur station-master what was happening. The station-master arrived on the platform and took Zakir Husain and Haq into his office. Before entering the room, Zakir Husain turned and heatedly told the Gurkhas that their duty was to protect passengers, not to menace them; the soldiers seemed not to hear.

Kapur, who had been searching for the Gurkhas' commander, found a young Sikh officer, Captain Gurdial Singh, and brought him to the station-master's office. When he saw the uniformed officer, Zakir Husain berated him for the role of his men. Looking anxious and ashamed, Gurdial Singh said, "I will take you to a safe place, sir." "Find our luggage," said Zakir Husain. Ordering the Gurkhas not to let anyone enter the station-master's room, Singh went to look for the luggage. Returning without it, he said to Zakir Husain and Haq, "Please forget about the luggage and come with me."

Despite Singh's threats, the youths who had accompanied the burly man molested Zakir Husain, Haq and Manzoor. The three got to Singh's army truck, but a crowd surrounded it and asked Singh to hand over the Muslims. He said he could not. "You can take away the bearded man," said someone in the crowd, "but the other fellow belongs to Jullundur. Give him to us." Singh said he would order his men to fire, the crowd retreated, and the truck got away. Kapur the Hindu, Singh the Sikh and Manzoor the Muslim had saved Zakir Husain's life.

The next day he returned to Delhi. Rejecting advice, he travelled again by train though, on Manzoor's entreaty, he moved away from a seat by the window. The train reached Old Delhi station at 3 a.m. All the waiting-rooms were full. Zakir and Manzoor spent the next hours on the roof of a cheap hotel near the station—its rooms were dirty and airless. They had to push to one side some goats they had found on the roof. After sunrise they took a bus to Okhla, and, to avoid being seen, Jamia's father walked across the fields to his home. That day or the next he met Nehru and Patel, and an incensed Jawaharlal flew immediately to Jullundur to chastise the town's administration.

Unwilling to face enemies or friends, Zakir Husain hid himself for a few days in Mujeeb's house. Soon, however, disturbances started in Delhi. Many Muslims living in villages near Okhla were looted and killed, not by their Hindu neighbours, who had a long relationship of friendship with the Muslim villagers and with Jamia, but by organized groups from outside. Some Jamia men were attacked too. Shafiqur Rahman and Hamid Ali Khan, who was in charge of Jamia's publications, barely escaped with their lives. Led by Zakir Husain, who was obliged to forget his weariness and depression, the Jamia community organized the protection of its women and children and harboured a number of Muslims who had fled from their homes in surrounding areas. Nehru visited Jamia in the middle of one night; General Cariappa, head of the army, came and left behind a platoon of the Madras Regiment. "Keep the garden in trim," Zakir Husain told Mujeeb. "If we are forced to vacate, let those who occupy this place after us feel that we loved it."[56]

From Calcutta, where a fast by him had restored security, Gandhi, 78, arrived in Delhi. His first question to those who met him at the station was, "Is Zakir Husain safe, is the Jamia safe?" The next day he went to Okhla. Later Zakir Husain recalled the visit:

> His fingers had got crushed in the door of the car and he was suffering great pain. In spite of this he laughed and provoked others to laugh, he infused courage into us, and advised us to stay where we were. He talked to the Muslim refugees on the terrace of the Secondary School, took an orphaned child in his arms and hugged and kissed her. Then he left, saying that he would do all that was necessary for our safety or perish in the attempt.[57]

Though on occasion he referred to Gandhi as his guru, or teacher, Zakir Husain was not a "follower" of the Mahatma. In his life Gandhi was, in Mujeeb's phrase, "a powerful influence," and he told Mujeeb that what he admired most in the Mahatma was "his capacity to laugh at himself,"[58] but, as we have seen, there were times when Zakir Husain frankly disagreed with Gandhi. Always, however, it would seem, there was affection between them.

On January 10, 1948, at Shafiqur Rahman's initiative, a number of Hindu and Sikh refugees from Pakistan, men, women and children, were invited to "come and meet and eat fruits and sweets together with Muslim children and parents."[59] Three days later, his pain at Hindu-Muslim violence unrelieved, Gandhi started another fast. Unlike many who urged Gandhi not to take the step, Zakir Husain told him that he had "chosen the right moment to urge . . . people to purify their hearts." "We are overwhelmed with shame," he added, "that free India should have nothing to offer you but bitterness and distress."[60] Delhi was safer after the fast, which was broken on January 18. Twelve days later Gandhi was killed.

* * *

The desire to leave Jamia entered Zakir Husain's heart some months after independence. Voices on the campus were critical of his non-Jamia involvements, which he was not willing to eschew. He hoped, in fact, for a wider role, and he thought that Jamia needed a change at its helm. Having to go for funds to Nehru and Azad, who was Education Minister, was not pleasing to him. He had made one request but the government had sat on it, and he did not like the idea of beseeching rulers again and again. Yet money was needed if Jamia was to grow. A Vice-Chancellor who did not mind going to Nehru and Azad with the begging-bowl was called for.

India, newly independent, required a person of Zakir Husain's qualities but his enlistment was delayed because of Azad's attitude to him. As a student in Etawah and Aligarh, Zakir Husain had been roused by Azad's writings. He would speak till his death of Azad's place in India's freedom movement but, at least during the last ten years of Azad's life, relations between them were not cordial. Azad, who was consulted by Nehru whenever the question of a Muslim candidate for a national role arose, seems seldom, if ever, to have raised Zakir Husain's name. He felt, as he once told Zakir Husain, that the latter was not strong enough, but more personal sentiments may have also played a part.

However, in November 1948, when Aligarh Muslim University (AMU) needed a new Vice-Chancellor, Azad asked Zakir Husain if he would serve. Zakir Husain said yes, provided the University Court elected him unanimously. This stipulation was met, and Zakir Husain took over at AMU at the end of November; three years later he was reappointed for a six-year term.

AMU was and is a campus of critical significance, which derives from its prestige in Muslim eyes and from the role, over the decades, of its teachers and students. A major blow for the Khilafat movement had been struck at AMU, thanks in fair part to Zakir Husain himself. Later, the campus had supported the League and Pakistan. As Zakir Husain put it in December 1951, before an audience headed by President Rajendra Prasad, the place of Muslims in India would be "largely determined" by "the way Aligarh works, the way Aligarh thinks" and by "the way India deals with Aligarh."[61] There was sweet irony in his return to the campus. In 1920 the police had removed him in a truck; his coming back was forbidden. But his emotions now had more to do with home-coming than with vindication or victory. He said:

> When I was a student, I looked up Aligarh as my all. It was my home, my garden, my native land. . . . We had founded the Jamia Millia after rebelling against this place, but we never regarded the Jamia as something apart. . . . There too I was working for Aligarh. I was convinced that one day we would return to Aligarh.[62]

His task was difficult and delicate. Replacements had to be found for the many faculty members who had gone to Pakistan. Some of those who remained had supported the League and Pakistan; they needed protection from victimization. A section of the students looked upon Zakir Husain as an intruder, even as one foisted by a government which, it was said, saw AMU as polluted because of its pro-Pakistan past and wished to "purify" it. The secretary of the students' union made biting remarks in a speech that was supposed to be one of welcome; and a whispering campaign contrasted Zakir Husain's salary as AMU's Vice-Chancellor with what he had been receiving at Jamia.

Zakir Husain responded with goodwill to his detractors and with a complete absence of curiosity about the previous sympathies of the staff. The spirits of a fearful, even tense, campus began to be rehabilitated. He recruited professors and young lecturers, many of them Hindu, from different parts of the land, expanded the budget and had a German-designed engineering college built. Drafting the help of Begum Qudsia Zaidi of Rampur and studying local trees and flowers himself, he brightened the campus with bougainvilleas, flowering shrubs and roses, and lined every street with trees.

Students were inevitably exhorted by him and, on occasion, rebuked, though only in roundabout language. And he used small instructive gestures. In the fashion of the day, students would at times call on him with their long coats unbuttoned above the waist. Saying nothing about it, the Vice-Chancellor would, while talking with them, quietly button up the coats.

A year after he came to Aligarh he had a heart attack that would have killed him had a physician not arrived in time. Henceforth he would not eat as he liked. Yet he and his family were at last enjoying some long-forgotten comforts. The Vice-Chancellor's house was large and adequately furnished; and several servants came with it. Zakir Husain was able to start a collection of fossils and to possess books that hitherto he could only borrow.

The Aligarh Muslim University Act of 1951 added to Zakir Husain's difficulties. Implementing a clause of India's new constitution, under which colleges receiving grants from the government could not make religious instruction compulsory, this Act made religious study optional at AMU. Some AMU Muslims were displeased. They objected, too, to another provision of the Act, which, for the first time, enabled the election of non-Muslims to the university court.

Not everyone at AMU praised Zakir Husain. Some of the meetings he had to conduct were unpleasant. There were insinuations that he had created a "new" Aligarh of the sort desired by New Delhi. Giving in to his unhappiness, Zakir Husain once said publicly that he had lost hope of anything worthwhile being done at AMU. In the middle of 1956, a year before his term was to end, he resigned.

* * *

Half of him hoped for privacy. The other half enjoyed life in public, prizing, for example, the nominated seat he occupied in the Rajya Sabha, the upper house of the Indian parliament, where his interventions had been rare but also of rare quality. He was still in Aligarh and wondering which half would be satisfied when Azad finally spoke to him and offered him the chairmanship of the University Grants Commission (U.G.C.), the body that oversaw and funded the nation's campuses. Intrigued, Zakir Husain began, as he frankly told a friend, "to desire the post." Some days later he heard on the radio that Chintaman Deshmukh had been appointed to the job. He felt "utterly disgusted."[63]

When Zakir Husain was back in his home in Delhi, a close associate of Azad, Humayun Kabir, called on him and said that Azad wanted to see him. The Pathan in Zakir Husain flared up. "Please tell Maulana Azad," he said, "that the distance from his house to mine is the same as the distance from my house to his."[64] Later Azad and Zakir Husain ran into each other at a public function and Azad offered the explanation that the U.G.C. needed a man who was ready to be harsh.

A year after Zakir Husain had left Aligarh Nehru decided to offer him the Governorship of Bihar. But nobody seemed to know where Zakir Husain was. Finally his whereabouts were discovered and a cable sent to Germany, where he was recuperating after surgery on an eye. Zakir Husain replied that he would give his answer on returning to India. It was yes.

Though he had visited Bihar to raise funds for Jamia, Zakir Husain did not really know the state. However, a Governor does not have to be knowledgeable about the state he presides over. He is spared—except when circumstances are deemed abnormal, when he is supplied with advisers—the tasks of deciding or executing policies. His duties are to be gracious to callers and wise before audiences and to keep ministers in harmony with one another. Zakir Husain played these roles with distinction.

By being what he was, he influenced politicians and charmed all who called on him, whatever their station in life. When invited to launch, or otherwise play a role in, a meeting, exhibition, performance, factory or whatever, many an Indian Governor, or other dignitary, has been content to utter impromptu banalities. With Zakir Husain it was a violation of culture to talk at random. Despite his distaste for writing out his talks, once he had agreed to go to an occasion, he would labour in order to make an intellectual contribution to it, reading up, if necessary for the first time, on yoga, or aspects of Jainism, or astronomy, or whatever. One of his significant talks was on Urdu:

> Urdu is the language which I first learnt from my mother, the language in which I still think, and from the literary and intellectual treasures of which I still derive benefit. . . . It is not the language of a community or a religion; it was not imposed by any government. . . . It is the language of the common people . . . and of the *faqirs* and saints who were anxious to communicate the love which overflowed their hearts to the common people who hung on their lips. . . . It is not startled by what is novel, it does not shy at innovation, it does not consider any words as polluted.[65]

While holding this view of Urdu, he used, in his formal speeches, a number of Sanskrit words, even when Urdu equivalents were current. Some Muslims in Bihar regarded this as a betrayal; to Zakir Husain the use of Sanskrit words was his way of showing that as Governor he represented not the *qaum* and Muslim culture alone but India and Indian culture as a whole. Still, his popularity among Muslims was affected. Hearing his Sanskrit words on the radio, many of them drew adverse conclusions about him. That as Governor he was helping a number of Muslim educational and cultural organizations was not known to them.

A Governor has to swallow his disagreements with the decisions of his ministers and legislators. Unless he resigns, he signs. Once Zakir Husain threatened to quit, and Bihar's ministers gave in. A Bill of theirs would have reduced the state's universities to insignificant departments of their government. When Zakir Husain said that he could not possibly assent to such a measure, it was substantially modified. Except in this instance, Zakir Husain signed each time. He had accepted a constitutional role, and was content to be gracious and wise and to help in modest ways.

* * *

When Azad died in 1958 there were rumours that Zakir Husain would take his place as Education Minister. Nehru talked with him but did not ask him into the cabinet. However, in 1962 Nehru proposed his name as Vice-President, to fill the place left by Sarvepalli Radhakrishnan. In May Zakir Husain was elected and sworn in.

A Vice-President has four tasks. He chairs the Rajya Sabha's sessions, receives and is received by rulers of other lands, lends prestige to ceremonies and functions, and is kind and encouraging to all who are able to call on him.

Though he could not forget that it was to Nehru that he owed his position, Zakir Husain was an impartial chairman, and more than fair in giving time to opposition MPs. In private conversation he rated their performance above that of most Congress MPs. He also learned, for the first time in his life, to bang the table, to shout and to order men to silence.

He journeyed to other lands, of course. Whether they met him at home or in India, foreign leaders used to the polite, sophisticated and predictable talk of international diplomacy were usually surprised to find that Zakir Husain was genuinely appreciative of, and curious about, their countries. This was not an attitude in which he was always backed by the foreign ministry, which arranged his tours or his appointments with visiting dignitaries.

Frequently, the ministry's draft of an address by him to an audience in another land was patriotic in a narrow and self-defeating sense; over-stressing India's contribution toward peace, culture and justice, it would underplay the host country's role. Zakir Husain would rewrite the speeches, for the sake both of fairness and of sound diplomacy.

Because he was Vice-President, Zakir Husain was besieged with invitations. Because he was polite he accepted many of them. Because he spread charm, he was importuned all the more. He told Mujeeb that his smile had become a fixed part of his face and that his jaws ached from constant grinning.[66] Not that he had turned into a machine. He would identify himself with the work of those he was with, writers, painters, musicians, or botanists, or young men and women aspiring to be such, and stimulate and encourage them.

And if he went to a place he had known before he had become so important, he would look out for the humble person there who knew him in the past, a *mali* perhaps, or a peon or a driver, who would be too diffident to come forward on his own to greet the Vice-President of India; on finding the person, Zakir Husain would grasp his hand, or embrace him. If, as happened but very rarely, someone called on him thinking of what he or she could do for Zakir Husain, and was curious about what was in his mind, he was very grateful. Such persons—he told Mujeeb—helped sustain his faith in human nature.

In power and popularity Zakir Husain was hopelessly outranked by Nehru. Yet in protocol the Vice-President was placed above the Prime Minister, and physically Zakir Husain was easily the taller of the two. Sometimes these factors made Zakir Husain a little uncomfortable in Nehru's company; he would try to compensate for it by being the deferential younger brother. Nehru died two years after Zakir Husain became Vice-President; Zakir Husain spoke movingly of his grief.

India and Pakistan clashed a year later. When the neighbours come into conflict, a Muslim citizen of India experiences thoughts that do not trouble his Hindu compatriot. He wonders, at times, whether his loyalty is being questioned; and he wonders too whether the conflict will hurt Hindu-Muslim relations in India. In Zakir Husain's case there was a third factor. A brother of his, Dr. Yusuf Husain, was a professor in Pakistan.

Shortly before the 1965 war, Zulfiqar Ali Bhutto, at the time an adviser to President Ayub of Pakistan, had visited New Delhi. At a lunch given for him at the International Centre, Zakir Husain sat in the middle. Placed to his right, Bhutto ignored him totally and talked past him to an I.C.S. officer sitting on the Vice-President's left. Zakir Husain sat through the lunch without turning to either side and without an expression on his face.[67]

* * *

The pact of Tashkent followed the 1965 war. The following morning Lal Bahadur Shastri died on Soviet soil. Zakir Husain stood with Radhakrishnan to receive Shastri's body and observed the selection, by Congress's leaders, of Nehru's daughter as Prime Minister.

A year later Congress was once more returned to power at the centre, but its majority was considerably reduced and it lost some important states to opposition parties. It had to choose a candidate for President. Radhakrishnan was expected to retire, and apparently wanted to. It was widely expected that Zakir Husain would succeed him. His performance as Vice-President had been without blemish. His elevation to Rashtrapati Bhavan would have conformed to what had happened five years earlier, when Radhakrishnan moved up from the Vice-Presidentship. Moreover, Zakir Husain seemed about the only man who might be acceptable to Congress and the opposition both; in view of the latter's increased strength, this was an important factor.

However, led by Kamaraj of the Tamil country, some of Congress's chiefs urged Radhakrishnan to offer himself for a second term. Their aim was to circumscribe the powers of Indira Gandhi, the Prime Minister, who was showing more independence than they had foreseen. In their belief Radhakrishnan was more likely than Zakir Husain to stand up to Indira; they proposed a re-election of the two in the positions they held. Stories appeared in the press that Radhakrishnan was willing to serve another term; true or false, they were not contradicted.

Zakir Husain now made an astute move, which also accorded with his sense of self-respect. He announced to the press that "he would under no circumstances" agree to remain Vice-President for a second term. This strengthened his position and that of Indira Gandhi, who had made plain her preference for Zakir Husain. Knowing that the opposition would capitalize on any impression that Congress had been unfair to Zakir Husain, Kamaraj and his allies yielded to Indira Gandhi's wish and called off their plea to Radhakrishnan. On April 9 Radhakrishnan announced his retirement; on April 10 Congress adopted Zakir Husain as its candidate. Some in the opposition said, with or without truth, that if Congress's leaders, including Mrs. Indira Gandhi, had gone about it the right way, Zakir Husain would have been everyone's candidate. However, either because Congress erred or because the opposition could not free itself from its habit of opposing, Zakir Husain's candidacy was contested. K. Subba Rao, shortly to retire as the Supreme Court's Chief Justice, was named as the opposition candidate.

Zakir Husain's prospects were not poor. Congress had a small but clear majority in the electoral college, which consisted of elected members of the assemblies of the states, as well as elected members of the two houses at the centre, whose votes had higher value. However, votes for Subba Rao from a few dozen Congress legislators would result in Zakir Husain's defeat. A few in Zakir Husain's circle of relatives and friends feared that some Congressmen would vote against Zakir Husain because he was a Muslim.

After he was nominated, Zakir Husain went to the U.S.A. to keep previously-made engagements. He returned three days before the election. There was some voting across party lines, but, on balance, it was in his favour. A few Congressmen did vote against him, but not, it would appear, because he was a Muslim. A larger number of opposition legislators voted for him, because he was Zakir Husain. Winning by a 4:3 ratio, he was sworn in on May 13, 1967. Friends poured into the Vice-President's residence on Maulana Azad Road to offer congratulations. A rejoicing but shy Shahjehan Begum served *barfis*.

* * *

At seven the next morning he went to Rajghat, to, in his words, "rededicate myself at the *samadhi* of the man who first showed me the way to devote myself to the service of my countrymen."[68] He recalled the expression Ram Raj, clarifying that Gandhi used it for a society where the down-trodden were uplifted. He said he was pledging himself "to the totality of my country's culture."[69] After his election, and before he was sworn in, he had called on the Hindu religious leader, the Sankaracharya of Sringeri, who was in Delhi, and on Muni Sushil Kumar, the Jain priest, and sought their blessings.

Some of these gestures disturbed the *qaum*. There were whispers that Zakir Husain was diluting or losing his faith to curry favour with Hindus.

Wasn't Ram Raj a Hindu term? Should a Muslim seek a Hindu's, or a Jain's, blessings? Zakir Husain's explanation that Gandhi employed Ram Raj as a phrase for a caring society was ignored. Criticism continued and was biting. "People only torture with their tongues now," he told Mujeeb, who noticed that a letter from a Musim had wounded Zakir Husain. The President quoted Ghalib to Mujeeb:

> I speak the truth, the ignorant
> lash at me with their tongues.
> Oh God, have judges now eschewed
> the scaffold and the noose?[70]

Zakir Husain was much too refined to employ gestures or expressions as a means of gaining cheap popularity among Hindus. Having attained India's highest office, he did not even stand in need of it. (The Prime Ministership was no doubt a more powerful office, but Zakir Husain's health and aptitudes ruled out any desire in that direction.) He said what he said and did what he did because he wanted to show Hindus and Muslims alike that an Indian, and not just a Muslim, had become President. He wanted to honour, and to be seen to honour, "the totality of Indian culture."

There was also, Mujeeb suggests, another factor. Zakir Husain seems to have felt that India's Muslims, who, rightly in his view, asserted their cultural identity, did not generally acknowledge a corresponding Hindu right. This might have been a reaction against Hindu attitudes. Even so, it amounted, in Zakir Husain's view, to a lack of generosity and a hardness of heart. He found several Hindus respecting his Muslimness; he wanted Muslims to respect Hindu culture. In his view they were not doing it, or not doing it enough; and he remembered how, back in 1920, some at Aligarh had been disrespectful in their talk about Gandhi. In Mujeeb's opinion, Zakir Husain wished, through the gestures that annoyed the *qaum*, to atone for Muslim shortcomings. Troubled by Hindu errors, Gandhi would fast. Pained by the *qaum's* narrowmindedness, as he saw it, Zakir Husain would go out of the way to show respect to Hindu culture.

Why did Zakir Husain not directly speak against the narrowness he perceived? His courteous nature came in the way. Yet courtesy is not always a wise guide. Frankness on his part, a direct word to the *qaum* that Hindu identity too needed to be respected, might have helped the *qaum* more, and offended it less, than his gestures.

* * *

At the end of 1967 he was to lay the foundation-stone for the Guru Govind Singh Bhavan of the Punjabi University at Patiala. As he tried to write a speech for the occasion, Zakir Husain remembered that Guru Govind Singh had been killed by a Muslim, and that the guru's father and sons had been executed at the behest of a Muslim ruler. Perhaps, too, he remembered his little Rehana, and his brothers, who died young. He remembered the long, sad tale of Sikh-Muslim violence. And he remembered how a Sikh officer had saved his life in 1947. Tears fell on his draft. He resolved to be strong while reading the speech but his eyes were wet again; so were the eyes of his largely-Sikh audience. Zakir Husain said:

> The whole life of Guru Govind Singh is a unique story of sacrifice, toil, educative activity, military talent, unrivalled valour, boundless graciousness, unfathomable love. There are in this story accounts of hardships suffered such as shake the heart and of success that fills it with hope. If anyone is innocent enough to believe that successes can be achieved without enduring hardships, this story will make it clear to him that the life of a man of God, a beautiful, pure and noble life, cannot be bought cheap.

> For what was there that this man of God did not bring as an offering before God's throne? His father; the light of his eyes, his beloved sons; recklessly brave comrades, to whom he was more gracious than to his own offspring; all were offered up by him.[71]

He travelled to India's far corners and to many a distant land. He spoke wisely, inaugurated patiently, received graciously, and observed acutely. After visiting Hungary and Yugoslavia he told the journalist Durga Das: "These two societies are changing and the winds of change are blowing. Nobody looks there any longer for doctrinaire, socialist solutions. But here we cling to slogans."[72]

He tried to promote harmony. Indira Gandhi talked to and listened to him; so did Morarji Desai and others in the cabinet who would, after Zakir Husain's death, fall out with Mrs. Gandhi. He saw self-centredness and desires to split, hurt or control. He could not cure what was wrong but at least he played a part in delaying a break-up of Congress. Occasionally he passed on opposition points of view to a Prime Minister who had a will of her own.

He liberally exercised the President's powers to commute a death sentence into one for life. Rashtrapati Bhavan never lacked gardens; in Zakir Husain's time they seemed prettier than ever. At a book fair he casually asked if the Maktaba Jamia—Jamia's publication wing—had a stall. Delighted to be told that it did, he went to it. The books were plentiful and tastefully displayed; his eyes were moist once more.

He was due for a routine check-up, in his room, on the morning of

May 3, 1969. The doctors arrived. Excusing himself, he went to the bathroom. When he did not come out for some minutes, his servant Ishaq, who had looked after him ever since his heart-attack twenty years earlier, knocked at the door; when there was no answer Ishaq hoisted himself and looked through a ventilator. India's President lay huddled by the door. He was dead.

Once, after a funeral they had attended together, Zakir Husain had said to Mujeeb: "If things are done as shabbily as this when I am being buried, I warn you that I shall get up and start shouting."[3] He had not known then that he would die as President. Many of the world's rulers came to the dignified, orderly funeral of Zakir Husain, who now rests within Jamia's campus, a school to his east, a library to the west and a mosque to the north.

CHAPTER 10

CONCLUSION

Do the eight lives say anything to us? Our times differ from theirs. As a result of the 1947 and 1972 divisions and the population flows that began in 1947, Hindus outnumber Muslims by 15 to 2 in India* and Muslims similarly outnumber Hindus in Bangladesh and even more decisively in Pakistan. Yet on the subcontinent even small ratios translate into immense communities. If Hindu-Muslim incompatibility is proved and incurable, we should expect large numbers to be separated by walls or hurt by gunfire. Any light that the lives shed on the Hindu-Muslim question is therefore relevant.

Not synonymous with Hindus but largely representing them, Congress was, we saw, ungenerous in that crucial year, 1937. Blindness lay behind its failure to give Muslims a visible share in its ministries. It did not realize that Congress rule could be taken as Hindu rule by the bulk of the qaum. This blindness was not new. We saw in Sayyid Ahmed's story that as far back as the 1880s most Hindus associated with the founding of Congress were unaware of Muslim fears of one-man-one-vote.

If Congress in 1937 was "a powerful organization which did not suffer from any lack of arrogance,"[1] as Rajagopalachari, then Congress's Premier of Madras, was to confess in 1965, we can also fairly accuse Jinnah of making excessive demands in the period between 1939 and 1947. As Wavell, not unsympathetic to him, said of Jinnah in 1946, "I think he has

---

*The Muslim rate of growth is, however, somewhat higher than the Hindu rate. Between 1971 and 1981 India's Muslim population increased by 30.59 percent, the Hindu by 24.15 percent. (Figures of the Census Commissioner of India quoted in *Indian Express*, Madras, July 21, 1985.)

been too unyielding."[2] His insistence on a bar against Congress's Muslims and his claim to Assam and the Hindu-majority portions of Punjab and Bengal were unreasonable positions; they damaged the cause of Hindu-Muslim understanding.

If arrogance (Congress's) and extremism (the League's) were hurtful, so was partisanship. Few on either side transcended the divide. From being an ambassador of Hindu-Muslim unity Jinnah withdrew into the *qaum*. Even Gandhi, who said that one of his functions was "to unite parties riven asunder,"[3] was only spasmodic in his strivings for a Hindu-Muslim alliance. He dramatically promoted it, we saw, in 1919–22 but seemed to lose faith in it after the mid-twenties, and in 1929, with remarkable candour, he told Lord Irwin, the Viceroy, that "however much they argued," Indian parties discussing the communal question "could not reach a policy which would be acceptable to all."[4] In 1937, however, he expressed his regret that Jinnah had not used him "as a bridge" between Congress and the League. To this Jinnah's reply was that Gandhi had identified himself with Congress.

Though called an appeaser of Muslims by the Hindu group that disliked him for years and finally killed him, Gandhi was seen as a Hindu leader by the bulk of the *qaum*, not as a bridge, except during two phases: 1919–22 and the last months of his life. Spelling out the *qaum*'s perception of the Mahatma, Chaudhri Muhammad Ali writes:

> That Gandhi, or any other Hindu leader, did not harm the individual Muslim, or actually served him loving care, was irrelevant to the political issue. It could not justify the exercise of (Hindu) political power over Muslims. . . . Gandhi had some admirers and partisans among the Muslims, but the more he praised them, the more they were looked upon as traitors. . . .[5]

The polarization at the top reflected grassroots sentiment. If opinion in the *qaum* prevented Jinnah from accepting the Motilal Nehru Report in 1928, which was another significant year, Sikh and Hindu feeling in Punjab restrained Gandhi and others in Congress from accepting Jinnah's substitute proposals.

Partisanship and polarization were accompanied by a sense of self-righteousness. A core of truth lay at the heart of Wavell's sweeping condemnation of Congress and the League in 1946:

> There was no constructive statesmanship or compromise. No Hindu admitted that a Muslim could possibly have a grievance or any other reason for mistrusting the 'democratic' predominance of the Congress;

no Muslim would admit any possibility of justice or fairness from Hindu hands.[6]

This self-righteousness, we saw, continued after partition. If Congress was certain that Muslims would be secure in India, to Jinnah and Liaqat it was unthinkable that Pakistan's Hindus and Sikhs had anything to fear. Neither in India nor in Pakistan was this confidence, soon to be drowned in the blood of the innocent, based on existing facts. Hindus denied the possibility of violence against Muslims not because anti-Muslim feelings did not exist among them—these feelings were alive and aflame—but out of the belief that Hinduism was tolerant; they quoted ancient texts about the world being a family or about different roads leading to God.

Likewise, despite the 1947 killings, Liaqat could speak in 1949 of "the great record of tolerance" of Muslim nations in times past, and of the "tolerance envisaged by Islam, wherein a minority does not live on sufferance but is respected."[7] The confidence, in other words, rested on Hinduism's finest thought or on Islam's finest age, on what sages once composed and a Prophet envisaged, not on what ordinary mortals were designing or doing at the time. Judging their own community by its highest *ideals*, both Hindus and Muslims nonetheless judged the other community by its lowest *deeds*.

Personality conflicts intensified these general weaknesses. Jinnah, we saw, felt that Gandhi had ousted him from the centre of the national stage; later Gandhi was to feel that Jinnah barred him from the stage before which the *qaum* sat. Sectionalism is strengthened when a gifted man is deprived of a nationwide role and does not forgive.

Congress's inability to speak in an Indian rather than a Hindu idiom gave a fillip to separatism. Most members elected in the elections of 1937 belonged to Congress; most Congress ministers were Hindus; deliberately or unconsciously, they presented their Hindu face. The fasts of their guide, the Mahatma, his use of the term Ram Rajya for the ideal society of the future, the description by some ministers of schools as temples of learning, the singing, at government functions, of songs that were patriotic to the Hindus but sounded Hindu to the *qaum*'s ear, and the use by ministers of Sanskritized Hindi—these were part of a Hindu idiom that lent some credibility to the League's cry of Hindu rule.

This effect was not foreseen. The aim of Congress's exercises was not to beat the Hindu drum but to touch or stir the average man. A Hindu metaphor or song was capable of having this effect on three citizens out of four; the Indian Hindu, like the Indian Muslim, was responsive to messages possessing a religious flavour. But the exercises resulted in persuading the fourth citizen that one-man-one-vote would lead to a Hindu state.

It may be asked whether this has any bearing on today's India, where four out of five are Hindus and only a fifth of the population can find a Hindu idiom strange. Yet a fifth of the Indian population is still a large and growing quantity of human beings, to whom our constitution guarantees the rights enjoyed by the majority. The building up of metaphors and motifs that can affect them as well as the Hindu majority is surely a matter of importance.

What is called for is an idiom that bears an Indian rather than a Hindu (or Muslim, Christian, Sikh or Buddhist) stamp while yet being in harmony with the values of Hinduism, Islam, Christianity, Sikhism, Jainism, Buddhism and Zoroastrianism; and one, moreover, that can stir the average citizen as deeply as religious motifs stir him. It is of course a major challenge, but not one that those who care about India's unity can afford to evade. It is beyond present scope to enlarge on this challenge or propose ways of meeting it.

If our study teaches Hindus in politics or government to consider their metaphors with greater care, and to weigh how Muslims might perceive them, it also suggests that Muslims need not regard every recourse to a Hindu motif as a sign of religious imposition. To do this suited the League's strategy but Hindu-Muslim understanding suffered. Thanks to the League's sustained rhetoric about Hindu rule, the bulk of the *qaum* failed to see that Congress's Hindu idiom was primarily intended to touch Hindus and not to Hinduize Muslims. Much of it was spontaneous and could have been accepted as such. To tolerate the other man's religious idiom may be as important a need as the building up of a non-religious all-India idiom.

Another lesson is that, rhetoric notwithstanding, separatists often want a division of power rather than separation. Jinnah's conviction that Pakistan was entitled to Assam and the Hindu-majority portions of Punjab and Bengal, his disappointment at the departure of Hindus from Sind and his unhappiness at their suffering showed that a say in the subcontinent's affairs was more his goal than the *qaum*'s separation. He knew that complete separation was impossible, and so it turned out. The divorce he obtained with rare skill and tenacity was partial: about 40 per cent of India's Muslims remained in India after Pakistan was formed, and the 60 per cent who separated could not leave the neighbourhood. The problem of cultivating Hindu-Muslim understanding did not disappear. Even if warmth is deemed unattainable, a working relationship within and between the nations is indispensable.

We saw, too, that Hindu-Muslim unity was a jealous mistress, exploding when Indians tried to embrace another goal, even a goal as noble as that of liberty. In 1924 Gandhi and Jinnah separately noted that Hindu-Muslim unity was a pre-condition for independence. Jinnah said that the "one essential requisite condition to achieve Swaraj is the political unity between Hindus and Muslims,"[8] while Gandhi wrote: "I see no way of achieving anything in this country without a lasting heart unity between Hindus and Mussalmans."[9]

However, though unity had not been achieved, Gandhi initiated mass movements in the early 1930s and again in the early forties. These movements may have brought independence nearer; they stirred and united "nationalist" Indians, including a section of Muslims; still, they alienated the bulk of the *qaum*; and more than once the Raj sought to justify its continuance by citing the *qaum*'s attitude. What was true of India vis-a-vis Britain may have some relevance today to the subcontinent vis-a-vis the super powers. Co-ordination among the nations of the region may be the wisest way to keep the super powers out; individual moves widen the subcontinent's gulfs and can draw in the super powers.

Our study does not show that the Raj created the Hindu-Muslim divide. Though often acting wrongly, Britain was not the author of Indian divisions. Muhammad Ali's statement, "We divide and they rule," which he made in London in 1930, was the truth. Gandhi's view, also given, a year later, in London, that the Hindu-Muslim "quarrel is not old [but] . . . . . . .is coeval with the British advent"[10] was an idealisation of India's pre-British past. Amending his thinking, Gandhi said in August 1947:

> The British Government is not responsible for partition. The Viceroy has no hand in it. In fact he is as opposed to division as Congress itself. But if both of us, Hindus and Muslims, cannot agree on anything else, then the Viceroy is left with no choice.[11]

When Sarat Bose, Subhas's brother, brought up the "divide and rule" charge in a 1946 conversation with Wavell, the Viceroy countered, "We are trying to 'Unite and quit'."[12]

This claim was not valid either. Three members of Britain's cabinet no doubt spent three trying months in India in 1946, but the ministers failed to propose, let alone impose, an unambiguous compromise. Rejecting Pakistan and also rejecting a unitary India, they outlined a loose federation with a large "Pakistan" area that might have been a solution; but they allowed, indeed encouraged, both Congress and the League to misinterpret their proposal. The League was prompted by them to accept the loose federation "as a step on the road to Pakistan," while Congress was advised to "accept" their scheme with "its own interpretation." What the "wise men" proposed was one thing, what the League accepted another and what Congress agreed to a third. Yet H.M.G. accepted these "accept-ances," scarcely an inspiring "unite and quit" performance.

Even Wavell, despite his belief in a "masculine" and "blunt" approach[13] and his unhappiness with the methods of Pethick-Lawrence and Cripps, was in the end a party to the exercise. Moreover, as he admitted in his diary, he was "perhaps wrong . . . .not to press Jinnah more strongly about a Congress Muslim from the very start."[14] Wavell's feelings had been hurt, as he again admitted, by Congress's Quit India movement launched in the middle of the war with Japan, when he was Commander-in-Chief in the region; the hurt affected his impartiality. We learn from this episode that it is hazardous when administrators or arbitrators employ ambiguity to announce "success" or allow hurts to influence their judgement. You don't have to be an alien ruler to make such mistakes.

Congress and the League were free, of course, to settle on their own. They did not. A lack of trust was the main reason, but a lack of channels also proved crucial. No friendly broker, Indian or British, asked Jinnah if he would give up Pakistan if he obtained a large semi-sovereign Pakistan, or Gandhi, Nehru and Patel if they would concede such a Pakistan if Jinnah agreed to a significant centre. There is no proof that the two sides would have agreed on this basis; equally, there is no evidence that such a compromise was ever spelt out, considered and rejected.

Our study also discloses the pitfalls that accompany nationalism, whether linked to Islamic, Indian or British impulses. Muhammad Ali's wrath against Britain over Turkey and the Khilafat blinded him to the opposition within Turkey to the Khilafat. The Turks, not the British, destroyed the Khilafat; thereby they also robbed Muhammad Ali of his platform. The effect of his inability to see clearly has been well described by Muhammad Habib:

> Mr. Muhammad Ali's masterpiece was his "Choice of the Turks." I read it with tears and faith as an Aligarh undergraduate and it was not till the rise of Kemal Pasha that I discovered that his facts were completely wrong and that the fall of the Turkish leaders whom he supported was not worth a tear.[15]

The vision of Hindus too was blurred by nationalist pride. Quit India represented their hearts' desire in 1942 but it alienated both the Raj and the *qaum* and strengthened the likelihood of Pakistan. There would have been no Quit India, it is true, if Britain had offered India a real measure of independence after war was declared. Congress's 1937–39 co-operation with the Raj had prepared the ground for such an offer but Britain's imperialist pride came in the way. Churchill, the Prime Minister, and Linlithgow, the Viceroy, were unwilling to forget the hurts caused by Congress's earlier campaigns of disobedience. Instead of moving towards Congress, they encouraged the League; and Congress countered with Quit India.

Two successful alliances were conceivable: a Congress-League alliance that could have ended the Raj, or a Congress-Raj alliance that would have isolated the League. Dislike and mistrust prevented both and what remained was a choice between continuing conflict and a settlement involving all three sides.

The lives do not point to any clear relationship, direct or inverse, between so-called Islamic fundamentalism and Hindu-Muslim friendship, confirming Muhammad Ali's perception that "it is not the love of our religion that makes us quarrel, ...but self-love and petty personal ambition."[16] Of the eight the two who most leaned on the "fundamentalist" side were Iqbal and Azad. Purism and separatism seemed to grow together in Iqbal but he was never hostile to communal harmony. With more romance perhaps than realism, he saw a Muslim homeland on the subcontinent as a territory peopled by a homogeneous dynamic Muslim race; and he saw it too, as Liaqat also did, as a laboratory for Islam; but it is hard to describe Iqbal as anti-Hindu.

As for Azad, he was, in practice, the strongest advocate of Hindu-Muslim partnership. Also, he claimed Qur'anic sanction for his views. In his understanding, pure Islam allowed Muslims to cooperate freely with all monotheists, including Hindus, and encouraged them to seek the spirit, and not just the letter, of Islam's injunctions.

The least religious of the eight, Jinnah, was the one to show the most passion for a Muslim homeland, but after obtaining Pakistan he reverted to his belief in the normalcy of Hindu-Muslim co-existence. Fazlul Huq's oscillations between separation from Hindus and partnership with them had little to do with the extent of his orthodoxy as a Muslim.

We saw that members of the *qaum* did not automatically like, or think like, one another. The Huq-Jinnah, Jinnah-Azad and Azad-Zakir equations were all tense; and the Huq-Jinnah friction preceding and following the Lahore resolution was the first warning of the stress that would divide the Muslim land, or lands, the two jointly demanded in 1940.

At least three of the eight—Iqbal, Huq and Jinnah—had marital difficulties. Taking the eight together, we could not, while looking at their lives, look at their wives. Except for Liaqat's wife Raana and, while she and her husband were together, for Jinnah's wife Ruttie, the women were generally invisible. What significance this may have was outside the scope of our study.

The lives neither deny nor assure Hindu-Muslim compatibility, though it is significant that at one time or another *each* of the eight believed in it. They speak alternately of tension and trust between Hindus and the *qaum*. They speak, too, of mistakes, others' and their own, of injuries taken and given, victories won and missed, doors slammed shut and others unexpectedly opening, of griefs and joys, of hardness and tenderness, of the fist and the moist eye, of long days and nights in prison and long applause from the faithful, of quantities of sweat and of blood, of goals attained and satisfactions denied. They tell of human weaknesses and also of Sayyid Ahmed's sagacious head, Iqbal's songs of genius, Muhammad Ali's heart-on-a-sleeve, Jinnah's backbone of steel, Huq's store of sympathy, Azad's mind of courage, Liaqat, content at number two, and Zakir the gentle. Reflecting on these qualities, some Hindus may, God willing, find themselves moving closer to Muslims than they were, even as the writer of these pages did.

BIBLIOGRAPHY

Abbott, Freeland, *Islam and Pakistan*, Cornell University Press, Ithaca.

Abedin, A.K. Zainul, (ed.), *Memorable Speeches of Sher-E-Bangla*, Al Helal, Barisal, 1978.

Abedin, A.K. Zainul, (ed.), *Bengal Today*, Al Helal, Barisal, 1978.

Afzal, Rafique, (ed.), *Speeches and Statements of Quaid-e-Azam M.A. Jinnah*, Research Society of Pakistan, Lahore, 1966.

Afzal, Rafique, (ed.), *Speeches and Statements of Quaid-i-Millat Liaqat Ali Khan*, Research Society of Pakistan, Lahore, 1967.

Ahluwalia, B.K., (ed.), *Zakir Husain*, Sterling, New Delhi, 1970.

Ahmad, J., (ed.), *Speeches and Writings of Mr. Jinnah*, Sh. M. Ashraf, Lahore, 1947.

Ahmad, J., (ed.), *Historic Documents of the Muslim Freedom Movement*, Publishers United, Lahore.

Ahmad, J., *Middle Phase of the Muslim Political Movement*, Publishers United, Lahore, 1969.

Ahmad, J., *Creation of Pakistan*, Publishers United, Lahore, 1976.

Ali, Chaudhri Muhammad, *The Emergence of Pakistan*, Columbia, New York, 1967.

Ali, Mohamed, *My Life: A Fragment*, Sh. Muhammad Ashraf, Lahore, 1966.

Allana, Ghulam Ali, *Quaid-e-Azam Jinnah*. Ferozsons, Lahore, 1967.

Azad, Abul Kalam, *India Wins Freedom*, Orient Longmans, Calcutta, 1959.

Baig, M.R.A., *The Muslim Dilemma in India*, Vikas, New Delhi, 1974.

Bakhsh, Ilahi, *With the Quaid-i-Azam During His Last Days*, Quaid-i-Azam Academy, Karachi, 1978.

Banerjee, A. C., *Two Nations*, Concept, New Delhi, 1981.

Bolitho, Hector, *Jinnah*, Greenwood Press, Westport, Connecticut.

Bose, S.C., *The Indian Struggle*, Asia, Bombay, 1964.

Brass, Paul R., *Language, Religion and Politics in North India*, Vikas, New Delhi, 1975.

Brecher, Michael, *Nehru*, Oxford University Press, London, 1959.

Brown, Judith, *Gandhi's Rise to Power*, Cambridge University Press, Cambridge, 1972.

Butt, Abdullah, (ed.), *Aspects of Abul Kalam Azad*, Maktaba-i-Urdu, Lahore, 1942.

Campbell-Johnson, Alan, *Mission With Mountbatten*, Robert Hale, London, 1951.

Chagla, M.C., *Roses in December*, Bharatiya Vidya Bhavan, Bombay, 1974.

Chandra, Kailash, *Tragedy of Jinnah*, Sharma, Lahore, 1941.

Chattopadhyay, Gautam, *Bengal Electoral Politics and Freedom Struggle*, New Delhi, 1984.

Chaudhuri, B.M., *Muslim Politics in India*, Orient, Calcutta, 1946.

Chishti, Anees, *President Zakir Husain*, Rachna, New Delhi, 1967.

Das, Durga, (ed.), *Sardar Patel's Correspondence* (10 Volumes), Navajivan, Ahmedabad.

Datta, V.N., and Cleghorn, B., *A Nationalist Muslim in Indian Politics*, Macmillan, New Delhi, 1974.

De, Amalendu, *Islam in Modern India*, Maya, Calcutta, 1982.

Desai, Mahadev, *Maulana Abul Kalam Azad*, Shiva Lal Agarwala, Agra, 1940.

Dwarkadas, Kanji, *Ruttie Jinnah*, Bombay, 1963.

Dwarkadas, Kanji, *Ten Years to Freedom*, Popular Prakashan, Bombay, 1968.

Gandhi, Rajmohan, *The Rajaji Story*, Bharatiya Vidya Bhavan, Bombay, 1984.

Glendevon, John, *The Viceroy at Bay*, Collins, London, 1971.

Graham, G.F.I., *The Life and Work of Sir Syed Ahmed Khan*, London, 1885. Reprinted.

Haq, Mushir U., *Muslim Politics in Modern India*, Meenakshi, Meerut, 1971.

Hardy, P., *Partners in Freedom and True Muslims*, Student Litteratur, Lund, Sweden, 1971.

Hardy, P., *The Muslims of British India*, Cambridge University Press, Cambridge, 197

Hasan, Mushirul, *Congress Muslims and Indian Nationalism: 1928–1934*, Occasional Paper No. 23 (unpublished), Nehru Memorial Museum and Library, New Delhi, 1985.

Hassnain, S.E., *Indian Muslims*, Lalvani, Bombay, 1968.

Hodson, H.W., *The Great Divide*, Hutchinson, London, 1969.

Husain, S. Abid, *The Destiny of Indian Muslims*, Asia, Bombay, 1965.

Husain, Zakir, *President Zakir Husain's Speeches*, Publications Divisions, New Delhi, 1973.

Iftikharuddin, Mian, *Speeches and Statements*, Nigarishat, Lahore, 1971.

Ikram, Sheikh Muhammad, *Modern Muslim India and the Birth of Pakistan*, Institute of Islamic Culture, Lahore.

Ikramullah, Shaista, *From Purdah to Parliament*, Crescent Press, London, 1963.

Iqbal, Afzal, *Mohamed Ali*, Idarah-i-Adabiyat, Delhi, 1978.

Iqbal, Javid, (ed.), *Notebook of Allama Iqbal*, Lahore, 1961.

Ispahani, M.A.H., *Quaid-e-Azam As I Knew Him*, Forward Publications Trust, Karachi, 1968.

Iyer, Subramonia, (ed.), *Role of Maulana Azad in Indian Politics*, Azad Oriental Research Institute, Hyderabad.

Jilani, S.G., *Fifteen Governors I Served With*, Lahore, 1979.

Jinnah, Fatima, *Speeches, Messages and Statements*, Research Society of Pakistan, Lahore, 1976.

Jinnah, Quaid-i-Azam M.A., *Speeches as Governor-General*, Karachi, 1962.

Kabir, Humayun, (ed.), *Abul Kalam Azad*, Publications Division, New Delhi.

Karandikar, M.A., *Islam in India's Transition to Modernity*, Orient Longmans, New Delhi, 1968.

Khaliquzzaman, Choudhry, *Pathway to Pakistan*, Pakistan Longman, Lahore, 1961.

Khan, Liaquat Ali, *Pakistan: The Heart of Asia*, Ministry of Education, Islamabad.

Khan, Mohammad Ayub, *Friends Not Masters*, Oxford University Press, London, 1967.

Lalljee, H.A., *Shia Muslims' Case*, Bombay, 1945.

Lelyveld, David, *Aligarh's First Generation*, Princeton, 1977.

Lokhandwalla, S.T., (ed.), *India and Contemporary Islam*, Indian Institute of Advanced Study, Simla, 1971.

Malik, Hafeez, *Moslem Nationalism in India and Pakistan*, Public Affairs Press, Washington D.C., 1963.

Malik, Hafeez, (ed.), *Iqbal: Poet-Philosopher of Pakistan*, Columbia, New York, 1971.

Malik, Hafeez, *Sir Sayyid Ahmed Khan and Muslim Modernization*, Columbia, New York, 1980.

Malsiani, Arsh, *Abul Kalam Azad*, Publications Division, New Delhi, 1976.

Mansergh, N., and Lumby, E.W.R., *The Transfer of Power* (12 Volumes), Her Majesty's Stationery Office, London, 1970–83.

Mehta, Asoka, and Nair, Kusum, *The Simla Triangle*, Padma, Bombay, 1945.

Menon, V.P., *The Transfer of Power in India*, Orient Longmans, Calcutta, 1957.

Merriam, Allen Hayes, *Gandhi vs Jinnah*, Minerva, Calcutta, 1980.

Mirza, B.A., *The Hindu-Muslim Problem*, Thacker, Bombay, 1944.

Montagu, E.S., *An Indian Diary*, Heinemann, London, 1930.

Moon, Penderel, *Divide and Quit*, University of California Press, Berkeley, 1962.

Moon, Penderel, (ed.), *Wavell: A Viceroy's Journal*, Oxford University Press, London, 1973.

M.R.T., *Pakistan and Muslim India*, Home Study Circle, Bombay, 1943.

Muhammad, Shan, *Sir Syed Ahmed Khan*, Meenakshi, Meerut, 1969.

Mujahid, Sharif Al, *Quaid-i-Azam M.A. Jinnah: Studies in Interpretation*, Quaid-i-Azam Academy, Karachi, 1981.

Mujeeb, Muhammad, *The Indian Muslims*, George Allen and Unwin, London.

Mujeeb, Muhammad, *Dr. Zakir Husain*, National Book Trust, New Delhi, 1972.

Naim, C.M., (ed.), *Iqbal, Jinnah and Pakistan*, Maxwell School of Public Affairs, Syracuse University, 1979.

Nasr, S.H., *Ideas and Realities of Islam*, Allen and Unwin, London, 1975.

Nehru, Jawaharlal, *Discovery of India*, John Day, New York, 1946.

Nehru, Jawaharlal, *Selected Works* (ed. S. Gopal), Orient Longman, New Delhi.

Noon, Feroz Khan, *From Memory*, Ferozsons, Lahore, 1966.

Peerzada, S.S., (ed.), *Foundations of Pakistan: All-India Muslim League Documents*, National Publishing House, Karachi, 1969.

Peerzada, S.S., (ed.), *Leaders' Correspondence with Mr Jinnah*, Taj Office, Bombay, 1944.

Pirzada, S.S., (ed.), *Quaid-i-Azam's Correspondence*, East and West, Karachi, 1977.

Pirzada, S.S., *Some Aspects of Quaid-i-Azam's Life*, National Commission on Historical and Cultural Research, Islamabad, 1978.

Prakasa, Sri, *Pakistan: Birth and Early Days*, Meenakshi, Meerut, 1965.

Prasad, Beni, *The Hindu-Muslim Question*, Kitabistan, Allahabad, 1941.

Prasad, Rajendra, *Autobiography*, Asia, Bombay, 1957.

Pyarelal, *The Last Phase* (Volumes 1 and 2), Navajivan, Ahmedabad, 1958.

Qureshi, Ishtiaq Husain, *The Muslim Community of the Indo-Pakistan Subcontinent*. Mouton and Co., The Hague, 1962.

Rab, A.K. Abdur, *A.K. Fazlul Huq*, Ferozsons, Lahore, 1967.

Rahim, Enayetur, *Bengal Election, 1937*, Journal of the Asiatic Society of Bangladesh, Dacca, 1977.

Rahim, Enayetur, *Provincial Autonomy in Bengal*, Rajshahi University, Rajshahi, 1981.

Rahman, Fazlur, *Islam*, University of Chicago Press, Chicago, 1979.

Rajagopalachari, C., *The Defence of India*, Rochouse, Madras, 1942.

Rajagopalachari, C., *The Way Out*, Oxford, Bombay, 1943.

Rajagopalachari, C., *Reconciliation*, Hind Kitabs, Bombay, 1946.

Rajput, A.B., *Maulana Abul Kalam Azad*, Lion, Lahore, 1946.

Rao, B. Shiva, *India's Freedom Movement*, Orient Longman, New Delhi, 1972.

Ray, Amalendu, *Inconsistencies in Azad*, Bangavarati Granthalaya, Howrah, 1968.

Robinson, Francis, *Separatism Among Indian Muslims*, Vikas, New Delhi, 1975.

Saiyid, M.H., *M.A. Jinnah*, Sh. M. Ashraf, Lahore, 1945.

Setalvad, M.C., *Bhulabhai Desai*, Publications Division, New Delhi, 1968.

Shahid, M.H., (ed.), *Quaid-i-Azam M.A. Jinnah*, Sang-e-Meel, Lahore, 1976.

Shakir, Moin, *Khilafat to Pakistan*, Kalamkar, New Delhi.

Sharma, M.S.M., *Peeps into Pakistan*, Pustak Bhandar, Patna, 1954.

Sinha, Sachchidananda, *Iqbal*, Ram Narain Lal, Allahabad, 1947.

Sitaramayya, Pattabhi, *The History of the Congress*, Congress Working Committee, Allahabad, 1935.

Smith, Vincent A., *The Oxford History of India*, Oxford, 1967.

Smith, Wilfred Cantwell Smith, *Modern Islam in India*, Victor Gollancz, London, 1946.

Smith, Wilfred Cantwell Smith, *Islam in Modern History*, Princeton, 1957.

Stephens, Ian, *Horned Moon*, Chatto and Windus, London, 1954.

Suleri, Z.A., *My Leader*, Lion, Lahore, 1946.

Symonds, Richard, *The Making of Pakistan*, Faber and Faber, London, 1950.

Tendulkar, D.G., *Mahatma* (8 Volumes), Times of India Press, Bombay, 1951.

Troll, Christian, *Sayyid Ahmed Khan: Reinterpretation of Muslim Theology*, Vikas, New Delhi, 1978.

Wolpert, Stanley, *Jinnah of Pakistan*, Oxford University Press, New York, 1984.

REFERENCES AND NOTES

Chapter 1: Hindus and Muslims

1. Quoted in Hafeez Malik, *Moslem Nationalism in India and Pakistan* (Public Affairs Press, Washington D.C., 1963), p. 12.

2. Ibid.

3. Quoted in Muhammad Mujeeb, *The Indian Muslims* (George Allen and Unwin, London), p. 234.

4. I.H. Qureshi, *The Muslim Community of the Indo-Pakistan Subcontinent* (Mouton and Co., The Hague, 1962), p. 348.

5. Malik, *Moslem Nationalism*, p. 298.

6. R.C. Majumdar and others, *The Delhi Sultanate* (Bharatiya Vidya Bhavan, Bombay, 1960), quoted in Malik, *Moslem Nationalism*, p. 299.

7. Malik, *Moslem Nationalism*, p. 294.

8. Ibid. p. 295.

9. Ibid. p. 296.

10. Quoted in Richard Symonds, *The Making of Pakistan* (Faber and Faber, London, 1950), p. 53.

11. Malik, *Moslem Nationalism*, p. 299.

12. Quoted in Qureshi, *The Muslim Community*, p. 349.

13. Malik, *Moslem Nationalism*, p. 300.

14. Hafeez Malik, *Sir Sayyid Ahmed Khan and Muslim Modernization* (Columbia, New York, 1980), p. 256.

15. Quoted in Ghulam Ali Allana, *Quaid-e-Azam Jinnah* (Ferozsons, Lahore, 1967), p. 319.

16. Quoted in Choudhry Khaliquzzaman, *Pathway to Pakistan* (Pakistan Longman, Lahore, 1961), p. 319.

17. Sheikh Muhammad Ikram, *Modern Muslim India and the Birth of Pakistan* (Institute of Islamic Culture, Lahore), p. 71.

18. Ibid.

19. Ibid.

20. Ibid., p. 64–71.

21. Mujeeb, *Indian Muslims*, p. 536.

22. Khaliquzzaman, *Pathway to Pakistan*, p. 319.

23. Ibid., pp. x-xi.

24. Vincent A. Smith, *The Oxford History of India* (Oxford, 1967), pp. 358–9.

25. Ikram, *Modern Muslim India*, p. 72.

26. Khaliquzzaman, *Pathway to Pakistan*, p. 319.

27. Ibid., pp. 307–8.

28. Quoted in Mujeeb, *Indian Muslims*, p. 233.

29. Malik, *Moslem Nationalism*, p. 86.

30. Mujeeb, *Indian Muslims*, p. 557.

31. Quoted in Malik, *Moslem Nationalism*, p. 295.

32. Qureshi, *The Muslim Community*, p. 135.

33. Ibid., p. 164.

34. Ibid., pp. 135–7.

35. Mujeeb, *Indian Muslims*, pp. 10–19.

36. Ibid., p. 388.

37. Malik, *Moslem Nationalism*, p. 15.

38. Mujeeb, *Indian Muslims*, p. 173–4.

39. Quoted in Khaliquzzaman, *Pathway to Pakistan*, p. 237.

40. Afzal Iqbal, *Mohamed Ali* (Idarah-i-Adabiyat, Delhi, 1978), p. 381.

41. Mujeeb, *Indian Muslims*, p. 556.

Chapter 2: Sayyid Ahmed Khan

1. Introduction by Zaituna Umer in G.F.I. Graham, *The Life and Work of Sir Syed Ahmed Khan* (London, 1885. Reprinted.), p. xvii.

2. Graham, *Life and Work*, p. 266.

3. Christian Troll, *Sayyid Ahmed Khan: Reinterpretation of Muslim Theology* (Vikas, New Delhi, 1978), p. 221 fn.

4. Details from Hafeez Malik, *Sir Sayyid Ahmed Khan*.

5. Ibid., p. 72.

6. Malik, *Sir Sayyid Ahmed Khan*, p. 74.

7.. Mujeeb, *Indian Muslims*, p. 447.

8. Quoted in Malik, *Sir Sayyid Ahmed Khan*, p. 58.

9. Sayyid Ahmed, *History of the Revolt in the District of Bijnor*, pp. 309–10, quoted in Malik, *Sir Sayyid Ahmed Khan*, pp. 107–8.

10. Ibid.

11. Quoted in Malik, *Sir Sayyid Ahmed Khan*, p. 79.

12. Graham, *Life and Work*, p. 12.

13. Ibid., p. 21.

14. Ikram, *Modern Muslim India*, p. 28.

15. Altaf Husain Hali, *Hayat-i-Javid*, p. 117, quoted in Malik, *Sir Sayyid Ahmed Khan*, p. 77.

16. Ibid.

17. Quoted in Troll, *Reinterpretation*, p. 9.

18. Malik, *Sir Sayyid Ahmed Khan*, p. 80.

19. Ibid., p. 121.

20. Ikram, *Modern Muslim India*, p. 25.

21. Ibid., p. 23.

22. See ibid., p. 26.

23. Malik, *Sir Sayyid Ahmed Khan*, p. 87.

24. Speech in Ghazipur, Jan. 9, 1864, quoted in Graham, *Life and Work*, p. 53.

25. Graham's words at inauguration, ibid., p. 49.

26. Ibid. p. 48.

27. Malik, *Sir Sayyid Ahmed Khan*, p. 230.

28. Ibid., p. 237.

29. In 1884. Ibid., p. 245.

30. David Lelyveld, *Aligarh's First Generation* (Princeton, 1977), p. 311.

31. Graham, *Life and Work*, p. 62.

32. On Jan. 9, 1864. Ibid., pp. 56–7.

33. Ibid., pp. 59–62.

34. Malik, *Sir Sayyid Ahmed Khan*, p. 93.

35. Letter of Apr. 29, 1870, quoted in Ikram, *Modern Muslim India*, p. 32.

36. Hali, *Hayat-i-Javid*, quoted in Ikram, *Modern Muslim India*, p. 32.

37. Letter of Apr. 29, 1870, Ibid., p. 32.

38. Ibid., p. 72.

39. Ibid.

40. Graham, *Life and Work*, , p. 79.

41. Ibid.

41 to 45. Ibid., pp. 76–105.

46. Letter of Oct. 15, 1869. Ibid., p. 132.

46 and 47. Letter of Oct. 15, 1869. Ibid., p. 132.

48. Ibid., pp. 125–6.

49. Letter to Duke of Argyll, July 28, 1869. Ibid., p. 68.

50. Malik, *Sir Sayyid Ahmed Khan*, p. 295.

51. Letter of Oct. 15, 1869. Graham, *Life and Work*, p. 127.

52. Ibid., p. 157.

53. Ibid., pp. 136–7.

54. Mujeeb, *Indian Muslims*, pp. 449–51. See also Freeland Abbott, *Islam and Pakistan* (Cornell University Press, Ithaca, New York), p. 129.

55. Ikram, *Modern Muslim India*, p. 36.

56. Quoted in Malik, *Moslem Nationalism*, p. 207.

57. Graham, *Life and Work*, p. 172.

58. Ibid., p. 218.

59. Malik, *Moslem Nationalism*, p. 213.

60. College prospectus, quoted in Shan Muhammad, *Sir Sayyid Ahmed Khan* (Meenakshi Prakashan, Meerut, 1969), p. 82.

61. Graham, *Life and Work*, p. 167.

62. Ibid., p. 223.

63. See Ikram, *Modern Muslim India*, p. 54.

64. Shan Muhammed, *Sir Syed*, p. 57.

65. Malik, *Sir Sayyid Ahmed*, p. 170.

66. Ibid., p. 214.

67. Ibid., pp. 167–72.

68. Shan Muhammad, *Sir Syed*, pp. 56–7.

69. Quoted in Ikram, *Modern Muslim India*, p. 15.

70. Graham, *Life and Work*, p. 219.

71. Ikram, *Modern Muslim India*, p. 38.

72. Graham, *Life and Work*, p. 140.

73. Ibid., p. 227.

74. See Shan Muhammad, *Sir Syed*, pp. 233–6.

75. Graham, *Life and Work*, pp. 229–30.

76. Quoted in Ikram, *Modern Muslim India*, p. 42.

77. Ibid., pp. 34–5.

78. Quoted in Symonds, *The Making of Pakistan*, p. 35.

79. Ibid., pp. 34–5.

80. Shan Muhammad, *Sir Syed*, p. 142.

81. Ibid., p. 144.

82. Ikram, *Modern Muslim India*, p. 45.

83. Shan Muhammad, *Sir Syed*, pp. 145–6.

84. Ibid., Letters of Jan. 13, 1888 and Feb. 2, 1888. Ibid., pp. 147–8.

85. Letter of Feb. 18, 1888. Ibid., pp. 148–9.

86. Letter of Sept. 4, 1888. Ibid., p. 152.

87. Nehru, *Discovery of India*, pp. 410–11, quoted in Shan Muhammad, *Sir Syed*, p. 228.

88. Wilfred Cantwell Smith, *Modern Islam in India* (Victor Gollancz, London, 1946), p. 25.

89. Malik, *Moslem Nationalism*, p. 211.

90. J.N. Dass, quoted in Shan Muhammad, *Sir Syed*, p. 149.

91. Ibid., p. 150.

92. Ibid., p. 157.

93. Ikram, *Modern Muslim India*, p. 48.

94. Ibid., p. 48.

95. Foreword, Shan Muhammad, *Sir Syed*, p. viii.

96. Ibid., p. 169.

97. Quoted in ibid., p. 168.

98. Lelyveld, *Aligarh's First Generation*, p. 195.

99. Ibid., p. 196.

100. Ibid., p. 217.

101. Ibid., p. 310.

102. Morison's description, quoted in ibid., p. 218.

103. Ibid., pp. 218–9.

104. Ikram, *Modern Muslim India*, p. 46.

105. Lelyveld, *Aligarh's First Generation*, p. 276.

106. Shan Muhammad, *Sir Syed*, p. 160.

107. Ikram, *Modern Muslim India*, p. 49.
108. Shan Muhammad, *Sir Syed*, p. 163.
109. Ibid., p. 172 fn.
110. Ibid., p. 162.
111. Ibid., p. 172 fn.
112. Troll, *Reinterpretation*, pp. xvi and 318.
113. Ikram, *Modern Muslim India*, p. 50.
114. Troll, *Reinterpretation*, p. 318.
115. Ibid., p. 332.
116. Abbott, *Islam and Pakistan*, p. 125.
117. Troll, *Reinterpretation*, p. xvi.
118. Ibid., p. 233.
119. Mujeeb, *Indian Muslims*, p. 448.
120. Troll, *Reinterpretation*, p. xvi.
121. Ibid., p. 314.
122. Mujeeb, *Indian Muslims*, p. 449.
123. Ibid.
124. Troll, *Reinterpretation*, p. 317.
125. Ibid., p. 313.
126. Ibid., p. 229.
127. Ibid., p. 221 fn.
128. Malik, *Moslem Nationalism*, p. 196.
129. Malik, *Sir Sayyid Ahmed Khan*, pp. 278–9.
130. Mujeeb, *Indian Muslims*, p. 451.
131. Ikram, *Modern Muslim India*, p. 54.
132. Troll, *Reinterpretation*, p. 17.
133. Ibid., p. 60.
134. Graham, *Life and Work*, p. 78.
135. Troll, *Reinterpretation*, p. 292.
136. Quoted in Malik, *Sir Sayyid Ahmed Khan*, p. 279.
137. Hector Bolitho, *Jinnah* (Greenwood Press, Westport, Connecticut), p. 38.
138. See comments by Percival Spear and S.M. Ikram in Ikram, *Modern Muslim India*, p. xiii.
139. Jan. 27, 1884. Quoted in Shan Muhammad, *Sir Syed*, p. 246.
140. Feb. 4, 1884. Ibid., p. 245.
141. *Aligarh Institute Gazette*, Apr. 7, 1888. Ibid., p. 239.
142. *The Reformer*, 1880. Troll, *Reinterpretation*, p. 303.
143. *Aligarh Institute Gazette*, Nov. 24, 1888. Ibid., p. 236.
143. *Aligarh Institute Gazette*, June 12, 1897. Shan Muhammad, *Sir Syed*, p. 238.
144. *Aligarh Institute Gazette*, Nov. 24, 1888. Ibid., p. 236.
145. Ibid., p. 237.
146. Ibid., p. 240.
147. Quoted in ibid., p. 233.
148. Qureshi, *The Muslim Community*, p. 286.

149. Graham, *Life and Work*.

150. Lelyveld, *Aligarh's First Generation*, p. 272.

Chapter 3: Iqbal

1. Mujeeb, *Indian Muslims*, p. 452.

2. Fazlur Rahman, *Islam* (University of Chicago Press, Chicago, 1979), p. 234.

3. W.C. Smith, *Modern Islam in India*, p. 20 and pp. 105–6.

4. Ibid., p. 103.

5. Ibid., p. 109.

6. W.C. Smith, *Islam in Modern History* (Princeton University Press, Princeton, 1957), p. 54 and p. 63 fn.

7. Mujeeb, *Indian Muslims*, p. 454.

8. Barbara Metcalf in C.M. Naim (ed.), *Iqbal, Jinnah and Pakistan: The Vision and the Reality* (Maxwell School of Public Affairs, Syracuse University, 1979), p. 140.

9. From *Ramuz-i-Bekhudi*, quoted in Hafeez Malik (ed.), *Iqbal: Poet-Philosopher of Pakistan* (Columbia University Press, New York, 1971), p. 8.

10. Ibid., p. 12.

11. Ibid., p. 11.

12. Quoted in Mujeeb, *Indian Muslims*, p. 484.

13. Ibid., p. 485.

14. Malik (ed.), *Iqbal*, p. 17.

15. From *Asrar-i-Khudi*, published in 1915, quoted in Malik (ed.), *Iqbal*, p. 18.

16. Ibid., p. 18.

17. Quoted in Ibid., p. 22.

18. Ibid., p. 23.

19. W.C. Smith's phrase, in Smith, *Modern Islam in India*, p. 102.

20. From *Payam-i-Mashriq*, quoted by Anikeyev in Malik (ed.), *Iqbal*, p. 270.

21. Foreword to first edition (1915) of *Asrar-i-Khudi*, quoted in Malik (ed.), *Iqbal*, p. 72.

22. Quoted by Freeland Abbott in Malik (ed.), *Iqbal*, p. 177.

23. Quoted by Riffat Hassan in Malik (ed.), *Iqbal*, p. 143.

24. Ibid., p. 148.

25. Rahman, *Islam*, p. 220.

26. From *Bang-i-Dara*, published in 1924, quoted in Ikram, *Modern Muslim India*, p. 169.

27. Ibid., p. 170.

28. Letter of March 28, 1909, quoted in Ikram, *Modern Muslim India*, p. 170.

29. Malik (ed.), *Iqbal*, p. 10.

30. Ibid., pp. 24–5.

31. Quoted in Ikram, *Modern Muslim India*, p. 168.

32. Ibid.

33. A.S. Nuruddin in Malik (ed.), *Iqbal*, p. 295.

34. S.H. Nasr, *Ideas and Realities of Islam* (Allen and Unwin, London, 1975), p. 122.

35. Rahman, *Islam*, p. 143.

36. Ibn al-Arabi, quoted by Nuruddin in Malik (ed.), *Iqbal*, p. 291.

37. Rahman, *Islam*, p. 141.

38. W.C. Smith, *Islam in Modern History*, p. 38.

39. Rahman, *Islam*, p. 140.

40. Ibid., p. 144.

41. Quoted by Nuruddin in Malik (ed.), *Iqbal*, p. 291.

42. See Nasr, *Ideas and Realities of Islam*, p. 137.

43. Nuruddin in Malik (ed.), *Iqbal*, p. 291.

44. Rahman, *Islam*, p. 145.

45. Ibid., p. 164.

46. Ibid., p. 155.

47. Quoted by Freeland Abbott in Abbott, *Islam and Pakistan*, p. 27.

48. Malik (ed.), *Iqbal*, p. 75.

49. Ibid.

50. Quoted by Sachchidananda Sinha in Sinha, *Iqbal* (Ram Narain Lal, Allahabad, 1947), pp. 432–3.

51. Malik (ed.), *Iqbal*, p. 76. Taken from *Ramuz-i-Bekhudi* ("The Mysteries of Selflessness"), published in 1918.

52. Javid Iqbal in Malik (ed.), *Iqbal*, p. 56.

53. Quoted by Annemarie Schimmel in Malik (ed.), *Iqbal*, p. 313.

54. Quoted by Rahbar in Malik (ed.), *Iqbal*, p. 53.

55. Quoted by Nuruddin in Malik (ed.), *Iqbal*, p. 294.

56. Ibid., p. 299.

57. Quoted by Mujeeb in Mujeeb, *Indian Muslims*, p. 490.

58. Quoted by Rahman in Rahman, *Islam*, p. 225.

59. Quoted by Rahbar in Malik (ed.), *Iqbal*, p. 54.

60. Ibid., p. 53.

61. Rahman, *Islam*, p. 225.

62. Smith, *Modern Islam in India*, p. 110.

63. Metcalf in Naim (ed.), *Iqbal, Jinnah and Pakistan*, p. 139.

64. Quoted in Sinha, *Iqbal*, p. 345.

65. Ibid.

66. Ibid., pp. 381–2.

67. Smith, *Modern Islam in India*, p. 115.

68. Quoted by Nuruddin in Malik (ed.), *Iqbal*, p. 296.

69. Ibid., p. 297.

70. Quoted by Sinha in Sinha, *Iqbal*, p. 319.

71. Quoted by Stepanyants in Malik (ed.), *Iqbal*, p. 303.

72. Anikeyev in Malik (ed.), *Iqbal*, p. 273.

73. Ibid.

74. Malik in Malik (ed.), *Iqbal*, p. 31.

75. Quoted by Gordon-Polonskaya in Malik (ed.), *Iqbal*, p. 132.

76. Quoted by Jan Marek in Malik (ed.), *Iqbal*, p. 168.

77. Symonds, *Making of Pakistan*, p. 39.

77. Letter to Nicholson, Jan. 24, 1927, quoted in Symonds, *Making of Pakistan*, p. 39.

78. Quoted by Jan Marek in Malik (ed.), *Iqbal*, p. 163.

79. Smith, *Modern Islam in India*, p. 140.

80. Quoted in Rahman, *Islam*, p. 234.

81. Smith, *Modern Islam in India*, p. 140.

82. Quoted by Mujeeb, *Indian Muslims*, p. 489.

83. Sheila McDonough in Naim (ed.), *Iqbal, Jinnah and Pakistan*, pp. 121–2.

84. Mujeeb, *Indian Muslims*, p. 454.

85. Quoted by Riffat Hassan in Malik (ed.), *Iqbal*, p. 150.

86. Ibid., pp. 148–9.

87. Smith, *Modern Islam in India*, p. 114.

88. Quoted by Hassan in Malik (ed.), *Iqbal*, p. 147.

89. Quoted in Sinha, *Iqbal*, p. 326.

90. Ibid., p. 327.

91. Javid Iqbal in Malik (ed.), *Iqbal*, p. 61.

92. Quoted in Malik (ed.), *Iqbal*, p. 31.

93. Quoted by Rahbar in Malik (ed.), *Iqbal*, p. 55.

94. Quoted in Ikram, *Modern Muslim India*, p. 171.

95. Javid Iqbal (ed.), *Notebook of Allama Iqbal* (Lahore, 1961), pp. 14–5.

96. Ikram, *Modern Muslim India*, p. 182.

97. Ibid., p. 172.

98. Ibid., p. 182.

99. Ibid., p. 173.

100. Quoted in Malik (ed.), *Iqbal*, p. 27.

101. Letter to Akbar Najibabadi, Apr. 12, 1925, quoted in Ikram, *Modern Muslim India*, p. 183.

102. Ibid., p. 186.

103. Mujeeb, *Indian Muslims*, p. 456.

104. Smith, *Modern Islam in India*, pp. 135–6.

105. Quoted in Smith, *Modern Islam in India*, p. 136.

106. See Freeland Abbott, *Islam and Pakistan*, p. 172.

107. Maudoodi quoted in ibid., p. 182.

108. Ibid., p. 182.

109. Quoted by Gordon-Polonskaya in Malik (ed.), *Iqbal*, p. 127.

110. Ikram, *Modern Muslim India*, p. 186.

111. Letter to Sir Francis Younghusband, quoted in Ikram, *Modern Muslim India*, p. 185.

112. Quoted by Jan Marek in Malik (ed.), *Iqbal*, p. 172.

113. Quoted by Hassan in ibid., pp. 156–7.

114. Javid Iqbal in ibid., p. 60.

115. Rahbar in ibid., p. 36.

116. Quoted by Javid Iqbal in ibid., p. 58.

117. Quoted by Rahbar in ibid., p. 39.

118. Ibid., p. 38.

119. Ibid., p. 39.

120. Quoted by Schimmel in ibid., p. 323.

121. Ibid.

122. Ibid., p. 19.

123. Javid Iqbal in ibid., p. 62.

124. Ibid., p. 39.

125. Ibid., p. 40.

126. Malik in ibid., p. 26.

127. Ibid., p. 40.

128. Javid Iqbal in ibid., p. 59.

129. Ibid.

130. Quoted in Allen Hayes Merriam, *Gandhi vs Jinnah* (Minerva, Calcutta, 1980), p. 17.

131. Quoted by Hassan in Malik (ed.), *Iqbal*, p. 148.

132. Ikram, *Modern Muslim India*, p. 175.

133. Hassan in Malik (ed.), *Iqbal*, p. 152.

134. Ibid., p. 151.

135. Quoted in Symonds, *Making of Pakistan*, p. 40.

136. Ibid.

137. Letters of May 28 and June 21, 1937, Malik (ed.), *Iqbal*, pp. 385–8.

138. Nehru, *Discovery of India* (John Day, New York, 1946), p. 355.

139. Quoted by Naim in Naim (ed.), *Iqbal, Jinnah and Pakistan*, p. 186.

140. See Ikram, *Modern Muslim India*, p. 382.

141. Malik (ed.), *Iqbal*, pp. 103–4.

142. Ibid., p. 327.

143. Ibid., p. 329.

144. Quoted by Rahbar in ibid., p. 47.

145. Ibid., p. 46.

146. Quoted by Hassan in ibid., p. 152.

147. Malik (ed.), *Iqbal*, p. 34.

148. Javid Iqbal in ibid., p. 62.

149. Ibid., pp. 64–5.

Chapter 4: Muhammad Ali

1. Ikram, *Modern Muslim India*, p. 158.

2. Professor Khuda Baksh, quoted in Smith, *Modern Islam in India*, p. 58.

3. Quoted in S.S. Peerzada (ed.), *Foundations of Pakistan: All-India Muslim League Documents, 1906–1947* (National Publishing House, Karachi, 1969), p. 533.

4. Afzal Iqbal, *Life and Times of Mobamed Ali* (Idarah-i-Adabiyat, Delhi, 1978), p. 19.

5. Ibid.

6. Mohamed Ali, *My Life: A Fragment* (Sh. Muhammad Ashraf, Lahore, 1966), p. 27.

7. Iqbal, *Mobamed Ali*, pp. 32–3.

8. Mohamed Ali, *My Life*, p. 29.

9. Ibid., p. 30.

10. Iqbal, *Mobamed Ali*, p. 45.

11. Ibid., p. 38.

12. Ibid.

13. Mohamed Ali, *My Life*, p. 32–3.

14. Ibid.

15. Iqbal, *Mohamed Ali*, p. 56.
16. Ibid., p. 55.
17. Ibid., pp. 39–40.
18. Ibid., p. 42.
19. Ibid.
20. Quoted in ibid., p. 41.
21. Ibid., p. 43.
22. Ibid., p. 60.
23. Ibid., p. 63.
24. Quoted in ibid., p. 62.
25. Mujeeb, *Indian Muslims*, p. 537.
26. Iqbal, *Mohamed Ali*, pp. 47–8.
27. Quoted in ibid., p. 93.
28. Khaliquzzaman, *Pathway to Pakistan*, p. 17.
29. Iqbal, *Mohamed Ali*, p. 86.
30. Ibid., p. 53.
31. Ibid., p. 85.
32. Ibid.
33. Quoted in ibid., p. 108.
34. Mohamed Ali, *My Life*, pp. 35–6.
35. Ibid., p. 49.
36. Ansari quoted in Iqbal, *Mohamed Ali*, p. 76.
37. Ibid., p. 74.
38. Mujeeb, *Indian Muslims*, p. 536.
39. See Iqbal, *Mohamed Ali*, pp. 96–8.
40. Khaliquzzaman, *Pathway to Pakistan*, p. 18.
41. Iqbal, *Mohamed Ali*, p. 105.
42. Ibid., p. 110.
43. Khaliquzzaman, *Pathway to Pakistan*, p. 28.
44. Ibid., p. 29.
45. Ibid., p. 31.
46. Ibid.
47. Ibid.
48. Iqbal, *Mohamed Ali*, p. 111.
49. Mohamed Ali, *My Life*, p. 41.
50. Iqbal, *Mohamed Ali*, p. 152.
51. Ibid., p. 159.
52. Quoted in ibid., p. 129.
53. Khaliquzzaman, *Pathway to Pakistan*, p. 33.
54. Letter of 25.4.18, quoted in Iqbal, *Mohamed Ali*, p. 159.
55. Quoted in ibid., p. 146.
56. Ibid.
57. Ibid., p. 142.
58. Ibid., pp. 124–5.

59. Pattabhi Sitaramayya, *The History of the Congress* (Congress Working Committee, Allahabad, 1935), p. 310.

60. Iqbal, *Mohamed Ali*, pp. 191–2.

61. Ibid.

62. Ibid., p. 403.

63. Mujeeb, *Indian Muslims*, p. 537.

64. Iqbal, *Mohamed Ali*, p. 197.

65. Ibid., p. 199.

66. Ibid., p. 228.

67. Ibid., p. 203.

68. Ibid., p. 210.

69. Ibid., p. 227.

70. Sitaramayya, *History of Congress*, p. 307.

71. Quoted in Iqbal, *Mohamed Ali*, p. 256.

72. Ikram, *Modern Muslim India*, p. 160.

73. Iqbal, *Mohamed Ali*, p. 236.

74. Ibid., pp. 237–8.

75. Letter, dated Feb. 1, 1921, from Knapp, Chief Secretary, Government of Madras, to Government of India, File 43 of 1921, Home, National Archives, New Delhi.

76. Letter in March 1921 from Reading, Viceroy, to the Secretary of State, in Iqbal, *Mohamed Ali*, p. 255.

77. Ibid., p. 201.

78. Ibid., p. 280.

79. Quoted in ibid., p. 267.

80. Ikram, *Modern Muslim India*, p. 160.

81. Iqbal, *Mohamed Ali*, p. 394.

82. Ibid., p. 256.

83. Ibid., p. 257.

84. See ibid., p. 267.

85. Ibid., pp. 266–70.

86. Figures given in Michael Brecher, *Nehru* (Oxford University Press, London, 1959), pp. 97–8.

87. Iqbal, *Mohamed Ali*, p. 271.

88. Ibid.

89. Ibid., p. 276.

90. Ibid., pp. 277–8.

91. Jamiluddin Ahmad, *Middle Phase of the Muslim Political Movement* (Publishers United, Lahore, 1969), p. 34.

92. D.G. Tendulkar, *Mahatma* (Bombay, 1951), Vol. 2, p. 89.

93. Sitaramayya, *History of Congress*, p. 373.

94. Letter to Abdul Hamid Said in Rome, quoted in Iqbal, *Mohamed Ali*, p. 281.

95. Ibid., pp. 279–80.

96. Tendulkar, *Mahatma*, Vol. 2, p. 106.

97. *Young India*, Feb. 2, 1922.

98. *Young India*, March 2, 1922.

99. Brecher, *Nehru*, p. 79.

100. Iqbal, *Mohamed Ali*, p. 285.

101. M. Ali's remark after release. Quoted in ibid., p. 305.

102. Ibid., pp. 298–9.

103. Ibid., p. 301.

104. Mujeeb, *Indian Muslims*, p. 538.

105. Iqbal, *Mohamed Ali*, p. 323.

106. Mujeeb, *Indian Muslims*, p. 538.

107. On March 9, 1922, quoted in Iqbal, *Mohamed Ali*, p. 294.

108. Letter from M.H. Kidwai to M.A. Ansari, quoted in ibid., p. 289.

109. In the middle of 1922. Quoted in ibid., p. 290.

110. In 1925. Ibid., p. 332.

111. In 1923. Ibid., p. 308.

112. Ibid., pp. 310–11.

113. Ibid., p. 308.

114. Quoted in foreword by Muhammad Habib in Moin Shakir, *Khilafat to Pakistan* (Kalamkar, New Delhi), p. xviii.

115. Iqbal, *Mohamed Ali*, pp. 312–13.

116. Mujeeb, *Indian Muslims*, p. 538.

117. Diary entry dated Feb. 17, 1924. Iqbal, *Mohamed Ali*, pp. 314–15.

118. Letter dated June 15, 1924. Ibid., p. 314.

119. Ibid., p. 315.

120. Ibid., pp. 318–19.

121. Ibid., p. 280.

122. Tendulkar, *Mahatma*, Vol. 2, p. 198.

123. Iqbal, *Mohamed Ali*, p. 320.

124. Ibid.

125. Rajagopalachari to Devadas Gandhi, Sep. 26, 1924. Devadas Gandhi Papers, Madras.

126. Iqbal, *Mohamed Ali*, p. 321.

127. Ibid., p. 331.

128. In 1926, quoted in ibid., p. 341.

129. Note by J.W. Hore to Edwin Montagu. Quoted in ibid., p. 212.

130. Ibid., p. 311.

131. Ibid., p. 338.

132. Ibid., p. 332.

133. Mujeeb, *Indian Muslims*, p. 539.

134. Khaliquzzaman, *Pathway to Pakistan*, p. 37.

135. Ibid., p. 99.

136. Ibid., p. 98.

137. Ibid.

138. Ibid.

139. Iqbal, *Mohamed Ali*, p. 344.

140. Ibid., p. 360.

141. Ibid., p. 371.

142. Ibid., p. 376.

143. Ibid., p. 379.

144. London remarks from ibid, pp. 379–82.

145. Mujeeb, *Indian Muslims*, p. 536.

Chapter 5: Jinnah

1. Hector Bolitho, *Jinnah: Creator of Pakistan* (Greenwood Press, Westport, Connecticut), p. 8.

2. Ibid.

3. Ibid., p. 13.

4. Ibid., pp. 8–9.

5. Ibid., p. 14.

6. Ibid., p. 15.

7. Ibid., p. 18.

8. Ibid.

9. Ibid., pp. 20–21.

10. Ibid., p. 18.

11. Ibid., p. 19.

12. Quoted in ibid., pp. 21–22.

13. Ibid., p. 48.

14. Ibid.

15. Ibid., p. 55.

16. Ibid.

17. Ibid., p. 51.

18. Ibid., p. 58.

19. Ibid., p. 64.

20. Ibid., p. 64.

21. B. Shiva Rao, *India's Freedom Movement* (Orient Longman, New Delhi, 1972), p. 125.

22. Michael Brecher, *Nehru* (Oxford University Press, London, 1959), p. 60.

23. Montagu quoted in Tendulkar, *Mahatma*, Vol. 1, p. 264.

24. Edwin S. Montagu, *An Indian Diary* (Heinemann, London, 1930), pp. 57–8.

25. Ibid.

26. Ibid., p. 67.

27. Letter from Sarojini Naidu to Syed Mahmud, quoted in V.N. Datta and B. Cleghorn (ed.), *A Nationalist Muslim in Indian Politics* (Macmillan, New Delhi, 1974), p. 31.

28. Bolitho, *Jinnah*, p. 76.

29. Ibid., p. 78.

30. Ibid.

31. Ibid., p. 80.

32. Gandhi's remark in *Young India*, Nov. 8, 1928.

33. Bolitho, *Jinnah*, p. 80.

34. Allen Hayes Merriam, *Gandhi vs Jinnah* (Minerva, Calcutta, 1980), p. 45.

35. Ibid.

36. Judith H. Brown, *Gandhi's Rise to Power* (Cambridge University Press, Cambridge, 1972), p. 263.

37. S.S. Pirzada (ed.), *Foundations of Pakistan: All-India Muslim League Documents* (National Publishing House, Karachi), Vol. 1, pp. 542–4.

38. Ronaldshay, Governor of Bengal, to Montagu, Secretary of State, Sep. 22, 1920, quoted in Brown, *Gandhi's Rise to Power*, p. 265.

39. See Bolitho, *Jinnah*, p. 85.

40. Bolitho, *Jinnah*, pp. 83–4.

41. Brown, *Gandhi's Rise to Power*, p. 295.

42. Bolitho, *Jinnah*, p. 85.

43. Ibid.

44. Brown, *Gandhi's Rise to Power*, p. 297.

45. Merriam, *Gandhi vs Jinnah*, p. 47 and Bolitho, *Jinnah*, p. 87.

46. Bolitho, *Jinnah*, p. 83.

47. Ibid., p. 84.

48. Ikram, *Modern Muslim India*, p. 362.

49. Bolitho, *Jinnah*, p. 89.

50. Merriam, *Gandhi vs Jinnah*, p. 47.

51. Bolitho, *Jinnah*, pp. 89–90.

52. Quoted in Ikram, *Modern Muslim India*, p. 363.

53. J. Ahmad, *Middle Phase*, p. 92.

54. Ibid., pp. 94–5.

55. K.M. Munshi, *Pilgrimage to Freedom* (Bharatiya Vidya Bhavan, Bombay, 1967), p. 24.

56. Ahmad, *Middle Phase*, pp. 94–5.

57. Bolitho, *Jinnah*, pp. 94–5.

58. Khaliquzzaman, *Pathway to Pakistan*, p. 98.

59. Quoted in Ikram, *Modern Muslim India*, p. 366.

60. M.H. Saiyid, *Mohammad Ali Jinnah* (S.M. Ashraf, Lahore, 1945), p. 433.

61. See P. Hardy, *The Muslims of British India* (Cambridge University Press, 1972), p. 433.

62. From notes of Afzal Haque, who was present, quoted in G.A. Allana, *Jinnah*, p. 213.

63. Bolitho, *Jinnah*, p. 91.

64. Ibid., p. 92.

65. Ibid., p. 95.

66. Ibid., p. 96.

67. Quoted in Allana, *Jinnah*, p. 179.

68. Quoted in Ikram, *Modern Muslim India*, p. 368.

69. Jinnah to Ikram, quoted in ibid., p. 372.

70. To Aligarh students in 1938, quoted in Bolitho, *Jinnah*, p. 100.

71. Quoted in Ahmad, *Middle Phase*, pp. 129–30.

72. Bolitho, *Jinnah*, p. 102.

73. Ahmad, *Middle Phase*, p. 140.

74. *Hindu*, Sept. 5, 1941.

75. Ikram, *Modern Muslim India*, p. 372.

76. Bolitho, *Jinnah*, pp. 104–5.

77. Ikram, *Modern Muslim India*, p. 377.

78. Ibid., p. 376.

79. Ahmad, *Middle Phase*, p. 170.

80. Letter of May 22, 1937, quoted in Peerzada (ed.), *Leaders' Correspondence with Mr Jinnah* (Taj Office, Bombay, 1944), p. 37.

81. Khaliquzzaman, *Pathway to Pakistan*, p. 167.

82. Abul Kalam Azad, *India Wins Freedom* (Orient Longmans, Calcutta, 1959), p. 161.

83. Ikram, *Modern Muslim India*, p. 381.

84. Pyarelal, *Mahatma Gandhi: The Last Phase* (Navajivan, Ahmedabad, 1958), Vol. 1, p. 76.

85. Quoted in Merriam, *Gandhi vs Jinnah*, p. 57.

86. Penderel Moon, *Divide and Quit* (University of California Press, Berkeley, 1962), p. 15.

87. Munshi, *Pilgrimage to Freedom*, p. 48.

88. *Hindu*, Jan. 1, 1938.

89. Ikram, *Modern Muslim India*, p. 381.

90. Ibid., p. 382.

91. Merriam, *Gandhi vs Jinnah*, p. 58.

92. Bolitho, *Jinnah*, p. 115.

93. Khaliquzzaman, *Pathway to Pakistan*, p. 172.

94. Ikram, *Modern Muslim India*, pp. 381–2.

95. Extracts taken from Peerzada (ed.), *Leaders' Correspondence*, pp. 38–50.

96. Merriam, *Gandhi vs Jinnah*, p. 62.

97. Ibid.

98. Ibid., p. 61.

99. Bolitho, *Jinnah*, pp. 116–17.

100. Merriam, *Gandhi vs Jinnah*, p. 62.

101. Bolitho, *Jinnah*, pp. 119–20.

102. Ibid., p. 119.

103. Ibid., p. 118.

104. Merriam, *Gandhi vs Jinnah*, p. 62.

105. Bolitho, *Jinnah*, pp. 117–18.

106. Letter of Oct. 19, 1939, Linlithgow Papers, India Office Library, London.

107. Merriam, *Gandhi vs Jinnah*, p. 67.

108. Remarks made in Oct. 1939 and March 1940. Quoted in Rajmohan Gandhi, *The Rajaji Story* (Bharatiya Vidya Bhavan, Bombay, 1984), pp. 50–51 and p. 64.

109. Merriam, *Gandhi vs Jinnah*, pp. 64–5.

110. Ibid., p. 67.

111. Quoted in Naim (ed.), *Iqbal, Jinnah and Pakistan*, p. 186.

112. John Glendevon, *The Viceroy at Bay* (Collins, London, 1971), p. 119.

113. Merriam, *Gandhi vs Jinnah*, p. 68.

114. Ibid., p. 66.

115. Ibid., p. 68–73.

116. J. Ahmad (ed.), *Historic Documents of the Muslim Freedom Movement* (Publishers United, Lahore), p. 372.

117. Merriam, *Gandhi vs Jinnah*, p. 98.

118. Ibid., p. 78.

119. Telegram from Jinnah, July 12, 1940. Exchange quoted in Peerzada (ed.), *Leaders' Correspondence*, p. 213.

120. Naim (ed.), *Iqbal, Jinnah and Pakistan*, p. 68.

121. J. Ahmad, *Creation of Pakistan* (Publishers United, Lahore, 1976), pp. 74–5.

122. Ibid., p. 75.

123. Merriam, *Gandhi vs Jinnah*, p. 64.

124. Bolitho, *Jinnah*, p. 84.

125. Enayetur Rahim, *Provincial Autonomy in Bengal: 1937–1943* (Rajshahi University, Bangladesh, 1981), pp. 232–5.

126. Merriam, *Gandhi vs Jinnah*, p. 77.

127. Gandhi's comments in *Harijan*, June 7, 1942 and June 21, 1942.

128. Nehru quoted in Shiva Rao, *India's Freedom Movement*, p. 182.

129. Azad, *India Wins Freedom*, p. 76.

130. R. Gandhi, *The Rajaji Story*, p. 87.

131. Merriam, *Gandhi vs Jinnah*, p. 79.

132. Ibid., p. 81.

133. Ibid., pp. 80–81.

134. Kanji Dwarkadas, *Ten Years to Freedom* (Popular Prakashan, Bombay, 1968), p. 79.

135. Merriam, *Gandhi vs Jinnah*, p. 88.

136. Based on Bolitho, *Jinnah*, p. 145, and on report of trial in *Times of India*, Bombay, quoted in Muhammad Haneef Shahid (ed.), *Quaid-i-Azam M. A. Jinnah* (Sange-e-Meel Publications, Lahore, 1976).

137. Merriam, *Gandhi vs Jinnah*, p. 90.

138. Ibid., p. 88.

139. Ibid., pp. 91–2.

140. R. Gandhi, *The Rajaji Story*, pp. 95–6 and p. 102.

141. Bolitho, *Jinnah*, p. 146.

142. Merriam, *Gandhi vs Jinnah*, p. 93.

143. Bolitho, *Jinnah*, p. 147.

144. Ibid., p. 148.

145. Azad, *India Wins Freedom*, p. 93.

146. Penderel Moon (ed.), *Wavell: the Viceroy's Journal* (Oxford University Press, London, 1973), p. 87.

147. Merriam, *Gandhi vs Jinnah*, pp. 94–108.

148. Ibid., p. 105.

149. Ibid., p. 106.

150. Bolitho, *Jinnah*, p. 152.

151. Merriam, *Gandhi vs Jinnah*, p. 108.

152. Khaliquzzaman, *Pathway to Pakistan*, pp. 316–8.

153. Merriam, *Gandhi vs Jinnah*, p. 101.

154. Khaliquzzaman, *Pathway to Pakistan*, p. 278.

155. Merriam, *Gandhi vs Jinnah*, p. 104.

156. Moon (ed.), *Wavell*, p. 120.

157. Ibid., p. 141.

158. From letter of July 8, 1946, quoted in ibid., p. 494.

159. Merriam, *Gandhi vs Jinnah*, pp. 117–8.

160. Bolitho, *Jinnah*, p. 154.

161. Ibid., p. 153.

162. Ibid., p. 158.

163. M.A.H. Ispahani, *Quaid-e-Azam As I Knew Him* (Forward Publications Trust, Karachi, 1966), p. 123.

164. Bolitho, *Jinnah*, p. 142.

165. Ibid.

166. Quoted in Brecher, *Nehru*, p. 309.

167. Moon (ed.), *Wavell*, p. 475 and p. 478.

168. Remark on Apr. 3, 1946, quoted in J. Ahmad (ed.), *Speeches and Writings of Mr Jinnah* (Ashraf, Lahore, 1947), Vol. 2, p. 384.

169. Moon (ed.), *Wavell*, p. 475 and p. 478.

170. Ahmad (ed.), *Historic Documents*, pp. 522–3.

171. N. Mansergh and E.W.R. Lumby (ed.), *The Transfer of Power*, Vol. 7, pp. 686–7.

172. Moon (ed.), *Wavell*, p. 488.

173. Ibid., p. 490.

174. Ibid., p. 305.

175. Ibid.

176. Quoted in Ahmad (ed.), *Historic Documents*, p. 528.

177. J. Ahmad, *Creation of Pakistan*, p. 274.

178. Ibid.

179. Bolitho, *Jinnah*, pp. 164–5.

180. Ahmad, *Creation of Pakistan*, p. 278.

181. Ibid.

182. Chaudhri Muhammad Ali, *The Emergence of Pakistan* (Columbia University Press, New York, 1967), p. 69.

183. Bolitho, *Jinnah*, pp. 165–6.

184. *Statesman*, Calcutta, Aug. 20, 1946.

185. On Aug. 21, 1946. Quoted in Durga Das (ed.), *Sardar Patel's Correspondence* (Navajivan, Ahmedabad), Vol. 3, p. 40.

186. Ahmad (ed.), *Historical Documents*, pp. 545–6.

187. *New York Herald-Tribune*, Oct. 29, 1946.

188. Brecher, *Nehru*, p. 325.

189. In a letter to Cripps, Dec. 15, 1946, quoted in Durga Das (ed.), *Patel's Correspondence*, Vol. 3, pp. 313–5.

190. Ibid.

191. Moon (ed.), *Wavell*, p. 406.

192. Ibid., pp. 422–3.

193. Pyarelal, *The Last Phase*, Vol. 1, p. 565.

194. Moon (ed.), *Wavell*, p. 421.

195. R. Gandhi, *The Rajaji Story*, p. 130.

196. Pyarelal, *The Last Phase*, Vol. 2, p. 169.

197. Azad, *India Wins Freedom*, p. 187.

198. Stanley Wolpert, *Jinnah of Pakistan* (Oxford University Press, New York, 1984), p. 317.

199. Muhammad Ali, *Emergence of Pakistan*, p. 148.

200. Ibid., p. 128.

201. Merriam, *Gandhi vs Jinnah*, p. 128.

202. Muhammad Ali, *Emergence of Pakistan*, p. 125.

203. Ibid., p. 126.

204. Ibid., pp. 142–3.

205. Ibid.

206. Alan Campbell-Johnson, *Mission With Mountbatten* (Robert Hale, London, 1951), p. 93.

207. Bolitho, *Jinnah*, pp. 194–5.

208. Ibid.

209. Muhammad Ali, *Emergence of Pakistan*, p. 114.

210. Ikram, *Modern Muslim India*, p. 389.

211. Ibid., p. 396.

212. Muhammad Ali, *Emergence of Pakistan*, p. 61.

213. Sharif Al Mujahid, *Quaid-i-Azam Jinnah, Studies in Interpretation* (Quaid-i-Azam Academy, Karachi, 1978), p. 171.

214. Muhammad Ali, *Emergence of Pakistan*, p. 61.

215. Ibid., p. 87 and pp. 145–8.

216. Bolitho, *Jinnah*, p. 183.

217. Muhammad Ali, *Emergence of Pakistan*, p. 144.

218. Durga Das (ed.), *Patel's Correspondence*, Vol. 3, pp. 313–5.

219. Azad, *India Wins Freedom*, p. 174.

220. See Ahmad, *Creation of Pakistan*, p. 339.

221. Muhammad Ali, *Emergence of Pakistan*, p. 73.

222. Ahmad, *Creation of Pakistan*, p. 339.

223. Khaliquzzaman, *Pathway to Pakistan*, p. 396.

224. Bolitho, *Jinnah*, p. 189.

225. Khaliquzzaman, *Pathway to Pakistan*, p. 321.

226. Letter from Suhrawardy to Khaliquzzaman, quoted in *Pathway to Pakistan*, pp. 397–8.

227. Bolitho, *Jinnah*, p. 198.

228. Quoted in Bolitho, *Jinnah*, p. 197 and Khaliquzzaman, *Pathway to Pakistan*, p. 321.

229. Bolitho, *Jinnah*, p. 197.

230. Ahmad (ed.), *Historic Documents*, p. 380.

231. Khaliquzzaman, *Pathway to Pakistan*, p. 321.

232. Naim in Naim (ed.), *Iqbal, Jinnah and Pakistan*, p. 181.

233. Merriam, *Gandhi vs Jinnah*, p. 135.

234. M.S.M. Sharma, *Peeps Into Pakistan* (Pustak Bhandar, Patna, 1954), p. 182.

235. Ibid., p. 188.

236. Bolitho, *Jinnah*, p. 95.

237. Sharma, *Peeps into Pakistan*, pp. 182–3.

238. Ikram, *Modern Muslim India*, p. 460.

239. Ibid., pp. 460–1.

240. Sharma, *Peeps into Pakistan*, p. 187.

241. Quoted in Ikram, *Modern Muslim India*, p. 463.

242. Qureshi in Naim (ed.), *Iqbal, Jinnah and Pakistan*, p. 35.

243. Muhammad Ali, *Emergence of Pakistan*, p. 238.

244. Naim (ed.), *Iqbal, Jinnah and Pakistan*, p. 36.

245. Ibid.

246. Muhammad Ali, *Emergence of Pakistan*, p. 385.

247. Ibid., p. 383.

248. Ibid., p. 386.

249. Naim (ed.), *Iqbal, Jinnah and Pakistan*, p. 68.

250. Ibid., p. 98.

251. Ibid., p. 97.

252. Muhammad Ali, *Emergence of Pakistan*, p. 297.

253. Ibid.

254. Ibid., p. 290.

255. Ibid., pp. 292–3.

256. Ibid., p. 297.

257. Bolitho, *Jinnah*, p. 208.

258. Ibid., p. 209.

259. Muhammad Ali, *Emergence of Pakistan*, p. 296.

260. See Alan Campbell-Johnson, *Mission with Mountbatten*, p. 283.

261. Bolitho, *Jinnah*, p. 210.

262. Naim (ed.), *Iqbal, Jinnah and Pakistan*, p. 22.

263. Ispahani, *Jinnah As I Knew Him*, p. 119 and p. 125.

264. Ibid.

265. Ibid.

266. Ibid., p. 107 and p. 112.

267. Bolitho, *Jinnah*, p. 208.

268. Ibid., p. 166.

269. Ibid.

270. Hicks to author.

271. Bolitho, *Jinnah*, p. 212.

272. Ibid., p. 180.

273. Ibid., p. 212.

274. See Merriam, *Gandhi vs Jinnah*, p. 108, and Pyarelal, *The Last Phase*, Vol. 1, p. 251.

275. S.S. Pirzada, *Some Aspects of Quaid-i-Azam's Life* (National Commission on Historical and Cultural Research, Islamabad, 1978), p. 37.

276. Naim (ed.), *Iqbal, Jinnah and Pakistan*, p. 22.

277. *Dawn*, March 12, 1948, quoted in Ikram, *Modern Muslim India*, p. 499.

278. Eid Day broadcast, Nov. 13, 1939, quoted in Naim (ed.), *Iqbal, Jinnah and Pakistan*, p. 101.

279. Ispahani, *Jinnah As I Knew Him*, p. 118.

280. Bolitho, *Jinnah*, p. 216.

281. Ibid., p. 212.

282. Ibid., p. 221.

283. Ibid., p. 223.

284. Ibid., p. 224.

Chapter 6: Fazlul Haq

1. Letter of Dec. 3, 1937, quoted in Enayetur Rahim, *Provincial Autonomy in Bengal: 1937–1943* (Institute of Bangladesh Studies, Rajshahi University, Bangladesh, 1981), p. 109.

2. Jinnah's remark, Feb. 15, 1942, in ibid., p. 235.

3. Shaista S. Ikramullah, *From Purdah to Parliament* (The Crescent Press, London, 1963), p. 104.

4. B.D. Habibullah in introductory remarks in A.K. Zainul Abedin (ed.), *Memorable Speeches of Sher-e-Bangla* (Al Helal Publishing House, Barisal, 1978),

5. Ibid.

6. Ikram, *Modern Muslim India*, p. 89.

7. A.S.M. Abdur Rab, *A.K. Fazlul Huq* (Ferozsons, Lahore, 1967), p. 5.

8. Abedin (ed.), *Speeches of Sher-e-Bangla*, p. 27.

9. Rab, *Huq*, p. 31.

10. Ibid., pp. 32–33.

11. Ibid., p. 40.

12. Ibid., p. 43.

13. Rahim, *Provincial Autonomy*, p. 59.

14. Letter to Sarat Bose, Feb. 22, 1921, in Rab, *Huq*, pp. 56–7.

15. Ibid., pp. 56-8.

16. Gautam Chattopadhyay, *Bengal Electoral Politics and Freedom Struggle* (New Delhi, 1984), p. 56.

17. Ibid., pp. 62–3.

18. Rab, *Huq*, p. 47.

19. Speech at the 1931 Round Table Conférence in London, quoted in ibid., p. 83.

20. See Chattopadhyay, *Bengal Politics*, p. 112 and p. 115.

21. Enayetur Rahim, "*Bengal Election, 1937*," *Journal of the Asiatic Society of Bangladesh* (Dacca, August 1977), p. 101.

22. Ibid.

23. Rahim, *Provincial Autonomy*, p. 59.

24. Rab, *Huq*, pp. 74–5.

25. Ibid., p. 79.

26. Ibid., p. 84.

27. Ibid., p. 82.

28. Abedin (ed.), *Speeches of Sher-e-Bangla*, pp. 132–4.

29. See Rahim, *Bengal Election, 1937*, pp. 105–6, and Chattopadhyay, *Bengal Politics*, p. 140.

30. Rahim, *Bengal Election, 1937*, p. 103.

31. Ibid., p. 98.

32. *Star of India*, Oct. 5, 1936, quoted in ibid., p. 108.

33. Ibid., p. 110.

34. Ibid.

35. *Star of India*, Oct. 30, 1936, quoted in ibid., p. 113.

36. Rab, *Huq*, pp. 88–9.

37. Chattopadhyay, *Bengal Politics*, p. 142.

38. Abul Mansur Ahmed, quoted in ibid., pp. 146–7.

39. Quoted in ibid., p. 147.

40. Rahim, *Bengal Election, 1937*, p. 117.

41. Letter of March 9, 1937, quoted in ibid., p. 117.

42. Rahim, *Provincial Autonomy*, p. 126.

43. Ibid., p. 130.

44. Ibid., p. 135.

45. Ibid.

46. Abedin (ed.), *Speeches of Sher-e-Bangla*, p. 11.

47. Rahim, *Provincial Autonomy*, p. 136.

48. Ibid.

49. Ibid., p. 141.

50. Ibid., p. 216.

51. Abedin (ed.), *Speeches of Sher-e-Bangla*, pp. 135–6.

52. Ibid., p. 138.

53. 1931 census figures, Quoted in Rahim, *Provincial Autonomy*, p. xii.

54. Rahim, *Bengal Election, 1937*, p. 122.

55. Rab, *Huq*, pp. 97–8.

56. Rahim, *Provincial Autonomy*, p. 231.

57. Ibid.

58. Quoted in Amalendu De, *Islam in Modern India* (Maya, Calcutta, 1982), p. 147.

59. Ibid.

60. Letter of Sep. 8, 1941, quoted in ibid., p. 153.

61. Ibid., p. 152.

62. Chattopadhyay, *Bengal Politics*, p. 173.

63. Ispahani, *Jinnah As I Knew Him*, p. 125.

64. A.K. Zainul Abedin (ed.), *Bengal Today* (Al Helal, Barisal, 1978), p. 6.

65. De, *Islam in Modern India*, p. 159.

66. Chattopadhyay, *Bengal Politics*, p. 173.

67. Sarat Bose, *I Warned My Countrymen* (Calcutta, 1968), quoted in Chattopadhyay, *Bengal Politics*, p. 173.

68. Quoted in Rab, *Huq*, p. 129.

69. Rahim, *Provincial Autonomy*, p. 234.

70. Ibid., p. 235.

71. Ibid., p. 236.

72. On Feb. 27, 1943, Bengal Legislative Assembly Proceedings quoted in Chattopadhyay, *Bengal Politics*, p. 188.

73. Abedin (ed.), *Bengal Today*, pp. 27–8.

74. Ibid., pp. 40–41.

75. From letters of Linlithgow to Amery, Secretary of State, Apr. 2 and 4, 1943, in Mansergh and Lumby (ed.), *Transfer of Power*, Vol. 3, quoted in Chattopadhyay, *Bengal Politics*, pp. 191–2.

76. Abedin (ed.), *Bengal Today*, pp. 44–5.

77. Moon (ed.), *Wavell*, pp. 31–2.

78. Ibid.

79. Ibid.

80. Letter to M. Shahjehan, dated Oct. 13, 1945, quoted in Rab, *Huq*, pp. 159–61.

81. Ibid., pp. 195–6.

83. Ibid., p. 18.

84. Ibid., pp. 205–6.

85. Ibid., p. 207.

86. On Apr. 8, 1943, quoted in Abedin (ed.), *Speeches of Sher-e-Bangla*, p. 144.

87. Rahim, *Provincial Autonomy*, p. 111.

88. Rab, *Huq*, p. 165.

89. Ibid., p. 167.

90. Abedin (ed.), *Speeches of Sher-e-Bangla*, p. 183.

91. S.G. Jilani, *Fifteen Governors I Served With* (Lahore, 1979), p. 7.

92. Rab, *Huq*, p. 170.

93. Jilani, *Fifteen Governors*, p. 40.

94. Ibid., p. 45.

95. Letter of Oct. 13, 1956, quoted in Abedin (ed.), *Speeches of Sher-e-Bangla*, p. 192.

96. Jilani, *Fifteen Governors*, p. 47.

97. Ibid., p. 48.

98. Letter from Huq to Ataur Rahman, Oct. 13, 1956, quoted in Abedin (ed.), *Speeches of Sher-e-Bangla*, pp. 192–3.

99. Ibid., pp. 186–7.

100. To Hashim Ali Khan, Feb. 2, 1956, ibid., p. 188.

101. Letter to Yusuf Ali, Feb. 28, ibid., p. 194.

102. Rab, *Huq*, p. 186.

103. Ibid. pp. 189–90.

Chapter 7: Abul Kalam Azad

1. Mushir U. Haq, *Muslim Politics in Modern India: 1857–1947* (Meenakshi, Meerut, 1970), p. 69.

2. Arsh Malsiani, *Abul Kalam Azad* (Publications Division, New Delhi, 1976), p. 2.

3. Quoted in ibid., pp. 14–15.

4. Ibid.

5. Abul Kalam Azad, *India Wins Freedom* (Orient Longmans, Calcutta, 1959), p. 4.

6. Ibid.

7. Ibid., p. 5.

8. Ibid., p. 7.

9. Smith, *Modern Islam in India*, p. 218.

10. Haq, *Muslim Politics*, p. 70.

11. Ikram, *Modern Muslim India*, p. 141.

12. K.A. Faruqi, quoted in Malsiani, *Azad*, p. 20.

13. *Al Hilal*, Dec. 18, 1912, quoted in Haq, *Muslim Politics*, p. 101.

14. Ibid., p. 79.

15. *Al Hilal*, Sept. 8, 1912, in ibid., p. 79.

16. *Al Hilal*, Sept. 11, 1912, in ibid., pp. 81–3.

17. Ibid.

18. *Al Hilal*, date not given, in Malsiani, *Azad*, pp. 25–6.

19. *Al Hilal*, Sept. 9, 1912, in Haq, *Muslim Politics*, p. 72.

20. Quoted in Mujeeb, *Indian Muslims*, p. 458.

21. Haq, *Muslim Politics*, p. 88.

22. *Al Hilal*, Dec. 3, 1913, in ibid., p. 90.

23. Quoted in ibid., pp. 94–5.

24. Ibid.

25. Malsiani, *Azad*, p. 30.

26. Azad, *India Wins Freedom*, p. 9.

27. Mujeeb, *Indian Muslims*, p. 441.

28. S.S. Pirzada, *Some Aspects of Quaid-i-Azam's Life* (National Commission on Historical Research, Islamabad, 1978), p. 62.

29. Haq, *Muslim Politics*, p. 96.

30. Mahadev Desai, *Maulana Abul Kalam Azad* (Shiva Lal Agarwala, Agra, 1940), p. 83.

31. Haq, *Muslim Politics*, p. 98.

32. Ibid., p. 118.

33. Mujeeb, *Indian Muslims*, p. 463.

34. Fatwa quoted in Haq, *Muslim Politics*, p. 102.

35. Ibid.

36. Azad, *India Wins Freedom*, p. 16 and p. 21.

37. Malsiani, *Azad*, p. 39.

38. Gandhi quoted in ibid., p. 40.

39. Desai, *Azad*, pp. 50–51.

40. Malsiani, *Azad*, pp. 49–50.

41. Azad, *India Wins Freedom*, p. 18.

42. Letter of Feb. 19, 1922, quoted in Brown, *Gandhi's Rise*, p. 328.

43. Ibid.

44. Kripalani quoted in Humayun Kabir (ed.), *Abul Kalam Azad* (Publications Division, New Delhi), p. 32.

45. Quoted in Malsiani, *Azad*, pp. 43–4.

46. Desai, *Azad*, pp. 82–6.

47. Mujeeb, *Indian Muslims*, p. 462.

48. Mujeeb's interpretation. Ibid., p. 461.

49. Ibid., p. 463.

50. *The Qur'an*, 5:48. Quoted in Abbott, *Islam and Pakistan* p. 169.

51. Abbott, *Islam and Pakistan*, pp. 168–9.

52. Mujeeb, *Indian Muslims*, p. 457.

53. Ibid., pp. 462–3.

54. Mujeeb's paraphrasing of Azad, ibid., p. 462.

55. Ibid., p. 463.

56. Ikram, *Modern Muslim India*, p. 152.

57. Ibid.

58. Desai, *Azad*, p. 25.

59. Ikram, *Modern Muslim India*, p. 152.

60. Ibid., p. 149.

61. Smith, *Modern Islam in India*, p. 128.

62. Mujeeb, *Indian Muslims*, p. 460.

63. Malsiani, *Azad*, p. 95.

64. Desai, *Azad*, p. 97.

65. Azad's remark quoted in Munshi, *Pilgrimage to Freedom*, p. 24.

66. Malsiani, *Azad*, p. 45.

67. Subramonia Iyer (ed.) *Role of Maulana Abul Kalam Azad in Indian Politics* (Azad Oriental Research Institute, Hyderabad), p. 57.

68. Khaliquzzaman, *Pathway to Pakistan*, p. 105.

69. Azad, *India Wins Freedom*, pp. 161–2.

70. Khaliquzzaman, *Pathway to Pakistan*, p. 167 and pp. 187–8.

71. Ibid., p. 197.

72. Ibid., p. 211.

73. Ibid., last page.

74. Muhammad Ali, *Emergence of Pakistan*, p. 112.

75. Khaliquzzaman, *Pathway to Pakistan*, p. 211.

76. Desai, *Azad*, p. 1.

77. Quoted in ibid., p. 102.

78. R. Gandhi, *The Rajaji Story*, p. 37.

79. Quoted in Malsiani, *Azad*.

80. Smith quoted in Merriam, *Gandhi vs Jinnah*, p. 70.

81. Khaliquzzaman, *Pathway to Pakistan*, p. 251.

82. Merriam, *Gandhi vs Jinnah*, p. 68.

83. Desai, *Azad*, p. 124.

84. Azad, *India Wins Freedom*, p. 37.

85. Ibid., p. 39.

86. R. Gandhi, *The Rajaji Story*, p. 76.

87. Ibid.

88. Ibid.

89. Azad, *India Wins Freedom*, p. 44.

90. Ibid., pp. 58–9.

91. Ibid., p. 233.

92. Ibid., pp. 65–6.

93. Ibid., p. 71.

94. Ibid., p. 74.

95. Malsiani, *Azad*, p. 158.

96. Ibid., pp. 158–9.

97. R. Gandhi, *The Rajaji Story*, p. 91.

98. Azad, *India Wins Freedom*, p. 81.

99. Ibid., pp. 83–4.

100. Ikram, *Modern Muslim India*, p. 149.

101. Malsiani, *Azad*, pp. 105–6.

102. Ibid., pp. 104–5.

103. Ibid., pp. 158–63.

104. Azad, *India Wins Freedom*, p. 93.

105. Khaliquzzaman, *Pathway to Pakistan*, p. 251.

106. Azad, *India Wins Freedom*, p. 100.

107. Ibid., p. 104.

108. Moon (ed.), *Wavell*, p. 154.

109. Azad, *India Wins Freedom*, p. 100.

110. Ibid., p. 141.

111. Ibid., p. 153.

112. Ibid., p. 128.

113. Ibid., pp. 153–5.

114. Ibid., p. 175.

115. Moon (ed.), *Wavell*, p. 336.

116. Azad, *India Wins Freedom*, pp. 179–80.

117. Ibid., pp. 143–4.

118. Ibid.

119. Ibid., p. 185.

120. Ibid.

121. Ibid., p. 185.

122. Ibid., p. 197.

123. Pyarelal, *The Last Phase*, Vol. 2, p. 252.

124. Azad, *India Wins Freedom*, p. 211.

125. Taken from Malsiani, *Azad*, pp. 164–9 and S.T. Lokhandwalla (ed.), *India and Contemporary Islam* (Indian Institute of Advanced Study, Simla, 1971), p. 51.

126. A.B. Rajput, *Maulana Abul Kalam Azad* (Lion Press, Lahore, 1946), pp. 199–201.

127. Mujeeb, *Indian Muslims*, p. 442.

128. Ikram's description of Daryabadi, Ikram, *Modern Muslim India*, p. 151.

129. Ibid.

130. Rajput, *Azad*, p. 203.

131. Mujeeb, *Indian Muslims*, p. 442.

132. Haq, *Muslim Politics*, p. vi.

133. Rajput, *Azad*, p. 202.

134. Azad, *India Wins Freedom*, p. 227.

135. Haq, *Muslim Politics*, p. 149.

136. Azad, *India Wins Freedom*, p. 227.

137. Ibid., p. 198.

138. Mujeeb, *Indian Muslims*, p. 441.

139. Mujeeb, *Dr Zakir Husain* (National Book Trust, New Delhi), p. 183 and p. 195.

140. Azad, *India Wins Freedom*, p. 217.

141. Ibid., pp. 219–20.

142. Ibid., p. 222.

143. Ikram, *Modern Muslim India*, p. 151.

144. Muhammad Ali, *Emergence of Pakistan*, p. 273.

145. Azad, *India Wins Freedom*, p. 184.

146. Nehru quoted in Malsiani, *Azad*, p. 175.

147. Abdullah Butt (ed.), *Aspects of Abul Kalam Azad* (Maktaba-i-Urdu, Lahore, 1942), pp. 32–3.

148. Malsiani, *Azad*, p. 177.

149. Tyabji in *Seminar on Gandhi and Azad* (Azad Oriental Research Institute, Hyderabad, 1969), p. 27.

150. Malsiani, *Azad*, p. 89.

151. Mujeeb, *Indian Muslims*, p. 442.

Chapter 8: Liaqat Ali Khan

1. Ikram, *Modern Muslim India*, p. 472.

2. M. Rafique Afzal (ed.), *Speeches and Statements of Quaid-i-Millat Liaquat Ali Khan* (Research Society of Pakistan, University of Punjab, Lahore, 1967), p. iv.

3. Mushirul Hasan, *Congress Muslims and Indian Nationalism: 1928–1934* (Occasional Paper No. 23, Nehru Memorial Museum and Library, New Delhi, 1985), p. 49.

4. Nawab of Chhatari, *Yad-i-Ayyam*, p. 262, quoted in Ikram, *Modern Muslim India*, p. 473.

5. Afzal (ed.), *Speeches*, p. v.

6. Bolitho, *Jinnah*, p. 105.

7. Ibid.

8. Afzal (ed.), *Speeches*, p. v.

9. Bolitho, Jinnah, pp. 105–6.

10. *Civil and Military Gazette*, Lahore, March 3, 1936, quoted in Ikram, *Modern Muslim India*, p. 244.

11. Ispahani, *Jinnah As I Knew Him*, p. 19, quoted in Afzal (ed.), *Speeches*, p. vi.

12. Statement in *Afaq*, Urdu daily of Lahore, Oct. 17, 1952, quoted in Afzal, *Speeches*, p. vi.

13. Khaliquzzaman, *Pathway to Pakistan*, p. 190.

14. Afzal (ed.), *Speeches*, p. vii.

15. Bolitho, *Jinnah*, p. 154.

16. C.M. Naim (ed.), *Iqbal, Jinnah and Pakistan* (Maxwell School of Public Affairs, Syracuse University, 1979), p. 186.

17. *Indian Annual Register*, 1943, Vol. 1, p. 278, quoted in Afzal (ed.), *Speeches*, p. viii.

18. S. Abid Husain, *The Destiny of Indian Muslims* (Asia, Bombay, 1965), p. 74.

19. J. Ahmad (ed.), *Speeches and Writings of Mr Jinnah*, Vol. 1, p. 574.

20. Afzal (ed.), *Speeches*, p. xi.

21. Moon (ed.), *Wavell*, p. 116.

22. Phrase of Sir Muhammad Yamin Khan, quoted in Sharif Al Mujahid, *Jinnah: Studies in Interpretation*, p. 403 fn.

23. Ibid.

24. According to Khalif Bin Sayeed, quoted in ibid., p. 404 fn.

25. Moon (ed.), *Wavell*, p. 114.

26. Syed Mahmud to Bhulabhai in Datta and Cleghorn (ed.), *A Nationalist Muslim in India* (Macmillan, New Delhi, 1974), p. 250.

27. Afzal (ed.), *Speeches*, p. ix.

28. M.C. Setalvad, *Bhulabhai Desai* (Publications Division, New Delhi, 1968).

29. V.P. Menon, *The Transfer of Power in India* (Orient Longmans, Calcutta, 1957), p. 178.

30. Ibid., p. 177.

31. Moon (ed.), *Wavell*, p. 144.

32. Menon, *Transfer of Power*, pp. 177–8.

33. Moon (ed.), *Wavell*, p. 116.

34. Afzal (ed.), *Speeches*, p. x.

35. Moon (ed.), *Wavell*, p. 114.

36. *Deccan Times*, Sept. 9, 1945, quoted in Mujahid, *Jinnah*, p. 404 fn.

37. Mujahid, *Jinnah*, p. 404 fn.

38. Munshi, *Pilgrimage to Freedom*, p. 94.

39. Mujahid, *Jinnah*, p. 404 fn.

40. Menon, *Transfer of Power*, p. 214.

41. Moon (ed.), *Wavell*, pp. 207–8.

42. Ibid., p. 220.

43. Ibid., p. 259.

44. Ibid., p. 366.

45. Ibid., p. 413.

46. Ibid., p. 430.

47. Afzal (ed.), *Speeches*, p. xii.

48. On Nov. 23, 1946, Moon (ed.), *Wavell*, p. 381.

49. Ibid., p. 391.

50. Mujahid, *Jinnah*, p. 405.

51. Afzal (ed.), *Speeches*, p. xii.

52. Moon (ed.), *Wavell*, p. 375.

53. Ibid., p. 366.

54. Ibid., p. 372.

55. Menon, *Transfer of Power*, p. 358.

56. Afzal (ed.), *Speeches*, p. xiv.

57. Ibid.

58. Ibid. p. xv.

59. Ibid., p. xviii and p. 209.

60. Quoted in ibid., p. xix.

61. Ibid., p. 210.

62. Menon, *Transfer of Power*, p. 431.

63. Ibid., p. 418.

64. Afzal (ed.), *Speeches*, p. 211.

65. Menon, *Transfer of Power*, p. 419.

66. Afzal (ed.), *Speeches*, p. 211.

67. Ibid.

68. Sharma, *Peeps Into Pakistan*, p. 183.

69. Afzal (ed.), *Speeches*, p. 209.

70. Quoted in Wolpert, *Jinnah*, p. 356.

71. See Ikram, *Modern Muslim India*, p. 477.

72. Quoted in Afzal (ed.), *Speeches*, pp. xix-xx.

73. Ibid., p. 211.

74. Ibid., p. xx.

75. Moon (ed.), *Wavell*, p. 443.

76. Afzal (ed.), *Speeches*, p. 220.

77. Ibid., p. 219.

78. Ibid., p. xxi.

79. Ikram, *Modern Muslim India*, pp. 477–8.

80. *Free Press Journal*, Sept. 19, 1949, quoted in ibid., p. 489.

81. Ikram, *Modern Muslim India*, p. 489.

82. Afzal (ed.), *Speeches*, p. 228.

83. Ibid., pp. 228–44.

84. Mian Iftikharuddin, *Speeches and Statements* (Nigarishat, Lahore, 1971), p. 365.

85. See Afzal (ed.), *Speeches*, pp. 228–44 and Ikram, *Modern Muslim India*, pp. 483–8.

86. Afzal (ed.), *Speeches*, p. 241.

87. *Hindu*, August 26, 1951, quoted in Ikram, *Modern Muslim India*, p. 492.

88. Liaquat Ali Khan, *Pakistan: The Heart of Asia* (Ministry of Education, Islamabad), p. 97.

89. Liaqat's statement of Apr. 29, 1949. Quoted in Afzal (ed.), *Speeches*, p. 249.

90. Statement made in March 1951. Ibid., p. 538.

91. Ibid., p. xxvi.

92. Nehru-Liaqat correspondence in Afzal (ed.), *Speeches*, pp. 577–639.

93. Mohammad Ayub Khan, *Friends Not Masters* (Oxford University Press, London, 1967), p. 40.

94. Letter of Jan. 5, 1948, quoted in Afzal (ed.), *Speeches*, p. 587.

95. In March 1949, quoted in ibid., pp. 241–2.

96. *Statesman*, Apr. 23, 1950, quoted in Ikram, *Modern Muslim India*, p. 480.

97. Ayub, *Friends Not Masters*, pp. 36–7.

98. Letter to Z.A. Bokhari, Controller of Broadcasting, in Fatima Jinnah, *Speeches, Messages and Statements* (Research Society of Pakistan, Lahore, 1976), p. 37.

99. Ayub, *Friends Not Masters*, pp. 40–41.

100. *Indian Express*, Madras, Oct. 18, 1951.

101. Ayub, *Friends Not Masters*, p. 42.

102. Afzal (ed.), *Speeches*, p. xxix.

103. Ayub, *Friends Not Masters*, p. 41.

Chapter 9: Zakir Husain

1. M. Mujeeb, *Dr. Zakir Husain* (National Book Trust, New Delhi, 1972), pp. 4–5.

2. Ibid., p. 11.

3. Anees Chishti, *President Zakir Husain* (Rachna Prakashan, New Delhi, 1967), p. 20 and Mujeeb, *Zakir Husain*, p. 17.

4. Mujeeb, *Zakir Husain*, p. 17.

5. Ibid., p. 20.

6. Quoted in B.K. Ahluwalia (ed.), *Zakir Husain: A Study* (Sterling, New Delhi, 1970), p. 28.

7. Mujeeb, *Zakir Husain*, p. 24.

8. Ibid., p. 25.

9. Ibid.

10. Ibid., p. 28.

11. Ibid., p. 29.

12. R. Gandhi, *The Rajaji Story*, p. 241.
13. *President Zakir Husain's Speeches* (Publications Division, New Delhi, 1973), p. 180.
14. Mujeeb, *Zakir Husain*, p. 32.
15. Ibid., p. 33.
16. Ibid., p. 34.
17. Ibid., p. 38.
18. Ibid., p. 39.
19. Ibid., p. 33.
20. Ibid., p. 35.
21. Ibid., p. 36.
22. Ibid., p. 38.
23. Ibid.
24. Ibid., pp. 39–40.
25. Ibid., p. 43.
26. Ibid., p. 50.
27. Ibid., p. 43.
28. Ibid., p. 44.
29. Ibid., p. 46.
30. Ibid.
31. Ibid., p. 58.
32. Ibid., p. 60.
33. Ibid., p. 57.
34. Ibid., pp. 66–7.
35. Ibid., p. 55.
36. In 1935. Ibid., p. 87.
37. Ibid.
38. Ibid., p. 84.
39. Ibid.
40. Ibid., p. 81.
41. Smith, *Modern Islam in India*, p. 129.
42. Mujeeb, *Zakir Husain*, p. 88.
43. Ibid., p. 90.
44. Ibid.
45. Ibid.
46. Ibid., p. 94.
47. Smith, *Modern Islam in India*, p. 131.
48. See article by Mujeeb in Ahluwalia (ed.), *Zakir Husain*, p. 46.
49. Ibid., p. 45.
50. Mujeeb, *Zakir Husain*.
51. Ibid., p. 98.
52. Ibid., p. 98 fn.
53. Moon (ed.), *Wavell*, p. 296.
54. Mujeeb, *Zakir Husain*, p. 137.
55. Ibid., p. 138.

56. Ibid., p. 247.
57. Ibid., p. 145.
58. Ibid., p. 67.
59. Ibid., p. 148.
60. Ibid.
61. Ibid., p. 160.
62. Ibid., p. 173.
63. Ibid., p. 182.
64. Ibid.
65. Ibid., pp. 205–6.
66. Ibid., p. 228.
67. Ibid., p. 211.
68. Ibid., p. 236.
69. *President Zakir Husain's Speeches*, p. 2.
70. Mujeeb, *Zakir Husain*, p. 240.
71. Ibid.
72. Article by Durga Das in Ahluwalia (ed.),*Zakir Husain*, p. 69.
73. Mujeeb, *Zakir Husain*, p. 180.

Chapter 10: Conclusion

1. R. Gandhi, *The Rajaji Story*, p. 337.
2. Moon (ed.), *Wavell*, p. 368.
3. Merriam, *Gandhi vs Jinnah*, p. 31.
4. See Wolpert, *Jinnah*, p. 111.
5. Muhammad Ali, *Emergence of Pakistan*, p. 145.
6. Moon (ed.), *Wavell*, p. 311.
7. Afzal (ed.), *Speeches*, pp. 231–2.
8. Merriam, *Gandhi vs Jinnah*, p. 40.
9. Ibid., p. 47.
10. Round Table Conference proceedings, quoted in Wolpert, *Jinnah*, p. 128.
11. Quoted in Menon, *Transfer of Power*, p. 382.
12. Moon (ed.), *Wavell*, p. 352.
13. Ibid., p. 314.
14. Ibid., p. 313 and p. 494.
15. Introduction by Habib in Moin Shakir, *Khilafat to Pakistan* (Kalamkar, New Delhi), p. xii.
16. Iqbal, *Mohamed Ali*, p. 38.

INDEX

READ MORE IN PENGUIN

In every corner of the world, on every subject under the sun, Penguin represents quality and variety – the very best in publishing today.

For complete information about books available from Penguin – including Puffins, Penguin Classics and Arkana – and how to order them, write to us at the appropriate address below. Please note that for copyright reasons the selection of books varies from country to country.

In India: Please write to *Penguin Books India Pvt Ltd, 706 Eros Apartments, 56 Nehru Place, New Delhi, 110019*

In the United Kingdom: Please write to *Dept. JC, Penguin Books Ltd, Bath Road, Harmondsworth, West Drayton, Middlesex, UB7 ODA, UK*

In the United States: Please write to *Penguin USA Inc., 375 Hudson Street, New York, NY 10014*

In Canada: Please write to *Penguin Books Canada Ltd, 10 Alcorn Avenue, Suite 300, Toronto, Ontario M4V 3B2*

In Australia: Please write to *Penguin Books Australia Ltd, 487 Maroondah Highway, Ring Wood, Victoria 3134*

In New Zealand: Please write to *Penguin Books (NZ) Ltd, 182–190 Wairau Road, Private Bag, Takapuna, Auckland 9*

In the Netherlands: Please write to *Penguin Books Netherlands B.V., Keizersgracht 231 NL–1016 DV Amsterdam*

In Germany : Please write to *Penguin Books Deutschland GmbH, Metzlerstrasse 26, 60595 Frankfurt am Main, Germany*

In Spain: Please write to *Penguin Books S. A., Bravo Murillo, 19-1' B, E-28015 Madrid, Spain*

In Italy: Please write to *Penguin Italia s.r.l., Via Felice Casati 20, I–20124 Milano*

In France: Please write to *Penguin France S. A., 17 rue Lejeune, F–31000 Toulouse*

In Japan: Please write to *Penguin Books Japan, Ishikiribashi Building, 2-5-4, Suido, Tokyo 112*

In Greece: Please write to *Penguin Hellas Ltd, Dimocritou 3, GR–106 71 Athens*

In South Africa: Please write to *Longman Penguin Southern Africa (Pty) Ltd, Private Bag X08, Bertsham 2013*